The New Economics of Outdoor Recreation

The New Economics of Outdoor Recreation

Edited by

Nick Hanley

Professor of Environmental Economics, University of Glasgow, UK

W. Douglass Shaw

Associate Professor, Department of Applied Economics and Statistics, University of Nevada, Reno, USA

Robert E. Wright

Professor of Economics, University of Stirling, UK

Edward Elgar
Cheltenham, UK • Northampton, MA, USA

Published by
Edward Elgar Publishing Limited
Glensanda House
Montpellier Parade
Cheltenham
Glos GL50 1UA
UK

Edward Elgar Publishing, Inc.
136 West Street
Suite 202
Northampton
Massachusetts 01060
USA

A catalogue record for this book
is available from the British Library

Library of Congress Cataloguing in Publication Data

The new economics of outdoor recreation/edited by Nick Hanley, W. Douglass Shaw, Robert E. Wright
  p. cm.
 Includes bibliographical references and index.
  1. Outdoor recreation—Economic aspects. 2. Outdoor recreation—
Environmental aspects. 3. Econometrics. I. Hanley, Nick. II. Shaw,
W. Douglass. III. Wright, Robert E., 1958– .
GV191.6.N49 2003
333.78—dc21   2002035402

ISBN 1 84064 985 2

Printed and bound in Great Britain by MPG Books Ltd, Bodmin, Cornwall

Contents

PART II   FORESTS

PART III   RIVERS AND THE SEA

Figures

Tables

Contributors

Wiktor (Vic) Adamowicz, Department of Rural Economy, University of Alberta, Canada

Begona Alvarez-Farizo, SIA-DGA, Zaragoza, Spain

Ian J. Bateman, Programme on Environmental Decision-Making, Centre for Social and Economic Research on the Global Environment (CSERGE), University of East Anglia, Norwich, United Kingdom

Robert P. Berrens, Department of Economics, University of New Mexico, USA

Peter C. Boxall, Department of Rural Economy, University of Alberta, Canada

Julie S. Brainard, Programme on Environmental Decision-Making, Centre for Social and Economic Research on the Global Environment (CSERGE), University of East Anglia, Norwich, United Kingdom

William S. Breffle, Stratus Consulting Inc., Boulder, CO, USA

Susan M. Chilton, Economics Department, University of Newcastle-on-Tyne, UK

Jeffrey Englin, Department of Applied Economics and Statistics, University of Nevada, Reno, USA

Therese Grijalva, Department of Economics, Weber State University, Utah, USA

Nick Hanley, Economics Department, University of Glasgow, Scotland

W. George Hutchinson, Department of Agricultural and Food Economics, Queen's University Belfast, UK

Paul M. Jakus, Department of Economics, Utah State University, Logan, UT, USA

Andrew P. Jones, Programme on Environmental Decision-Making, Centre for Social and Economic Research on the Global Environment (CSERGE), University of East Anglia, Norwich, United Kingdom

Douglas M. Larson, Department of Agricultural and Resource Economics, University of California, Davis, USA

Jordan Louviere, Department of Marketing, University of Sydney, Australia

Andrew A. Lovett, Programme on Environmental Decision-Making, Centre for Social and Economic Research on the Global Environment (CSERGE), University of East Anglia, Norwich, United Kingdom

D. Matthew Massey, National Center for Environmental Economics, US EPA, Washington DC, USA

Trevor McCallion, Biometrics Division, Department of Agriculture and Rural Development for Northern Ireland

Nicola Milne, Renfrew Enterprise, Scotland

Edward R. Morey, Department of Economics, University of Colorado, Boulder, USA

George R. Parsons, College of Marine Studies and Department of Economics, University of Delaware, USA

Mary Riddel, Center for Business and Economic Research, University of Nevada, Las Vegas, NV, USA

Geoff Riddington, Department of Economics, Glasgow Caledonian University, Scotland

Robert D. Rowe, Stratus Consulting Inc., Boulder, CO, USA

Riccardo Scarpa, Environment Department, University of York, United Kingdom

W. Douglass Shaw, Department of Applied Economics and Statistics, University of Nevada, Reno, USA

J. Scott Shonkwiler, Department of Applied Economics and Statistics, University of Nevada, Reno, USA

Colin Sinclair, Department of Economics, Glasgow Caledonian University, Scotland

Sabina L. Shaikh, Faculty of Agricultural Sciences, University of British Columbia, Canada

Joffre Swait, Department of Marketing, University of Florida, USA

Tiziano Tempesta, Department of Environmental and Agro-food Economics and Policy, University of Milan, Italy

Mara Thiene, Department of Land and Agri-forestry Systems (TESAF), University of Padua, Italy

Donald M. Waldman, Department of Economics, University of Colorado, Boulder, USA

David O. Watson, Northern Forestry Centre, Edmonton, Canada

Michael Williams, Intelligent Marketing Systems

Robert E. Wright, Economics Department, University of Stirling, Scotland

Acknowledgements

We thank the publishers of the *Journal of Environmental Economics and Management* for permission to reproduce Chapter 9 of this book; the publishers of the *Journal of Environmental Management* for permission to reproduce Chapter 15 of this book; the publishers of the *Canadian Journal of Forest Research* for permission to reproduce Chapter 11 of this book; the publishers of *Environmental and Resource Economics* for permission to use Chapter 4; and the publishers of the journal *Land Use Policy* for permission to use Chapter 3.

1. Introduction

Nick Hanley, W. Douglass Shaw and
Robert E. Wright

This introductory chapter sets out to accomplish four objectives. The first is to explain why outdoor recreation is a relevant and interesting subject of study for economists. Second, the chapter provides a short history of this field of study. Third, we very briefly detail the main methods for estimating the demand for and value of outdoor recreation, and how demand may change when environmental conditions change. Fourth and finally, we preview the chapters that follow this one.

1.   WHY AN ECONOMICS OF OUTDOOR RECREATION?

One of the first areas of study in the emerging discipline of environmental economics in the 1960s was that of outdoor recreation. Why? It seems to us that there are several possible reasons.

First, outdoor recreation was a fast-growing activity in the 1960s and remains so today. The great outdoors became more accessible as incomes grew, allowing households more leisure time, or at least easier access by automobiles. Accompanying this were interests in fitness and special activities such as fishing and hunting. This increasing demand for recreation brought with it its own pressures, such as congestion and potential environmental impacts. In addition, recreational activities were often in direct conflict with other demands on natural areas, such as mining, hydro-electric developments, farming, property development and afforestation. Economists were naturally interested in the relative costs and benefits of these different, often mutually-exclusive, land uses (for example Krutilla and Fisher, 1975). Perhaps what also helped stimulate economists to work on this issue was that outdoor recreation demands were often for activities on publicly-owned land, such as US Forest Service or UK Forestry Commission land. Such public agencies were interested in pursuing a wider set of objectives than simple timber production and, as such, demanded information from academic economists on the non-market benefits of the resources. Much early work on the economics of outdoor recreation was funded by public agencies concerned with land management. Again, this remains true today. Economists, meanwhile, found that recreation demands could be brought within the paradigm of neo-classical welfare economics and demand theory with few modifications to the basic ideas.

Finally, recreation modeling offered a productive link between people (their preferences and behavior) and the environment, which was a useful coincidence during a period when government initiatives were raising environmental quality levels or at least reducing environmental degradation in most countries. In the United States much of this effort was tied to conflicts over development of enormous western water projects. Damming rivers and streams was being done at a furious pace in the Pacific Northwest, in the Colorado River Basin, and in several parts of California, and environmentalists cried out for help in preserving them. Hells Canyon, Idaho and the Mineral King Controversy were famous examples involving recreation losses and gains. Such preservation or quality increases were in most cases costly, but were the benefits of preserving a river at the expense of forgone benefits from development commensurable? Recreational demand modeling provided some answers.

The benefits of water quality improvements could be estimated by studying impacts on the demand for sport fishing, whether these improvements were due to reduced point source emissions to water from sewage works, from reduced non-point emissions from farmland, or from reduced acid rain depositions. The hypothesis was simply that better water quality could improve the fishery, which in turn could improve the angler's experience and lead to measurable economic benefits. The increasing desire to place environmental policy-making under the spotlight of cost–benefit analysis provided another driver for increased activity in such work.

These issues are still very much to the fore in environmental valuation work today, whilst additional motivating factors have emerged, such as natural resource damage assessment (for example Hausman et al., 1995). This need for work to calculate economic benefits, coupled with increasing technical refinements in recreational demand methods (see, for example, Herriges and Kling, 1999), has meant and will continue to mean a rising volume of work. But before we look at the methods currently available to recreational economists, it is worth looking back to see how we got to the point we are at today.

2. A BRIEF HISTORY

It is an interesting coincidence that perhaps the two most practiced non-market valuation tools we have today, the Contingent Valuation Method (CVM) and Travel Cost Models (TCM), were originally proposed the same year. In 1949, Harold Hotelling wrote a letter to the National Park Service, outlining a method where the park visitor's round trip distance could be used to proxy the recreation trip price, so that consumer's surplus estimates might be recovered. The idea was to obtain the net benefit for outdoor recreation for a particular geographic area. The CVM method was suggested in the same year in an article by Ciriacy-Wantrup, although the first actual application of the method (to deer hunting in Maine) was by Robert Davis in his Harvard PhD dissertation, in 1963.

Some time after Hotelling's letter was sent, Wood and Trice (1958) and Marion Clawson (1959), who was working at Resources for the Future (RFF), applied the travel cost modeling idea to some actual data. Early TCMs used distance from some zone of origin to the destination point, a recreational area. The total number of visitors from the origin zone was the dependent variable in such models, and the travel cost from the zone to the area was a key explanatory variable. These applications became known as zonal travel cost models, and the unit of observation became the zonal aggregate population. Some ideas were taken from the regional economics 'gravity' models, typically used to model commuting decisions.

While novel and practical, it soon became clear that there were statistical or econometric problems with these zonal models. In particular, large population zones had a better chance of having larger variations in visitors to a recreation destination, but this fact was not typically considered, at least early on (although later versions of the zonal approach switched to visits per capita as the dependent variable). Vaughan and Russell and several others recognized that the assumption of homoskedastic errors would be suspect, and recommended corrections in the zonal model for the presence of heteroskedasticity.

Concerns about these early recreation TCMs and their somewhat shaky links to microeconomic theory led to the introduction of the idea that an individual recreational user might be a better unit of observation than an entire zone's population (Brown and Nawas, 1973). An individual user's demand for a trip to a recreation destination allowed more careful consideration of underlying microeconomic theory, but also required that more extensive data be collected. Once individual-specific data collection was contemplated the door was open to collecting data on the individual's income, her labor market situation, the length of her stay at an area, and even more detail on the activities she engaged in at each area visited. The limit, of course, would be dictated by the survey mechanism and amount of information collectible before exhausting the respondent. Suddenly, travel cost modeling took a huge leap from the days of collecting only the origin location off the license plate on the back of an automobile.

Another important breakthrough with individual survey data related to modeling trips to more than one destination. Once data could be collected on trips to multiple sites, a modeler could think of entire systems of demand equations, or at least partial (recreation) demand systems. Burt and Brewer's classic article, published in 1971, applied just this idea. And so, connections between individual-specific data, better adherence to microeconomic theory, and sophisticated econometric techniques launched the new wave of travel cost and recreation demand modeling. Thorny issues quickly emerged to complicate the modeling and data collection, but resolution of these details made the models' predictive ability stronger.

These difficult technical issues included how to treat the time spent in travel to and from the recreation destinations, the time spent on site, the length of a stay at the site, how to assign values to the time spent, whether more than one destination was visited on a single 'trip', whether and which substitute site trip costs should be included in the model, and how to model congestion or overcrowding at some destinations. Progress was made on most of these issues, but something was still missing.

Perhaps the next major development in travel cost modeling was to incorporate site characteristics to help explain variation in trip-taking behavior beyond the travel cost itself. Up to a point in history, the only feature of the recreation destination that uniquely mattered in the models was the cost of getting to it and back. Why would a potential visitor pay attention to only this one detail? Surely an angler would care about how good the fishing at a lake was, or a hunter would wish to know that the destination offered excellent opportunities for success. Thus emerged the need to introduce recreation site characteristics, which obviously only would work empirically with adequate variation in the data. Hypotheses quickly emerged: better fishing, better hunting, more beautiful scenery, all lead to more trips, ceteris paribus.

There were other modelers who suggested this application of Lancaster's basic idea, but the best known of these early characteristics studies is by Morey (1981), who considered features of ski slopes and how these would contribute to the skier's choice of ski areas. This modeling more carefully considered what features of a recreation destination were important to the potential visitor beyond the trip price or travel cost. Morey went further than many and also introduced the ability of the recreational user as a factor pertaining to the enjoyment of the ski area. Novice skiers would have little interest in double-black diamond (for experts only) ski terrain.

Extensions of the characteristics idea also allowed a great deal of focus on how to connect these models to the environment, considering welfare measures for specific water quality improvements and the like.

Finally, the falling cost of desktop computers with high performance allowed careful consideration of the data generation process underlying recreation destination choice and the trip data. Two important approaches provided impetus for years of research to follow. One avenue pursued discrete choice modeling and we have seen Michael Hanemann's and Peter Caulkin's PhD dissertations (at Harvard and the University of Wisconsin, respectively) cited as examples of pioneering work in this discrete choice modeling area. Nancy Bockstael, Ted McConnell, and their colleagues at Maryland were also major contributors in this regard, stemming from their work funded by the US EPA on marine recreation. This work on recreation issues carried on through several major contributors from Maryland, including Maryland graduates Doug Larson and Cathy Kling, and as seems true for nearly every idea in environmental economics, Kerry Smith dove into the pool as well.

The other main development in travel cost modeling recognized that if the respondent understood what it meant to take a 'trip' and reported it consistently in integer units, then the data followed a count data process. Trips cannot take negative values and unless the visitor reports taking something like 1.5, or 1.25 trips, cannot take anything but integer-reported trips. Count models are then logical for nonzero positive integer data, and can be developed to handle zero reported trips. The Poisson distribution and its variants were used to represent the distributions of these trips. Daniel Hellerstein worked to develop this approach in his PhD dissertation at Yale along with Rob Mendelsohn, and the count data approach has since been extensively applied (for example, Hellerstein, 1991; Englin et al., 1997; Shonkwiler and Shaw, 1996; Haab and McConnell, 2002).

This nearly brings us up to the present. In the past ten years or so there has been increasing sophistication, even involving some dabbling in travel cost modeling by an economist who has now won the Nobel Prize in economics, though naturally we understand that the prize was not given for this particular work (see Hausman et al., 1995). The highest compliment ever received by one of the authors after a seminar was in the form of a question something like: 'Recreation economics has all the challenges that labor supply economics does, but it is much harder because of all the issues and unobservables, isn't it?' Indeed today, recreation demand modeling often looks little different from the most advanced labor supply modeling at the individual level. This is for good reason, in that much of the micro-econometrics used in modeling an individual's labor supply is also used in modeling recreation demand, and of course because one might think of recreation demand as a special case of the entire labor–leisure choice decision.

Despite application of interesting and promising econometrics, and more careful adherence to the microeconomic theory underlying welfare measures, many challenges remain. We still cannot identify any manuscript that adequately deals with congestion and overcrowding in an empirical model using revealed preference data. There are many good reasons for this and we are not suggesting recreation economists have been lazy in this regard: it may be that modeling congestion adequately will require development of game-theoretic empirical models. In addition, though some have made recent contributions on incorporating the role of time (for example Feather and Shaw, 1999), there is still no agreement on the best way of handling this difficult issue. Proper treatment of time suggests the need to model all of the individual's activities carefully, a task that even more general microeconomic theorists have failed to do. A few other challenges ahead that we can think of include handling corner solutions (taking zero trips, trips to site A, site B, sites A and B, and so on) with more than a small number of recreation destinations, dealing with potential survey and sampling bias, linking choice occasions together to allow patterns in behavior to be reflected, and more generally, handling dynamic aspects of decision making over time.

3.   A QUICK OVERVIEW OF METHODOLOGICAL APPROACHES

In this section we look at two issues: what do we typically want to value, and how can we actually estimate these values?

3.1   What Do We Want to Value?

To begin, for the uninitiated, we want to dispel the notion that recreation economists wish to value coca-colas, sandwiches, sun hats, and locally purchased gasoline. Many, many times we recreation economists have had to spend time convincing the public that expenditures in areas where recreation destinations are located is *not* our primary focus. Their mistake is in thinking that more local expenditure means a highly valued recreation destination, and such may not be the case. It is the job of the regional economist to ascertain what impact, if any, recreational visitors have on local areas when they visit. But recreational and environmental economists are more interested in the value of a lake itself, which does not include the value of the soft drinks purchased while there.

Economic values are defined over some potential or actual change in prices or the quality or quantities of goods and services that affect utility. For recreational destinations the earliest focus was on the implied value of a recreational resource (forest, lake . . .), rather than do without it. As such, these early studies typically focused, at least implicitly, on price changes. What is found in many early studies is an estimate of ordinary consumers' surplus, calculated as the area under the estimated demand curve for the recreational resource. Perhaps without fully realizing it, the topic of interest was actually whether a site-charge or entry fee might lead to a loss in benefits to the visitors. These points can be made clearer with a quick and simple formal discussion.

Let utility be a function of the trip price (P), income (Y), and quality attributes of the sites (q). Demand for trips will be X. The usual utility maximization problem, subject to constraints, leads to an indirect utility function $V(P,q,Y)$. Most travel cost modeling uncovers the consumer's surplus measure, the maximum willingness to pay (WTP). Typically WTP is hoped to be a compensating variation (CV) measure to prevent a price increase or quality decrease. It is possible, as seen later in the book, to uncover an equivalent variation measure (EV) also, but doing so requires careful consideration of income effects. For a given price increase in a site price at a national park used for recreation, WTP is defined by:

$$V(\mathbf{P_0}, \mathbf{q}, Y - \text{WTP}) = V(\mathbf{P_1}, \mathbf{q}, Y) \qquad (1.1)$$

where $\mathbf{P}$ is a price vector of all market goods, $\mathbf{q}$ is a vector of quality attributes or environmental goods, Y is income, and where the price is changing from P_0 to P_1. WTP is the most income an individual would give up to prevent an undesirable change in P, and is defined by this indifference condition.

As stated, in early work by recreation economists, most emphasis was on price changes, in the sense that most modeling efforts were aimed at estimating WTP or consumers' surplus for recreational experiences from a baseline of current conditions. Sometimes the assumptions were not explicit. The modelers often simply estimated a linear or log-linear demand function for one or more sites, and then calculated the area under this demand function. The notion, whether done properly or not, was that the entire area under the supposed demand function is consumer's surplus. This is naturally true if the demand function is truly connected to some underlying utility function (that is, it 'IS' a demand function as we know it), and if the implicit goal is to examine the consumer's surplus related to a choke price, say P^*. P^* is assumed to be that trip price that forces demands to zero, that is it is that trip price where all, or at least most, visitors will no longer visit the site. Another way of looking at the possible meaning of these estimates is that they reveal peoples' WTP to maintain access to a recreational site, and many assume that such a value is in fact the value of the recreational destination itself.

When averaged across a sample of individuals, the CS measure above yields the average WTP for the recreational area. Many early economists also reported such estimates after dividing by some number of reported or estimated trips, and such estimates became known as the value or CS per trips. A CS per trip measure that is logical does flow from count data models. However, in later years several economists, starting with Morey (1994), questioned the meaning of early CS per trip measures, showing that the derivation of these as well as the change being contemplated are of critical importance. One of Morey's points is that, for example, if we estimate the annual WTP to increase water qualty at some lake and find this consumer's surplus to be an average of $80, then does it make much sense to divide this by some number of trips, breaking the environmental quality change across trips? The reason that policy-makers today still cling to per-trip welfare measures in recreation is both their apparently simple information content (the value of an average trip), and that the data collected for a benefits transfer often lend themselves to doing back-of-the-envelope estimates with such values.

Contingent valuation methods have also been widely used to measure WTP to preserve the right to visit a recreation destination, such as a forest. Since values are only defined over changes, some change must be at least implicit in these types of calculation: the implicit change early on was once again the removal of the right to access these recreational areas. For example, the earliest use of contingent valuation in the UK to look at forest recreation values (Hanley, 1989) asked people their WTP to preserve the right to walk in the Queen Elizabeth Forest Park in Scotland (P_0, above), versus not being able to walk in the woods in the future (P_1, above).

Today, in the context of managing recreational resources, the earlier type of 'use as is' value may be of rather less policy relevance than it used to be. Rarely do we see the potential complete loss of a recreation destination, unless it relates to extinction of a resource, or to access restrictions.[1] The choke-price models and results do enable the non-market rate of return from such resources to be calculated, and to be compared across forest types (say), but a rather more useful focus from a management viewpoint is likely to be tied to quality changes within a recreational resource. Questions that arise today are, how does acid rain affect a lake or forest? How does non-point source pollution affect the value of recreation on a river? And, do toxins that lead to fish consumption advisories harm all anglers and their experiences, or some smaller group of those who actually eat fish they catch?

The above formal derivation of a WTP can be simply modified to produce the WTP to prevent such a quality decline from q_0 to q_1, or to bring about an improvement in quality from some baseline point. In assessing the benefits of reducing pollution in a lake which will likely improve fishing conditions from 'fair' to 'good', it is best to have estimates of consumers' surplus for this change. If all we know is the value of consumers' surplus per fishing trip under current conditions, say \$25 per fishing trip, this may be of limited value to the researcher or policy-maker.

Attention has therefore increasingly focused on estimating the value of site quality changes. Applications have led to hundreds of travel cost studies too numerous to cite here. Water quality changes are probably the most common application, but travel cost studies of forest-based recreation and recreation tied to hunting and species habitat are growing in number.

Another recent focus of valuation has been to look at the welfare impacts of measures to limit access. For instance, if site managers are worried about increasing erosion of footpaths on a popular mountain site, they may introduce alternative measures to discourage visits, such as increasing access fees (if possible), or making access more difficult or more time consuming. Such actions can be expected to diminish the utility of a trip to those people who still visit the site, but also to displace visits to other, substitute sites. Some types of recreational demand models (for example, repeated nested logit models) can be used to study both of these potential impacts.[2]

Finally, although recreational demand studies have very much focussed on the welfare of people who actually visit sites (users), newer models allow recovery of values to those who do not currently use the recreation destinations. The 'non-users' fall into two groups: those who are potential users, but who do not visit the destination today, and those who are neither users now, nor will be in the future. Many travel cost models allow recovery of values for potential users (see Hellerstein's 1992 work on this, or the theoretical discussion by Shonkwiler and Shaw), but it is still true today that the stated preference methods are the only way to recover values for non-users. For instance, protecting woodland habitats for caribou which some people like to hunt might also increase utility for those who just like to know that caribou are benefiting from their habitat being protected. Many studies have tried to estimate what these non-use values might be for recreational resources (for example Adamowicz et al., 1998).

Having explained what types of value we might want to measure, we now want to briefly look at the range of empirical methods available for actually estimating these values.

3.2   Methods for Estimating Recreational Values

Methods for estimating environmental values are conventionally divided
into *stated preference* and *revealed preference* approaches. In the former
case, researchers make use of questionnaire surveys to directly question
respondents about their WTP for the option to use recreational resources,
or with regard to quality changes to these resources. Two types of stated
approach are available. The first, and most widely used, is the *contingent
valuation method* (CVM). In a CVM survey, respondents are asked their
WTP to either obtain (for welfare-increasing changes) or avoid (for welfare-
decreasing changes) an environmental change. For example, people might
be asked their WTP for a program which improves water quality at a
popular lake where swimming and fishing activities are pursued. WTP
values may be obtained in a number of ways, for example as a referendum
('if the cost to you was $y, would you approve the scheme?'), or using a iter-
ative format ('would you pay £x? Yes? Well then, would you pay £2x?'). A
full discussion of the method can be found in Bateman and Willis (1999),
or in Bateman et al. (2002). CVM has proved very popular amongst both
academic researchers and the policy community due to its very wide applicability, and its relative simplicity. Both use and non-use values can be estimated with the technique.

An alternative stated preference approach which is gaining increasing
use in recreation economics is *choice modeling* (CM) (Adamowicz et al.,
1994). Choice modeling, as used by economists, is based on Lancaster's
attribute theory of value, and can be developed using random utility theory
and the random utility model (RUM). The environmental resource in question is described in terms of its attributes. For example, suppose we want
to estimate the value of increasing species diversity in forests used by
walkers. Any particular forest might be described in terms of, say, four
attributes: species diversity, the extent of trails, the proportion of forest as
open space, and the age of the forest. Different forest management plans
could be described in terms of differing levels of these attributes. In order
to derive welfare measures, it is also necessary to include a cost attribute.
Two 'forest profiles' might look as shown in Table 1.1. Respondents would
be asked to make choices between pairs such as this, with a 'visit neither'
option also being included. By making such choices, respondents reveal the
marginal utility they place on each attribute: this is derived in some models
from the estimated parameter for a given attribute in a probabilistic model
describing actual choices (typically, a simple conditional multinomial logit
model).

The parameter on the cost attribute in the simple MNL can be interpreted as the marginal utility of income: dividing any attribute parameter

Table 1.1   Attributes of hypothetical forests

	Forest A	Forest B
Species diversity	Low	High
Extent of trails	10km	10km
Proportion of forest as open space	5%	10%
Mean age	75 years	45 years
Travel cost per visit	$5	$9

by this value gives an 'implicit price', which can be interpreted as a marginal WTP value. Finally, welfare effects for changes in attributes (for instance, for a program which increases both species diversity and the extent of trails) can be calculated using a 'log-sum' expression:

$$-\left(\frac{1}{\beta_c}\right)\left[\ln \sum \exp(V_i^1) - \ln \sum \exp(V_i^2)\right] \qquad (1.2)$$

where β_c is the parameter on the 'price' attribute (and thus $1/\beta_c$ can be interpreted as the marginal utility of income), and V^1 and V^2 are the indirect utility associated with pre- and post-change attribute bundles respectively. Such equations must be modified for different assumptions, including whether income effects are present. For a full account of the CM approach, see Bennett and Blamey (2001), Louviere et al. (2000), or Hanley et al. (2001). Like CVM, CM can measure both use and non-use values.

One common objection to stated preference approaches today is that they produce estimates of value that are not founded in actual behavior. People's responses to both CVM and CM questions are not actually budget-constrained, no matter how ingenious the questionnaire design. A worry exists that stated preference estimates of value are thus somehow less 'real' than other economic values, or at the very least are biased upwards. It should thus be apparent that basing value estimates on actual behavior might be an attractive alternative.

Revealed preference approaches are based on actual behavior. Founded on pioneering theoretical work by Maler (1974), economists have been able to show how behavior in related markets can be used to estimate use values for non-market goods such as recreational resources. Unfortunately, non-use values cannot be so estimated, as they leave no 'behavioral trail' behind. The main related market of interest in our context is for travel. People are observed to spend money on fuel, cars and so on in order to be able to 'consume' outdoor recreational experiences. The idea is simply this. Although I pay no entrance fee to climb Ben Nevis (a popular mountain in Scotland), I do have to spend money on petrol in order to drive there from where I live. By tracing out a relationship between such expenditures and visit rates (trips per annum, for example), economists can estimate demand curves for such sites. Another type of price recreational users pay in accessing outdoor sites is related to the use of their time. Time is a scarce commodity with an economic value (de Serpa, 1971), and people spend time both in accessing a site whilst actually going for a walk, going fishing, going canoeing, and so on. How exactly to include such time values in revealed preference models has, however, proved a tricky issue, as noted earlier.

Two or three basic approaches can be identified for the *travel cost* modeling (TCM) approach to recreational valuation. The first stems from the origin of the methods used by Wood and Trice and by Clawson and Knetsch (see the history lesson). The idea here is simply to estimate one or more demand equations, hopefully which are consistent with economic theory. The most popular approach is now referred to as *count modeling*.[3] Far and away the most common in the literature is a single-site count model, however, actual site quality cannot be included in a single site model as it is a constant. Systems of demand equations allow variation in site quality, and are possible in the count framework, as Chapter 6 shows. Others develop systems of demand equations based on other empirical assumptions, as Chapter 14 shows.

In all such demand models whether to use objective or subjective measures of these characteristics has proved another tricky issue (Englin et al., 1997). Naturally economists do not wish to introduce endogeneity in the right-hand side variables, so one must be careful if the explanatory variable is constructed from subjective assessments of a recreation destination's characteristics. This is also a problem with modeling congestion, as what seems crowded to one person may not seem so to another (see the discussion in Jakus and Shaw, 1998).

Count models focus on predicting participation (trips) at sites, and on consumers' surplus per trip. The second approach to travel costs models takes a somewhat different approach. Random Utility Models (RUMs) are probabilistic in nature, and revolve around the allocation of a fixed quantity of trips across substitute sites within a 'choice set', as site qualities change. The welfare effects of such quality changes can again be calculated (for example, Morey et al., 1993). Haab and McConnell (2002) provide a good discussion of the econometric issues involved. One problem with site-choice RUMs is that total trips to all sites in the choice set are fixed by assumption. Two ways around this limitation have been developed. The first is to use a repeated RUM model, where both the number of trips and trip destination are modeled simultaneously. A limiting assumption with this approach is that the number of choice occasions has to be fixed. A second alternative is to combine RUM and count models, and estimate the system simultaneously. One of the first efforts along these lines was undertaken by Yen and Adamowicz (1994). A discussion on alternative ways of approaching this task is given in Parsons et al. (1999) and theoretical considerations are in Shaw and Shonkwiler (2000).

Finally, it is possible to combine revealed and stated preference approaches (Bateman et al., 2002). For instance, suppose we constructed a CM approach to forest valuation based on the choice sets in Table 1.1. We could now also estimate a revealed preference RUM by sampling visitors to the forests, finding out their trips to each forest, and then obtaining measures of each attribute for each forest in the choice set. Two categories of observation now exist on peoples' preferences across different recreational forests, one based on stated preferences (the CM experiment), and one on actual behavior (the travel cost model). These can now be pooled together, and a joint model estimated (see, for example, Adamowicz et al. in Chapter 9). A second approach is to combine travel cost models of site visits with questions on how respondents' behavior would change should site characteristics change (for example species diversity is improved). This allows revealed preference models to 'look beyond' existing site quality levels using stated intentions. For examples of this type of approach, see Grijalva et al. (2002), Englin and Cameron (1996) and, most recently, Hanley, Bell and Alvarez-Farizo (2003).

The above discussion by no means exhausts the list of all of the important contributors to recreation demand modeling. To keep this chapter short we cannot provide a complete discussion, but we would be remiss in at least not mentioning the omitted names of Frank Cesario, Mike Creel, Ken Willis, John Loomis, and Guy Garrod and of course the newest contributors to the field of recreation modeling, too numerous now to specifically mention.

4. AN OUTLINE OF THE BOOK

We have divided the book into sections that relate to the resources being analysed. Part One of the book is concerned with the mountains. Mountains have been extremely important as recreational resources in Europe over the last 150 years, and are of growing importance in the United States and elsewhere. In Chapter 2, Therese Grijalva and Robert Berrens use contingent valuation to estimate the value of ensuring access to a particular type of rock climbing, known as 'bouldering', at Hueco Tanks Texas State Park. Hueco Tanks is a world-renowned bouldering site. Across varying levels of park access, a scope test is conducted on willingness to pay (WTP) to protect rock-climbing and bouldering access. This means testing whether WTP estimates are sensitive to the quantity/quality of environmental good 'on offer'. Scope tests have become important as one way of assessing the validity of contingent valuation applications. The empirical results indicate that the WTP for protecting rock climbing and boudering access is indeed sensitive to changes in scope.

A rather different approach to valuing changes in access to rock climbing sites is reported in Chapter 3, where Nick Hanley, Begona Alvarez-Farizo and Douglass Shaw use a repeated nested logit approach to value the welfare impacts of different policies to manage rock-climbing sites in Scotland. This approach also allows the authors to produce predictions of the change in the number of visits made to each climbing area when policies are introduced; the policies studied comprise car parking fees, and making access more time-consuming. Scottish rock-climbers are also the subject of Chapter 4, where Nick Hanley and Robert Wright use the choice experiment method to investigate which characteristics of climbing sites determine the demand for climbing. The chapter also investigates a methodological issue in choice experiments, namely the effects of changing choice task complexity.

In Chapter 5, Paul Jakus, Mary Riddel and Douglass Shaw investigate the fascinating subject of climbers' attitudes to risk. Most non-climbers probably view climbers as being off their heads, but the authors argue that climbers' actual choices show quite consistent and economically-rational decisions under risk. Italian mountaineers are the focus of Chapter 6, in which Riccardo Scarpa, Tiziano Tempesta and Mara Thiene apply a sophisticated system of count models to trips to the North-Eastern Alps. The method used here is particularly appealing in terms of the close relationship between econometric method and the classical theory of demand. Finally in this section, Geoff Riddington, Colin Sinclair and Nicola Milne apply a conventional Random Utility Model to the choice of sites by downhill skiers in Scotland. They find that two distinct groups of skiers exist: overnight stayers and daytrippers. For the former, the quality and price of the skiing is relatively unimportant. The key determinant in this market seems to be accommodation. For day-trippers snow cover, cost and, to a lesser extent, journey length, were the critical factors. Interestingly sites which for the day-tripper are competitors become, for the overnight customer, complementary.

Part Two of the book concerns forest recreation. In Chapter 8, George Hutchinson and co-authors use a regional travel cost model to estimate the spatial distribution of positive and negative welfare effects arising from the implementation of a number of policies for managing forest recreation in Northern Ireland. Using a travel cost model based on choice probability and count modeling, the chapter develops a method to estimate the welfare effects of adjustments in charging and site quality, and of how these effects are distributed across the 26 district council areas in the region. This kind of distributional analysis is rather uncommon in travel cost models. In Chapter 9, Vic Adamowicz and colleagues employ a combined stated-revealed preference approach to study the preferences of moose hunters for forest sites in Alberta. This study compares perceptions with objective measures of site attributes. Results suggest that the model based on perceptions slightly outperforms the models based on objective attribute measures. However, issues such as the definition of the choice set and the measurement of welfare present significant challenges when using perceptions data.

Benefits transfer is an important area of research in environmental valuation, and in Chapter 10 Ian Bateman and friends report on an extensive programme of work at the University of East Anglia which investigates the use of Geographic Information Systems (GIS) in this context. They employ GIS techniques in an increasingly-sophisticated array of models to predict visitor numbers and consumers' surplus for public forests in the UK. This work is very important in terms of the wider use of environmental valuation in the management of natural resources. A rather different focus is provided by Peter Boxall, David Watson and Jeff Englin in Chapter 11. They study the recreational demands of backcountry recreationists, primarily canoeists, in Nopiming Provincial Park in eastern Manitoba. This work is undertaken in the context of a need to estimate the relative values of economic value of four forest ecosystems, fire-damaged forests and several park management features. One of their most interesting findings is that whilst park management variables play a role in determining recreation values, the ages and types of forests located at recreation sites are more important.

Part Three takes to the water. In Chapter 12, George Parsons and Matt Massey estimate a random utility site choice model for beaches in the Mid-Atlantic region of the US. They study the relative importance of site attributes such as travel cost, beach width and beach facilities on people's decisions as to which beaches to visit. Using the model estimates, they are able to estimate the economic loss associated with both beach closures and beach erosion in the region. The main focus of Shonkwiler and Shaw in Chapter 13 is to extend random utility modeling to allow for the analysis of income effects on demand. The case study they choose centers around reservoir recreation along the Columbia river. The conventional random utility model assumes that the marginal utility of income is constant. Income effects are therefore not present in the individual's choice among alternatives and this has strong implications for welfare measures; yet in many applications that require examination of rather large changes in prices or attributes of the alternatives, allowing for income effects would seem desirable. The chapter therefore presents an important methodological advance for recreation demand modeling using the RUM approach. Methodological enhancements are also the focus of Larson and Shaikh in Chapter 14, this time in the context of a system of count models. They use whalewatching trips to three northern Californian sites as their empirical focus. Finally, Chapter 15 moves us back to random utility modeling, but now in the context of a motivation for environmental valuation which became increasingly important in the US in the 1990s: natural resource damage assessment. Morey, Breffle, Rowe and Waldman report on a natural resource damage assessment for the State of Montana. Mining wastes have caused significant reductions in trout stocks in a 145-mile stretch of Montana's Silver Bow Creek and Clark Fork River. To estimate economic damages from decreases in catch rates, the authors develop and estimate an individual-based utility-theoretic model of where and how often an angler will fish as a function of travel costs, catch rates, and other influential characteristics of the sites and individuals. The model includes resident and non-resident anglers who currently fish in Montana, and allows them to have different preferences. The chapter is an excellent example of the usefulness of recreational demand models for this type of damage assessment.

We hope you enjoy reading this book, and that you will find it useful as well. We have certainly enjoyed working on this project, and wish to thank all the authors for their contributions, as well as Maggie Dewar for her help in putting together the final version of the book. Douglass Shaw thanks the Colorado School of Mines for their hospitality during his sabbatical, and the girls for putting up with his hiding in the basement.

NOTES

1. One such example is when a lake dries up, as can happen in the arid western United States. At some point the lake becomes useless for recreational fishing, boating and other uses. Fadali and Shaw (1998) considered such a problem for a dying lake in Nevada.
2. Chapter 3 is an example of such a model.
3. For a discussion of the econometric issues involved in estimating such models, see Haab and McConnell (2002).

REFERENCES

Adamowicz, W., J. Louviere and M. Williams (1994), 'Combining revealed and stated preference methods for valuing environmental amenities', *Journal of Environmental Economics and Management*, **26**: 271–92.

Adamowicz, W., P. Boxall, M. Williams and J. Louviere (1998), 'Stated preference approaches for measuring passive use values: choice experiments and contingent valuation', *American Journal of Agricultural Economics*, **80**(1): 64–75.

Bateman, I. and K. Willis (1999), *Valuing Environmental Preferences: Theory and Practice of the Contingent Valuation Method in the US, EU, and Developing Countries*, Oxford and New York: Oxford University Press.

Bateman, I. et al. (2002), *Economic Valuation with Stated Preference Techniques*, Cheltenham: Edward Elgar.

Bennet, J. and R. Blamey (2001), *The Choice Modeling Approach to Environmental Valuation*, Cheltenham: Edward Elgar.

Bockstael, N.E., W.M. Hanemann and I.E. Strand Jr. (1987), *Measuring the Benefits of Water Quality Improvements using Recreation Demand Models*, Vol. III, Report to the U.S. EPA, Dept. of Agricultural and Resource Economics, University of Maryland.

Brown, W.G. and F. Nawas (1973), 'Impact of aggregation on the estimation of outdoor recreation demand functions', *American Journal of Agricultural Economics*, **55**: 246–9.

Burt, O. and D. Brewer (1971), 'Estimation of net social benefits from outdoor recreation', *Econometrica*, **39** (September): 813–28.

Clawson, M. (1959), *Methods of Measuring the Demand for and the Value of Outdoor Recreation*, reprint No. 10, Washington DC: RFF.

Davis, R. (1963), 'Big game hunting in the Maine woods', *Natural Resources Journal*, **3**: 239–49.

De Serpa, A.C. (1971), 'The theory of the economics of time', *Economic Journal*, **81**: 828–46.

Englin, J. and T.A. Cameron (1996), 'Augmenting travel cost models with contingent behavior data: Poisson regression analyses with individual panel data', *Environmental and Research Economies*, **7** (March): 133–47.

Englin, J., D. Lambert and W.D. Shaw (1997), 'A structural equations approach to modeling consumptive recreation demand', *Journal of Environmental Economics and Management*, **33**: 33–43.

Fadali, E. and W.D. Shaw (1998), 'Can recreation values for a lake constitute a market for banked agricultural water?', *Contemporary Economic Policy*, **16**(4): 433–41.

Feather, P. and W.D. Shaw (1999), 'Estimating the cost of leisure time in recreation demand models', *Journal of Environmental Economics and Management*, **38**(1): 49–65.

Grijalva, T., R. Berrens, A. Bohara and W.D. Shaw (2002), 'Testing the validity of contingent behavior trip responses', *American Journal of Agricultural Economics*, **84**(2) (May): 401–14.

Haab, T. and K.E. McConnell (2002), *Valuing Environmental and Natural Resources: the econometrics of non-market valuation*, Cheltenham: Edward Elgar.

Hanley, N.D. (1989), 'Valuing rural recreation benefits: an empirical comparison of two approaches', *Journal of Agricultural Economics*, September, 361–74.

Hanley, N., D. Bell and B. Alvarez-Farizo (2003), 'Valuing the benefits of coastal water quality improvements using contingent and real behaviour', *Environmental and Resource Economics*, forthcoming.

Hanley, N., S. Mourato and R. Wright (2001), 'Choice modelling: a superior alternative for environmental valuation?', *Journal of Economic Surveys*, **15**(3), 453–62.

Hausman, J., G. Leonard and D. McFadden (1995), 'A utility-consistent, combined discrete choice and count data model: assessing recreational use losses due to natural resource damage', *Journal of Public Economics*, **56** (January): 1–30.

Hellerstein, D. (1991), 'Using count data models in travel cost analysis with aggregate data', *American Journal of Agricultural Economics*, **73**: 860–67.

Hellerstein, D. (1992), 'The treatment of nonparticipants in travel cost analysis and other demand models', *Water Resources Research*, **28**(8): 1999–2004.

Herriges, J.A. and C. Kling (1999), *Valuing Recreation and the Environment*, Cheltenham: Edward Elgar.

Hotelling, Harold (1949), 'A Reply Letter to a U.S. Park Service Request in The Economics of Public Recreation', mimeograph, Roy A. Prewitt (ed.), Washington DC: National Park Service.

Jakus, P.M. and W.D. Shaw (1998), 'Congestion at recreation areas: empirical evidence on perceptions, mitigating behavior, and management preferences', *Journal of Environmental Management*, **50**(4): 389–402.

Krutilla, J.V. and A.C. Fisher (1975), *The Economics of Natural Environments*, Baltimore: Johns Hopkins University Press.

Louviere, J., D. Hensher and J. Swait (2000), *Stated Choice Methods: Applications in Marketing, Transportation and Environmental Evaluation*, Cambridge: Cambridge University Press.

Maler, K.G. (1974), *Environmental Economics: a theoretical enquiry*, Baltimore: Johns Hopkins Press.

Morey, E.R. (1981), 'The demand for site-specific recreational activities: A characteristic approach', *Journal of Environmental Economics and Management*, **8** (December): 345–71.

Morey, E.R. (1994), 'What is consumer's surplus per day of use, when is it a constant independent of the number of days of use, and what does it tell us about consumer's surplus?', *Journal of Environmental Economics and Management*, **27** (May): 257–70.

Morey E., R. Rowe and M. Watson (1993), 'A repeated nested logit model of atlantic salmon fishing', *American Journal of Agricultural Economics*, **75**: 578–92.

Parsons, G.R., P.M. Jakus and T. Tomasi (1999), 'A comparison of welfare estimates from four models for linking seasonal recreational trips to multinomial logit models of site choice', *Journal of Environmental Economics and Management*, **38**: 143–57.

Shaw, W.D. and J.S. Shonkwiler (2000), 'Brand choice and total purchases revisited: an application to recreation behavior', *American Journal of Agricultural Economics*, **82** (August): 515–24.

Shonkwiler, J.S. and W.D. Shaw (1996), 'Hurdle count data models for recreation demand analysis', *Journal of Agricultural and Resource Economics*, **21**(2): 210–19.

Smith, V.K. (1989), 'Taking stock of progress with travel cost recreation demand methods: theory and implementation', *Marine Resource Economics*, **6**: 279–310.

von Ciriacy-Wantrup, S. (1947), 'Capital returns from soil conservation practices', *Journal of Farm Economics*, **29**: 1181–96.

Wood, S. and A. Trice (1958), 'Measurement of recreation benefits', *Land Economics*, **34**: 195–207.

Yen, S.T. and W.L. Adamowicz (1994), 'Participation, trip frequency and site choice: a multinomial-Poisson hurdle model of recreation demand', *Canadian Journal of Agricultural Economics*, **42**: 65–76.

PART I

The Mountains

2. Valuing rock climbing and bouldering access

Therese Grijalva and Robert P. Berrens

1. INTRODUCTION

Information on the economic benefits of recreational activities can assist public agencies in managing multiple uses on public lands (Loomis, 1993). For some common outdoor recreation activities, such as wildlife viewing, hunting and fishing, there are now numerous studies on relative nonmarket use values. These estimates have accumulated over the last three decades or more, and are now routinely incorporated in various policy and planning processes (Loomis, 1999; Rosenberger and Loomis, 2001). While outdoor rock climbing is a sport with considerable history, it is generally considered to have undergone significant growth in the last decade in the US and elsewhere. Due to the rapid increase in popularity, and associated concerns over congestion and site impacts, there have been a number of conflicts over rock climbing access at US federal and state parks. These concerns have resulted in various public agency actions and proposals, and have made rock climbing access a controversial issue in the 1990s (Cavlovic, 2000). While estimates of the nonmarket value of rock climbing can be an important informational input in addressing management conflicts and access issues, only a handful of published studies on the value of rock climbing exist (Shaw and Jakus, 1996; Hanley et al., 2001 and 2002; Grijalva et al., 2002a and b).

This study uses the survey-based contingent valuation (CV) method to estimate the value of access to a particular type of rock climbing, known as 'bouldering', at Hueco Tanks Texas State Park. Hueco Tanks, located approximately thirty miles east of El Paso, TX, is a premier bouldering destination, but also contains historic rock art found throughout the park. In efforts to protect ecological and archeological resources, park managers severely restricted open-rock climbing access at Hueco Tanks. A mail survey of climbers was conducted in the spring of 1998, and used an open-ended (OE) elicitation format to ask climbers who had visited Hueco Tanks about their willingness to pay (WTP) under alternative hypothetical policy rules. A number of tests of scope were conducted on the WTP responses for ensuring various levels of access to rock climbing and bouldering opportunities. To be clear, Hueco Tanks is divided into four significant mountain areas, each with various numbers of bouldering and climbing opportunities. Initially, Park managers proposed gradual restrictions in access – first one area and then adding other areas to the list. The test of scope specifically analyses this proposal. It is expected that climbers would be willing to pay more to secure access to more areas than access to fewer areas.

2. ROCK CLIMBING, BOULDERING AND HUECO TANKS PARK

While rock climbing has existed on public lands for the past century, recreational demand for climbing in the US and elsewhere is perceived to have grown significantly over the last several decades. Results from a 1994–95 US Forest Service survey showed that approximately 7 million (3.7 per cent) US citizens (age 15 and older) had gone rock climbing that year (Cavlovic, 2000). In 1995, it was estimated that approximately 100 000 US citizens try climbing each year (*Economist*, 1995); thus, the pool of potential rock climbers is believed to be much larger than 7 million.[1] This growth has led to a variety of new climbing management and access proposals in the US (NPS 1993). In 1993, the National Park Service (NPS) was the first US public land agency that explicitly recognized recent climbing activities and growth on public lands:

> While rock climbing has been a long accepted recreational activity in most park areas. . . . An explosive growth of rock climbing in recent years, along with increased impacts to park resources because of this activity, suggest that regulations and guidelines need to be developed to protect park resources while providing for a quality experience. (NPS, 1993, 32878–80)

By 1998, the US Forest Service began initiating new climbing access rules that would become the source of considerable controversy. Most prominently, the US Forest Service proposed to ban the use and placement of fixed anchors in federal wilderness areas. Due to widespread concern over the impacts to recreational climbing, the ban was later suspended, and the US Forest Service initiated a rulemaking process open to negotiation and input from climber groups.

Climbing access conflicts have occurred not just on federal public lands, but also at state lands and parks, which are separately managed in the US. For example, during the spring of 1999, park managers proposed to prohibit fixed climbing anchors at the Garden of the Gods state park in Colorado. Perhaps the most significant state climbing access issue is the case at Hueco Tanks located in Texas. While relatively small in size, Hueco Tanks is a high desert mountain park and unique for the type of climbing favored there.

During the 1980s and 1990s, Hueco Tanks became known to climbers as a premier climbing destination providing numerous types of climbs including traditional rock climbs, sport climbs, and especially what are referred to as boulder problems. Hueco Tanks is particularly famous for its quality and quantity of boulder problems, and ideal winter climbing conditions (that is, dry and warm).

Unlike most types of rock climbing, bouldering does not require ropes, climbing protective gear (for example, fixed gear), or knowledge about climbing protection. Strong, agile climbers climb on boulder problems generally not higher than 10 feet. Foam crash pads (approximately three inches thick and nine square feet) and spotters (that is, other climbers) protect climbers from a fall. Climbers can generally walk off the back of boulders to descend. The 'V' grading system is used to identify the difficulty of boulder problems and a climber's ability level (for example, the ratings range from V0 through V14, where V0 represents the easiest rated boulder problem).

Due to increases in recreational use (predominately rock climbing) during the 1980s and 1990s, the Texas Parks and Wildlife Department (TPWD) became concerned about the potential recreational impacts on ecological and archeological resources at the park.[2] To give one example, the 1997 management plan stated:

> Park planners with TPWD began to realize, even as they planned for increased recreational use . . . , that conflicts were going to occur between park users and there was a great need to protect the priceless rock art found throughout the park. The place was literally being loved to death by thousands of hikers, climbers, and picnickers. Increasing use by rock climbers from around the world is beginning to impact the park permanently . . . (Hueco Tanks State Historic Park 1997)

In 1997, TPWD proposed a management plan recommending gradual restrictions in open-recreational access (TPWD, 1997). On September 1, 1998, TPWD closed three of four mountain areas in Hueco Tanks to open-recreational access (TPWD, 1998). Consequently, TPWD has greatly reduced access to a unique, world-class bouldering area. Severe restrictions in access can cause significant loss in economic value to outdoor rock climbers. To be completely clear, there may be other nonmarket values affected by proposed policy changes, which should be included in any full benefit–cost analysis. But the focus here is on valuing the protection of access for the predominant group of recreational users at the site.

3.   VALUATION ISSUES AND THE TESTS OF SCOPE

Nonmarket valuation refers to the assessment of economic values for goods and services that are not typically priced and traded in functioning markets (for example, outdoor recreation, air and water quality, species and wilderness preservation). Environmental economists have invested considerable effort over the last four decades into developing and refining a battery of techniques for measuring nonmarket values (both use and non-use). These techniques can be divided into revealed preference (RP) and stated preference (SP) approaches. RP approaches, such as the travel cost method (TCM) and related random utility models (RUMs), rely on observed individual behavior, often *revealed* in survey instruments, to infer values for environmental goods or services. A variety of SP techniques are used to assess the economic value of nonmarket environmental goods and services, the most prominent of which is the contingent valuation (CV) method (Mitchell and Carson, 1989; Freeman, 1993; Boyle, 2002).

In CV, survey respondents are asked to make statements about their willingness to pay (WTP), or to accept compensation, for proposed changes in environmental quality or access. Common elicitation formats for asking valuation questions include both open-ended (OE), and closed-ended formats. The latter includes the common dichotomous choice (DC) format, where respondents must either accept or reject a given payment amount for the proposed change in environmental quality or access. DC formats include the hypothetical referendum format, as advocated by Arrow et al. (1993) for assessing non-use values in natural resource damage assessments. For recreational use value studies, which are considerably less controversial than assessments of non-use values (Smith, 2000; Carson et al., 1996), applications of both OE and DC elicitation formats remain common. Somewhat surprisingly, the accumulated evidence to date is that OE formats tend to produce conservative WTP estimates relative to DC formats (Schulze et al., 1996). While some sources attribute this difference to inherent 'yea-saying' in the DC format, the caveat is that the OE format may tend to produce 'fair-share' or 'reasonable' WTP responses (Bishop et al., 1995). This may be particularly the case when respondents have cost information about providing the good (Bohara et al., 1998). As recently reviewed by Boyle (2002), the case supporting DC as the commonly preferred elicitation format remains ambiguous relative to a range of alternatives. In this applied CV study, we use the OE format, and following the suggestion of Boyle (2002) apply the Tobit model, which doesn't allow negative WTP values and accommodates a probability spike at zero (\$0).[3]

Following the prompting of Arrow et al. (1993) and others, the number of validity tests of CV has grown rapidly (Smith, 2000). These include considerable numbers of criterion (or external) validity tests (for example, see List and Gallet, 2001), and construct validity tests, such as tests of scope or temporal reliability (for example, see reviews in Carson, 1997; Carson et al., 1999). Construct validity involves the degree by which a measure relates to other measures as predicted by theory (American Psychological Association, 1974; Mitchell and Carson, 1989, 191). Scope refers to the size or level of some chosen dimension of the environment (for example, number of species, geographic scale), which will be affected by the proposed policy change (Whitehead et al., 1998).

As argued by Arrow et al. (1993), valid CV surveys should demonstrate sensitivity in response to the 'scope of the environmental insult'; that is, they must pass a scope test.[4] For example, suppose an individual is confronted with a change in the level or scope of an environmental good from Q_0 to Q_1, where $Q_1 > Q_0$. Given strictly positive marginal utility for the good, then it is expected that the individual would value Q_1 more than Q_0 (Carson and Mitchell, 1995, 156). Within the general frame of construct validity, a test of scope is conducted in this study using varying levels of rock climbing and bouldering access.

More specifically, the test of scope is conducted by treating Hueco Tanks as a categorically nested good (Carson and Mitchell, 1995).[5] Categorical nesting exists when a good G is composed of two or more objects, such as g and its complement g', where neither g nor g' is an empty set and their intersection is empty (Carson and Mitchell, 1995). For example, a park area G may be comprised of several areas within the park, where g is a proper subset of those areas. Hueco Tanks is comprised of four separate areas within the park, where access to all areas constitute the good G, and access to some subset of areas would be g. It is always possible to have multiple levels of nests, but to maintain the property of categorical nesting, in each case the lowest category in the nest must be a proper subset of the next higher nest. Table 2.1 describes the three levels (A, B and C) of access to Hueco Tanks evaluated, and in each case the study design maintains the property of categorical nesting. Note that in terms of total boulder problems available, the change from A to B is fairly minor, while the change from B to C is much larger.

If recreational climbers are sensitive to the level of scope, then the values for different elements of a good G should vary according to the level of inclusion of the good. This means that the value of the good G should be greater than the value of a subset g. Because each level of access to Hueco

Table 2.1   Site access levels and open-ended annual WTP

Access level	Site access conditions	Number of available boulder problems (% of total at park)	Mean WTP (Standard deviation) [Minimum, maximum] {Number of zero-valued responses}
A	North Mountain East Spur Maze East Mountain West Mountain	1237 (100%)	40.40 (58.80) [0, 500] {45} N = 378
B	North Mountain East Spur Maze East Mountain	1127 (91%)	24.95 (42.14) [0, 500] {111} N = 379
C	North Mountain East Spur Maze	706 (57%)	11.46 (23.82) [0, 200] {212} N = 379

Tanks being evaluated maintains the property of categorical nesting, it is expected that respondents would value protecting access to more areas in the park higher than protecting access to fewer areas. Thus, against the null of no differences, our basic hypothesis is that reductions in site access at Hueco Tanks will decrease a climber's willingness to pay (WTP). Against the null hypothesis of no difference, the alternative hypotheses can be stated as:

$$H_1: WTP_A \geq WTP_B,$$
$$H_2: WTP_B \geq WTP_C,$$

where WTP_A represents the protection of full access, and WTP_B and WTP_C represents the protection of progressively smaller levels of access. Testing H_1 and H_2 each constitutes a test of scope for a categorically nested good. However, H_2 involves a much larger change in access.

4. SURVEY INSTRUMENT AND DATA COLLECTION

In order to assess the values of rock climbing and bouldering, and implement our testing strategy concerning the level of access, a mail survey was conducted in April of 1998. It is important to note that all surveys were completed before August 24, 1998, the date TPWD announced it was restricting access at Hueco Tanks beginning September 1, 1998.

The survey collected standard socioeconomic and demographic information, climbing experience indicators, and a series of questions regarding willingness to pay for protecting climbing access. It also included questions regarding details of climbers' trips to Hueco Tanks including length of stay, lodging and travel expenses, travel accommodations (for example, by car or airplane), the number of people traveling together on a trip, climber preferences for different climbing areas in Hueco Tanks, purposes of visiting Hueco Tanks, knowledge of proposed policy changes, and opinions about substitute sites. (Approximately 90 per cent of 413 respondents did not list any substitute sites.) In the design stage, several dozen climbers reviewed the survey. These climbers anonymously provided edits and clarifications, and made recommendations to use examples to clarify difficult questions.

Recreational climbers were first identified, and contact information collected, by on-site sampling over an eight month period in 1997 and 1998.[6] The full survey was mailed first class to 752 climbers. A follow-up reminder letter was sent to nonrespondents four weeks after the original survey mailing. In addition, a follow-up survey and reminder letter was mailed to 100 random climbers who had not yet responded. The adjusted response rate (adjusted for 15 undeliverable surveys) was 56 per cent, providing a potential usable sample of 413 climbers. Of these 413 climbers, thirteen were from Canada and ten were from overseas. The valuation section of the survey begins with the following introduction:

> Texas Parks and Wildlife Department (TWPD) is responsible for the management of Hueco Tanks State Park. TWPD is considering limiting access for climbing and bouldering at Hueco Tanks in order to restore and preserve the historical and natural resources of the park. At the moment, there are no definite changes in rules that would limit access.

Then respondents were asked a variety of questions about current use (with full access, A), and possible changes in use under different access conditions (B and C).[7] Climbers were also asked whether they believe recreational users at Hueco Tanks should be required to pay for access. Next, respondents were asked to consider their annual willingness to pay into a voluntary fund to be used by TWPD in managing the climbing areas in a safe fashion, and with no changes in access (from what then existed). Specifically, the valuation question for level A read:

> Q: What would be your annual maximum willingness to pay to such a fund if it ensured that climbers could continue to boulder at the four mountain areas? $_____

Then, respondents were presented with valuation questions for level B:

> Q: Now suppose that West Mountain is closed. What would be your annual maximum willingness to pay to such a fund if it ensured that climbers could continue to boulder at the other three mountain areas in Hueco Tanks? $_____

And then for level C:

> Q: Now suppose that both West Mountain and East Mountain are closed. What would be your annual maximum willingness to pay to such a fund if it ensured that climbers could continue to boulder at the other two mountain areas in Hueco Tanks? $_____

These three valuation questions were presented sequentially, after the respondent had already answered the same sequence of changes concerning contingent trip behavior (how their trip-taking behavior might change in response to proposed changes). To assist climbers in answering the set of valuation questions, a map of Hueco Tanks, and a table listing notable boulder problems by mountain area were provided in the survey.

5.   MODELING CONSIDERATIONS

In testing H_1 and H_2, we estimate several single equation WTP models:

$$WTP_i = \beta' x_i + e_i, \tag{2.1}$$

where x is a vector of characteristics of climber i, and β is the vector of corresponding parameters to be estimated. A primary consideration in estimating WTP is that WTP responses from survey data often consist of numerous zeroes and nonnegative values. Because a considerable fraction of observations of the dependent WTP variable are zero-valued, classical linear regression methods should not be used (Boyle, 2002; Greene, 1997). As shown in Table 2.1, there were 45 zero responses (11.9 per cent) for level

A, 111 for level B (29.3 per cent) and 212 (55.9 per cent) for level C. Therefore, several single equation Tobit models are used to handle the numerous zeroes and estimate the WTP function. The Tobit model is formulated in terms of an index function,

$$WTP_i^* = \beta'\mathbf{x}_i + e_i, \qquad e_i \sim N(0, \sigma_e^2), \qquad i = 1, \ldots, N \text{ climbers}$$
$$WTP_i = 0 \text{ if } WTP_i^* = 0, \tag{2.2}$$
$$WTP_i = WTP_i^* \text{ if } WTP_i^* > 0.$$

In addition to single equation models, WTP responses for policies A, B and C, were pooled in a single Tobit model, where a vector of dummy variables were included to control for hypothetical access conditions (that is, $\alpha'DUM_t$ is included in equations (2.1) and (2.2).

Definitions and descriptive statistics for the explanatory variables used in the various WTP models are shown in Table 2.2. In addition to socio-economic and demographic characteristics, there are a number of independent variables specific to rock climbing at Hueco.

The variable BOULD indicates whether a climber identified herself as primarily a boulderer. It is also argued that the number and difficulty of boulder problems or climbs actually available at a site, given the respondent's skill level, will influence a climber's WTP. Because it is believed that climbers select areas at Hueco Tanks that offer boulder problems comparable with their skills, the variable BPROBLEM is constructed to take into account climber skill differences and site access conditions; thus, BPROBLEM is an individual-specific continuous variable that measures actual bouldering opportunities. Further, the mean for BPPROBLEM will vary by equation. The mean level of boulder problems for policies A, B, and C are 966, 877 and 546, respectively. In the pooled model, the mean level of BPROBLEM is 753.

For the pooled Tobit regression model, dummy variables are included to measure differences in WTP depending on access levels. The interactions of these variables with a number of other explanatory variables are also included. As corollaries to H_1 and H_2, the absolute value of the β coefficients on the various dummy variables should follow:

$$H_3: \alpha_{\text{constant}} \geq \alpha_{\text{DUM-B}},$$
$$H_4: \alpha_{\text{DUM-B}} \geq \alpha_{\text{DUM-C}}.$$

Against the null of no differences, hypotheses H_3 and H_4 relate to whether WTP responses exhibit statistically significant differences across substantial changes in site access.

Table 2.2   Description of independent variables (n =377)

Variable	Description	Mean (Standard Deviation)
DUM-A	Dummy variable – 1 if access level A, 0 otherwise. This is the base category (full access) dropped during estimation of pooled models.	—
DUM-B	Dummy variable – 1 if access level B, 0 otherwise.	—
DUM-C	Dummy variable – 1 if access level C, 0 otherwise.	—
YRCLIMB	Number of years climbing experience/100.	0.075 (0.065)
BOULD	Dummy variable – 1 indicates whether the person primarily is a boulderer, 0 otherwise.	0.09 (0.28)
BOULD*B	Access level indicator DUM-B × BOULD	—
BOULD*C	Access level indicator DUM-C × BOULD	—
AGE	Age of climber. Variable scaled by 100.	0.30 (0.08)
MALE	Dummy variable – 1 male, 0 female.	0.79 (0.41)
INC1	Dummy variable – 1 indicates that annual income is less than $25000, 0 otherwise. This is the base category for estimation.	0.52 (0.50)
INC2	Dummy variable – 1 indicates that annual income is $25000 through $44999, 0 otherwise.	0.23 (0.42)
INC3	Dummy variable – 1 indicates that annual income is $45000 through $79999, 0 otherwise.	0.17 (0.37)
INC4	Dummy variable – 1 indicates that annual income is greater than $79999, 0 otherwise.	0.09 (0.28)
BPROBLEM	Number of boulder problems available at Hueco Tanks based on different site access conditions and a climber's ability range using the 'V' rating system. Variable scaled by 1000.	0.753 (0.320)
KNOW	Dummy variable – 1 indicates the climber had information prior to taking a trip regarding the intent of the TPWD to propose a climbing management plan for Hueco Tanks, 0 otherwise.	0.66 (0.47)
KNOW*B	Access level indicator DUM-B × KNOW	—
KNOW*C	Access level indicator DUM-C × KNOW	—
USERFEE	Dummy variable – 1 indicates that the climber believes that recreational users of Hueco Tanks should be required to pay for access, 0 otherwise.	0.79 (0.41)
TCP	Dummy variable – 1 indicates the climber owned a Texas Conservancy Pass, which allowed them to enter Hueco at a user fee discount, 0 otherwise.	0.23 (0.42)
TCP*B	Access level indicator DUM-B × TCP	—
TCP*C	Access level indicator DUM-C × TCP	—
ENVIRON	Dummy variable – 1 indicates the climber is a member of an outdoor recreational or environmental group, 0	0.75 (0.44)

6.   EMPIRICAL RESULTS

Assuming normal distributions and independence, we can test for differences in stated means. From Table 2.1, the mean WTP for level A is $40.40, and $24.95 and $11.46 for levels B and C, respectively. Using a one-tailed test, the stated mean WTP for level A significantly exceeds the stated mean for level B (0.005 level). Similarly, for the more substantial change in access, the stated mean WTP for level B significantly exceeds the stated mean for level C (0.025) level. Thus, without controlling for any other factors, the evidence supports hypotheses H_1 and H_2 (rejects the null); the observed WTP values demonstrate significant sensitivity in scope across the three levels of access.

Similarly we can also test for differences in the proportion of zero responses in Table 2.1 (those unwilling to pay anything for access protection at the different levels). Using a one-tailed population proportions test (McLave and Deitrich, 1985), and assuming independence, the proportion of zero responses for level B significantly exceeds the proportion of zeroes for level A (0.005 level). Similarly, for the more substantial change in access, the proportion of zeroes for level C significantly exceeds the proportion of zeroes for level B (0.005 level). These results support the general hypothesis of significant sensitivity to scope. As access level decreases, the proportion of zero WTP responses significantly increases. Given these preliminary results, we turn to the WTP modeling.

Estimation results for a set of four Tobit models of WTP are presented in Table 2.3. First, three separate models are estimated for each of the three levels of access (A, B and C). After eliminating overseas and Canadian surveys, and those with missing WTP responses, the number of available observations is 378 for WTP_A, and 379 for WTP_B and WTP_C. Additionally, we combine the data and run a pooled Tobit model, which includes the dummy indicator variables DUM-B and DUM-C (with level A as the base category).[8]

In terms of explanatory variables, there are a number of results that are consistent across all models in Table 2.3. The estimated coefficient on BOULD is always positive and significant (0.10 level), indicating that respondents who consider themselves primarily boulderers (about 10 per cent of the sample), are willing to pay more for protecting access. The estimated coefficient on TCP is always positive and significant (0.10 level), indicating that respondents who hold a Texas Conservation Pass, and thus are accustomed to paying for guaranteed access (and not pay the activity fee), also have a higher WTP for protecting access at Hueco.

Focusing on the pooled models (n = 1136), the coefficients on DUM-B and DUM-C are both negative and statistically significant at either the 0.05

Table 2.3   *Parameter estimates for single equation and pooled Tobit*
              models

Variable	WTP$_A$	WTP$_B$	WTP$_C$	Pooled Model I	Pooled Model II
Intercept	−22.78	−13.37	2.55	1.91	−1.54
	(−1.01)	(−0.66)	(0.14)	(0.14)	(−0.11)
DUM-B	—	—	—	−20.72***	−16.52**
				(−5.01)	(−2.27)
DUM-C	—	—	—	−42.69***	−31.25***
				(−7.38)	(−3.78)
YRCLIMB	−19.71	16.14	76.59	17.03	18.99
	(−0.30)	(0.27)	(1.47)	(0.46)	(0.52)
BOULD	19.05*	30.74***	24.96***	25.26***	20.69**
	(1.66)	(3.09)	(2.98)	(4.11)	(2.04)
BOULD*B	—	—	—	—	10.50
					(0.74)
BOULD*C	—	—	—	—	3.49
					(0.24)
AGE	−24.74	−9.91	−65.16	−30.41	−31.23
	(−0.43)	(−0.19)	(−1.42)	(−0.95)	(−0.98)
MALE	−2.90	−1.43	−1.26	−3.11	−2.78
	(−0.35)	(−0.19)	(−0.19)	(−0.68)	(−0.61)
INC2	0.92	0.83	7.73	3.34	3.22
	(0.11)	(0.11)	(1.18)	(0.72)	(0.70)
INC3	16.01*	5.06	10.28	11.38**	11.24**
	(1.68)	(0.60)	(1.39)	(2.16)	(2.15)
INC4	40.17***	0.27	7.26	18.25***	17.92***
	(3.11)	(0.02)	(0.71)	(2.53)	(2.45)
BPROBLEM	46.69***	12.67	−25.22	25.34***	23.30***
	(3.27)	(0.91)	(−1.28)	(2.82)	(2.59)
KNOW	7.41	9.55	3.97	6.77*	10.35*
	(1.03)	(1.51)	(0.72)	(1.72)	(1.66)
KNOW*B	—	—	—	—	−1.94
					(−0.22)
KNOW*C	—	—	—	—	−9.44
					(−1.03)
USERFEE	5.13	12.77*	11.15*	9.59**	9.81**
	(0.66)	(1.85)	(1.80)	(2.23)	(2.29)
TCP	33.76***	18.25***	11.02*	21.33***	35.00***
	(4.44)	(2.71)	(1.87)	(5.11)	(5.14)
TCP*B	—	—	—	—	−17.16*
					(−1.77)
TCP*C	—	—	—	—	−26.32***
					(−2.58)

Table 2.3   (continued)

Variable	WTP$_A$	WTP$_B$	WTP$_C$	Pooled Model I	Pooled Model II
ENVIRON	−0.21	−6.82	−5.23	−4.25	−4.21
	(−0.03)	(−1.05)	(−0.92)	(−1.05)	(−1.05)
σ	59.23***	50.88***	40.85***	53.86***	53.55***
	(25.41)	(22.15)	(16.63)	(37.75)	(37.74)
LnL	−1870.67	−1519.85	−980.55	−4397.74	−4392.92
Likelihood Ratio Index	58.46***	33.59***	22.49**	237.30***	246.95***

Notes: Numbers in parentheses are aysmptotic t-statistics; ***, **, and * denote significance at the 0.01, 0.05, and 0.10 levels, respectively.

and 0.01 levels. The magnitudes of the coefficients indicate WTP is lower for lower levels of access (relative to full access level A). This result provides general support for the hypothesis of scope sensitivity. Further, climbers who have access to more boulder problems based on their individual skill level (BPROBLEM) are willing to pay more for access. Overall these results suggest that WTP responses exhibit statistically significant differences across substantial changes in site access. Results again show that that those climbers that consider themselves primarily boulders (BOULD) are willing to pay more for protecting access; and the coefficients on informational and attitudinal variables, KNOW and USERFEE, are positive and significant at the 0.10 and 0.01 levels, respectively. Climbers with knowledge about possible access restrictions or who believe that climbers or other recreational users of Hueco Tanks should be required to pay for access are willing to pay more for secured access. Additionally, climbers who hold a TCP are willing to pay more for secured access; the coefficient on TCP is positive and significant (0.01 level). With substantial reductions in access (access levels C), however, the amount by which TCP ownership influences WTP estimates is significantly less. The only socioeconomic variable that affects WTP is income. Climbers falling into income categories 3 and 4 are willing to pay more to secure access.

The predicted WTP estimate from each of the three separate Tobit models (Table 2.3) corresponds closely with the observed WTP estimate for each level (see Table 2.1). As predicted by the individual Tobit models and after scaling coefficients for marginal effects, the respective values for expected WTP are: E(WTP$_A$) = $47.27, E(WTP$_B$) = $29.04, and E(WTP$_C$) = $12.59. The expected WTP from the pooled model is $29.92.

Differentiating by access level, the predicted values from the pooled models are: $E(WTP_A) = \$42.27$, $E(WTP_B) = \$30.25$, and $E(WTP_C) = \$17.50$ for Pooled Model I; and $E(WTP_A) = \$42.35$, $E(WTP_B) = \$30.25$, and $E(WTP_C) = \$17.25$ for Pooled Model II.

Although Hueco Tanks provides access to traditional rock climbs, sport climbs and boulder problems, it is best known for the latter. Thus, it is interesting to use the BOULD (1 or 0) variable to separately estimate WTP values for those who identify themselves as primarily boulders. For boulders, the predicted WTP values rise to (using the separate Tobit models): $E(WTP_A) = \$59.57$, $E(WTP_B) = \$46.13$, and $E(WTP_C) = \$21.86$.[9] Of note, $E(WTP_B)$ represents 88 per cent and $E(WTP_C)$ represents 55 per cent of the full access value. These percentages compare very closely to the proportions of boulder problems available in access levels B and C (91 per cent and 57 per cent), respectively, as shown in Table 2.1. Again, this evidence supports the general hypothesis of scope sensitivity. To test hypotheses tests H_3 and H_4, a Wald test is conducted to explore differences in parameter estimates from the pooled models. In testing the null hypothesis corresponding to H_3 ($\alpha_{constant} = \alpha_{DUM-B}$), the chi-squared values are 2.24 (p-value of 0.13) and 0.74 (p-value of 0.39) for Pooled Models I and II, respectively. In either of the pooled models, the null hypothesis corresponding to H_3 cannot be rejected. Failure to reject the null hypothesis of no difference between $\alpha_{constant}$ and α_{DUM-B} suggests that when West Mountain (which represents only 9 per cent of the boulder problems) is excluded from a climbers site options at Hueco Tanks, WTP to secure access to the remaining three areas will likely be comparable to WTP to secure access to all four areas. In testing the null hypothesis corresponding to H_4 ($\alpha_{DUM-B} = \alpha_{DUM-C}$), the chi-squared values are 17.17 (p-value of 0.001) and 3.28 (p-value of 0.07) for Pooled Models I and II, respectively. Rejecting the null hypothesis of no difference between α_{DUM-B} and α_{DUM-C} suggests that WTP to secure access to three areas (1127 boulder problems, or 91 per cent of total) will be greater than a climber's WTP to secure access to two areas (706 boulder problems, or 57 per cent of total).

7. DISCUSSION

For several important reasons, we believe our WTP results may be relatively conservative estimates of the value of protecting rock climbing and bouldering access at the site (approximately $500000 aggregate annual benefits).[10] First, the valuation questions ask respondents their WTP to *ensure* a particular level of access (A, B or C), and thus wouldn't necessarily be viewed as the full value of access, but more simply as the value of an insurance policy. This doesn't negate the test of scope, but as in any CV study the values can only be connected to what is actually asked. Second, the open-ended responses to a voluntary fund mechanism may be particularly susceptible to 'fair-share' type responses, and thus themselves be conservative estimators of value (see Bishop et al., 1995; Bohara et al., 1998). With these caveats in mind, our estimated WTP value to ensure full access to Hueco Tanks ($47 for all climbers, and $60 for boulders, from Table 2.3) does compare favorably to the seasonal value estimate of $56.27 from a national-level RUM when dropping Hueco Tanks from a set of 60 US climbing sites (Grijalva et al., 2002b). However, the estimates here are much lower, by an order of magnitude, than the range of seasonal compensating surplus estimates from the single-site travel cost models for Hueco Tanks of Grijalva et al. (2002a), where traditional travel cost trip data is combined with contingent behavior responses to various policy changes.

We speculate that the reason for the difference in estimates is because the travel cost model and the valuation models may be measuring different values. The estimates from the single-site travel costs models, which may fail to fully account for substitution effects, represent climbing use values; whereas the estimates from this study may have been viewed as representing the value of an insurance policy to protect access. More similarly to the results found here though, the single-site TC models also demonstrate significant sensitivity to changes in scope.

8.   CONCLUSIONS

The sport of outdoor rock climbing has experienced considerable growth in the US and elsewhere over the last decade. Despite a number of ongoing controversies in the US over public lands access, available estimates of the nonmarket value of rock climbing remain scarce (see Rosenberger and Loomis, 2001). Further, like other general categories of recreational activity (for example, hunting and fishing, and so on), there are various *types* of rock climbing. This study has attempted to provide an initial recreational value estimate from a site favored for a particularly unique variant of rock climbing – bouldering. Given current conflicts over rock climbing access at Hueco Tanks state park, the value estimates for protecting access may provide an important input to a full-blown benefit–cost analysis and the larger policy process.

The value estimates from any particular CV study take on additional credence when they can pass some basic tests of validity (Arrow et al., 1993). As an indicator of construct validity, the experimental design of this study allowed several tests of scope; the tests were conducted by comparing the value estimates for protecting different levels of recreational access at the site. Results demonstrate that climbers' WTP responses are generally sensitive to changes in the scope of rock climbing and bouldering access. While we find some mixed evidence (depending on the test) in the case of a small percentage change in access to bouldering problems, the results are unambiguous in the case of the large discrete change in access to bouldering problems. To place our results in a general context, insensitivity in valuation responses to changes in the scope of a nonmarket good remains a common criticism of the CV method (for example, Desvouges et al., 1996; Blamey, 1998). However, the results of this study support the accumulating evidence that CV studies of *use* values will typically pass a scope test (Carson, 1997; Carson et al., 1999; Boyle, 2002).

NOTES

1. For a review of estimates of the population of US rock climbers see Cavlovic (2000). As discussed there, a 1998 national telephone survey of over 1000 US households asked: 'Have you ever participated in outdoor technical rock climbing that required ropes and rock climbing protective gear, or outdoor bouldering that required crashpads and spotters?' The question was answered affirmatively by 9.7 per cent of the respondents. From a probit model, significant positive determinants of climbing participation included: gender (males more likely), education level, and environmental group membership. There was no evidence of any income effects on participation.
2. The park has been publicly owned and managed for recreational access since the early 1970s. The area was the site of a number of failed development schemes in the 1960s, including construction of a recreation lake (200 acres) and earthen dam. Previously, the site was used for military personnel training. Many of these activities had negatively affected the cultural integrity of the site. See discussion in Cavlovic (2000).
3. Negative values are ruled out in the voluntary contribution context, since individuals can always choose not to contribute to the fund (or use the site), but zero values are clearly possible. For other CV applications of the Tobit see: Berrens et al. (1998), Desvouges et al. (1992), Goodwin et al. (1993), and Halstead et al. (1991).
4. Carson (1997) provides a long list of CV studies that have detected significant scope effects. But as Boyle (2002) argues, a review of this list reveals a paucity of evidence relating to non-use values. For an example where a CV study demonstrated significant sensitivity to scope and was assumed to be primarily motivated by non-use values, see Berrens et al. (2000).
5. There are a number of nesting, sequencing, and embedding phenomenan loosely referred to as scope effects (Brown and Duffield, 1995). Following Carson and Mitchell (1995), we conduct a scope test of component sensitivity for geographically nested goods. This corresponds to Kahneman and Knetsch's (1992) concept of perfect embedding.
6. For complete details of the sampling design, and a copy of all introductory letters, the full survey instrument, and so on, see Cavlovic (2000). Data collected from parts of this survey sample have been combined elsewhere with: (1) similarly structured surveys conducted in Tennessee and Nevada to estimate a national RUM on US rock climbing and the loss of federal wilderness access (Grijalva et al., 2002b); and (2) a set of follow-up surveys at Hueco Tanks to test the validity of contingent behavior responses (Grijalva et al., 2002a). The CV data used here has never been previously analysed.

7. Full access in 1997–98 included the following conditions: (1) all four mountain areas were open to recreational access; (2) the park was limited to 60 vehicles at any one time, but there was no restriction on the number of individuals in the park; (3) the entrance fee was $2 per person, with an additional $2 climbing activity fee, with the latter not required if the climber purchased a seasonal Texas Conservancy Pass (TCP); and (4) climbers were not allowed to climb near or on prehistoric pictographs.

8. Additional specifications and modeling approaches were also evaluated, including a seemingly unrelated regressions (SUR) model. If the disturbances among the WTP equations are correlated, then SUR will yield more efficient estimates than ordinary least squares (Greene, 1997), but results showed little effect on estimated WTP and qualitative model conclusions.

9. For those respondents who did not identify themselves as primarily boulderers, the predicted WTP values lower to: $E(WTP_A) = \$46.07$, $E(WTP_B) = \$27.41$, and $E(WTP_C) = \$11.68$.

10. On average, our sample of climbers took 5.45 trips to Hueco Tanks during the season of April 1997 through April 1998. Schlacter (1999) reports that in the mid 1990s total annual visitation at the site was approximately 75000, and then declined after site closures to 17000 for the fiscal year 1999 (ending August 31). Given general visitation patterns, and the predominance of rock climbing, we assume that the difference was solely attributable to climbers and provides a conservative estimate of climbing trips (58000). So, there were approximately 10642 climbers in the 1997–98 season (58000/5.45). Assuming our sample is representative, then the aggregate annual benefit of protecting site access is approximately $503047 ($47.27 × 10642).

REFERENCES

American Psychological Association (APA) (1974), *Standards for Educational and Psychological Tests*, Washington, DC: APA.

Arrow, K.J., R. Solow, P.R. Portney, E.E. Leamer, R. Radner and H. Schuman (1993), 'Report of the NOAA Panel on contingent valuation', *Federal Register*, **58**: 4601–14.

Berrens, R., A. Bohara, C. Silva, D. Brookshire and M. McKee (2000), 'Contingent values for New Mexico instream flows: with tests of scope, group-size reminder and temporal reliability', *Journal of Environmental Management*, **58**: 73–90.

Berrens, R., D. Brookshire, P. Ganderton and M. McKee (1998), 'Exploring non-market values for the social impacts of environmental policy change', *Resource and Energy Economics*, **20**: 117–37.

Bishop, R., P. Champ and D. Mullarkey (1995), 'Contingent Valuation', in D.W. Bromley (ed.), *The Handbook of Environmental Economics*, Cambridge, MA: Basil Blackwell.

Blamey, R. (1998), 'Decisiveness, attitude expression, and symbolic responses in contingent valuation', *Journal of Economic Behavior and Organization*, **34**: 577–601.

Bohara, A., M. McKee, R. Berrens, H. Jenkins-Smith, C. Silva and D. Brookshire (1998), 'Effects of total cost and group-size information on willingness to pay responses: open-ended versus dichotomous choice', *Journal of Environmental Economics and Management*, **35**: 142–63.

Boyle, K. (2002), 'Contingent Valuation in Practice', in P. Champ, K. Boyle and T. Brown (eds), *A Primer on Nonmarket Valuation*, Kluwer: Boston.

Brown, T. and J. Duffield (1995), 'Testing part-whole valuation effects in contingent valuation of instream flows', *Water Resources Research*, **31**: 2341–51.

Carson, R.T. (1997), 'Contingent Valuation Surveys and Tests of Scope Insensitivity', in R.J. Kopp, W. Pommerhene and N. Schwartz (eds), *Determining the Value of Non-Marketed Goods: Economic, Psychological, and Policy Relevant Aspects of Contingent Valuation Methods*, Boston: Kluwer.

Carson, R. and R. Mitchell (1995), 'Sequencing and nesting in contingent valuation surveys', *Journal of Environmental Economics and Management*, **28**: 155–73.

Carson, R., N. Flores, K. Martin and J. Wright (1996), 'Contingent valuation and revealed preference methodologies: comparing the estimates from quasi-public goods', *Land Economics*, **72**: 80–99.

Carson, R., N. Flores and R. Mitchell (1999), 'The Theory and Measurement of Passive-Use Value', in I.J. Bateman and K.G. Willis (eds), *Valuing Environmental Preferences: Theory and Practice of the Contingent Valuation Method in the US, EU, and Developing Countries*, New York: The Oxford University Press.

Cavlovic, T. (2000), 'Valuing the loss in access: an institutional and welfare analysis of rock climbing on US public lands', Ph.D. Diss., University of New Mexico.

Desvouges, W., S. Hudson and M. Ruby (1996), 'Evaluating CV Performance: Separating the Light from the Heat', in D. Bjornstad and J. Kahn (eds), *The Contingent Valuation of Environmental Resources: Methodological Issues and Research Needs*, London: Edward Elgar.

Desvouges, W., F.R. Johnson, R. Dunford, K. Boyle, S. Hudson and K. Nicole (1992), *Measuring Nonuse Values Using Contingent Valuation: An Experimental Evaluation of Accuracy*, RTI Monograph, 92–1, Research Triangle, NC: Exxon.

Economist (1995), 'Climbing Up the Wall', March 11.

Freeman, A.M. (1993), *The Measurement of Environmental and Resource Values: Theory and Methods*, Washington DC: Resources for the Future.

Goodwin, B., L. Offenbach, T. Cable and P. Cook (1993), 'Discrete/continuous contingent valuation of private hunting access in Kansas', *Journal of Environmental Management*, **39**: 1–12.

Greene, W. (1997), *Econometric Analysis*, New Jersey: Prentice Hall.

Grijalva, T., R. Berrens, A. Bohara and W.D. Shaw (2002a), 'Testing the validity of contingent behavior trip responses', *American Journal of Agricultural Economics*, **84**(2): 401–14.

Grijalva, T., R. Berrens, A. Bohara, P. Jakus and W.D. Shaw (2002b), 'Valuing the loss of access to rock climbing in wilderness areas: a national-level random utility model', *Land Economics*, **78**(1): 103–20.

Halstead, J., B. Lindsay and C. Brown (1991), 'Use of the Tobit model in contingent valuation: experimental evidence from the Pemigewasset wilderness area', *Journal of Environmental Management*, **33**: 79–89.

Hanley, N., B. Alvarez-Farizio and W.D. Shaw (2002), 'Rationing an open-access resource: mountaineering in Scotland', *Land Use Policy*, forthcoming.

Hanley, N., G. Koop, R. Wright and B. Alvarez-Farizio (2001), 'Go climb a mountain: an application of recreation demand models to rock climbing in Scotland', *Journal of Agricultural Economics*, **52**(1).

Hueco Tanks State Historic Park (1997), *Hueco Tanks SHP Resource Management Plan*, draft 3.2.

Kahneman, D. and J. Knetsch (1992), 'Valuing public goods: the purchase of moral satisfaction', *Journal of Environmental Economics and Management*, **22**: 57–70.

Loomis, J. (1993), *Integrated Public Lands Management: Principles and Applications to National Forests, Parks, Wildlife Refuges, and BLM Lands*, New York, NY: Columbia Press.

Loomis, J. (1999), 'Contingent Valuation Methodology and the US Institutional Framework', in I. Bateman and K. Willis (eds), *Valuing Environmental Preferences: Theory and Practice of the Contingent Valuation Method in the US, EU, and Developing Countries*, Oxford, UK: Oxford University Press.

List, J. and C. Gallet (2001), 'What experimental protocol influence disparities between actual and hypothetical stated values?', *Environmental and Resource Economics*, **20**: 241–59.

McLave, J. and F. Deitrich (1985), *Statistics*, 3rd edn, San Francisco: Dellen Publishing.

Mitchell, C.M. and R.T. Carson (1989), *Using Surveys to Value Public Goods: The Contingent Valuation Method*, Washington, DC: Resources for the Future.

Rosenberger, R. and J. Loomis (2001), 'Benefit Transfer of Outdoor Recreation Use Values: A Technical Document Supporting the Forest Service Strategic Plan' (2000 Revision), Gen. Tech. Report. RMRS-GTR-72, Fort Collins, CO: US Dept. of Agriculture, Forest Service.

Schlacter, B. (1999), 'Rock Art vs. Rock Climbers Limits on Use of State Park Protected', *Fort Worth Star Telegram*, October, Pg. 1.

Schulze, W., G. McClelland, D. Waldman and J. Lazo (1996), 'Sources of Bias in Contingent Valuation', in D. Bjornstad, and J. Kahn (eds), *The Contingent Valuation of Environmental Resources: Methodological Issues and Research Needs*, Cheltenham, UK: Edward Elgar Publishing.

Shaw, W.D. and P. Jakus (1996), 'Travel cost models of the demand for rock climbing', *Agricultural and Resource Economics Review*, **25**(2): 133–42.

Smith, V.K. (2000), 'JEEM and nonmarket valuation', *Journal of Environmental Economics and Management*, **39**: 351–74.

Texas Parks and Wildlife Department (TPWD) (1997), *Hueco Tanks State Historical Park Draft Public Use Plan*, Austin, TX.

Texas Parks and Wildlife Department (TPWD) (1998), *Hueco Tanks State Historical Park Public Use Plan*, Austin, TX.

US National Park Service (NPS) (1993), *Federal Register*, **58**(112): 32878–80.

Whitehead, J., T. Haab and J. Huang (1998), 'Part-whole bias in contingent valuation: will scope effects be detected with inexpensive survey methods', *Southern Economic Journal*, **65**: 160–68.

3. Using economic instruments to manage access to rock-climbing sites in the Scottish Highlands

Nick Hanley, Begona Alvarez-Farizo and W. Douglass Shaw

1. INTRODUCTION

Many outdoor recreation areas are characterized by open access, in that users pay no direct fee to gain entry to the site. This is especially true in Northern Europe, where the cultural tradition of 'free' access to such areas is strong, whether they are publicly or privately owned. Access is of course costly and not free, since users must pay certain costs to access such sites, notably time and out-of-pocket travel costs. However, any moves to ration access to some European areas (such as National Parks in England and Wales) through direct entry fees are highly unlikely from a political perspective. At public parks and other lands in the US entry fees are a longstanding tradition, but recent suggestions by federal lands managers to impose new or additional fees are also causing protests from outdoor recreational users.

It is becoming increasingly evident that in many parts of the UK, open-access conditions, coupled with a rising demand for outdoor activities, are creating problems at outdoor recreation areas. These problems are twofold. First, higher visitor numbers may lead to overcrowding, and reduced utility per visit.[1] Second, higher visitor numbers may place more pressure on the natural environment. This environmental externality is manifested in the disruption of wildlife sites (for instance, in relation to breeding waders such as Dotterel and Golden Plover), and increased erosion of footpaths. Erosion problems in the UK due to hill-walking have been extensively studied, for example in the Lake District (Colman, 1979), and the Mourne Mountains in Northern Ireland (Ferris et al., 1993, Bloomfield, 1999). Examples in Scotland include erosion on the Cairngorm plateau (Bayfield, 1971), and in Coire Laggan in Skye (Wightman, 1996). With regard to impacts on flora and fauna, Sidaway and Thompson (1991) have noted the relative scale of impacts from recreation on upland plant communities across upland areas of the UK, whilst Cole and Knight (1991) report conflicts between wilderness recreation and wildlife preservation in the US.

Taken together, these problems have led to calls for action to be taken to manage access. The purpose of this chapter is to simulate the impacts of two different possible policy instruments for managing access, using data from a study of Scottish rock-climbers.

In the Highlands of Scotland, a principal outdoor recreation activity is mountaineering, a term which includes hill-walking, rock-climbing and ski-mountaineering. Increasing numbers of people are heading for the hills, as evidenced for example by the increase in the number of people annually registered as completing all 284 mountains over 3000 feet (the 'Munros') from 10 per year in 1960 to 140 per year in 1990 (Crofts, 1995). Figure 3.1 shows some additional indicators of the rising demand for mountaineering (although these indicators relate to a range of mountain uses, and not just rock climbing as studied in this chapter). This trend has led to increased congestion in the most popular mountain areas, and increased environmental pressures.

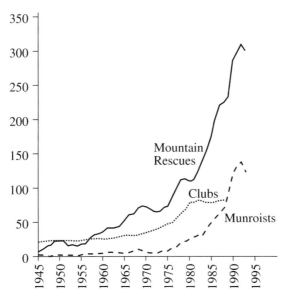

Source: Base data derived from annual listings of mountain rescues and Munro completions in the *Scottish Mountaineering Club Journal*, and from the records of the Mountaineering Council of Scotland (Wightman, 1996).

Figure 3.1   Three indices of growth in mountain recreation, 1945–94 (3-year running mean)

Since direct entry fees to mountain areas are culturally inconceivable and also impractical, attention has recently focussed on alternative mechanisms of limiting access and its potentially negative impacts. The first of these is to levy car-parking charges at principal access points in some high-pressure locations. Most mountain areas are privately-owned, so this would constitute a source revenue for private estates, who complain that they are expected to maintain access routes for no direct compensation (some mountain areas are owned by trusts, such as Glencoe, owned by the National Trust for Scotland, and Bla Bheinn and Knoydart, owned by the John Muir Trust). Currently there are extremely few examples of such parking charges being levied. Charges were threatened by private estate owners in Arran, a move which led to the establishment of the Arran Access Trust to restore footpaths. Car park charges have been introduced at Glen Muick by the Upper Deeside Access Trust, and are a 'reserved power' in the Visitor Management Plan produced for the Northern Cairngorms at Coire Cas. Car park charges are also levied at the Grey Mairs Tail site in the Southern Uplands.

The second, and more popular alternative, is the so-called 'long walk-in' policy (Cairngorms Working Party, 1993). This involves making access to the mountains more time-consuming, by closing off parking areas close to popular sites, closing private estate roads to public vehicles, demolishing foot bridges (such as the Coire Gabhail and Coire nan Lochan bridges in Glencoe), and restricting mountain bike use along access tracks. The idea is that by increasing the time price of access, demand will be reduced, and so pressure from overuse will also be diminished. The only actual long walk-in policy so far introduced in Scotland is in the Southern Cairngorms at Linn of Dee, where mountain bikes are banned from using estate tracks. Mountain bikes are also discouraged at Ben Lawers in Perthshire, in order to protect remote and fragile areas from increasing visitor pressure.

In this chapter, we model the impacts of each of these policy alternatives using a revealed preference model for one important group of mountaineers, namely rock-climbers. An additional consideration in choosing this focus was that climbers constitute an easy-to-define group of users for sampling purposes. Whilst climbers constitute a rather small percentage amongst total 'hill users' (around 11 per cent, according to the survey reported in HIE, 1996), we use this group to illustrate how the impact of different policy levers can be modelled in the mountain environment. In what follows, Section 2 describes the empirical approach taken, Section 3 describes the way in which data was collected, and Section 4 presents results. The final section provides a discussion, focussing on policy implications.

2. EMPIRICAL APPROACH

We assume that rock climbers make two behavioural decisions that are relevant to issues in this study. These are how many total climbing trips to take in a season (participation), and where to take these trips from amongst a set of possible sites (site choice). We expect both these decisions to be potentially affected by the rationing measures of interest here. Increasing access times at certain sites may directly or indirectly effect both participation and site choice, as may the imposition of car-parking charges.

We apply the familiar travel cost method (TCM), which is used in modelling recreation behaviour and which is a standard non-market valuation technique. There are a host of possible specific versions of the TCM from which to choose, and each has advantages and disadvantages in terms of accurately predicting behaviour, and producing meaningful welfare measures. We apply a nested random utility model as it seems an appropriate modelling strategy here, given that it controls for both site choice and participation and may be consistent with utility maximization and standard consumer theory (see Kling and Herriges, 1995).

As is common to all random utility approaches, we assume that utility is determined by both deterministic and stochastic components. The latter are assumed to follow the extreme value distribution, and this partially determines the exact and specific version applied here, the repeated nested multinomial logit (hereafter RMNL). This approach controls for both participation and site choice as a function of both site-specific and individual-specific parameters, in a linked way, and allows recovery of seasonal, rather than per-choice occasion, welfare measures. The RMNL approach has been recently used in several published recreation demand studies including Montgomery and Needelman (1997), Shaw and Ozog (1999), Fadali and Shaw (1998), Parsons and Needelman (1992), Needelman and Kealy (1995), and Morey et al. (1993). A host of unpublished reports and papers also use this approach (see many references in Fadali and Shaw, op. cit.). The reader is cautioned to note differences between repeated and non-repeated multinomial logit models. The latter can be nested, but not repeated because the participation, or 'go' versus 'not go' decision is not modelled.

In applications of the RMNL the top or first level of the nest examines the individual's decision whether or not to participate in any given period, yielding estimates of the total number of trips taken. This is assumed to be dependent on climber-specific attributes such as climbing ability, and takes into account the inclusive value (expected maximum utility) of lower level decisions. It is also assumed that each choice occasion is independent from any other,[2] and that the decision process repeats throughout the season. In the second level, climber's choices over trip destinations are modelled as a function of site attributes. In our model these include travel costs, approach time (the time taken to reach the start of the climb from the car park) and a number of site-specific constant terms. Policies that impact approach time directly affect the approach time variable. Policies that affect car-parking fees increase the trip price, or travel cost. As is conventional, this is composed of estimated out-of-pocket distance-related costs (return trip-distance multiplied by 10 pence per mile) and car parking fee, if any exists or is proposed at the destination parking area. A recent paper suggests that omission of a money-equivalent time cost may be consistent with the assumption that demands are conditional on, and separable from, labour–leisure choice variables (see Shaw and Feather, 1999).

Earlier RMNL models were estimated sequentially, so that the second stage destination decision is estimated separately from the participation decision, and then results are fed into the participation model (see, for example, Montgomery and Needelman (1997) and Parsons and Kealy, 1992). However, it is quite possible given a manageable number of destinations to estimate both parts of the model simultaneously using Full Information Maximum Likelihood (FIML) techniques. Examples of this approach are Fadali and Shaw (1998), Shaw and Ozog (1999), and Morey et al. (1993), and we adopt that approach here. Using FIML, the log likelihood function estimated is:

$$L = \sum_{h=1}^{H} \sum_{n=1}^{M} \sum_{i=1}^{J} y_{hni} \ln[\mathbf{Prob}\,(hni)] \tag{3.1}$$

where:

$$\mathbf{Prob}(ni) = \frac{\exp(sV_{ni}) \left[\sum_{j=1}^{J} \exp(sV_{nj})\right]^{1/s-1}}{\sum_{m=1}^{M} \left[\sum_{j=1}^{J} \exp(sV_{ij})\right]^{1/s}} \tag{3.2}$$

In equation (3.1), the letter i indexes individuals, m is the number of sites available to the climber as a choice of where to visit, h refers to the two decisions the climber can make on any choice occasion in terms of go climbing/stay at home, and y is the number of times they choose any alternative site in the choice set of all climbing areas. Equation (3.1) says that the (log) likelihood for y is the sum of the individual's probabilities of choosing an alternative, weighted by the number of times they choose that alternative. Equation (3.2) is the conditional probability that person i chooses to visit site n. In (3.2), V_{ni} is the conditional indirect utility function given the choice of a visit to the ith destination, which may include the indirect utility function evaluated for the non-participation decision. We assume that V_{ni}

is linear in its arguments. The s exponent in equation (3.2) is known as a 'nesting parameter', and it is common to first assume that it is not equal to one. If $s = 1$, then the independence of irrelevant alternatives (IIA) assumption holds, and one may just as well include the non-participation (stay at home) alternative in the same group of alternatives as the destinations (see Morey et al. 1991). This, as seen below, is a testable hypothesis.

The RMNL leads to the ability to calculate the seasonal welfare measure, CV_{seas}. This is simply accomplished by multiplying the per-choice occasion welfare measure, CV_{pco} by the assumed number of choice occasions, T. Thus, the longer the season (the higher the value of T), the greater will be the estimate of CV_{seas}. CV_{pco} is in turn calculated using the usual formula, which examines the difference in the expected maximum utility evaluated at each policy scenario being compared (Morey, 1999). In the linear RMNL the marginal utility of income is assumed constant, and is the price parameter, β. The CV_{pco} is simply found using the formula:

$$CV_{pco} = 1/\beta[V(0) - V(1)] \qquad (3.3)$$

where V indicates the indirect utility function evaluated at the initial (0) and subsequent (1) levels being assessed. V depends on site attributes: thus any change in these attributes (for example approach time) will change V, and thus the estimate of CV_{pco}. Finally, a complete modelling of congestion impacts is not possible given our data set. When individuals make decisions over whether or not to visit a given site, they form some expectation of the level of crowding: however, we have no measure of expected congestion in our data set. What is more, the positive impact on the utility per visit of those who keep visiting a site once the number of visits by others has been reduced by some management means cannot be modelled here. Our results should be read with this limitations in mind.

3. DATA AND SAMPLING

The initial steps in this study were to identify the choice sets climbers face. To accomplish this, focus groups were conducted with climbers from university mountaineering clubs in Edinburgh and Stirling. Discussions with the Mountaineering Council of Scotland (MCS) also helped in this process. Eight principal climbing areas were identified. These were the Northern Highlands (Torridon and Wester Ross), Creag Meagaidh, Ben Nevis (including Glen Nevis), Glen Coe (including Glen Etive), Isle of Arran, Arrochar, the Cullins of Skye, and the Cairngorms. Figure 3.2 shows the location of these sites.

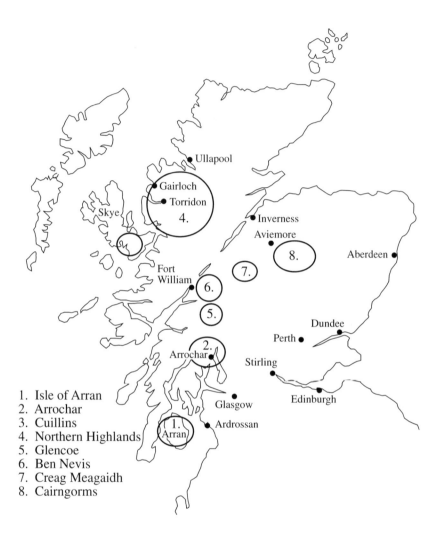

Figure 3.2   Climbing areas used in the study

A sampling frame was provided by MCS through a list of climbing club members in Scotland. As has been mentioned before (Shaw and Jakus, 1996), randomly drawing individuals who undertake specialised activities such as climbing from the general population of households is cost-prohibitive. A random sample of these addresses was selected, and questionnaires mailed to these individuals, who were asked to complete and return the questionnaire. A donation of £2 was promised to the John Muir

Trust (a charity which exists to conserve wilderness areas in Scotland) for every questionnaire returned as an incentive. To widen the sample in terms of being representative of the general population of climbers, question-naires were also administered at indoor climbing walls in Edinburgh, Glasgow and Falkirk. One major problem which became apparent with the sampling frame was that we had no way of identifying which members of a given club were actually rock climbers, and which were just hill walkers.[3] This resulted in a very large number of questionnaires being returned by hill-walkers since many of the questions did not apply to them, and thus in a number of additional mail-outs being necessary. Nevertheless, a sample of 267 useable responses from contacted climbers was eventually acquired.

Climbers were asked questions relating to their total climbing trips in the last twelve months in both summer and winter climbing to each of the 8 areas; to evaluate each area in terms of approach time; to provide infor-mation on their climbing abilities and experience; to identify their home location; and finally, to provide us with standard socio-economic informa-tion.

3.1 Descriptive Statistics for the Sample

Some 55 per cent of all climbers questioned were in the 25–40 years age bracket, which exhibited twice as many climbers as in any other age group. Nineteen per cent and 24 per cent of climbers were in the age brackets under 25 years and 41–55 years respectively. The majority of those inter-viewed were male (79 per cent). Of the sample 55 per cent were single, whilst 29 per cent of those interviewed had children. The majority of climbers (71 per cent) were university degree holders with a further 16 per cent having completed a certificate or diploma. The mean household income before tax was £27111. Over 58 per cent of climbers had been climbing for 10 years or less, with another 28 per cent outlining they had been climbing for between 10 and 20 years. Overall respondents had been climbing for a minimum of 1 year, a maximum of 56 years with the mean at 11 years. In terms of participation, 36 per cent of all respondents completed 25 climbs or less in a year, with the next largest group of 31 per cent of respondents completing from 26 to 50 climbs. Overall the mean number of climbs com-pleted per year (any given year) was 57, with the median at 40 and mode at 100 climbs. Climbers were asked how many of a sample of the eight key Scottish climbing sites they had visited at any time in the past. As indicated in Table 3.1, the climbing areas most visited by respondents in the preced-ing summer were Cairngorms, Glencoe, the Northern Highlands and Ben Nevis.

Table 3.1   Visits to climbing sites in Scotland in the past: summer trips

Site	Number of people climbing in area in last 12 months in sample	Mean trips as visit days per respondent in last 12 months *
Arran	57	0.78
Arrochar	76	0.77
Ben Nevis	134	1.12
Cairngorms	170	2.61
Creag Meagaidh	64	0.12
The Cuillins	106	1.77
Glencoe	173	3.20
Northern Highlands	127	2.68

Notes: * excludes three outliers with >60 days per season for any one site.
Sample size = 247.

4.   ESTIMATING THE MODEL

As mentioned above, we employ the standard RMNL to predict climbers' choices over participation and site choice. We restricted our attention to summer climbing trips only, since summer climbing on rock and winter climbing on ice and snow may be different sports, and erosion and congestion problems are greatly reduced in winter. Each of these levels is now described in more detail, and results presented.

4.1   Participation

The participation decision was assumed to depend on climber-specific attributes. At this level of the nest, climbers can choose to stay at home instead of climbing on any choice occasion. The main determinant of participation is taken to be the climber's own ability, as measured by the maximum grade they can lead. We expect more skilful (and therefore probably more committed) climbers to take more trips. Income influences the decision to stay home, but a separate parameter on income is not estimated, as in the linear version of the RMNL income effects are lost. Total choice occasions (T) were set equal to the maximum number of observed summer trips in the sample, which is 144 per season. Other things being equal, the total number of choice occasions should be set to be in accordance with an assumed one trip per choice occasion, and to avoid dropping individuals in the sample. However, a large number of choice occasions leads to a smaller welfare per choice occasion, while a small number may increase the welfare per choice occasion, and barring some influences in the tails, the modeller's choice of T is balanced out in calculation of the seasonal welfare measure.

4.2 Site Choice

Site choice was assumed to depend on site-specific attributes. These were measured as (i) out-of-pocket travel costs from the respondent's home to each site, represented as round-trip distance calculated from post-codes using AUTOROUTE multiplied by 10 pence per mile (an estimate of the marginal cost of motoring for the UK[4]); (ii) approach time for each site, measured as estimated minutes from parking the car to reaching the foot of the climb; and (iii) a range of site-specific dummies. These site dummies represent the somewhat unique physical characteristics of each climbing area.[5] In addition, approach time–site interaction dummies were included for two sites, Arran and the Cuillins, since access to both of these island sites requires a short sea crossing. For these two areas, the costs of the sea crossing were included as a fixed cost item in out-of-pocket costs.

Table 3.2 gives estimation results for both levels of the nested model, using Full Information Maximum Likelihood. Travel costs are strongly significant determinants, with climbers preferring cheaper sites; whilst approach time is strongly significant also, showing climbers to prefer shorter walk-in times (since this leaves more time in the day for actual climbing). Most of the site dummies are significant as well, including the approach interaction dummies for Arran and the Cuillins. In terms of participation, the individual climber's ability level, as measured by the maximum grade she can climb, is positively related to the participation decision. The scale parameter is significantly different from zero, but that is of less interest than whether it is significantly different from one. As mentioned above, $s = 1$ indicates that a simple MNL (non-nested) could be estimated, and staying at home is just another alternative to any one of the J destinations. Assuming that errors are asymptotically normal, we use a simple t-test, giving a t-value of 0.34. This implies that s is not in fact significantly different from one, so that we could have estimated a non-nested model with non-participation as one of any of the alternative destinations for a visit. This may be due to the fact that the stay at home decision for this sample of climbers is not fundamentally different from the site choice decision.

Table 3.2   *Repeated nested multinomial logit for summer trips*
              (N = 244)

Variable	Estimated Coefficient (White's Std. Errors)
Price (£)	−0.082 (0.012)*
Approach time (minutes)	−0.005 (0.001)*
Site 1 constant	0.487 (0.173)*
Site 2 constant	−1.70 (0.352)*
Site 5 constant	−1.39 (0.710)*
Site 6 constant	−2.40 (0.447)*
Site 7 constant	−0.251 (0.542)
Site 8 constant	0.198 (0.121)
Site 5 approach interaction dummy	0.016 (0.004)*
Site 7 approach interaction dummy	0.011 (0.003)*
Max grade can climb	0.056 (0.03)
Log likelihood at convergence	−14793.19
Scale parameter	0.94 (0.191)

Note: * Significant at the one per cent level. White's standard errors are robust to specification choices.

5. SIMULATING POLICY ALTERNATIVES

The main objective of this chapter is to estimate the welfare effects of alternative rationing policies for climbers' access to popular mountain areas in Scotland. We also want to illustrate the changes in participation related to these policy alternatives. Accordingly, we look at five alternatives, focussing on three of the most popular (and most crowded) sites, Glencoe, the Cairngorms and Ben Nevis. These are briefly detailed below:

Ben Nevis: Ben Nevis is the highest mountain in Scotland, and the site of a number of very popular climbing areas. The policy options simulated here are the introduction of car parking fees at the only two feasible parking locations; and banning car parking at current sites. Climbers would then face a much longer walk in. Accordingly the policy options are specified as: Option A: impose £5/day car parking fee. Option B: increase access time by 2 hours/day.

Glencoe: The pass of Glencoe contains a number of climbing areas, including the Three Sisters, which are very popular due to their proximity to the road and general high quality. However, overall visitor pressure is now viewed as a serious problem by the National Trust for Scotland, who own the land: the Trust is just completing a £230 000 footpath repair programme in the glen. The Trust is considering a move to restrict car parking in Glencoe itself. One option is to require hill-walkers/climbers to park in Glencoe village (at the end of the pass) and then either walk or use a shuttle bus to access the hills. There has also been an on-going debate about the desirability of taking down foot bridges over the River Coe to make access to the hills behind more difficult (NTS/MCoS, 1997). Accordingly, we specify Option C as increasing access time to the main climbing sites in Glencoe by 2 hours/day.

Cairngorms: The Cairngorms form the largest continuous high-level massif in Scotland, and contain many of Scotland's highest mountains. Climbing is greatly aided by the presence of a high-level car park belonging to the Cairngorm Mountain Company, which operates downhill ski-ing activities on the northern slopes. Parking in this area is currently free for anyone. However, concern over increasing levels of erosion on the plateau, the building of a new 'funicular' access to the plateau, and the future designation of the Cairngorms as a national park, have produced pressure for change. Car-parking fees have been suggested in Coire Cas (Option D: levy parking fee of £5/day), whilst future options could include forcing mountaineers to park at a more distant site (Option E: increase approach time by 2 hours/day). Although there are no current plans to charge for use of the Coire Cas car park at Cairngorm, this option has been retained as a 'reserved powers' by the Cairngorm Mountain Company in their draft Visitor Management Plan, so that parking charges could well be introduced at some point in the future (Scottish Mountaineer, 2001).

Given the structure of the RMNL approach, welfare estimates are produced as per season compensating variation.[6] Results are given in column 2 of Table 3.3. As may be seen, for the three policy options which increase access time by two hours, welfare losses are similar for Glencoe and Cairngorms, which in turn are about double that for Ben Nevis. For the scenarios involving car-parking fees, losses are again much higher at the Cairngorms site than for Ben Nevis. This does not necessarily mean that the utility of an average trip to Ben Nevis is much less than for the Cairngorms, however, since attributes other than access time are assumed to contribute (positively or negatively) to utility.

Table 3.3   Predicted welfare changes

(1) Policy option	(2) Change in seasonal compensating variation per climber[1]	(3) Change in aggregate seasonal compensating variation[2]
A: £5/day car parking fee at Ben Nevis	−£13.00	£161 525
B: 2-hour extra walk-in time, Ben Nevis	−£12.50	£155 312
C: 2 hour extra walk-in time, Glencoe	−£24.00	£298 200
D: £5/day car parking fee in Northern Cairngorms	−£20.00	£248 500
E: 2 hour extra walk-in time, Northern Caingorms	−£23.00	£285 775
All of the above simultaneously	−£40.00	£497 000

Notes:
[1] All figures rounded to nearest £0.50.
[2] Based on population of 12 425 active climbers living in Scotland.

We can also make some qualified statements about impacts on aggregate welfare. Since our model controls for both participation and site choice, and since non-participation is allowed for, per-season welfare change estimates from the sample can be aggregated to the population of Scottish climbers, assuming our sample is broadly representative. The most recent survey of total UK visits to the Highlands is that reported in HIE (1996), and gives a figure of 767 000 mountaineers. This includes English, Welsh and Irish respondents as well as Scottish respondents. Of this total, 10.7 per cent gave the main purpose of their trips as climbing, implying 82 836 climbers visiting the area. A reasonable guess would be that around 15 per cent of these individuals live in Scotland (our sample refers only to climbers living in Scotland). This implies a total of 12 425 climbers resident in Scotland. Taking this figure as suitable for indicative purposes, we arrive at the aggregate welfare losses in column 3 of Table 3.3, which allow both for changes in participation and site substitution under any of the policy scenarios. Combining all policies results in an aggregate welfare loss per season of just under £0.5 million. It should be noted that the figure of 12 425 used for the relevant population is probably an underestimate since many of those giving their 'main purpose' as other than climbing (almost 90 per cent of the sample) will climb occasionally. The aggregate welfare estimates are probably thus on the low side.

It is also interesting to look at the implications for each policy option for predicted trips for each site in the choice set (ie to dis-aggregate the quantity changes implicit in column 3 of Table 3.3). Estimates are given in Table 3.4, where for each site we show predicted trips under each policy option relative to the baseline predicted trips. Column one shows the site name and predicted trips to this site under the baseline conditions. Columns 2–6 then show changes in trips to each site under each policy option. Column 2 shows changes in predicted trips to all sites when a £5 car-parking fee is imposed at Ben Nevis. This reduces trips to Ben Nevis from 4.18 to 2.88 per climber per summer season, and increases predicted trips per season at most other sites. However, since total participation also changes, the reduction in mean trips to Ben Nevis is larger than the aggregate increase in mean predicted trips to all other sites. Trips to Arrochar and Arran, for example, are unaffected in any of the scenarios, but this is not unexpected since both are far away from any of the three study sites. A somewhat greater reduction in visits to Ben Nevis occurs with a two-hour approach time increase: again, knock-on effects at other sites are predicted. In terms of proportionate impacts, a £5 car parking fee at the Cairngorms is predicted to reduce rock climbing trips to the Cairngorms by 31 per cent, which may be compared with a 44 per cent reduction achieved by a two-hour increase in approach time. A two-hour increase in approach time in Glencoe is predicted to cut climbing trips to Glencoe by 44 per cent. These are all significant impacts on behaviour.

One unanswered question is the exact extent to which use ideally needs to be reduced at different sites. Currently, mountain ecologists have not come up with such estimates. Furthermore, we do not know the damage

Table 3.4   *Changes in predicted trips**

		Policy option				
Site/Mean baseline predicted trips	A: Fee increase at Ben Nevis	B: Two hour approach increase at Ben Nevis	C: Two hour approach time increase at Glencoe	D: Fee increase at Cairngorms	E: Two hour approach time increase at Cairngorms
(1) North Highlands 4.09	4.13	4.14	4.17	4.17	4.20
(2) Creagmeagaidh 0.97	0.98	0.98	0.99	0.98	0.99
(3) Ben Nevis 4.18	2.88	2.33	4.28	4.25	4.27
(4) Glencoe 7.77	7.83	7.86	4.35	7.87	7.91
(5) Arran 0.66	0.66	0.66	0.67	0.66	0.67
(6) Arrochar 0.002	0.002	0.002	0.002	0.002	0.002
(7) Cullins 2.04	2.06	2.07	2.09	2.08	2.09
(8) Cairngorms 7.881	7.97	7.90	7.99	5.41	4.39

Note: * Trips are predicted using the repeated nested multinomial logit model.

cost functions for access: it is thus not possible to comment on optimal levels of time-price or parking fee. However, one interesting aspect is to look at the different policy measures in terms of the combined effect of reductions in numbers of visitors and the consumers' surplus, to obtain a cost-effectiveness measure. To do this, we estimate the aggregate reduction in visits per season at each site, and divide this into the aggregate consumer surplus loss. This gives the results in Table 3.5. Taking Ben Nevis as an example, it may be seen that the car parking fee (option A) has a higher welfare loss per reduced visit than the increase in access time (option B), since the former imposes a higher per-climber welfare loss but is less effective in reducing visits. The per-reduced visit cost for Glencoe is, however, higher than for Ben Nevis. Car parking fees seem less cost-effective than increasing access time on this criteria for the Cairngorms as well. However, it is impossible to say whether this superior cost-effectiveness for long walk-in policies is transferable to other mountain contexts.

Table 3.5   Cost-effectiveness indicators for the policy alternatives

Policy option/site	Reduction in seasonal visits per climber, dV	Aggregate dV	Aggregate welfare loss, £/season	Welfare loss per reduced visit, £
A: Ben Nevis	1.3	16152	161525	10.00
B: Ben Nevis	1.85	22986	155312	6.76
C: Glencoe	3.42	42493	298200	7.02
D: Cairngorms	2.47	30689	248500	8.09
E: Cairngorms	3.49	43363	285775	6.59

6.   CONCLUSIONS

The demand for outdoor recreation can be expected to increase over time as real incomes rise. As Krutilla and Fisher (1975) pointed out many years ago, this has implications for the management of what are essentially open-access resources in many countries. In Scotland, increasing use of mountains is having undesirable impacts on landscape quality (through erosion) and wildlife (through disturbance), as well as imposing a crowding exter-nality. In this chapter, we show how the Repeated Nested Logit model can be used to predict the effects of alternative management policies on both participation and site choice, where direct pricing of users is not possible. Although we do this for a branch of mountaineering where environmental damages are somewhat less apparent and significant than for, say, hill-walking, the approach here could be applied to any mountain activity, including mountain biking and downhill skiing.

Car-parking fees are investigated in this chapter as a disincentive to use, in the sense that the purpose of levying the fee is to reduce demand for a particular site. However, the current debate over car parking fees in Scotland is oriented around a different primary purpose, namely to raise revenues for footpath maintenance. Any fee raises revenue. However, fees could be set low enough that they have little impact on visits, and yet raise significant monies for footpath restoration. One's intuition is that such fees are less likely to encounter opposition if mountain users know that they are being used entirely for footpath restoration purposes. Long walk-in policies seem more attractive in the sense that they avoid 'pricing the hills'. Our analysis also shows them to be cost-effective in reducing visits at a given site. However, long walk-in policies can be difficult to implement, both in terms of policing/enforcing restrictions (such as a ban on mountain bike use), or because of worries over safety issues: this was a major concern in discussions over getting rid of footbridges in Glencoe. It is also crucial to be aware of knock-on effects, whereby visits are simply displaced to alternative sites. An advantage of the methodology we use here is that such displacement effects are explicitly modelled.

One difficult issue which we have been unable to address satisfactorily in this chapter is the feedback effect from crowding. As measures are taken to reduce visits to a given site, those climbers still visiting the site may gain higher utility per visit. However, this reduction in expected crowding would also impact on participation decisions, that is whether to visit a given site. To adequately model this behaviour and its welfare implications would require a measure of expected congestion X, which would in turn require measures of the probability of X. We have no such measure, and our model assumes certainty, so we cannot address this issue satisfactorily.

Investigations of options for mountain management would appear to be particularly relevant given the new legislative interest in reforming access arrangements to the Scottish mountains. A draft Scottish Outdoor Access Code and the draft Land Reform (Scotland) Bill were recently published by the Scottish Executive: the fact that over 3500 responses to this consultation were made indicates a substantial public interest in this issue. The involvement of many stakeholder groups in the Access Forum, which led up to the publication of this code and bill, is also indicative of great interest on the part of all those who use Scotland's mountain areas in reducing future conflicts. This chapter has shown how economic instruments, which bear on the time or money cost of access, can be used to address one such conflict, namely that between rising participation in mountaineering, and the environmental pressures which result from this.

ACKNOWLEDGEMENTS

We thank the UK Economic and Social Research Council for funding this work under the Global Environmental Change Initiative; the Mountaineering Council of Scotland for providing access to membership lists of Scottish climbing clubs; and the John Muir Trust. We also thank Scott Shonkwiler and two anonymous referees for helpful comments, and Hilary Kirkpatrick for providing information on environmental impacts. This paper first appeared in *Land Use Policy* (2002), **19**: 167–76. We thank the publishers for permission to reproduce an edited version here.

NOTES

1. It is interesting to note that Hardin (1968) pointed to this problem in national parks as one example of his 'tragedy of the commons'. However, charging was notably absent from his list of suggested remedies.
2. This is one of the main weaknesses of the RMNL model, however, unless one has data on the timing of trips within a season, it is a necessary assumption.
3. Hill walkers in Scotland would be equivalent to that group of people in the US who hike or walk up mountains without the benefit of technical mountain climbing equipment.
4. Based on petrol consumption, but excluding insurance and depreciation.
5. See Hanley et al. (2001) for an investigation of the impact of dis-aggregating site attributes on site choice.
6. Again, recall that in this model with no income effects, the $CV = EV$ (Herriges and Kling, 1999).

REFERENCES

Bayfield, N. (1971), 'Some Effects of Walking and Ski-ing at Cairngorm', in E. Duffey and A.S. Watt (eds), *The Scientific Management of Animal and Plant Communities for Conservation*, Oxford: Basil Blackwell, pp. 469–85.

Bloomfield, C.P. (1999), 'Erosion hazard assessment in the High Mourne Mountains', unpublished PhD dissertation, Queens University of Belfast.

Cairngorms Working Party (1993), *Common Sense and Sustainability: A Partnership for the Cairngorms*, Scottish Office, Edinburgh.

Cole, D.N. and R.L. Knight (1991), 'Wildlife preservation and recreational use: conflicting goals of wildland management', *Transactions North American Wildlife and Natural Resources Society*, **56**: 233–7.

Colman, R. (1979), 'Effects of recreation and environment on the erosion of mountain footpaths in the Lake District', Unpublished PhD thesis, University of Sheffield.

Crofts, R. (1995), *The Environment: Who Cares?*, Scottish Natural Heritage, Battleby, Perth.

Fadali, E. and W.D. Shaw (1998), 'Can recreation values for a lake constitute a market for banked agricultural water?', *Contemporary Economic Policy*, **XVI** (October): 433–41.

Ferris, T., K. Lowther and B. Smith, (1993), 'Changes in footpath degradation 1983–1992: a study of the Brandy Pad, Mourne Mountains', *Irish Geography*, **26**(2): 133–40.

Hanley, N., G. Koop, R. Wright and B. Alvarez-Farizo (2001), 'Go climb a moun-
    tain: an application of recreation demand models to rock-climbing in Scotland',
    Journal of Agricultural Economics, **52**(1): 36–51.
Hardin, G. (1968), 'The tragedy of the commons', *Science*, **162**: 1243–8.
Herriges, J.A. and C.L. Kling (1999), 'Nonlinear income effects in random utility
    models', *Review of Economics and Statistics*, **81**(1): 62–72.
Highlands and Islands Enterprise (HIE) (1996), *The Economic Impacts of
    Hillwalking, Mountaineering and Associated Activities in the Highlands and
    Islands of Scotland*, Produced by Jones Economics and published by Highlands
    and Islands Enterprise, April.
Kling, C. and J. Herriges (1995), 'An empirical investigation of the consistency of
    nested logit models with utility maximization', *American Journal of Agricultural
    Economics*, **77**: 875–84.
Krutilla, J.V. and A.C. Fisher (1975), *The Economics of Natural Environments*,
    Washington, DC: Resources for the Future.
Montgomery, M. and M. Needelman (1997), 'The welfare effects of toxic contam-
    ination in freshwater fish', *Land Economics*, **73**(2): 211–23.
Morey, E. (1999), 'Two RUMS uncloaked: nested logit models of site choice and
    participation', in J. Herriges and C. Kling (eds), *Valuing Recreation and the
    Environment*, Cheltenham: Edward Elgar.
Morey, E., W.D. Shaw and R. Rowe (1991), 'A discrete-choice model of recreation
    participation, site-choice and activity valuation', *Journal of Environmental
    Economics and Management*, **20**: 181–201.
Morey, E., R. Rowe and M. Watson (1993), 'A repeated nested logit model of
    Atlantic salmon fishing', *American Journal of Agricultural Economics*, **75**(3):
    578–92.
Needelman, M. and M.J. Kealy (1995), 'Recreational swimming benefits of New
    Hampshire Lake Water Quality Policies: an application of a repeated discrete
    choice model', *Agricultural and Resource Economics Review*, **24**: 78–87.
NTS/MCoS (1997), *Glencoe: Developing the Mountaineering View*, Report of a
    meeting to discuss the future management of Glencoe, National Trust for
    Scotland/Mountaineering Council of Scotland.
Parsons, G. and M.J. Kealy (1992), 'Randomly drawn opportunity sets in a random
    utility model of lake recreation', *Land Economics*, **68**(1): 93–106.
Parsons, G. and M. Needleman (1992), 'Site aggregation in a random utility model
    of recreation', *Land Economics*, **68**: 418–33.
Scottish Mountaineer (2001), March issue. Perth: Mountaineering Council of
    Scotland.
Shaw, W.D. and P. Feather (1999), 'Possibilities for including the opportunity costs
    of time in recreation demand systems', *Land Economics*, **75**: 592–602.
Shaw W.D. and P. Jakus (1996), 'Travel cost models of the demand for rock climb-
    ing', *Agricultural and Resource Economics Review*, October, 133–42.
Shaw, W.D. and M. Ozog (1999), 'Modelling overnight recreation trip choice: appli-
    cation of a repeated nested multinomial model', *Environmental and Resource
    Economics*, **13**: 397–414.
Sidaway, R. and D. Thompson (1991), 'Upland recreation: the limits of acceptable
    change', *ECOS*, **12**(1): 31–9.
Wightman, A. (1996), *Scotland's Mountains: An Agenda for Sustainable
    Development*, Perth: Scottish Countryside and Wildlife Link.

4. Valuing recreational resources using choice experiments: mountaineering in Scotland

Nick Hanley and Robert E. Wright

1. INTRODUCTION

The inability to place monetary values (prices) on goods and services that are not bought and sold in the market makes it difficult (if not impossible) to use economic theory to guide decisions related to their allocation. Pricing is important – it conveys information about relative values, which can then be used in decisions over the appropriate level of supply of such public goods. Numerous approaches have been developed which aim to collect information about non-traded goods and service through indirect means. Broadly speaking, the methods developed fall into two categories. The first involves inferring values for public goods through related markets, and thus relying on revealed preferences. The second category, which we focus on in this chapter, relies instead on constructed or hypothetical markets. These approaches can be termed 'stated preference' methods, with the Contingent Valuation Method (CVM) and Choice Modelling (CM) currently being the most popular in applied work.

This chapter is concerned with investigating the potential of choice experiments for modelling the demand for recreation. More specifically, the data that we examine are based on a survey of mountaineers and climbers in Scotland, with the recreational activity in question being technical climbing (the data was collected in the same survey used by Hanley, Alvarez-Farizo and Shaw in Chapter 3 of this volume). Mountaineering and climbing are increasingly popular sports in Scotland. Figures from Highlands and Islands Enterprise suggest that 767000 mountaineers from the UK visited the Highlands and Islands for hillwalking, technical climbing, ski mountaineering or high level cross-country skiing in 1996 (HIE, 1996).

Climbers pay no access fees for accessing the Scottish hills. In contrast to many other countries (such as the United States), participants are not required to pay user or other fees nor are there any quota or permit systems in place. In this sense access is 'free', although travel and time costs ration demand. There is nothing that resembles a 'market for mountaineering services'. The main aim of this chapter is to attempt to price mountaineering services using the choice experiment method. Multinomial and nested logit models are estimated which relate the preferences of climbers for alternative sites to site characteristics (attributes) and personal characteristics. The parameters of these models are used to derive implicit prices for these attributes. Some testing is carried out to establish whether results are sensitive to the complexity of the choice task and the underlying rationality of respondents' behaviour.

The remainder of this chapter is organised as follows. Section 2 sets out the basic choice experiment approach. Section 3 discusses the design of the survey used to collect our data, along with several tests incorporated into the design. Section 4 presents results. Concluding comments follow in Section 5.

2.   CHOICE EXPERIMENTS

The Choice Experiment (CE) approach was initially developed by Louviere and Hensher (1982) and Louviere and Woodworth (1983), and is one option in a family of empirical stated preference approaches known as choice modelling (for a review, see Hanley et al., 2001). Respondents are asked to choose between alternative goods, defined in terms of their attributes. CE share a common theoretical framework with other environmental valuation approaches in the random utility model (Thurstone, 1927; McFadden, 1973). According to this framework, the indirect utility function for each respondent i (U_i) can be decomposed into two parts: a deterministic element (V), which is typically specified as a linear index of the attributes (X) of the j different alternatives in the choice set, and a stochastic element (e), which represents unobservable influences on individual choice:

$$U_{ij} = V_{ij}(X_{ij}) + e_{ij} = bX_{ij} + e_{ij} \qquad (4.1)$$

The probability that any particular respondent prefers option g in the choice set to any alternative option h, can be expressed as the probability that the utility associated with option g exceeds that associated with all other options:

$$P[(U_{ig} > U_{ih}) \forall h \neq g] = P[(V_{ig} - V_{ih}) > (e_{ih} - e_{ig})] \qquad (4.2)$$

In order to derive an explicit expression for this probability, it is necessary to know the distribution of the error terms (e_{ij}). A typical assumption is that they are independently and identically distributed with an extreme-value (Weibull) distribution, which implies that the probability of any particular alternative g being chosen as the most preferred can be expressed in terms of the logistic distribution (McFadden, 1973). This specification is known as the conditional logit model:

$$P(U_{ig} > U_{ih}, \forall h \neq g) = \frac{\exp(\mu V_{ig})}{\sum_j \exp(\mu V_{ij})} \qquad (4.3)$$

where μ is a scale parameter, inversely proportional to the standard deviation of the error distribution. Once parameter estimates have been obtained, a willingness-to-pay (WTP) compensating variation welfare measure that conforms to demand theory can be derived using the formula given by (4.4) where V_0 represents the utility of the initial state and V_1 represents the utility of the alternative state. The coefficient b_y gives the marginal utility of income and is the coefficient of the cost attribute:

$$\textit{Welfare Measure} = -\frac{1}{b_y}(V_0 - V_1) \qquad (4.4)$$

The value of a marginal change in any of the attributes can be expressed as the ratio of coefficients given in the estimation of (4.1), where b_C is the coefficient on any of the attributes. These ratios are often known as implicit prices:

$$WTP = \frac{-b_C}{b_y} \qquad (4.5)$$

An important implication of this standard specification is that selections from the choice set must obey the 'independence from irrelevant alternatives' (IIA) property (or Luce's Choice Axiom; see Luce, 1959). This property states that the relative probabilities of two options being selected are unaffected by the introduction or removal of other alternatives, and follows from the independence of the Weibull error terms across the different options contained in the choice set. If a violation of the IIA hypothesis is observed, then more complex statistical models are necessary that relax some of the assumptions used, such as the random parameters logit model (Train, 1998) and the heterogeneous extreme value logit (Bhat, 1995). We test for violations of the IIA assumption below using a test developed by Hausman and McFadden (1984).

CE have now been fairly widely applied in the environmental economics literature (for a survey, see Hanley, Wright and Adamowicz, 1998; and

Hanley et al., 2001). Previous applications to recreation include: Adamowicz et al. (1994) on water-based recreation in Alberta; Boxall et al. (1996) and Adamowicz et al. (Chapter 9, this volume) on moose hunting in Alberta; Bullock et al. (1998) on deer hunting in Scotland; and Hanley et al. (1998) on environmentally sensitive areas in Scotland.

3. STUDY DESIGN

Climbs are classified according to a two-tier grading system in Britain, which describes both the overall difficulty and exposure of a route, and the degree of difficulty in making the hardest move on the climb (the crux). Climbers' appreciation of routes, though, extends beyond this technical grading, to include aspects such as length of climb, scenic quality, and degree of crowding on a route. One may thus think of individual climbs as different bundles of a given set of attributes, although it may be hard for the researcher to completely describe a particular climb using this set. Climbers make choices from the set of all climbs in Scotland in deciding on where to go on a particular trip: a natural way to model this choice problem is thus to make use of random utility theory (although for an alternative view, see Loewenstein, 1999).

The initial steps in this study were to identify the choice alternatives and their relevant attributes. To accomplish this, focus groups were conducted with climbers from university mountaineering clubs in Edinburgh and Stirling. Six attributes of climbs were established by the focus groups as being central to the choice decision. The appropriate levels for these attributes were decided on both though the focus groups, and through use of local climbing guidebooks. The chosen attributes were:

Length of the climb. The hypothesis is that (*ceteris paribus*) longer climbs are preferred to shorter climbs. The attribute has four levels: (1) 50 metres; (2) 100 metres; (3) 200 metres; and (4) 300 metres.

Approach time. This attribute refers to the amount of time required to walk to the base of the climb from a place where a car may be parked. The hypothesis is that (ceteris paribus) shorter approaches are preferred to longer approaches. The reason being that given a fixed allocation of time, a shorter approach time leaves more time for climbing. There are four levels; (1) 3 hours; (2) 2 hours; (3) 1 hour; and (4) 30 minutes.

Crowding on the climb. This refers to whether on not other climbers are present on the chosen climb. Crowded climbs are more dangerous and crowding usually results in slower climbing times as queues develop. The hypothesis is that (ceteris paribus) less crowded climbs are preferred to more crowded climbs. This attribute has two levels: (1) crowded; and (2) not crowded.

Overall 'quality' of the climb. It is common for most guidebooks to employ a 'star rating system' which provides information on the overall quality of the climb. This attribute has four levels: (1) no stars; (2) 1 star; (3) 2 stars; and (4) 3 stars. The hypothesis is that (ceteris paribus) climbs with more stars are preferred.

Scenic quality. This refers to the area where the climb is located, and is meant to capture the relative beauty of the landscape that surrounds the climb. This attribute has four levels: (1) not at all scenic; (2) not scenic; (3) scenic; and (4) very scenic. The hypothesis is that (ceteris paribus) more scenic climbs are preferred to less scenic climbs.

Distance as a proxy for cost. This refers to the distance that the climb is away from one's home and is used to estimate indirectly the cost or price of the climbing package. This attribute has six levels: (1) 30 miles; (2) 70 miles; (3) 110 miles; (4) 160 miles; (5) 200 miles; and (6) 250 miles. After the questionnaires were administered, this mileage distance measure was converted into a travel cost or price (*Cost*) using the following simple formula: *Cost = 2 × Distance in miles * 10 pence per mile*, based on an estimate of the marginal cost of motoring provided by the Royal Automobile Club. The hypothesis is that (ceteris paribus) 'cheaper' climbs are preferred to more 'expensive' climbs.

The sampling frame was provided by the Mountaineering Council of Scotland through a list of climbing club members in Scotland. A random sample of these addresses was selected, and questionnaires mailed to these individuals, who were asked to complete and return the questionnaire. A donation of £2 was promised to the John Muir Trust (a charity which exists to conserve wilderness areas in Scotland) for every questionnaire returned as an incentive. Questionnaires were also administered at climbing walls in Edinburgh, Glasgow and Falkirk. A sample of 267 useable responses from climbers in total was acquired.

It is hard to judge the representativeness of the sample since very little information exists on the population of interest. The only alternative data which we are aware of relates to the survey reported in Highlands and Islands Enterprise (1996). It focussed on Scottish visits by mountaineers in general, with only 11 per cent of these being rock-climbers. Relative to this 1995 sample, our sample seems to consist of a higher proportion of men (79 per cent versus 66 per cent); to contain fewer older participants; and to have a higher figure for climbing trips per year (22 compared with 14). Income per respondent is only suggested in HIE (1996) by socio-economic classification, with 64 per cent of the sample being in social classes A, B or

C1. Since this scale is calculated by occupation, we cannot compare it with our sample. Finally, mean local spending per day in HIE was £18.71: this compares with a figure of £10.92 in our sample. Given all of this, it would be wise to take a cautious view as to how representative our sample is of the population of Scottish rock-climbers.

Climbers were asked questions to complete a number of choice experiments, ranging from four to eight choice pairs; to provide information on their climbing abilities and experience; and to provide standard socioeconomic information. An example choice set is given in Table 4.1. As may be seen, respondents are asked to choose between two routes described in terms of their attributes, including price; or choose to consume neither (for example 'stay at home'). Choice sets were produced using a fractional factorial design, and climbers were instructed to assume that all routes described in the choice experiment were within their technical ability.

Table 4.1   Illustrative choice experiment question

Which of the two routes described below would you rather visit? Please tick one of the options shown at the foot of the page:

Characteristics of route	Route A	Route B
Length of climb in metres	100 metres	200 metres
Approach time (The time it takes you to walk to the base of the climb from where you leave the road)	3 hours	2 hours
Quality of climb (i.e. no. of stars)	2 stars	0 stars
Crowding at route (How many other people there are on the route you are climbing, i.e. Crowded/Not crowded)	Crowded	Not crowded
Scenic quality of route (Very scenic/Scenic/Not scenic/Not at all scenic)	Not at all scenic	Not at all scenic
Distance of route from home (The time it takes to travel from home to where you leave the road)	160 miles	110 miles

I WOULD CHOOSE ROUTE A	—
I WOULD CHOOSE ROUTE B	—
I WOULD CHOOSE NEITHER, AND STAY AT HOME	—

As mentioned above, climbers were presented with either four or eight choices. This split was used in order to test whether the complexity of the choice task (as measured by the number of choice sets the respondent had to complete) has an effect on measures of preferences. Evidence in the literature on the impact of choice complexity is somewhat mixed (see, for example, Swait and Adamowicz, 1996). We also included two simple tests of the rationality behind respondents' answers. The first was to include for a sub-set of respondents a choice pair where one alternative strictly dominates the other. This was achieved by making these alternatives identical except for price (that is, travel cost). Respondents would be expected to reject the more expensive option. The second was to include, for a different subset of individuals, identical choice pairs as their first and fourth choice occasion. The answer which respondents gave in the first instance was expected to be the same as the answer they gave when the pair was repeated.

4. RESULTS

4.1 Multinomial Logit Model

Columns 1 and 2 in Table 4.2 are the parameter estimates for the multinomial or conditional logit model (MNL). Column 1 is for a model that does not include any individual-specific covariates. Column 2 is for the model that includes four covariates: the respondent's income; whether the respondent is married; whether the respondent has children; and the respondent's age. The parameter estimates associated with these covariates are not shown since they are of no direct substantive importance. Both specifications include alternative-specific constant terms (that is α(Option A) and α(Option B) in Table 4.1).

The first point to note is that the parameter estimates associated with each of the attributes are very similar across the two specifications suggesting that the model is robust to the inclusion of individual-specific covariates. In both models all the site-choice attributes are statistically significant at conventional threshold levels, with the only exception being for the 'two-stars' climb quality attribute. In addition all the attributes have the expected signs and their changes in magnitude are consistent with the hypotheses discussed above. More specifically, climbers are shown to prefer longer climbs with shorter approach times, climbs which are not crowded, and climbs in more scenic areas. The star rating of climbs in the guidebooks is also important, with 'three-star' climbs attracting the highest probability of visit. The cost variable has a negative sign which is in agreement with the

The mountains

Table 4.2 Parameter estimates (absolute values of t-statistics in parentheses)

	(1)	(2)	(3)	(4)
Estimator:	MNL	MNL	NL	NL
Covariates?:	No	Yes	No	Yes
Length	0.00372	0.00379	0.00450	0.00447
	(6.5)	(6.5)	(6.4)	(6.4)
Approach time	−0.384	−0.391	−0.454	−0.451
	(6.8)	(6.9)	(6.8)	(6.8)
Not crowded	0.602	0.613	0.692	0.691
	(11.3)	(11.4)	(10.2)	(10.1)
Not scenic	−0.309	−0.317	−0.331	−0.337
	(3.6)	(3.7)	(3.3)	(3.6)
Scenic	0.354	0.357	0.415	0.411
	(3.8)	(3.8)	(4.0)	(4.0)
Very Scenic	0.826	0.843	0.990	0.989
	(8.7)	(8.9)	(8.3)	(8.3)
One star	−0.162	−0.168	−0.228	−0.226
	(1.9)	(1.9)	(2.4)	(2.4)
Two stars	0.127	0.136	0.236	0.231
	(1.3)	(1.4)	(1.9)	(1.9)
Three stars	1.019	1.037	1.120	1.125
	(11.6)	(11.7)	(11.3)	(11.4)
Cost	−0.0334	−0.0337	−0.0361	−0.0361
	(9.5)	(9.5)	(9.6)	(9.5)
α(Option A)	1.679	2.231	2.207	2.816
	(9.4)	(10.1)	(7.7)	(7.8)
α(Option B)	1.361	1.839	1.873	2.415
	(7.7)	(8.4)	(6.7)	(6.9)
γ (Yes)	—	—	0.725	0.753
			(10.1)	(9.0)
Pseudo-R^2	0.30	0.31	0.39	0.39
χ^2	724	762	1296	1331
N =	1332		3996	
IIA χ^2 =	83.25		—	

hypothesis that 'cheaper' climbs are preferred to 'more expensive' climbs after other characteristics of climbs are held constant.

Implicit prices associated with the MNL model that includes covariates are shown in Column 1 of Table 4.3. These prices were calculated for each of the attributes by applying equation (4.5) and may be interpreted as willingness-to-pay amounts. An extra metre of length adds £0.11 to the

Table 4.3   Implicit prices (£), (standard errors) and [95 per cent confidence bands]

	(1)	(2)
Estimator:	MNL	NL
Covariates	Yes	Yes
Length	0.11	0.12
	(0.02)	(0.02)
	[0.07 to 0.15]	[0.08 to 0.17]
Approach time	−11.61	−12.49
	(2.04)	(2.22)
	[−15.62 to −7.60]	[−16.84 to −8.13]
Crowding:		
Crowded	−18.22	−19.14
	(4.24)	(2.60)
	[−23.10 to −13.34]	[−24.24 to −14.05]
Not crowded	18.22	19.14
	(4.24)	(2.60)
	[−34.56 to −17.94]	[14.05 to 24.24]
Scenic quality:		
Not at all scenic	−26.25	−29.41
	(4.24)	(4.67)
	[−34.56 to −17.94]	[−38.57 to −20.25]
Not scenic	−9.43	−9.34
	(2.63)	(2.77)
	[−14.59 to −4.27]	[−14.78 to −3.91]
Scenic	10.62	11.37
	(3.06)	(3.06)
	[4.62 to 16.62]	[5.47 to 15.37]
Very scenic	25.06	27.38
	(3.89)	(4.14)
	[17.43 to 32.68]	[19.26 to 35.50]
Quality of climb:		
No stars	−29.85	−31.27
	(3.75)	(3.77)
	[−37.19 to −22.51]	[−38.66 to −23.88]
One star	−5.00	−6.27
	(2.70)	(2.80)
	[−10.28 to 0.29]	[−11.75 to −0.78]
Two stars	4.03	6.40
	(3.0)	(3.51)
	[−1.84 to 9.91]	[−0.49 to 13.28]
Three stars	30.81	31.14
	(3.66)	(3.73)
	[23.64 to 37.99]	[23.83 to 38.46]

value of a climb. A one-hour reduction in approach time adds £11.61. Big increases in value are also found for moving from crowded to not crowded climbs, with the latter adding £18.22 in value. Scenic quality also matters. Climbers are willing to pay more for climbs that are located in areas with better scenic quality. 'Very scenic' climbs add £25.06 in value. The quality of climb as described by the star rating system is also important. 'Three stars' climbs are highly valued, adding £30.81 to the value of a climb.

4.2   Nested Logit Model

As noted in Section 3, one critical assumption of the MNL model is the Independence of Irrelevant Alternatives. We tested for the validity of this assumption using a test developed by Hausman and McFadden (1984). The test is a chi-square test of the form:

$$\chi^2 = (\boldsymbol{\beta}_s - \boldsymbol{\beta}_f)'[V_s - V_f]^{-1}(\boldsymbol{\beta}_s - \boldsymbol{\beta}_f)$$

where $\boldsymbol{\beta}_s$ is a vector of parameter estimates from a model with a restricted 's' number of choices (that is two in our application) and $\boldsymbol{\beta}_f$ is a vector of parameter estimates from the model with the full f number of choices (that is three in our application). V_s and V_f are the estimates of the covariance matrices from the restricted and full models respectively. Degrees of freedom for this test are the number of attributes, 'K'. We applied this test and found that IIA assumption is firmly rejected. For example, a χ^2 value of 83.25 was found for a MNL model (without covariates) which drops the stay at home alternative from the choice set.

One possible solution to violation of IIA is to recast the model as a nested structure. We adopted such an approach by considering two levels of choice. The first level is: Option 1 – 'Stay at home' or Option 2 – 'Route A or B'. Conditional on Option 2 being chosen, in the second level there are two further options: Option 1 – 'Route A' or Option 2 – 'Route B'. With this structure, there are only two choice alternatives at each level and the notion of 'irrelevant alternatives' is no longer relevant. The structure of this nested model is summarised in Figure 4.1.

Columns 3 and 4 in Table 4.2 are the parameter estimates for the nested logit model (NL). Column 3 is for a model that does not include any individual-specific covariates while Column 4 is for the model that includes four individual-specific covariates discussed above. The γ(Yes) is a constant term for the first level of choice. A comparison of the four columns in Table 4.2 reveals that the parameter estimates (including the cost attribute) from the NL model are larger in absolute magnitude than the parameter estimates from the MNL model.

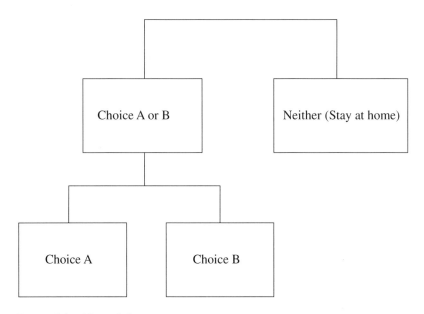

Figure 4.1   Nested choice structure

The MNL and NL models are more similar than the simple comparison of parameter estimates might suggest. This similarity becomes apparent when the implicit prices suggested by the two models are compared. The implicit prices for the NL model (with covariates) are shown in Column 2 of Table 4.3. When standard errors are taken into account, these implicit prices are not significantly different between the two models, as may be seen from the 95 per cent confidence intervals for implicit prices shown in Table 4.3. More importantly, the same substantive conclusions are reached with respect to the relative importance of the attributes. Despite the fact that the Hausman and McFadden test clearly rejects the IIA assumption, violation of this assumption does not appear to have much impact on the estimated implicit prices which for practical and policy purposes are of central interest.

4.3   Testing for the Effects of Choice Complexity

Does the complexity of the choice task matter? Our *a priori* hypothesis is that the complexity of the choice task, as measured by the number of choice sets to be completed, may impact on measures of preference. This could either be due to respondents learning how better to complete tasks as the number of tasks increase; or that respondents become fatigued and pay less attention to accurately completing tasks as the number of choice sets increases. If preference measures are sensitive to the number of choice tasks, then this means that welfare estimates can turn on questionnaire design decisions. In order to explore this issue separate MNL and NL models were estimated for respondents who were asked to complete four choice sets and these models were compared to MNL and NL models estimated separately for respondents who were asked to complete eight choices sets. A likelihood ratio test was carried out to test the hypothesis that the parameters between these four choice and eight choice models were not statistically different, that is we test:

$$H_0: \beta(4 \text{ choices}) - \beta(8 \text{ choices}) = 0,$$

where β are the relevant parameter vectors.

Using this likelihood ratio test approach, we find only weak evidence that the number of choices has a significant effect on preferences. In the MNL model (with covariates), the χ^2 test statistic is 27.9, with an associated prob-value of 0.11, suggesting that the equality of parameters cannot be rejected at the 10 per cent level. In the NL model, the χ^2 test statistic is 35.9 with associated prob-value of 0.06. This suggests that equality of parameters can be rejected at 5 per cent but not 10 per cent. Taken together, these tests do not present strong evidence that parameter estimates depend on whether the respondent was asked to complete four or eight choices.

Another way of comparing the effects of varying the number of choices is to look for significant differences in the implicit prices generated from the two treatments. Based on the 5 per cent level of statistical significance (and hence on 95 per cent confidence intervals), none of the confidence bands failed to overlap. In this sense, even though the likelihood ratio tests reject equality of the parameters at the 10 per cent level, the implicit prices (which are perhaps the most important information) are not different at the more stringent 5 per cent level. This would appear to be good news on the whole for the choice experiment method, in the sense that arbitrary design decisions have only small impacts on estimates of willingness to pay.

4.4   Testing for Rationality

Finally, we note the outcomes of the two informal tests for rationality in responses described in Section 3. As will be recalled, these were twofold. First, in four versions of the questionnaire, strictly-dominated alternatives were included, where in one of the choice pairs route A (B) was identical to route B (A) in every respect except price. Some 42 responses were returned from this distribution of questionnaire versions. Of these 42 responses, there was only one individual who chose the strictly-dominated alternative route rather than the identical-but-cheaper route. There were insufficient responses to perform any formal statistical tests of rationality.

Second, in two versions of the questionnaire, identical choices were included. In these cases, the first and fourth choice pair were identical to each other. An individual choosing A on the first occasion would be expected to choose A again on the second occasion. Only 22 responses were returned of this questionnaire version. In only one case out of these 22 did a respondent change their mind when the identical choice pair was repeated.

5.   CONCLUDING COMMENTS

This chapter reports results from a choice experiment study of rock-climbing in Scotland. Climbers' choices over substitute sites are modelled as a function of the attributes of these sites, plus an error term. A broad conclusion is that the CE approach succeeds in this case in adequately representing demand, in that the variation in site choice is explained in an intuitively-plausible manner by the logit models, which themselves represent an underlying process of probabilistic utility maximisation. We should not expect such representations to be exact, due to errors and inaccuracies in peoples' responses to the survey instrument, due to the limitations of the econometric techniques used, and due to Loewenstein's observation that the behaviour of climbers is probably not entirely assessable within the conventional economic model of utility maximisation anyway.

Using the logit model results, implicit prices were then obtained, showing the marginal utility of changes in site attributes. This might be useful information in two contexts: first, where there is a desire to estimate the economic costs or benefits of land-use changes which have an impact on climbing sites (such as an increase in access times or decreases in scenic quality); second, where management of outdoor recreation areas can be guided by knowledge of the relative economic values of those site attributes, which can be affected by management.

In terms of the wider development and use of the CE method in modelling recreation demand, this chapter has a number of interesting findings. First, the fact that moving to a nested model from an MNL model (due to the violation of IIA in the latter) produced relatively small changes in welfare measures or model coefficients. Second, that changes in the number of choice tasks which individuals were asked to perform had largely insignificant effects on parameter values in our estimated conditional indirect utility functions, and on implicit prices. Third, some limited (and informal) tests for rationality showed that the great majority of respondents behave rationally in answering choice questions.

ACKNOWLEDGEMENTS

We thank Vic Adamowicz and Douglass Shaw for many helpful comments on this project. Ceara Nevin provided excellent research assistance in the conduct of the survey. The ESRC provided funding under its Global Environmental Change programme. We thank the Mountaineering Council of Scotland and the John Muir Trust for their assistance. This chapter first appeared in the journal *Environmental and Resource Economics* (2002), **22**: 449–66; it is reproduced here with kind permission of Kluwer Academic Publishers.

REFERENCES

Adamowicz, W., J. Louviere and M. Williams (1994), 'Combining revealed and stated preference methods for valuing environmental amenities', *Journal of Environmental Economics and Management*, **26**: 271–92.

Bhat, C.R. (1995), 'A heteroskedastic extreme value model of intercity travel mode choice', *Transportation Research B*, **29**(6): 471–83.

Boxall, P., W. Adamowicz, J. Swait, M. Williams and J. Louviere (1996), 'A comparison of stated preference methods for environmental valuation', *Ecological Economics*, **18**: 243–53.

Bullock, C.H., D.A. Elston and N.A. Chalmers (1998), 'An application of economic choice experiments to a traditional land use – deer hunting and landscape change in the Scottish Highlands', *Journal of Environmental Management*, **52**(4): 335–51.

Hanley, N., D. MacMillan, R.E. Wright, C. Bullock, I. Simpson, D. Parsisson and B. Crabtree (1998), 'Contingent valuation versus choice experiments: estimating the benefits of environmentally sensitive areas in Scotland', *Journal of Agricultural Economics*, **49**(1): 1–15.

Hanley, N., S. Mourato and R. Wright (2001), 'Choice modelling: a superior alternative for environmental valuation?', *Journal of Economic Surveys*, **15**(3): 435–62.

Hanley, N., R. Wright and W. Adamowicz (1998), 'Using choice experiments to value the environment: design issues, current experience and future prospects', *Environmental and Resource Economics*, **11**(3–4): 413–28.

Hausman, J.A. and D. McFadden (1984), 'Specification tests for the multinomial logit model', *Econometrica*, **52**: 1219–40.

Highlands and Islands Enterprise (1996), *The Economic Impacts of Hill-walking, Mountaineering and Associated Activities in the Highlands and Islands of Scotland*, Inverness: HIE.

Loewenstein, G. (1999), 'Because it is there: the challenge of mountaineering for utility theory', *Kyklos*, **52**: 315–44.

Louviere, J. and D. Hensher (1982), 'On the design and analysis of simulated choice or allocation experiments in travel choice modelling', *Transportation Research Record*, **890**: 11–17.

Louviere, J. and G. Woodworth (1983), 'Design and analysis of simulated consumer choice or allocation experiments: an approach based on aggregate data', *Journal of Marketing Research*, **20**: 350–67.

Luce, R.D. (1959), *Individual Choice Behavior: A Theoretical Analysis*, New York: John Wiley & Sons.

McFadden, D. (1973), 'Conditional Logit Analysis of Qualitative Choice Behaviour', in P. Zarembka (ed.), *Frontiers in Econometrics*, New York: Academic Press.

Swait, J. and W. Adamowicz (1996), 'The effect of choice environment and task demands on consumer behaviour', paper presented at the Canadian Resource and Environmental Economics Study Group, Montreal.

Thurstone, L. (1927), 'A law of comparative judgement', *Psychological Review*, **34**: 273–86.

Train, K.E. (1998), 'Recreation demand models with taste differences across people', *Land Economics*, **74**(2): 230–39.

5. Are climbers fools? Modeling risky recreation

Paul M. Jakus, Mary Riddel and W. Douglass Shaw

1. INTRODUCTION

In this chapter we examine the recreational activity known as rock climbing, linking this activity to the economics of risk-taking. Nearly all economic studies of risk or uncertainty relate to financial risk and/or portfolio management. Recently, however, people engaged in the valuation of environmental amenities have recognized the need to allow their models to incorporate an individual's uncertainty about the environment or some decision that must be made and, at times, complex behaviors under risky conditions. Still, the vast majority of recreation studies have assumed no uncertainty or risk while explaining recreationists' behavior, even those that do examine recreational activities one might deem risky. For example, nearly all of the analyses of rock climbing apply the standard random utility or count data versions of the travel cost model of recreation demand, with none of them involving aspects of risk except in a very minor way (Ekstrand, 1994; Shaw and Jakus, 1996; Grijalva et al., 2002a, 2002b; Hanley et al., 2001; and Hanley et al., 2002).

Nearly all of these rock climbing studies examine access to climbing areas in the United States or Scotland, focusing on where participants go climbing and how often. These studies have been motivated by proposed climbing management plans that may restrict climbing access on public land used by climbers. In recent years managers of public lands have grown concerned that rock climbing harms resources or have become aware of potential conflicts between rock climbers and other types of public lands users.[1] The 'certainty' models used in previous studies typically explain how an individual's destination, trip-making frequency, or total seasonal participation may change under the new regulatory policies. Conventional welfare measures under certainty are derived to examine the losses or gains of some access restrictions. For example, Grijalva et al. (2002a and 2002b) examine the losses to climbers who visit Hueco Tanks near El Paso Texas and, more broadly, the losses to climbers for access restrictions in wilderness areas at a host of climbing areas around the United States.

Many researchers have attempted to lay out a framework for participation in risky recreation such as rock climbing or similar pursuits such as mountaineering, scuba diving, canoeing or white-water rafting, and big-game hunting, but most of this research focuses on *why* individuals become attracted to risky forms of leisure in the first place (for example, Slanger and Rudestam, 1997; Schreyer and White, 1979; Robinson, 1992).[2] The perception of risk by participants in risky activities has been studied by Cheron and Ritchie (1982). Jakus and Shaw (1996) explored trade-offs between technical difficulty and risk ratings communicated for particular climbing routes.

Risky recreation is clearly being undertaken by an increasingly large number of participants around the world; to the degree that risk attributes of the sport affect the choice of destination and trip frequency decisions, economists may need to develop models that incorporate this attribute of the behavioral decision process.[3] Our specific goal in this chapter is to consider whether it makes a difference if we model the demand for recreation with explicit recognition of the risk, as opposed to modeling the demand for climbing ignoring risks. The standard approach to modeling demand for recreation assumes that the individual has 'perfect' information regarding all choices, and that she or he is certain about outcomes. Climbers, in contrast, face many risks, including the risk of injury or death, the risk of not completing a route, and risks associated with weather and crowds. We show how a consideration of risk results in demand models that differ from the usual model of recreation activities. Our discussion is presented within the context of risks associated with injury or death because these are probably the most interesting and important aspects for both climbers and economists. While some authors have considered some type of uncertainty and risk in recreation, none have considered risk of injury, and none that we know of have used revealed preference data in the empirical modeling.[4]

Although rock climbing is the risky recreation examined in this chapter, our results can be generally applied to several other forms of recreation that involve risks. The economic model focuses not on the individual's motives to take up the sport in the first place, but on the determinants of the destinations, frequency of visits, and the willingness to incur risk. A parallel with other risky recreational pursuits can be found in the way that climbers sometimes refer to success as 'bagging' a route, which conjures up the hunter's claim of 'bagging' a deer or elk. Both involve uncertainty, with no guarantee of success.

The remainder of the chapter begins with details on the sport of rock climbing (Section 2). In Section 3 we present some preliminary empirical results that are relevant to modeling and understanding risky recreation. The information presented in Section 3 is used to motivate the risk-related travel cost demand models presented in Section 4. We do not actually estimate the parameters of a risky recreation demand model in this chapter because the data necessary to do so are not available to us at this time. Our focus, instead, is on the implications of risk for future welfare analysis. Section 5 summarizes the chapter and offers some suggestions for future research in this area.

2.   THE RISKY GAMES CLIMBERS PLAY

We begin this section with a description of the activity of rock climbing, so that the models proposed in Section 4 can be better understood. Though several scholarly papers on rock-climbing have been published, none completely explain what goes on in the sport, nor do they differentiate between the varieties of climbing (and risk) that can be experienced in a variety of settings and configurations of rock.

Technical rock climbing on smaller cliffs or 'crags' involves the choice of specific routes up the rockface.[5] Routes differ in their degree of difficulty, length and other aesthetic aspects, as well as the degree of risk involved. Technical climbing usually involves the use of ropes and climbing gear to protect the climber in the event of a fall.[6] The equipment used to protect the climber from hitting the ground or rock feature after falling varies from hardware (metal devices) placed permanently in the rock (a bolt or piton), to metal devices that can be temporarily inserted into cracks and fissures, and later removed. Using either one, as the 'leader' climbs, the rope is run through these devices, one of which will act as a fulcrum point in the event of a fall. The second climber (or 'second') holds (belays) the rope from the bottom. The leader advances using the features of the rock, with the climbing equipment used to protect against the consequences of a fall which would otherwise result in injury. After belaying the leader, the second advances up, also using rock features, but he or she is quite well protected by the rope above, and thus takes little or no risk of injury.

Specific climbs or 'routes' are often rated according to technical or gymnastic difficulty and also for their assessed risk. Technical ratings are initially proposed by the first ascent party but, as the route is climbed by others over the years, a consensus rating is determined. Such consensus ratings are published in readily available climbing guidebooks (for popular areas) or spread by word of mouth (for less popular areas). These are much like fishing guides or trail or hiking guides. Guidebooks note the location and length of a route, its technical difficulty, a quality rating, and whether the climb can be well protected or not (the risk scale).[7] In the United States, the risk ratings were developed in the 1970s, and were based on the letters used by the Motion Picture Association to designate suitability of a film for different viewers: G, PG, R, and X. Specific climbs or routes that the leader can protect safely are rated 'G' (excellent protection) or 'PG' (good protection). Rock climbs that cannot be well protected are typically rated with an 'R' or, when protection is extremely poor to non-existent, an 'X'. An R-rating indicates that should the climber fall, even with the use of protective equipment, the fall would likely result in serious injury. This is because the places in the rock for protection will likely cause the climber to climb long distances between protection points; if a fall occurs it will be a long one, which may heighten the probability of hitting the rock or the ground. An X-rating indicates protection possibilities that are so poor that, should the climber fall, death would be a near certainty. Other than this, little is communicated about risks in rock climbing on a widespread basis, at least in terms of information that climbers can readily access.[8] Based on our experience, we know that climbers often share details with others about routes they have done, and this information is passed along in the community, most often by word-of-mouth.

Given the information available about climbing routes, climbers may choose from a variety of potential outdoor climbing experiences. One climber may push her athletic limit by choosing a well-protected climb with a technical difficulty at or beyond her current technical limit. This climber may fall frequently, but safely, in her attempts. Another climber may play a more psychological game by choosing to lead an R- or X-rated climb, perhaps technically easier, but one which requires 'mind control' to complete the risky route. This climber would not wish to fall, since it would result in injury. Others may choose an 'easy' day at the crag, climbing only safe routes well within their technical ability, or maximizing the vertical distance or number of vertical feet successfully climbed. Finally, some may choose to minimize risk altogether by always choosing to climb with a rope from above. These activities are clearly in contrast to the assumption by some researchers that the sole goal in climbing is to 'get to the top' by any means necessary. Whereas this may be a reasonable assumption to make in considering the sport of mountain climbing or mountaineering, it is often inappropriate for rock climbing.

3. SOME RELEVANT PRELIMINARY EMPIRICAL RESULTS

In this section we present some preliminary empirical results relevant to modeling and understanding risky recreation. The data come from a Fall

1993 mail survey of members of the Mohonk Preserve in New York State and were used by Shaw and Jakus in their studies. We use these data to guide us in identifying which risk-related aspects of rock climbing behavior are important to climbers and, thus, important to those wishing to model such behavior.

The Mohonk Preserve offers some of the finest rock climbing in the United States and is visited by climbers from all over the world. Compared to other nationally-known climbing areas, the Preserve is somewhat unusual in that it maintains a policy of not allowing new bolts or pitons to be placed in the cliffs. Climbers must use their own protection, or the few existing permanent protection (bolts and pitons) that had been permitted in the past. Of the 892 respondents to the Mohonk Preserve survey, 221 stated that they took a climbing trip in 1993. The group who returned the survey is well educated and has a high average household income.

3.1   The Primary 'Goal' of Rock Climbers

Casual perusal of the Mohonk Preserve climbing guidebooks dissuades researchers of the notion that reaching the top of these routes is the most important goal. The area's guidebooks report the full description of a route followed, for example, by a statement that 'most people only climb the first rope-length'. This occurs because this section of the route contains the best (or hardest) quality climbing, with the remainder of the route being unpleasant or too easy. Results from the Mohonk Preserve sample of rock climbers also illustrate that 'getting to the top' is not a consideration for nearly half the respondents, and that route difficulty is sought out, not avoided. First, a majority of climbers (60 per cent) most frequently choose to do routes that are just at or above, not *below* the grade at which they are technically able to climb without falling. In addition, when asked how they 'normally' finished a climb, 51 per cent said they continue to the top, 11 per cent said they rappelled (descended on the rope) after one or more rope-lengths of climbing, and 38 per cent had no preference. Thus, fully half of our responding sample of climbers defined success as something other than completing the route. Respondents were also asked to rate the attractions of a trip to the Preserve on a 1 (most important) to 5 (least important) scale. A large number of climbers gave 'physical challenge' a score of 1 (60 per cent of those who responded). This supports earlier evidence (for example, Ewert, 1985) that the challenge is important to this group of individuals. These data suggest that an expected utility model based on the risky outcome of 'getting to the top' would be misdirected, at least for rock climbers.

3.2   Risk Attitudes, Risk-taking Behavior and the Probability of Failure

Climbers in the Preserve study were asked whether the Preserve's policy of no bolting should be maintained, or reconsidered. Recall that bolts very likely reduce the risks of injury or death, so one might assume climbers would be in favor of reconsidering this policy. Of those responding to the question, 68 per cent said it should be maintained. Only 1 per cent thought the policy should be revoked, while 31 per cent said it should be reconsidered, with the majority of these saying it should be reconsidered to increase safety. We learn several things here. First, there are ways of climbing safely without bolts, and a majority of Preserve climbers do not mind these alternatives. Second, attitudes toward bolting do not necessarily reveal a preference for taking risks because climbs with poor protection may be avoided. More careful questions have to be asked of the climbers to further explore this issue of bolting and how it relates to risk-taking and the experience.

The Mohonk questionnaire also asked climbers to describe a typical day at the Preserve. Of those who responded, only 7 per cent *always* climb on a toprope, which involves little or no risk because the rope is always above the climber to protect him. An additional 18 per cent said they usually toprope a specific route, with the remaining 75 per cent climbing with a toprope only infrequently. This shows that few climbers approach their sport in a manner in which they can always minimize risk.

Climbers were also asked whether they led climbs that were rated 'R' (serious injury if a fall is taken) or 'X' (death in the event of a fall) (see Jakus and Shaw, 1996). The responses clearly indicate that many climbers voluntarily assume risk of injury or death. Of those who answered, 31 per cent said they led R-rated climbs and 20 per cent said they led X-rated climbs, or climbed without a rope. The questionnaire also asked the level of difficulty at which the climber said he led the R or X climb. The risk in these endeavors, whether real or perceived, may decline if the climber leads a route that protects poorly, but is well below his or her level of ability.[9] Of those who said they led R-rated climbs, 30 per cent said they lead the same level of technical difficulty as they would for a G- or PG-rated climb. Fifty-one per cent said they lead one level lower than they report leading normally, and 11 per cent said they lead two levels lower. A similar comparison for leaders of X-rated climbs found that only 10 per cent said they lead at the same level of technical difficulty as a G- or PG-rated climb, 41 per cent said one level lower, and 39 per cent said two levels lower.

We note that the number who lead at the same level as their ability drops significantly when the outcome from the fall increases from injury (R) to death (X). This finding is consistent with two key aspects of behavior. First, climbers appear to avoid risk and second, the probabilities of failure are controlled to some degree by the climber (see Jakus and Shaw, 1996). Climbers are adjusting the difficulty downward when climbing an R- or X-rated route to decrease the probability of injury. Again, this behavior suggests the conventional expected utility model, which assumes exogenous risk probabilities, may be inappropriate unless ability and difficulty can be integrated with the probability of injury. It is also interesting to examine those individuals who lead R- and X-rated climbs and their responses on the questions pertaining to the bolting policy. We might expect that, if the thrill of the potential injury or death motivates them in choosing climbing routes, this group may be against any new bolts or pitons. However, for the 81 individuals who lead either R- or X-rated climbs, 40 per cent thought the policy should be reconsidered and 19 per cent of this group said so because of safety reasons.

3.3   Summary: Key Features of Climbers' Behavior to be Modeled

The behavioral data indicate the ways in which the empirical recreational demand model should be extended. First, consider the notion that an important risky attribute of climbing is the uncertainty associated with reaching the top of the cliff. This is unfounded. Climbers often seek out routes of such extreme difficulty that many falls are expected; recall that falling without injury is common. Further, climbers may focus on successfully completing only a portion of a route, choosing to return to the ground after completing this section. Second, 'falling' is part of the game because physical challenge is an important element of the sport. Third, the key risk that remains is the risk of injury or death. Climbers appear to recognize this as an integral element of the sport, but one that can be controlled to some degree through judicious selection of climbing routes. Thus, the risk of injury or death may, in some large part, be endogenous to the climber, at least in an *ex ante* sense. These facts guide us in model development.

4.   THE MODELS

4.1   Demand under Certainty

A wide variety of certainty-based (no risk) recreation demand models use the theory of consumer behavior and observed trip data to explain the choice of destinations and/or the number of trips to particular recreation areas. Typical models use the individual's travel costs to and from a recreation destination to proxy the market price of the good, and are thus often referred to as travel cost models (TCM). These are also called *revealed preference* models because they reveal the value of non-market resources (a site or site attribute) through actual behavior. These models allow the value, or maximum willingness to pay (WTP), for access to the recreation site(s) or the value of changes in site quality to be estimated. Modern methods allow estimation of the compensating (CV) or equivalent variation (EV) measures of consumers' surplus.

CV or EV are often used in the analysis of different policy scenarios. We assume the reader is familiar with this literature and do not make any attempt to comprehensively reference what must be hundreds of recreation demand studies. Recent advances in computing, econometric theory, and readily-available software, however, has led to widespread use of the random utility model (RUM) or count data models (the Poisson, negative binomial, and its variants) in travel cost modeling. Each of these techniques was adopted simply because the standard unit of consumption is a recreation 'trip' and a trip is a discrete random variable. As noted in the first chapter of this volume, recent concerns about correlation patterns have caused researchers to consider even more sophisticated econometric modeling approaches (random parameters logit, and so on).

The large strides made in the econometrics of travel cost modeling may not have been matched by corresponding developments in the microeconomic theory that underlies it. Few researchers seem willing to tackle difficult theoretical issues in travel cost modeling such as dealing with trips of different lengths, connections between the trips over a longer period of choice, the role that time plays in the choice of activities, and uncertainty or risks. We make no suggestion that these issues are trivial – they are very, very difficult aspects relating to behavior.

Despite the implication of its name, the 'random' part of the conventional RUM approach does not imply any sort of gamble on the part of individuals. When the individual makes a decision he weighs the utility he gets from recreating at site j against the utility he gets from visiting any other alternative site k: if utility is greatest at site j relative to all other sites k on some choice occasion, he goes to site j. Utility is random only from the researcher's perspective. The RUM-based WTP is the maximum amount of money the recreational user expects to pay to experience recreation at a site, knowing all conditions relating to whether he may or may not go to the site, or how many trips will be taken there. As will be demonstrated below, this is different from the WTP measure stemming from a model with uncertain outcomes or site conditions.

4.2 Demand under Uncertainty: Review

The derivation of the demand for goods and services in the presence of risk still owes much to the expected utility model (EUM) originally proposed by Bernoulli in 1738 and advanced by von Neumann and Morgenstern in 1947. To provide some intuition, we will apply this framework to a risky climbing situation. Let utility (U) for the individual (suppressing an indicator for individual i) be a function of some non-stochastic variables in a vector of goods $\mathbf{G}$ (including recreation trips), exogenous attributes of the climbing route or area (q), and a function of being healthy (state H, $H=1$), or injured or dead (state I, $H=0$). The attributes q could include route length, quality of the climbing, and the injury incurred in the event of a fall (that is, the R- or X-rating).[10] Assume, for the moment, that both states are such that the probabilities of state-dependent utilities can be accurately assessed by experts and are thus exogenous to the individual. Utility when healthy is given by $U_H = U_H(\mathbf{G}, q, H=1)$, and when injured it is $U_I = U_I(\mathbf{G}, q, H=0)$, and the probability of each state is π, and $1-\pi$ respectively. Then expected utility in this simple two-state world is:

$$EU = \pi\, U_H(\mathbf{G}, q, H=1) + (1-\pi)\, U_I(\mathbf{G}, q, H=0) \qquad (5.1)$$

Assuming the axioms of the expected utility model are satisfied one can maximize EU subject to the usual budget (m) constraint (see Starmer, 2000). The solution to the expected utility problem leads to expected demands for $\mathbf{G}$ from which welfare measures can be derived.

One of the often discussed welfare measures is the expected surplus, ES, which is simply the probability-weighted *ex post* consumers' surpluses summed together. Using the above, if one knew that consumers' surplus from some change when definitely injured was CS_I and when healthy was CS_H, then $ES = \pi\, CS_H + (1-\pi)\, CS_I$. As an example, consider what *ex post* ES tells us as researchers. Suppose a climber attempts a route with quality attributes q_0 and the climber stays healthy, which happens with a probability $\pi=0.75$. If CS_H is \$15 and CS_I is \$10, then the probability-weighted sum of the *ex post* surpluses is \$13.75, also known as the expected surplus (ES). If there were more than two outcomes (each with known probability), we would simply add these in the determination of ES over all outcomes.

The problem is that *ex post* surplus calculations imply a resolution to the uncertainty and, thus, the measure is of limited use in practice. For the decision involving, say, whether to attempt a risky climbing route, the choice must be made *ex ante*, and welfare measures involving this uncertainty should reflect this aspect of the choice. The option price (OP) has been found to be the most desirable welfare measure under uncertainty because it incorporates the idea that an *ex ante* payment could be made prior to the resolution of the uncertainty. The OP is most often defined for a price change, where the price faced by the consumer is uncertain. Graham (1981) defines OP in the context of collective risk and provision of a public good (a dam), where risk is associated with uncertain weather (dry or wet). Within the context of risky recreation, such a collective good could be rescue services (*RS*) in the event of an injury or bolt replacement for aging climbing anchors. For the purposes of the following exposition, let OP be the *ex ante* payment needed to assure that rescue services are available (*RS* = 1).

Injury may take various forms of severity; let the health status of the individual be described by some random variable *H*, where *H* is a function of climbing route and climber-specific attributes. In particular, let health status be a random variable and a function of three route attributes, the technical difficulty rating, *D*, the hazard warning *R* or *X*, and a climber's ability, *A*, so that for an *R*-rated route the function is,

$$H = H(D, R, A) \tag{5.2}$$

noting that this can also take on a distribution. We might in fact add an error term denoting the 'random' aspects of the climbing experience that can influence deterministic health status, but this is not necessary to introduce uncertainty. For example, a climber may be injured by rockfall, the route may have loose handholds and footholds or, perhaps, the climber may simply fail to successfully climb the route without falling. If *H* is a continuous random variable, then in the absence of rescue services expected utility could be defined as,

$$EU = \int U[m, H(D, R, A), D, R, A, RS = 0] \, dH \tag{5.3}$$

and utility has arguments income *m* and health status *H*.[11] The climber's ability *A* and route attributes *D* and *R* appear in the health state function and again in the utility function because these attributes may provide utility beyond that associated with health status. The *ex ante* OP payment that would keep expected utility with rescue services equal to that without rescue services,

$$\int U[m - OP, H(D, R, A), D, R, A, RS = 1) \, dH$$
$$= \int U[m, H(D, R, A), D, R, A, RS = 0) \, dH \tag{5.4}$$

Equations (5.3) and (5.4) treat the source of uncertainty as a continuously distributed random variable whereas Graham's presentation treated the uncertainty as a discrete, binomial distribution.

Equation (5.4) obscures an important difference between the two approaches, however. In this model the probabilities of each health state are endogenous to the climber because, although he or she is endowed with a

fixed level of ability, the other factors affecting health status (route difficulty and hazard) are choice variables.[12] If we were to revert to the simple
binomial outcome (Healthy or Injured), one could recast our model as in
equation (5.5),

$$
\begin{aligned}
&[\pi\,(D,\,R,\,A)\times U_H(M-OP,\,D,\,R,\,A,\,RS=1)]+\\
&[(1-\pi\,(D,\,R,\,A))\times U_I(M-OP,\,D,\,R,\,A,\,RS=1)]=\\
&[\pi\,(D,\,R,\,A)\times U_H(M,\,D,\,R,\,A,\,RS=0)]+\\
&[(1-\pi\,(D,\,R,\,A))\times U_I(M,\,D,\,R,\,A\ RS=0)]
\end{aligned}
\tag{5.5}
$$

The expression shows that the OP is the payment prior to resolution of the
uncertainty: the individual could be injured or healthy and does not know
which with certainty, but the OP that equalizes expected utility for the provision of rescue services can nevertheless be determined.

This model embodies a richness of recreational behavior not possible in
the standard expected utility model. First, previous analyses of climbers
have shown that risk is an important element of the recreational pursuit,
and that climbers do not seek complete elimination of risk. The fact that
many climbers attempt dangerous routes indicates that at least some climbers derive utility from overcoming the danger. Thus, route attributes enter
the utility function directly as choice variables.[13] Second, and perhaps more
important from a modeling standpoint, the 'injury' probabilities are endogenous to the climber. Again this is consistent with previous research, particularly Jakus and Shaw (1996), who found that climbers who attempted
dangerous routes adjusted the probability of injury by attempting routes
with a technical difficulty (D), well within the climber's technical ability (A).

Solving for the OP yields an expression that can be empirically tractable.
One can then examine how the OP changes with say, the change in route
attributes, or a climber's ability, that is, the probability of the risky outcome
itself. The way the optimal option price payment changes with changes in
risk relates directly to risk management programs is of interest to policy
makers. Smith shows (using our notation) how management decisions
affect OP via a change in the risk probability:

$$
\frac{dOP}{d\pi}=\frac{U_H[m,H(D,\,R,\,A),\,D,\,R,\,A]-U_I[m,H(D,\,R,\,A),\,D,\,R,\,A]}{\pi(D,\,R,\,A)\times U_{Hm}+[1-\pi(D,\,R,\,A)]\times U_{Im}}
\tag{5.6}
$$

where U_{Hm}, for example, is the partial of the 'healthy' utility function with
respect to income. Here one can see that the marginal utility of income,
whether healthy or injured, is perhaps as important a component of the
marginal value as changes in the probabilities or the degree of risk. If the
marginal utility of income is constant in both states, then the denominator

is quite simple, but this is generally not true (Cook and Graham, 1977); many in the health economics research area would argue that the marginal utility of income is different across the 'healthy' and 'injured' states. In fact a standard assumption is that the marginal utility of income is zero if dead, unless there are bequest motives built into the utility function.

Note that income and the shape of the expected utility function with respect to route attributes play an important role in determining how OP changes. The existence and sign of the second derivative of the utility function with respect to income or route attributes is one way to determine whether an individual is risk neutral, risk averse, or risk loving. In addition, this derivative determines the relationship between option price and the expected surplus arising from the certainty RUM. For example, if the expected utility function is concave in route attributes, Jensen's inequality implies that the OP will be greater than the expected surplus, ES. But we are sure of these relationships only when there is this one source of uncertainty. As seen below, there may be other sources of uncertainty and the second derivative with respect to only one variable does not tell the entire story.

Perhaps only when the strict assumptions of expected utility theory are met can one graph a locus of expected utilities, compare these to expected surplus, and analyse differences between OP and ES. Graham makes these assumptions explicitly or implicitly. An important outcome in this framework is that utility functions that are linear in income imply constant marginal utility of income (the second derivative is absent), and hence Graham's WTP locus is linear, and ES and OP will be the same unless there are other sources of risk. As a preview to what comes below, note that much of the existing RUM recreation demand literature reports surplus measures using utility functions that are linear in income.

The theoretical structure arising from the expected utility model has led many to examine the topic of behavior under risk, but only a few are *empirical* studies, and the majority of these do not estimate and report anything related to welfare measures (for example, Cicchetti and Dubin, 1994). To our knowledge most empirical studies that involve welfare estimation assume that *stated* values under uncertainty yield estimates of the OP and the technique applied is the contingent valuation approach.

Equation (5.4) can be used to derive a deterministic expression for OP and, with careful specification of the source of randomness, a stochastic expression for OP. Larson and Flacco (1991) point this out, but never derive an expression for OP that can be directly estimated using revealed preference (RP) data. Doing so may help one to understand the difficulties in moving from a deterministic to a stochastic OP. While there are many models of non-market valuation currently used in practice, we focus on the family of discrete choice models currently in vogue for stated preference and/or RP modeling.

4.3   Possible Empirical Models

RP data are most often used in recreation demand models to derive estimable welfare measures. The two most popular approaches seem to be the random utility model (RUM) and the single and multiple-site count data approach, though micro-theoretic systems of a different kind also occasionally appear in the literature. We speculate below on how to extend the RUM to allow for uncertainty, not because we think the RUM is 'best' among the model options, but because it allows a relatively straightforward discussion of the issues.

The conventional RUM assumes that conditional indirect utility functions are random because the investigator is unable to observe all the factors that influence decision making. Expected utility models can, in fact, look like conventional RUMs, but the source of the underlying randomness is quite different. Several scholars have explicitly or implicitly made the claim that the usual binomial logit or MNL assuming certainty can be used to estimate the OP (Edwards, 1988). This is not quite correct, as will be shown below. Alternatively, both Leggett (2002) and Ibañez (2000) introduce uncertainty associated with imperfect information in the context of discrete choice models. These authors follow the Foster and Just (1989) approach of using a restricted expenditure function, where expenditures depend on perceptions but expected utility involves true knowledge. However, the imperfect information framework still maintains the assumption that the individual has perfect information at the time a purchasing decision must be made. The fact that he or she could be 'wrong' when making a choice in an earlier stage because of imperfect information is a different issue from the one with which we are concerned.[14]

Cameron (2001) differs from the previous studies by generating an expression for OP based on differences in expected utilities. Suppose we let the uncertainty pertain to a change in the random variable q, then we want to examine the expected utility difference over a change in q, or $E_q[V_1 - V_0]$. Let q_1 be an improvement over q_0. Following Cameron, we may start with an indirect utility function specification that is log-linear in income m. Again, this is not necessary, nor is it required to let q change in various states, but the former allows for income effects while the latter assumption helps motivate the changing conditions that increase or decrease the uncertainty associated with injury or death. For sports such as rock climbing, one could assume q is the 'injury rate' associated with the risk rating for a climb (the R or X discussed above), so that it has a distribution, but is a characteristic for a route. A is a payment made to or by the individual so that they are indifferent between two levels of utility, where $V(\cdot)$ is the indirect utility function:

$$V_1(m - A, q_1) = \beta_0 \ln(m - A) + \beta_1 q_1 + \varepsilon_1$$
$$V_0(m, q_0) = \beta_0 \ln(m) + \beta_1 q_0 + \varepsilon_0 \tag{5.7}$$

where the ε terms are the conventional measurement error terms. As noted, if one prefers q can be held constant and the utility difference between health and injured (H and I) can be substituted, but to allow for risk, H and I must be random variables. Consider the expectation of these utility differences across outcomes for q:

$$E_q[V_1 - V_0] = \beta_0 \ln[(m - A)/m] + \beta_1(q_1 - q_0)\,dq + \varepsilon \tag{5.8}$$

where $\varepsilon = \varepsilon_1 - \varepsilon_0$. This shows that the density function for q enters the calculation of the optimal *ex ante* payment. Without some source of randomness due to uncertainty we are simply left with the errors arising from the conventional assumptions regarding ε, as before, so that the expected CV is the same as one would be under certainty. If the current state of q, say q_0, is known, then we are left with the integral on one variable, q_1, which may collapse to something as simple as the mean, $E(q_1)$. Cameron, using stated preference data, allows utility to depend on the subjective range in q provided by respondents. We briefly consider the dependence of the utility function on this range, and other possibilities for the source of uncertainty below.

First, consider the payment A. Because Cameron directly incorporates payment A into an expected utility framework, OP is the payment A that solves equation (5.8). Thus, under the simple assumptions made above, OP is quite similar to the CV in the certainty model except OP involves the density on q for each individual. We can solve equation (5.8) for the OP by setting it equal to zero, making the two expected utilities equal. Again, let the integral collapse to the mean $E[q_1]$. Solving for OP then yields:

$$OP = Y - Y \times \exp\{\varepsilon/\beta_0 - \beta_1/\beta_0\,[E(q_1) - q_0]\} \tag{5.9}$$

Empirically, it would now be necessary to find E[OP] for each individual.

The certainty CV has a closed form expression if it is linear in income, so that E[CV] can be recovered by finding the average over a sample of individuals. The OP in equation (5.9) is a bit more complicated than the measure a linear-in-income model would yield, and nonlinearities may lead to issues in somewhat complex expected welfare measures. Cameron offers a formula for the OP based on a moment generating function. The exploration of this is tangential to our theme of uncertainty, so we refer the reader to the work of McFadden (1999), Herriges and Kling (1999), and Karlstrom and Morey (2001). Of greater interest in this chapter are assumptions about the nature of the uncertainty and the strength and appropriateness of the EUM framework for application to risky recreation. It is worth exploring whether the concavity in the utility function, perhaps with respect to a risky argument in the utility function other than income, causes difficulties similar to those introduced by non-linearity of income. First, we consider a few variants on the EUM.

4.4   Alternatives to the Expected Utility Model

Many experiments have indicated that an individual's choices can violate expected utility theory, leading to alternative models of risk preferences. The alternatives are numerous and are nicely described by Starmer (2000). Probably the most popular alternative approaches are prospect theory (Kahneman and Tversky, 1979), regret theory (Loomes and Sugden, 1982), and prospective reference theory (Viscusi, 1989). The key concern for alternative theorists seems to be the independence axiom of the EU model. The axiom is frequently inconsistent with observed behavior because it forces the expected utility indifference curves (in probability space) to be parallel lines. Indifference curves may not be parallel if, for example, losses are considered in a much different manner from gains, or if the outcome magnitudes are large enough to cause changes in risk preferences. With rock climbing or other sports where injury or death are legitimate risks, participants may not equally trade off prospects where the worst outcome is a broken ankle and those where the worst outcome is death. In terms of the EU model, a climber would be unlikely to make equal trades where the probability of death is 1 in 10 million, versus a climb with a 1 in 4 chance of death. Empirical models of recreation risk should allow for such richness in behavior. In all alternatives to the EU model there *is* a gamble taken by an individual but the exact meaning of the resulting welfare measures is a matter of some debate. Some think, for example, that the alternative models yield a different *ex ante* welfare concept than what Graham intended with his linear-in-probabilities utility function. However, we believe a correct welfare measure is truly an *ex ante* one, and that consistency with theory should be considered (see Smith, 1992; or Shaw et al. 2002).

4.5   Other Aspects of Modeling Risk and Rock Climbing

Larson (1988) and others raise the possibility that virtually all experiences involve some uncertainty. Recreational fishing does not guarantee a fish caught, a hunter isn't guaranteed to bag an elk, and so on. In the same real sense all climbing is risky, depending on what one considers the goal of climbing, or the risky 'outcome'. If we call reaching the top of the climb the outcome, then each climbing route has the potential for a failure or success, especially if uncertain weather is introduced. Indeed, reaching the 'top' seems to be the thought behind the work by some of those who have explored the risk issues to date (Ewert, 1985; Robinson, 1992; Ewert and Hollenhorst, 1989), but we have seen that the outcome 'completing the route' makes little sense for rock climbing. Would a rock climber be willing to pay something *ex ante* to avoid failure? The advent of sport climbing, with its great emphasis on gymnastic skills, makes the answer less clear. It is likely *some* climbers would like success guaranteed, but the very struggle to overcome the difficulties of the route are linked to the enjoyment of the climbing experience – as suggested by our hypothetical example of the climber who purposefully chose to attempt a route whose technical difficulty was at or beyond her limit. Given the many games that climbers play, the analyst must first carefully define the risk to be modeled.

We must also emphasize the link between the probability of failure and the individual's ability and skill. Relative to a less experienced, less skilled climber, the more experienced and skilled climber has the greater probability of completing a climbing route of any given difficulty without injury. As documented in Jakus and Shaw (1996) we know that climbers simply do not ignore these risks. Further, risk-taking attitudes change for routes of different quality, over different days, with different climbing partners and as other factors in a climber's life change over long periods of time (we age, we have children, our willingness to gamble that a rock won't fall from above us changes, and so on). Again, it is likely that highly skilled climbers perceive lower risks of injury or death on a given route relative to less skilled climbers, though we know of no one who has extensively modeled this. Anecdotal evidence exists that a highly skilled climber simply does not believe he or she will fall on particular routes.

The probability of injury or death could be determined in a variety of ways. First, we could use the observed frequency of falls resulting in injury for this, or other climbs. Such statistics are available to a degree, from *Accidents in North American Mountaineering*, an annual survey published by the American Alpine Club and the Canadian Alpine Club. Many climbing area managers also keep such statistics. We could also rely on survey information reporting the climber's perceived probability of injury or death, but collecting such data would be a formidable task. If the route is rated R or X, then all climbers have some indication of the probability of injury or death, or at least they know that the probability is higher for the R- or X-rated route than for one rated G or PG. Whether there is a statistical relation between R- and X-rated climbs and the probability of failure remains to be seen. While the EU model uses expert-assessed risk estimates, are these the appropriate probabilities for use in modeling risky recreation? We think not in the case of rock climbing because it is subjective probabilities that directly influence observed choices. Thus, a subjective assessment of probabilities may be more appropriate, as in Cameron (2001); also see Machina 1987; Smith 1992; Shaw et al. (2003).

It is clear that skill and other characteristics of the individual should be linked to risk-taking behavior but this will not be easy. First, it would be inappropriate to assume many or all climbers are risk averse, so that the functional form used in estimation of OP is flexible enough to allow for different risk preferences across individuals. This type of flexibility is not so daunting in certainty models (hence the new wave of modeling individual-specific parameters with simulation methods), but may produce further difficulties in estimation in the context of uncertainty.

Second, analysts often have data linking only the number of climbing trips at a given travel cost to the destination area. While each area may vary a bit in its overall risk attributes, the typical data set would likely end up with too little variation in risks for given travel costs. Data that allows variation in the risk attributes of a given choice must be collected. This implies that we need to more finely tune our demand models and data collection efforts, collecting information on the actual routes chosen because the variation in risk will be across these routes, not areas.[15] In other words, what the climber does *during* a given trip becomes important, not just where the trip was taken.

All this may suggest that the hedonic travel cost model might be worth renewed interest. We are cognizant of the fact that the hedonic travel cost model (HTC) popularized by Brown and Mendelsohn (1984) is also subject to some debate in the economics literature (see Smith and Kaoru, 1987). Still, the HTC may have strong potential for modeling risky behavior because it could be used to explore the activities on a given trip, and to value each of the various characteristics of the risk recreation experience. As we have suggested, the probability of injury or death (risk) is a characteristic of climbing routes that may explain choices, that is, individuals can be observed to choose from among different climbing routes, just as an investor might change among assets with different risk levels. If travel costs (say approach times) vary across climbing routes we may infer the hedonic price, or the relevant *ex ante* marginal value for changes in risk from the observed data on route choice. The HTC model could be used to answer the question, 'What change in travel costs is observable at the margin when the risk changes?' The HTC assumes that the climber would trade off risk for travel cost (distance); data can be collected to recover this. Similarly, the marginal implicit prices yielded by the HTC may be used to find the route quality/route risk tradeoff.

5. SUMMARY AND SUGGESTIONS FOR FUTURE RESEARCH

Our exploration has been into risky recreation, particularly the sport of rock climbing. Information collected from rock climbers provides some interesting insights into modeling risky recreation. First, the data run counter to the belief that 'getting to the top' is a primary goal of all climbers, instead showing that 'how' one climbs a route is more important. Thus, the risky outcome is not, in general, the risk of route completion. The data also show that risk-taking is part of the climbing experience.

The theoretical discussion has shown why the risk and uncertainty models yield WTP measures that are different from models that do not incorporate uncertain outcomes. Empirical application of any uncertainty models will require information not normally collected by recreation demand modelers. We need information on choices made *during* a trip, not just where and how frequently trips are made. Revealed preference data has the potential to be used to model preferences and values under risk, even without use of stated values or preferences. For example, while others have used survey questionnaires that ask individuals to state their WTP for a reduction in risk, we might collect data on the actual route choices (or more generally some set of activities at the larger area) on a given trip, adding the amount of time it takes to get to a given route (the number of minutes they must walk, or wait to do a particular route). This will likely reveal much about the value for risk reduction. There may be others, but we know of only one study that relies solely on observed behavior to incorporate something about recreation risks (see Jakus and Shaw, 2003).

The interesting policy questions that relate to risk reduction for rock climbers, including emergency rescue management at a climbing area, can probably best be answered using a risky recreation model. Given the cost of rescues at sites such as Yosemite Valley, CA, one might well ask what climbers are willing to pay to reduce risks of injury or death. This could be used to find reasonable insurance payments, if desired.

5.1 Applications to Other Risky Sports

A good deal of what we have learned can be applied to other recreational activities that involve risks of some sort. Perhaps obvious to the reader at this point, a risk model can also be used explore site or recreation area congestion, about which recreationists might be uncertain (see Jakus and Shaw, 1997; Boxall and Adamowicz, 2000), or any other quality attribute which may involve uncertainty. The approach may also prove useful in the uncertainties associated with hunting or wildlife management. These include the risks of bagging the species or harvesting it, but may also include the risks of driving important species to population levels where their very survival is in question. Several scholars have estimated economic models that allow for some uncertainty in the hunting experience, yet we know of no empirical ones that fully do so.

Analysts need to collect more detailed information on recreation choices and how these relate to risks. Climbers (or other risky recreation participants such as white-water boaters) choose risk levels in three ways. First, they can choose to visit a recreational area with levels of risk across different specific activities that differ from the risks presented at some other area. Second, they can choose different activities within the selected recreation area. If distances vary to each possible activity, we may estimate a risk/dollar trade-off because a person might drive/walk further to be able to recreate in an activity with lower risk. Third, an individual can probably take steps to reduce his or her own risk of injury or death by mitigating activities: wearing a helmet, doing things like top-roping, employing a professional guide, and so on.

Finally, what is a fool? We aren't the first to ask this, as some economists have explored whether willing casino-goers are foolish. No matter what the definition, we think this chapter has shown that in taking risks all climbers are not fools; indeed the average climber is probably rational is his risk-related choices. Whether this is true for other risky sports remains to be seen. Despite our accumulated knowledge and the thousands of hours that each author has spent hanging from the side of cliffs, we wonder if there is any model based on rational behavior that can explain why some choose to jump off mountain tops wearing a tiny parachute . . .

ACKNOWLEDGEMENTS

Research partially supported by the Nevada and Utah Agricultural Experiment Stations, and the California Water Quality Control Board. The authors want to thank Therese Grijalva and all of our climbing partners and friends for their input, as well as Trudy Cameron and Kerry Smith for sharing their thoughts with us on the economics of risk.

NOTES

1. For example, Grijalva et al. (2002b) report the possible harm climbers do to Native American rock art.
2. For example, the 'why' of climbing has been considered by Ewert (1985; 1987) and by Slanger and Rudestam (1997).
3. Mountain and rock climbing drew an estimated 4.2 million participants in the US in 1991, and 17 per cent of the 1992 subscribers of the popular magazine *Backpacker* said they rock climbed (Lewis, 1993). Staff at a popular US climbing magazine estimate there are 100000 new climbers each year (Anonymous, *The Economist*, 1995).
4. One study estimates the willingness to pay (WTP) for white-water boating using the CVM, but does not directly address risk or risk reduction (Boyle et al. 1993). Another study estimates recreation WTP under uncertainty about congestion levels, again using what is more or less the CVM approach (Prince and Ahmed, 1988). Uncertainty or risk has been examined with respect to the probability of fish catch 'success' (Larson, 1988) or bagging big game (Johansson, 1990). We know of no models that use actual behavior or revealed preference (RP) data to derive welfare measures under risk until quite recently (Jakus and Shaw, 2002).
5. Our focus is on rock climbing, as opposed to climbing high mountains such as those found in Alaska or the Himalayas. A key difference is that rock climbing is usually done in fair weather on dry rock, so risks do not include freezing to death in a severe storm, injury or death due to avalanche, ice fall, falling into a crevice, or altitude-related illness. Choice of the type of climbing one does, in itself demonstrates some risk avoidance by certain types of climbers.
6. Some climbers may climb without a rope. This is called 'free soloing'; a fall while free soloing a reasonable distance above the ground will almost certainly result in death or serious injury.
7. The numerical scale for technical difficulty varies in different countries, but in the US the scale runs from the easiest technical climb at 5.0 to the (currently) most difficult, at 5.14. The technical rating is akin to the difficulty rating assigned to dives in diving competitions. Quality ratings usually range from zero stars (low quality) to three stars (high quality). The risk scale is described in the text. Despite different numerical and other classification schemes, the communication of difficulty, quality and risk can be translated from one country to another.
8. Various organizations do keep total statistics on fatalities and injuries. For example, the American Alpine Club reported an average of roughly 30 climbing-related deaths per year in the US during 1990–97. The Mountain Rescue Council states that six climbers were killed in England and Wales in 1993, out of perhaps as many as 150000 climbers in Britain (Anonymous, *The Economist*, 1995).
9. This might be compared to the perceived risk of one walking down a flight of stairs, that is, there is some risk associated with falling, but most of us perceive almost no risk because our abilities allow us to negotiate the stairway safely.
10. In addition to technical difficulty and the hazard warning, climbing guidebooks nearly always include a 'quality' rating of zero to three stars. Climbers, especially those climbing in the area for only a short period of time, will focus their efforts on climbs with two or three stars.
11. Here we treat all market goods as a numeraire.
12. Some would argue that because the probabilities are endogenous the expression for OP in (5.2) is not an option price at all. We are not prepared to argue this point in depth; we use the OP terminology because the payment is made prior to the resolution of the uncertainty.
13. This formulation of utility shares the notion put forth by Loewenstein (1999) that climbers derive utility from 'pleasures of skill'. We also note that the climbing community bestows recognition on those who ascend difficult and dangerous routes, so that the preference structure is also consistent with what Loewenstein calls 'self-signaling'.

14. Leggett assumes that the CV with imperfect information is still an outcome from utility maximization, where utility is again assumed linear in income.
15. Similarly, if one were interested in modeling white-water kayaking, the important 'location' information may be the particular reach (or reaches) of river that is run as opposed to the put-in point. Further, one may wish to learn if certain sections of the river were portaged rather than boated.

REFERENCES

Anonymous (1995), 'Climbing up the wall', *The Economist*, March 11th, 1995, p. 88.

Boyle, K. et al. (1993), 'The role of question order and respondent experience in contingent valuation studies', *Journal of Environmental Economics and Management*, 25(1): S-80–S-99.

Boxall, P.C. and W. Adamowicz (2000), 'Incorporating Endogenous Perceptions of Environmental Attributes in RUMs: The Case of Congestion', Presented at the International Institute of Fisheries and Trade Conference, Oregon State University, Corvallis, Oregon, July 2000.

Brown, G. Jr. and R. Mendelsohn (1984), 'The hedonic travel cost method', *Review of Economics and Statistics*, 66(3) (August): 427–33.

Cameron, T.A. (2001), 'Updated Subjective Distributions for Future Climate and Individual Option Prices for Climate Change Mitigation', Discussion paper, UCLA.

Cheron, E.J. and J.R. Ritchie (1982), 'Leisure activities and perceived risk', *Journal of Leisure Research*, 14(2): 139–54.

Cicchetti, C.J. and J.A. Dubin (1994), 'A microeconometric analysis of risk aversion and the decision to self-insure', *Journal of Political Economy*, 102(1): 169–86.

Cook, P.J. and D.A. Graham (1977), 'The demand for insurance and protection: the case of irreplaceable commodities', *Quarterly Journal of Economics*, 91(1) (Feb.): 143–56.

Edwards, Steven F. (1988), 'Option Prices for Groundwater Protection', *Journal of Environmental Economics and Management*, 15(4) (December): 475–87.

Ekstrand E. (1994), Unpublished PhD dissertation, Department of Agricultural Economics, Colorado State University, Fort Collins, CO.

Englin, J. and J. Shonkwiler (1995), 'Estimating social welfare using count data models: an application to long-run recreation demand under conditions of endogenous stratification and truncation', *Review of Economics and Statistics*, 77: 104–12.

Evans, W. and K. Viscusi (1991), 'Estimation of state-dependent utility functions using survey data', *Review of Economics and Statistics*, 83: 94–104.

Ewert, A. (1985), 'Why people climb: the relationship of participant motives and experience level to mountaineering', *Journal of Leisure Research*, 17(3): 241–50.

Ewert, A. (1987), 'Risk recreation poses new management problems', *Park Science*, 8(1): 7–8.

Ewert, A. and S. Hollenhorst (1989), 'Testing the adventure model: empirical support for a model of risk recreation participation', *Journal of Leisure Research*, 21(2): 124–39.

Foster, W. and R.E. Just (1989), 'Measuring welfare effects of product contamination with consumer uncertainty', *Journal of Environmental Economics and Management*, **17**: 266–83.

Freeman, A.M. (1991), 'Indirect methods for valuing changes in environmental risks with nonexpected utility preferences', *Journal of Risk and Uncertainty*, **4**: 153–65.

Freeman, A.M. (1993), 'Values in an Uncertain World', chapter 8 in *The Measurement of Environmental and Resource Values: Theory and Methods*, Washington, DC: Johns Hopkins Press for Resources for the Future.

Graham, D. (1981), 'Cost benefit analysis under uncertainty', *American Economic Review*, **71**: 715–25.

Grijalva, T.A. (formerly T.A. Cavlovic) (2000), 'Valuing the Loss in Access: An Institutional and Welfare Analysis of Rock Climbing on U.S. Public Lands', Unpublished PhD dissertation, University of New Mexico. Albuquerque, N.M.

Grijalva, T.A., R.P. Berrens, A. Bohara and W. D. Shaw (2002a), 'Testing for the validity of contingent behavior trip responses', *American Journal of Agricultural Economics*, **84**(2) (May): 401–14.

Grijalva, T.A., R.P. Berrens, A. Bohara, P. Jakus and W.D. Shaw (2002b), 'Valuing the Loss of Rock Climbing Access in Wilderness Areas: A National-level RUM', *Land Economics*, **78**(1) (February): 103–20.

Hanemann, W.M. (1994), 'Valuing the environment through contingent valuation', *Journal of Economic Perspectives*, **8**: 19–43.

Hanemann, W.M. and B. Kanninen (1999), 'The Statistical Analysis of Discrete CV Data', in Ian Bateman and Kenneth G. Willis (eds), *Valuing Environmental Preferences: Theory and Practice of the Contingent Valuation Method in the U.S., E.U. and Developing Countries*, Oxford: Oxford University Press.

Hanley, N., G. Koop, R. Wright and B. Alverez-Farizo (2001), 'Go climb a mountain: an application of recreation demand models to rock-climbing in Scotland', *Journal of Agricultural Economics*, **52**(1): 36–51.

Hanley, N., B. Alverez-Farizo and W.D. Shaw (forthcoming), 'Rationing an open-access resource: mountaineering in Scotland', *Land Use Policy*.

Herriges, J. and C. Kling (1999), 'Nonlinear income effects in random utility models', *Review of Economics and Statistics*, **81** (January): 62–72.

Ibañez, A.M. (2000), 'A Proposal to Measure the Value of Information in Discrete Choice Models: an application to Cartegena Bay', Unpublished PhD dissertation, University of Maryland, College Park, MD.

Jakus, P.M. and W.D. Shaw (1996), 'An empirical analysis of rock climbers' response to hazard warnings', *Risk Analysis*, **16**(4): 581–6.

Jakus, P.M. and W.D. Shaw (1997), 'Congestion at recreation areas: empirical evidence on perceptions, mitigating behaviour and management preferences', *Journal of Environmental Management*, **50**: 389–401.

Jakus, P.M. and W.D. Shaw (2003), 'Perceived hazard and product choice: an application to recreational site choice', *Journal of Risk and Uncertainty*, **26**(1): 77–92.

Johansson, P.O. (1990), 'Willingness to pay measures and expectations: an experiment', *Applied Economics*, **22**: 313–29.

Kahneman, D. and A. Tversky (1979), 'Prospect theory: an analysis of decisions under risk', *Econometrica*, **47**: 263–91.

Kaoru, Y., V.K. Smith and J.L. Liu (1995), 'Using random utility models to estimate the recreational value of estuarine resources', *American Journal of Agricultural Economics*, **77**: 141–51.

Karlstrom, A. and E. Morey (2001), 'Quickly and Accurately Calculating Welfare Measure in GEV Random Utility Models with Income Effects: a Primer', Discussion paper, Dept. of Economics, University of California, Berkeley (May).

Larson, D. (1988), 'Choice and Welfare Measurement Under Uncertainty: Theory and Applications to Natural Resources', Unpublished dissertation, University of Maryland.

Larson, D. and P.R. Flacco (1991), 'Measuring option prices from market behavior', *Journal of Environmental Economics and Management* (**22**): 178–98.

Leggett, C. (2002), 'Environmental valuation with imperfect information: the case of the random utility model', *Environmental and Resource Economics*, **23**(1): 343–55.

Lewis, B.G. (1993), *White paper for Outdoor Recreation Coalition of America*, Interaction Associates, 1918 Beulah Highway, Beulah, Michigan 49617.

Loewenstein, G. (1999), 'Because it is there: the challenge of mountaineering . . . for utility theory', *Kyklos*, **52**(3): 315–44.

Loomes, G. and R. Sugden (1982), 'Regret theory: an alternative theory of rational choice under uncertainty', *Economic Journal*, **92**: 805–24.

Machina, M.J. (1987), 'Choice under uncertainty: problems solved and unsolved', *Journal of Economic Perspectives*, **1**: 121–54.

McFadden, D. (1999), 'Computing Willingness to Pay in Random Utility Models', in J. Moore, R. Riezman and J. Melvin (eds), *Trade, Theory and Econometrics: Essays in Honour of John S. Chipman*, Routledge: London.

Morey, E.R. (1999), 'Two Rums Uncloaked', in J. Herriges and C. Kling (eds), *Valuing Recreation and the Environment*, Northhampton, MA: Edward Elgar Press.

McIntyre, N. (1992), 'Involvement in risk recreation: a comparison of objective and subjective measures of engagement', *Journal of Leisure Research*, **24**(1): 64–71.

Prince, R. and E. Ahmed (1988), 'Estimating individual recreation benefits under congestion and uncertainty', *Journal of Leisure Research*, **20**(4): 61–76.

Quiggin, J. (1982), 'A theory of anticipated utility', *Journal of Economic Behavior and Organization*, **3**: 323–43.

Robinson, D. (1992), 'A descriptive model of enduring risk recreation involvement', *Journal of Leisure Research*, **24**(1): 52–63.

Schreyer, R. and R. White (1979), 'A conceptual model of high-risk recreation', in *Proceedings of the 1st Annual National Conference on Recreation Planning and Development*, New York: American Society of Civil Engineers.

Shaw, W.D. and P.M. Jakus (1996), 'Travel cost models of the demand for rock climbing', *Agricultural and Resource Economics Review*, **25**(2): 133–42.

Shaw, W.D., M. Riddel and P.M. Jakus (2003), 'Sources of Randomness: an Update on Valuing the Environment in the Presence of Uncertainty', Discussion paper, University of Nevada, Reno.

Slanger, E. and K.E. Rudestam (1997), 'Motivation and disinhibition in high risk sports: self-seeking and self-efficacy', *Journal of Research in Personality*, **31**: 355–74.

Smith, V.K. (1992), 'Environmental Risk Perception and Valuation: Conventional Versus Prospective Reference Theory', Chapter 2 in D.W. Bromley and K. Segerson (eds), *The Social Response to Environmental Risk: Policy Formulation in an Age of Uncertainty*, Boston: Kluwer Academic Press, 217 p.

Smith, V.K. and Y. Kaoru (1987), 'The hedonic travel cost approach: a view from the trenches', *Land Economics*, **63**: 179–92.

Starmer, C. (2000), 'Developments in non-expected utility theory: the hunt for a descriptive theory of choice under risk', *Journal of Economics Literature*, **XXXVIII** (June): 332–82.

Viscusi, W.K. (1989), 'Prospective reference theory: toward an explanation of para-doxes', *Journal of Risk and Uncertainty*, **2**: 235–64.

6. Non-participation, demand intensity and substitution effects in an integrable demand system: the case of day trips to the North-Eastern Alps

Riccardo Scarpa, Tiziano Tempesta and Mara Thiene

1. INTRODUCTION

The mountain range of the Alps is a much celebrated destination for outdoor activities. Recreationists come from all over the world to enjoy the Alpine environment and the local traditions. Foreign as well as Italian visitors from non-Alpine regions share the benefits of this resource with local users, who also have a long-established tradition of outdoor recreation in the Alps.

Despite the tremendous popularity that the Alps enjoy as a destination for recreation, surprisingly few international research papers have attempted an estimation of the economic benefits associated with this natural resource. None, to our knowledge, focuses on non-specialist (or 'generic') outdoor recreation by local residents, such as day trips. The main objective of this chapter is to start filling this apparent vacuum. We attempt such an analysis by considering a set of Eastern Alps destinations and casting the problem as a demand system for day trips from residents of a neighbouring region. Day trips are normally taken for carrying out many diverse activities, such as rambling, hiking in ferrata routes and flora and fauna watching. The kind of trips we analyse are generic trips in the sense that they are not related to any particular mountain activity.[1]

The effort is timely, as the year 2002 is the year of the Mountains, and this has brought about more awareness as to the role of Alpine environments as suppliers of a number of non-market functions, such as their role in maintaining the hydro-geological conditions of the mountain slopes, upkeep of local cultural identities and traditions of land use, as well as locally managing a large volume of external demand for outdoor recreation. The Alps regularly attract more than 60 million tourists a year and 370 million overnight stays (Tschurtchenthaler, 2000, p. 62). This is estimated to produce €23 billion a year in terms of national product from tourism, corresponding to 5 per cent of the total world GDP from tourism (Moroder, 2000, p. 31).

However, the economic benefits from many visits escape the official accounts. A large fraction of these are day trips from neighbouring areas. These local trips are arguably a politically important component as the preferences of local residents determine the election of the regional authorities that are in charge of land use policies in the local mountain areas.

We present an empirical evaluation of the economic benefits provided by a section of the Eastern Alps to local users in a demand system consistent with the neoclassic results of economic theory for consumer behaviour (Mas-Colell et al., 1995). The good under valuation is the system of 18 mountain groups into which a main section of North-Eastern Alps can be identified for the purpose of outdoor recreation. The type of recreation under analysis is that concerning day trips from residents in Veneto, a region in direct proximity to the mountain region. Here the tradition of sustainable use of the Alps dates as far back as the time of the Serenissima Republic of Venice. Under this rule the Alpine land was managed to provide wood for its vast commercial and military fleets and for building the foundations for much of the buildings in Venice.

We simultaneously model both the participation decision to recreate at each site as well as the frequencies of day trips. The model clearly differs from models that are confined to one specific activity, such as skiing, rock-climbing, snowboarding, hunting and fauna and flora watching.

For each destination one can identify a first participation decision related to whether or not in the time period under consideration the destination k is visited. A second decision, given participation, determines the intensity of demand by visitor i at site k (that is the amount 'consumed' y_{ki}). A similar approach is often employed in multi-stage decision models employing, for example, the repeated random utility framework (Morey et al., 1993),[2] or via asymptotic results in models linking count and random utility models (Parsons et al., 1999; Romano et al., 2000), but less frequently so in demand systems. The non-participation or zero-demand observations are distinct in a 'pure' non-participation component and a second 'zero-demand' or 'corner solution' component. This is achieved by ascribing the excess zeros to a logistic probability explaining non-participation which is additional to the amount of zeros due to corner solutions and naturally accounted for by the count model process. FIML

(Full Information Maximum Likelihood) estimation allows for observed zero counts at each site to be endogenously shared between the two processes. For this type of generic outdoor use of the Alps, the 18 destinations under analysis compete in this type of market for recreation. As such they are treated as substitutes in consumption and the problem is cast as an incomplete system of independent demand functions to be simultaneously estimated.

In our empirical analysis we build on previous theoretical results from LaFrance and other empirical research on demand systems based on count models from Ozuna and Gomez (1994), Shonkwiler (1995, 1999) and Englin et al. (1998), to address both these issues. In particular, we explore the modelling choices available to the researcher to estimate demand in a slightly less restrictive fashion, yet maintaining the simultaneous system of equations theoretically consistent with economic theory, and the desirable count specification. In the empirical example we derive estimates of consumer surplus for the sample for each of the 18 destinations and retrieve the matrix of median predictions for the compensated substitution effects.

The remainder of the chapter is structured as follows. Section 2 is based on previous work by Ozuna and Gomez (1994), Shonkwiler (1995, 1999) and Englin et al. (1998), and it illustrates the practical implications of integrability for modelling in linear-in-the-variables semi-log demand systems, developing the link between the two distinct forms of zero counts and the various count heterogeneity options. Section 3 presents the area of study and the data employed for estimation. In Section 4 we provide details and a discussion of the econometric analysis, while Section 5 concludes.

2. THEORY AND METHODS

2.1 Count Processes in Recreation Demand

The use of count modelling was first introduced in the early 1990s (Creel and Loomis, 1990; Hellerstein, 1991; Hellerstein and Mendelsohn, 1993) and has now become a mainstay in the literature of applied research in individual travel cost analysis (Feather et al., 1995; Haab and McConnell, 1996; Gurmu and Trivedi, 1996). In this context, count specifications are theoretically desirable for their ability to model limited dependent variables that only take discrete non-negative values. Such is the nature of outcomes of outdoor recreation visits. Over a given time interval trips to various outdoor destinations take the form of zeros or small integers. More traditional approaches, such as ordinary least squares, are poorly suited to deal with dependent variables with such characteristics. Furthermore, it is a well-known result from mathematical statistics that the limiting behaviour of binomial events with fixed and low probability of success in a higher number of trials can be approximated with Poisson counts. Such an interpretation is consistent with observed recreation behaviour, in which the probability of choosing a given site as a destination for a recreational trip may be considered to be low, assuming that the choice opportunities for recreation are relatively numerous, at least over the typical time interval of interest (usually the year or 'good' season).

Count specifications have been widely used in modelling recreation demand via the individual travel cost approach. However, most empirical applications based on analyses supported by count models do not extend to modelling a system of demand for the set of substitutable sites while simultaneously estimating a participation process.

Englin et al. (1998), drawing on previous work by Ozuna and Gomez (1994) and by Shonkwiler (1995), propose a theoretically consistent system of demand functions for visits to wilderness parks in Canada, using a system of truncated Poisson counts. However, given the nature of the truncated nature of the on-site data employed, participation was not modelled. A further limitation of that study, upon which our study improves, was the lack of data for some potentially significant substitute sites. Shonkwiler (1995) provides a three-site example and some insightful theoretical discussion as to the superiority of Poisson with log-normal heterogeneity in data with high zero counts. His approach improves on Ozuna and Gomez in terms of his treatment of cross-price effects, and on Englin et al. as it accounts for the correlation structure of error terms across demand equations for different destinations. However, correlated log-normal heterogeneity is computationally practical only for demand systems with few sites as it requires approximating k-variate normal probabilities. A more practical approach to account for dependence across demand equations is outlined in Shonkwiler (1999), and is drawn from longitudinal data analysis from the biometrics literature.

In this study we adapt and extend the approach employed in their seminal work on incomplete demand systems by the above authors in two ways. First, we allow for an increasingly flexible form of heterogeneity in the system by using negative binomial specifications with variance functions that are linear (NB1), quadratic (NB2) and unconstrained (GNB) (Grijalva et al., 2002). Secondly, we simultaneously estimate a non-participation process using a logit-inflated zero-count in the count process, following the seminal work in this direction by Shonkwiler and Shaw and by Haab and McConnell on hurdle count models. Estimates of per day trip consumer's surplus and of compensated substitution effects are then reported and contrasted across models.

2.2   Integrability in Semi-logarithmic Demand Systems

The importance of integrability in demand systems for recreation, and the associated problem of path-dependency of integrals of welfare measures have long been a concern for applied economists (Burt and Brewer, 1971). Furthermore, the market for destinations faced by local residents wishing to take a day trip in the Alps is expected to show clear substitution effects, which a demand system approach can address.

In the typical travel cost setting to a single site k, the objective is that of estimating a demand function for the ith visitor, of the type:

$$y_{ki} = f(p_{ki}, \mathbf{p}_{k'i}, m_i, \mathbf{s}_i), \qquad (6.1)$$

where p_{ki} is the price of the good, that is the travel cost associated with the day trip to site k and visitor i, $\mathbf{p}_{k'i}$ is a vector of prices for the substitute sites k', m_i is income, and $\mathbf{s}_i$ is a vector of socio-economic shifters.

In the typical single site semi-log specification, with a linear-in-the-variables index, one has:

$$\ln(y_{ki'}) = \alpha + \beta_k p_{ki} + \Sigma_{k'} \gamma_{k'} p_{k'i} + \delta m_i + \Sigma_j \eta_j s_{ij}, \qquad (6.2)$$

where j indices the various socio-economic individual characteristics, such as age, education etc.; k' indices the substitutes for site k; and the Greek letters are all coefficients to be estimated from the sample data.

From this individual semi-log demand function for a single site, economic benefit measures can be obtained by integrating equation (6.2) over the own price interval between the present travel cost p_k^0 and the choke price p_k^1, to obtain the well known closed-form solution for per-trip consumer surplus: $CS = -1/\beta_k$.

While this expression is correct for a one-site demand function, this is inadequate to account for the integrability conditions resulting from economic theory in the case of an incomplete system of demand equations for a set of destinations.

Consider the case at hand of the Eastern Italian Alps. A number of 18 mountain groups can be identified (Table 6.1). The general system of semi-log demand equations can be written as:

Table 6.1   Descriptive statistics of excursions per head by destinations

Mountain groups	Mean	St. Dev.	Median	90th percentile	Excursions
1. Vette Feltrine. M. Sole	2.59	3.53	2	5	304
2. P. Dolomiti Pasubio	4.91	5.64	3	11	421
3. Cansiglio-Alpago	2.18	3.02	1	4	197
4. Altipiano Asiago	3.64	4.22	2	10	191
5. M. Grappa	2.7	2.99	2	5	312
6. Lessini-M. Baldo	5.03	8.68	2	13	255
7. Antelao	1.39	0.94	1	2	178
8. Pelmo	1.35	0.69	1	2	186
9. Tofane-Cristallo	1.86	1.42	1	3	130
10. Duranno-Cima Preti	1.45	0.72	1	2	31
11. Sorapiss	1.35	0.82	1	2	100
12. Agner-Pale San Lucano	1.31	0.72	1	2	89
13. Tamer-S. Sebastiano	1.64	1.06	1	3	127
14. Marmarole	1.7	1.66	1	3	104
15. Tre Cime-Cadini	1.8	1.29	1	3	319
16. Civetta-Moiazza	1.86	1.7	1	3	322
17. Pale di S. Martino	2.05	1.63	1	4	299
18. Marmolada	1.61	1.22	1	3	154

$$\ln(y_{1i}) = \alpha_1 + \beta_1 p_{1i} + \sum_{1'} \gamma_{1'} p_{1'i} + \delta_{1'} m_i + \sum_j \eta_{1'j} s_{ji}$$

$$\ln(y_{2i}) = \alpha_2 + \beta_2 p_{2i} + \sum_{2'} \gamma_{2'} p_{2'i} + \delta_{2'} m_i + \sum_j \eta_{2'j} s_{ji}$$

$$\vdots \qquad \vdots \qquad \vdots \qquad \vdots \tag{6.3}$$

$$\ln(y_{18i}) = \alpha_{18} + \beta_{18} p_{18i} + \sum_{18'} \gamma_{18'} p_{18'i} + \delta_{18'} m_i + \sum_j \eta_{18'j} s_{ji}$$

where the prime stands for 'different from' and refers to the site-specific substitutes.

Such a demand system can be simplified by imposing the necessary and sufficient integrability restrictions derived from consumer's theory.

LaFrance (1990), LaFrance and Hanemann (1989), Shonkwiler (1995, 1999) and Englin et al. (1998) show that these restrictions take a particularly simple form in the case of semi-logarithmic demand systems.[3] In the case of a linear-in-the-variables exponential index the sufficient restrictions are:

1. *Intercept restrictions*: $\alpha_k = \alpha_{k*}\beta_k/\beta_{k*}$, $\forall k$, where the asterisk indicates the arbitrarily chosen site for which the constant α_{k*} is estimated, and where k indices the sites, 1, 2, ..., 18.

These restrictions imply that only one constant term of the k possible is identified from the data in the system. All the others can be derived by applying the above identity.

2. *Zero cross-price effect of Marshallian demand restrictions*: Omitting the subscript i for each visitor, the generic cross-price effect is:

$$\frac{\partial y_k(p,m)}{\partial p_{k'}} = 0, \tag{6.4}$$

where k' is any site in the system different from k.

Using the well-known Slutsky relationship, this condition implies that Hicksian cross price effects are equal to the marginal income effect scaled by the amount of consumption of the substitute site:

$$\frac{\partial y_k(p,m)}{\partial p_{k'}} = 0 \Rightarrow \frac{\partial y_k^h(p,m)}{\partial p_{k'}} = \frac{\partial y_k(p,m)}{\partial m} y_{k'}. \tag{6.5}$$

3. *Single income effect restrictions*:

$$\frac{\partial y_k(p,m)}{\partial m_k} = \frac{\partial y_{k'}(p,m)}{\partial m_{k'}}, \forall\, k . \tag{6.6}$$

So there are no differences across the k income effects, and they can all be jointly grouped into a single effect called δ.

Combining equality (6.5) and the derivative property of semi-log functions the result is a conveniently simple form for the compensated substitution effect:

$$\frac{\partial y_k^h(p,m)}{\partial p_{k'}} = \frac{\partial y_k(p,m)}{\partial m_k} y_{k'} = \delta y_k y_{k'}, \qquad \delta > 0, \forall\, k \neq k'. \tag{6.7}$$

Purely for convenience, following the restriction on the income coefficient δ, in our implementation we also constrain all the coefficients for the socio-economic characteristics η to be the same across destination sites. Our theoretically consistent system of semi-log demand functions can therefore be written as:

$$\ln(y_{1i}) = \alpha_1 + \beta_1 p_{1i} + \delta m_i + \sum_j \eta_j s_{ji}$$

$$\ln(y_{2i}) = \beta_2 p_{2i} + \delta m_i + \sum_j \eta_j s_{ji}$$

$$\vdots \qquad \vdots \tag{6.8}$$

$$\ln(y_{18i}) = \beta_{18} p_{18i} + \delta m_i + \sum_j \eta_j s_{ji}$$

This system in our case requires the estimation of one site-intercept, conveniently chosen across the 18 sites, all own-price coefficients, one income effect, and j coefficients for the socio-economic shifters.

2.3 Non-participation, Corner Solutions and Positive Demand

In empirical travel cost data it is not unusual to have a number of zero counts that are higher than is consistent with the parametric count process at hand (Gurmu and Trivedi, 1996; Haab and McConnell, 1996; Shonkwiler and Shaw, 1996). Many Italian Alpine Club (CAI) members never visit some of the mountain destinations in the system during the time interval under consideration. The reasons for not doing so are varied, but two dominant motives are assumed here. The first is that $y = 0$ is the value truly resolving the individual's constrained maximization problem. That is, zero is a 'proper' corner solution (CS) in the demand for recreation at that site. This is economically rational, for example when the expected benefit from the visit is lower than the cost of access to the site. Alternatively, some visitors may simply not be in the market for that good and do not participate (NP). That happens, for example, when the site in question is not part of the utility function of the individual, maybe because the visitor does not know the site or does not consider it as a suitable substitute destination for the activities s/he has in mind. 'Non-participation' in day trips to a site is the second component of zero trips we identify and explain separately, yet simultaneously, but independently. This is important in a large system such as ours because the more sites the system includes, the higher the likelihood that one will observe zeros in consumed trips to some destinations over the period of interest.

As pointed out by Shonkwiler and Shaw (1996), some statistical specifications may account for both sources of zero counts, while others confound the two.[4] In this study we account for both, as follows:

$$\Pr(y = 0) = \Pr_{NP} + (1 - \Pr_{NP})\Pr_{CS} =$$
$$[e^{\theta'z} + f(y = 0 | \Xi, \mathbf{x})] [1 + e^{\theta'z}]^{-1}, \text{ for } y = 0, \tag{6.9}$$

$$\Pr(y>0)=(1-\Pr_{\mathrm{NP}})\Pr(y>0)=f(y>0|\Xi,\mathbf{x})$$
$$[1+e^{\theta'z}]^{-1}, y=1, 2, 3,\dots \tag{6.10}$$

where $f(\cdot)$ is a suitably restricted count process, such as Poisson, NB1, NB2 or GNB. For example, Englin et al. (1998) employ a Poisson system of zero-truncated demand functions, such that:

$$\Pr(y_{ki}=x|y_{ik}>0)=\frac{e^{-\lambda_{ki}}\lambda_{ki}^{y_{ki}}}{y_{ki}!(1-e^{-\lambda_{ki}})}, y_{ki}=1,2,3,\dots\ ; \ \lambda_{ki}=e^{\Xi'x}, \tag{6.11}$$

where $\Xi'\mathbf{x}$ is the linear demand index with proper restrictions imposed on α and δ. Clearly, in a Poisson process $E(y)=\mathrm{Var}(y)=\lambda$. This latter Poisson condition imposes that the conditional mean be equal to the conditional variance. This is often violated in practice. Furthermore, it does not accommodate an error term in the exponential demand index $\Xi'\mathbf{x}$. As illustrated in Cameron and Trivedi 1998, (p. 27), if the conditional mean is correctly specified, that is if $E(y|\Xi,\mathbf{x})=\exp(\Xi'\mathbf{x})$, then the maximum likelihood estimator for the Poisson regression model maintains consistency even under a misspecified density. However, a misspecification of the probability function implies variance misspecification, which in turn produces incorrect inference due to incorrect standard errors.

A standard result is that overdispersion can be accommodated by using a specification for $f(\cdot)$ that belongs to the family of negative binomial (NB) distributions, by virtue of a log-gamma multiplicative error term (Greene, 1997):

$$\lambda_{ki}^{NB}=\exp(\Xi_k'\mathbf{x}_{ki}+\varepsilon_{ki})=\exp(\Xi_k'\mathbf{x}_{ki})\exp(\varepsilon_{ki})=\lambda_{ki}^p\lambda_{ki}. \tag{6.12}$$

In these models the variance of the count variable can be expressed as a function of the mean and an additional dispersion parameter ψ^5: $\mathrm{Var}(y)=g(\lambda,\psi)$, but most frequently this is a linear function: $\mathrm{Var}(y)=\lambda(1+\psi^\omega)$. Commonly employed values for ω are 1 and 2, which imply respectively a linear in the mean (NB1) and quadratic in the mean (NB2) variance function. However, generalized forms (GNB) with hybrid properties between these two may also be estimated by allowing an extra parameter to take up optimal values. Grijalva et al. (2002, eq. 5, p. 406) show that setting $\omega=2-\kappa$, the extra parameter κ may be estimated from the data using full information maximum likelihood procedures. NB1 variance function is equivalent to restricting $\kappa=1$, while NB2 to restricting $\kappa=0$, with hybrid forms for values within the [0,1] interval.

The effects that the four count specifications have on the estimated coefficients of the systems of semi-logarithmic demand functions, and their policy implications, are to be evaluated empirically in Section 4.

3.   DATA

3.1   The North-East Alps

The eighteen mountain destinations are quite diverse from both a morpho-logical and mountaineering point of view, but they can provide non-specialist outdoor recreation, and so are all potential destinations for day trips. Two broad geographically determined groups can be distinguished. Destinations 1–6 (Table 6.1) belong to the pre-Alps, which are mountains with gentler slopes and lower peaks separating the plane from the proper Alps. Because of their closeness to the main urban centres, and the pres-ence of relative high difficulty hiking routes – even though the length of the paths is limited – the pre-Alps are the final destination of many local day trips.

Destinations 7–18 are in the North-Eastern Alps, in the mountain chain of the Dolomites, which is an extended rocky area mostly made of dolo-mite rocks. This rare and distinguished rock type is geologically well-defined as it originates from coral reefs. Mountains made of this rock are scenically quite attractive as they tend to show orange-pink reflections at sunset. These create those dramatic scenes for which the Dolomites are well-known all over the world.

3.2   Sample and its Characteristics

Because a great fraction of the Italian alpine visitors belong to the CAI,[6] and our interest was defining the benefits enjoyed by the local users, the sampling frame was based on the Veneto chapter of CAI members. This membership is quite popular across regular mountain users as the club pro-vides a great deal of locally relevant services, such as training courses, activ-ity maps, guides, rescue services and so on. The data for the study was collected with a survey from a sample of 904 members of the local chapter of the CAI, who reported on their mountain visits for the year 1999. The total number of trips reported is 10391, some descriptive statistics along with the list of destination are reported in Table 6.1.

Data were collected using a questionnaire. Typically a group of respon-dents was given the questionnaire along with an explanation of how to interpret and answer several questions. Then, each member of the group would fill the questionnaire independently on their own. Respondents were asked questions about their mountain abilities and experience, whether they attended mountaineering training courses; regularly trained in cliffs and indoor climbing walls; since when had they been hiking; other activ-ities practised such as ski-mountaineering and so on.

They were also asked their total number of day trips in the last twelve months to each of the 18 sites. Finally, they provided socio-economic information about the state of their households. Round-trip distances from own residence to each of the destinations in the choice set were calculated using the software package 'Strade d'Italia e d'Europa'. This data was used to estimate the individual travel cost for each trip.

Distance costs were converted into monetary values in tenths of €. Each reported visit was a 'one day trip', as customary for this form of local outdoor recreation. Usually in Italy, there is no cost attributed to travel time, mainly because the opportunity of producing extra income using spare time is very limited, and so the opportunity cost of time is assumed to be zero. This may well be one of the main limits in this study, which can be improved upon using a framework similar to that developed by Shaw (1992), or by Feather and Shaw (1999).

The definition of a complete set of substitute destinations for this kind of recreation is a thorny issue to resolve. However, in this instance, because of the proximity of these sites to the residence of the interviewed sample, we believe it is safe to assume that all the 18 destinations are substitutes, although this set is certainly not exhaustive. The short nature of the visits (day trips) makes the existence of complement sites unlikely, while the large number of destinations considered clearly induce a large non-participation rate.

The majority of the respondents in the sample are male (70 per cent) and quite young: half of them are under 40 years old. Most of them attended high school (52 per cent) and almost 16 per cent graduated from university programmes. About 45 per cent of the sample has a take-home income ranging from €17500 to €22500. The average family size is 3.1 people.

The statistics in Table 6.2 show that, at the time of the survey, 48 per cent of respondents had been hiking for at least eleven years, therefore a sizeable portion in the sample seems to be very experienced. Some of them occasionally practice more challenging activities, such as climbing, since almost 11 per cent of the respondents climb on cliffs and indoor walls and 25 per cent attended at least one mountaineering course. Although half of the respondents made less than 10 trips per year, almost 35 per cent took more than 20 day trips. No respondent reported zero day trips.

Seven sites are visited almost once a year by more than 30 per cent of those interviewed; these are Tre Cime di Lavaredo-Cadini, Civetta-Moiazza, Pale di S. Martino (which are located in the Dolomites), Vette Feltrine-Monti del Sole, Piccole Dolomiti-Pasubio, Altipiano d'Asiago, M. Grappa (which are in the Pre-Alps). Unsurprisingly, the most frequently attended destinations are those closest to urban areas.

Table 6.2   Sample statistics of travel cost to site and closest substitute, in €

Destinations	Travel cost to destination			Travel cost to closest substitute		
	Mean	St. Dev.	Median	Mean	St. Dev.	Median
1. Vette Feltrine. M. Sole	5.93	2.41	6.1	2.98	1.41	2.9
2. P. Dolomiti Pasubio	5.8	3.16	5.7	3.06	1.31	2.9
3. Cansiglio-Alpago	6.06	2.65	5.7	3.48	1.46	3.3
4. Altipiano Asiago	4.96	2.34	5.8	2.9	1.31	2.9
5. M. Grappa	3.36	1.86	8.8	2.9	1.76	4.1
6. Lessini-M. Baldo	5.96	2.38	5.0	3.63	1.68	3.2
7. Antelao	7.9	3.88	8.8	3.13	1.67	3.3
8. Pelmo	8.4	3.66	8.8	3.21	1.66	2.9
9. Tofane-Cristallo	10.97	4.61	11.7	2.77	1.63	2.9
10. Duranno-Cima Preti	5.5	3.45	6.6	2.68	1.92	2.9
11. Sorapiss	9.6	4.29	10.7	3.13	1.72	3.25
12. Agner-Pale San Lucano	8.76	3.16	9.1	3.14	1.45	2.9
13. Tamer-S. Sebastiano	6.7	2.52	7.4	2.3	1.56	2.9
14. Marmarole	8.24	4.22	9.5	2.85	1.78	2.9
15. Tre Cime-Cadini	11.63	4.52	11.5	3.06	1.57	2.9
16. Civetta-Moiazza	9.25	2.78	9.7	3.23	1.51	2.9
17. Pale di S. Martino	7.09	1.9	7.1	3.3	1.4	2.9
18. Marmolada	12.42	2.73	13.3	3.3	1.45	3.1

4.   ECONOMETRIC ANALYSIS

4.1   The General Framework

The event of taking at least a day trip to each of the eighteen destinations during the time period in consideration is a joint binary variable. Once all sites are considered, it becomes the joint event of 18 binary variables across n visitors. So, assuming independence[7] and an Extreme Value Type I in the participation linear index $z_{ki}'\theta + \varepsilon_{ki}$, the contribution to the log-likelihood for each individual in the sample is modelled as:

$$\ln L = I_{y=0}\ln L_{y=0} + I_{y>0}\ln L_{y>0},$$

where $I_{y=0}$ and $I_{y>0}$ are indicator functions, while:

$$L_{y=0} = \prod_{k=1}^{18}\left[\frac{\exp(\theta'z_{ki})}{1 + \exp(\theta'z_{ki})} + \frac{f(y_{ki} = 0|\Xi, x_{ki})}{1 + \exp(\theta'z_{ki})}\right] \text{ for } y_{ki} = 0 \quad (6.13)$$

$$L_{y>0} = \prod_{k=1}^{18} \frac{f(y_{ki}|\Xi,\mathbf{x}_{ki})}{1 + \exp(\theta'\mathbf{z}_{ki})}, \text{ for } y_{ki} = 1,2,3,.... \qquad (6.14)$$

where $f(\cdot)$ is the adequate count probability function, $\mathbf{z}_{ki}$ is a matrix of variables explaining non-participation for the ith individual to the kth site, $\mathbf{x}_{ki}$ is the matrix of variables for the semi-log demand system, and θ and Ξ are two adequately restricted vectors of coefficients to be estimated from the sample information. The count probability function $f(\cdot)$ was in turn Poisson, NB1, NB2 and GNB.[8]

It is noteworthy that the inclusion of travel cost to sites can plausibly affect the non-participation decision, and so does the cost to access substitutes sites. In our specification they both enter $\mathbf{z}$ along with other individual characteristics.

Starting from the trips reported by the 904 CAI members in the sample to the 18 mountain destinations, and after excluding 24 observations with incomplete socio-economic data, the total number of day trips went down to $n(k) = 880(18) = 15\,840$ participation choices in the summer 1999. The estimation was done by maximizing the log of the joint likelihood of these trips.[9]

Model specification was based on the Poisson results. All variables that gave the result significant or meaningful for the $\mathbf{z}_{ki}$ and $\mathbf{x}_{ki}$ vectors when $f(\cdot)$ was the Poisson were kept in the other 3 more flexible NB models. The estimated values are reported in Table 6.3 where, to avoid cluttering, and departing from convention, we marked with asterisks the few coefficient estimates which are *not* significantly different from zero.

4.2   Non-participation

The first vector of coefficient θ regards the matrix $\mathbf{z}$, which defines the set of variables determining the probability of non-participation (NP) in day trips to each given destination. We assumed that NP at a site is determined by travel cost to reach the site (T_COST), the cost of the closest substitute (TC_SUB), the number of years the visitor had been making day trips to the Alps (EXC_YRS a proxy for experience in the area), a dummy indicating that the visitor declared himself as occasionally practicing alpinism (which is generally intended as a more specialised outdoor activity than generic outdoor day trips) (OCC_ALP); a dummy indicating that day trips had been a regular activity during the season (REGULAR a proxy for continuity), rather than an occasional one. Finally, we included the two age groups which emerged as significant: 25–40 and 41–55.

All the above variables are significant in the Poisson version, with the exception of the dummy for age group 41–55, which is only marginally so.

Table 6.3   FIML estimates

Variable	Poisson		NB2	
	Estimate	Asy. z-value	Estimate	Asy. z-value
Non-participation parameters				
CONST	−0.095	−0.951	−1.454	−3.165
T_COST	0.010	13.635	0.023	8.655
TC_SUB	−0.013	−8.066	−0.124	−7.024
EXC_YRS	0.010	4.603	0.030	3.068
OCC_ALP	−0.464	−6.239	−0.588	−1.542
REGULAR	−0.470	−8.866	−0.214*	−0.788
AGE25_40	0.323	4.749	0.201*	0.723
AGE41_55	0.121*	1.832	−0.976	−2.341
System of demand parameters				
α_6	1.686	18.488	2.130	10.572
β_1	−0.016	−19.169	−0.020	−16.561
β_2	−0.004	−7.235	−0.009	−8.439
β_3	−0.021	−19.827	−0.025	−19.412
β_4	−0.008	−10.086	−0.012	−9.803
β_5	−0.025	−17.467	−0.029	−15.313
β_6	−0.032	−17.677	−0.046	−15.469
β_7	−0.022	−21.999	−0.024	−21.361
β_8	−0.020	−21.967	−0.022	−21.004
β_9	−0.014	−17.588	−0.018	−20.529
β_{10}	−0.052	−17.098	−0.054	−17.794
β_{11}	−0.022	−20.274	−0.025	−21.788
β_{12}	−0.028	−21.677	−0.031	−22.577
β_{13}	−0.030	−23.003	−0.034	−22.939
β_{14}	−0.023	−20.462	−0.027	−21.971
β_{15}	−0.009	−19.988	−0.011	−15.356
β_{16}	−0.011	−19.411	−0.013	−15.799
β_{17}	−0.015	−20.023	−0.019	−16.992
β_{18}	−0.013	−18.182	−0.017	−20.519
δ	0.016	16.068	0.006	3.700
EXC_YRS	0.011	11.156	0.008	4.863
OCC_ALP	0.218	7.071	0.439	7.426
REGULAR	0.408	15.655	0.607	14.508
AGE25_40	0.343	8.849	0.179	2.970
AGE41_55	0.324	8.006	0.170	2.731
AGE56_65	0.411	10.174	0.355	5.472
ψ	n.a.	n.a.	1.710	55.968
log-lik.	−15,436		−13,354	

Table 6.3   (continued)

Variable	NB1		GNB	
	Estimate	Asy. *z*-value	Estimate	Asy. *z*-value
Non-participation parameters				
CONST	−1.587	−3.476	−1.593	−3.198
T_COST	0.014	6.034	0.019	6.961
TC_SUB	−0.103	−8.191	−0.130	−7.964
EXC_YRS	0.032	4.053	0.036	3.883
OCC_ALP	−0.049*	−0.165	−0.281*	−0.752
REGULAR	0.719	2.508	0.314*	1.028
AGE25_40	0.136*	0.563	0.095*	0.335
AGE41_55	−0.443*	−1.534	−0.889	−2.254
System of demand parameters				
α_6	1.199	6.961	1.728	9.445
β_1	−0.021	−18.263	−0.022	−17.874
β_2	−0.011	−13.122	−0.011	−11.175
β_3	−0.027	−20.175	−0.028	−20.294
β_4	−0.015	−14.502	−0.015	−12.499
β_5	−0.036	−17.910	−0.035	−16.895
β_6	−0.036	−13.572	−0.043	−15.374
β_7	−0.021	−20.736	−0.025	−21.476
β_8	−0.020	−20.545	−0.023	−21.235
β_9	−0.018	−20.351	−0.020	−21.312
β_{10}	−0.054	−15.434	−0.058	−17.105
β_{11}	−0.023	−20.603	−0.027	−21.680
β_{12}	−0.030	−21.457	−0.034	−22.598
β_{13}	−0.033	−21.847	−0.037	−22.858
β_{14}	−0.025	−20.468	−0.029	−21.704
β_{15}	−0.010	−15.865	−0.012	−16.417
β_{16}	−0.013	−17.010	−0.015	−17.087
β_{17}	−0.019	−18.500	−0.020	−18.233
β_{18}	−0.017	−20.607	−0.018	−21.432
δ	0.010	6.789	0.009	5.416
EXC_YRS	0.007	4.203	0.008	4.707
OCC_ALP	0.411	7.709	0.448	7.785
REGULAR	0.680	16.057	0.684	16.051
AGE25_40	0.134	2.350	0.160	2.601
AGE41_55	0.157	2.528	0.176	2.722
AGE56_65	0.342	5.756	0.385	5.853
ψ	2.233	26.324	2.216	28.587
κ	n.a.	n.a.	0.376	11.014
log-lik.	−13,478		−13,304	

Note: * Indicate estimates *not* significant at conventional levels.

This was left in **z** because it resulted as significant in other specifications (for example NB2), and also because in a FIML estimation for a model with 34 parameters, and holding an α value of 10 per cent, about 3 otherwise significant variables may appear not significantly different from zero by the effect of chance alone.

The signs suggest that respondents aged 25–40 are those that have highest probabilities of non-participation. This implies that, at the margin, they visited a smaller variety of sites than respondents of age group 41–55, who in turn seem to have visited a larger set of sites than the baseline age groups (younger than 25 and older than 55).

Similarly, everything else equal, the number of years practicing day trips to the Alps (EXC_YRS) seems to increase selectiveness in choice of sites, as it is significantly associated with a larger probability of non-participation.

The travel cost (T_COST) to reach the destination also has a significant and positive effect on the probability of non-participation, while the travel cost to substitutes (TC_SUB) has a negative and significant effect. Both these results are consistent with economic theory.

Finally, making regular day trips during the season (REGULAR) or to have occasionally practised more specialized alpinist activities (OCC_ALP) decreases non-participation probability.

Few differences are observed in the coefficient estimates for the NP process across the various NB models. In particular, T_COST and TC_SUB maintain their significance and expected signs. EXC_YRS also maintain the positive effect and significance, while the significance of the other variables varies, and in one case (REGULAR in NB1) is significant, but with an opposite sign.

4.3 Demand System Estimates

Conditional on the visitor being in the market for a destination, the count specification $f(\cdot)$ is truncated at zero, so as to model integer numbers $y > 1$.

Once again, from these data the coefficient estimates Ξ for the matrix **x** are reported in the lower part of Table 6.3. The only intercept that was estimated was that for Lessini-Mount Baldo (site 6, or α_6), while the others can be computed using the equality $\alpha_k = \alpha_{k*} \beta_k / \alpha_{k*}$. As can be seen, in all models the estimated coefficients in Ξ are individually significant and all the travel cost coefficients are negative, as expected.

The estimated δ coefficients for income are positive in all specifications, which allows one to compute the compensated substitution effects using equation (6.7) for the whole system in all four specifications for the count $f(\cdot)$. The other socio-economic demand shifters in $\boldsymbol{\eta}$ all show a positive effect. Examining the magnitude of the coefficients in η for the Poisson system, it would seem that being a 'regular rambler' (REGULAR) has a relatively large impact on the number of day trips made in the season across all models. The estimated dummies for young age groups (25–40 and 41–55) are twice as large in the Poisson than in any of the 3 NB estimates, while those for older age groups (56–65) shows a more robust high value across models. Making generic day trips, which is generally seen as the least strenuous form of alpine activity, seems to be more intensely practiced in this age group. The number of years of practice shows a stable positive value across models, while the dummy variable for occasionally engaging in Alpinism gives estimates that are twice as large in the NB models than in the Poisson.

Given the large sample size, the improvement in the log-likelihood of each unrestricted model always produces a significant increase in fit. The estimated variance function from the most unrestricted NB process, the GNB, is $\lambda(1 + \psi^\omega) = \lambda(1 + 2.216^{1.624}) = \lambda 4.64$, which strongly suggests that our data violate the equidispersion assumption imposed by the Poisson specification, even after accounting for excess zeros.

4.4   Estimates of Consumer Surplus per Day Trip

In discussing the results, it is perhaps most interesting to investigate the differences in implied consumer surplus by the various count specifications of the demand system. These are estimates of per day trip CS given positive participation. Differences are visible at a glance from Figure 6.1. It is apparent that the CS implied by the Poisson specification are always higher than those of NB models. The difference is particularly large for two destinations: Piccole Dolomiti and Altipiano d'Asiago, where the Poisson predicts a CS of €24 and €13 versus an average of €9 and €7 respectively from the NB models.

The CS estimates for each destination vary little across the three NB models, although the GNB tends to produce the most conservative estimates.

In Figure 6.2 the approximate confidence intervals derived with the delta method are compared. The pattern illustrates that in general the GNB model provides the most accurate CS estimates.

4.5   Estimates of Substitution Effects

Hicksian compensated substitution effects are important measures of substitutability. In a context in which participation is probabilistic the correct computation of these effects must account for the predicted probability of

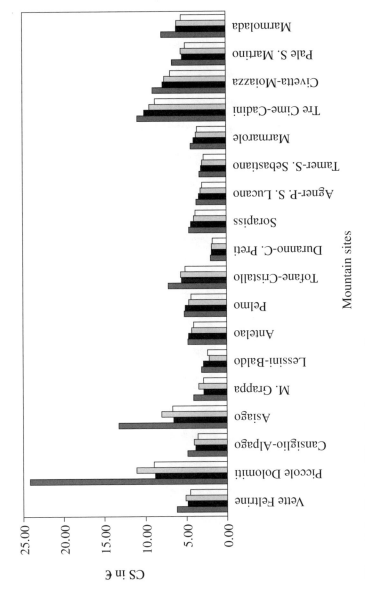

Figure 6.1   Per trip CS estimates across sites

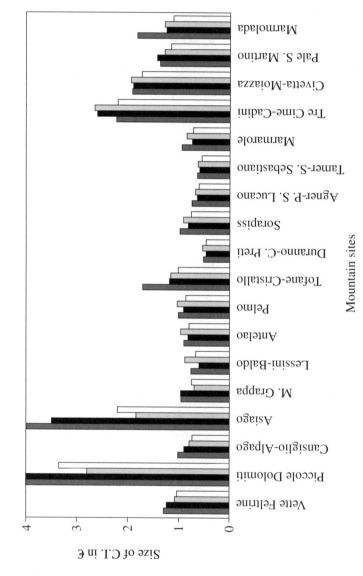

POISSON
NB1
NB2
GNB

Size of C.I. in €

Vette Feltrine
Piccole Dolomiti
Cansiglio-Alpago
Asiago
M. Grappa
Lessini-Baldo
Antelao
Pelmo
Tofane-Cristallo
Duranno-C. Preti
Sorapiss
Agner-P. S. Lucano
Tamer-S. Sebastiano
Marmarole
Tre Cime-Cadini
Civetta-Moiazza
Pale S. Martino
Marmolada

Mountain sites

Figure 6.2   Comparison of 96 per cent confidence interval around CS estimates across count models

116

participation. So, using the model estimates these can be computed for each observation as:

$$E\left[\frac{\partial y_k^h(p,m)}{\partial p_{k'}}\right] = \hat{\delta}[1 - \hat{Pr}(NP_{ki})]\hat{y}_{ki}[1 - \hat{Pr}(NP_{k'i})]\hat{y}_{k'i}, \quad \hat{\delta} > 0, \forall k \neq k', \quad (6.15)$$

where

$$\hat{Pr}(NP_{ki}) = \exp(\hat{\theta}'z_{ki})/[1 + \exp(\hat{\theta}'z)], \text{ and } \hat{y}_{ki} = \exp(\hat{\Xi}'x_{ki}). \quad (6.16)$$

Because of symmetry of the Slutsky substitution matrix only $(k^2 - k)/2 = [18(18) - 18]/2 = 153$ substitution effects need identification. These are illustrated by Figure 6.3, where the lower triangular matrix of median substitution effects[10] is plotted out. The top 4 median compensated substitute effects all involve site 17 (Pale di S. Martino). Everything else equal, and net of income effects, an increase in travel cost by €1 to Pale di S. Martino produces a median increase of the number of day trips of 1.02 to Tre Cime di Lavaredo-Cadini, of 0.67 to Piccole Dolomiti-Pasubio, 0.63 to Civetta-Moiazza. These results are consistent with the frequency of visits discussed at the end of Section 3.1. It also shows a value of 0.53 for Altipiano

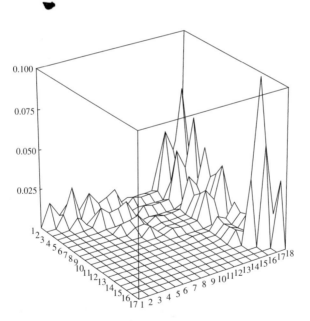

Note: Numbers 1–18 refer to sites as per Table 6.1.

Figure 6.3   Compensated median substitution effects

d'Asiago, which is quite a different destination (pre-Alps, high plane), and hence somewhat more difficult to rationalize.

The shape of the graph also shows that the group of sites 10–14 (Duranno-C.Preti, Sorapiss, Agner-P. S. Lucano, Tamer-S. Sebastiano, Marmarole) show particularly low substitution effects. These are destinations which share some traits. They all belong to the larger chain of the Dolomites, little known and with relatively high degrees of wilderness. It is plausible that visitors perceive each of these destinations as one with little substitutability.

Finally, the substitution patterns amongst geographically contiguous mountain groups is obvious, particularly amongst the destination sites 1–6, which all belong to the pre-Alps.

5. CONCLUSIONS

We started from the premise that although the commercial value of tourism in the Alps is a well studied issue, little is known of its local public value, as determined by the benefits of unspecialized outdoor recreation, such as generic day trips, to residents of neighbouring areas. In this study we have presented an attempt to estimate the benefits produced to local populations with a focus on the North-Eastern sector of the Alps and on days out for day trips. This is an unspecialized use of the resource, accessible to most and hence widely practiced.

In modelling such an activity we have drawn as much as we could from recent developments in travel cost modelling, giving the constraints of a large data-set with multiple destinations. For example, we decomposed zero-count in non-participation and corner solutions, and allowed for an increasingly flexible form of data dispersion in the semi-log demand system.

Data and other forms of limitation of this study include the following:

- Having used as sampling framework the Veneto chapter of the Club Alpino Italiano, rather than the general population, it can be argued that CAI members, who account for about 50000 users, versus an estimated total of 2 million visitors to the Alps from Veneto, may be self-selected and represent a segment with higher demand than that from the general population.
- Travel time was not accounted for in the travel cost variable, which probably implies an underestimation of the benefits from this type of recreation.
- Dependence across demand functions was ignored. In such a large

multi-site system it is certainly computationally impractical to compound the Poisson marginals with the multivariate log-normal distribution, as Shonkwiler did in his 1995 manuscript in a multi-site system with four demand equations. It is, however, probably feasible to account for correlation patterns by implementing a generalized linear model, following Shonkwiler (1999). Exploring the sensitivity of the policy relevant estimates of a demand system to the independence assumption can be an area of further empirical research.

- The estimated Hicksian substitution effects and welfare measures all hinge upon the validity of the assumption of a correct specification of the conditional mean.
- The magnitude of some estimated substitution effects are found difficult to rationalize.

For these reasons the results obtained here are of difficult generalization, and may best be regarded as pertaining to the CAI members, rather than to the whole of Veneto.

Despite these and probably other minor limitations, a number of points can be made. It is clear that the simultaneous estimation of the two zero-demand components (non-participation and corner solutions), is both conceptually desirable and has practical implications. Further, the (incomplete) system of semi-log demand functions estimated for the eighteen sites seems to be mildly sensitive to the functional form employed in the count process, especially between the Poisson results and the negative binomials. The latter approach produces similar consumer surplus estimates across NB1, NB2 and GNB variance functions, although the most flexible form (GNB) produces most accurate estimates. Allowing the variance to differ from the mean also corrects obvious anomalies, such as excessively high CS estimates obtained using the Poisson function for some sites, and increases efficiency, as illustrated by the tightened approximate confidence intervals.

The magnitude of most substitution effects implied by the model are also plausible and informative. This suggests that systems of demand functions may well constitute an alternative to more commonly employed random utility-based models when the focus is placed on substitution patterns unconditional on site attributes.

ACKNOWLEDGEMENTS

The authors are thankful for the various suggestions made by the editors and by research postgraduates attending the module in Environmental

Valuation at the Environment Department at the University of York in 2001–02.

NOTES

1. Although in the model specifications we do use some dummy variables to account for some activities undertaken by some visitors, but not all.
2. Although in repeated choice models a given number of choice opportunities is assumed, often 52 weekends in a year.
3. See also Von Haefen (2000) for a complete characterization which includes quasi-indirect and expenditure functions for common econometric specifications.
4. Morey et al. (1995) and Phaneuf et al. (2000) provide a discussion on and an empirical evaluation of the treatment of corner solutions in a random utility framework.
5. We use the symbol ψ here for the dispersion parameter which is commonly defined as α (for example Cameron and Trivedi, 1998) or in $1/\theta$ (for example Greene, 1993). This is in order to avoid confusion with the symbol α that we use to indicate the site-specific intercepts in the demand system. Further, $\lambda = \exp(\Xi'\mathbf{x})$ is often indicated as μ.
6. Some previous studies highlighted that about 25 per cent of the day trips in the studied area were completed by CAI members.
7. Multivariate probit could also be a possibility, but like count models with multivariate normal heterogeneity, it is only practical in correlated demand systems with fewer sites.
8. Formulae for Poisson and NB1 and NB2 are standard, while that for the GNB is reported Grijalva et al. (2002, p. 407, eq. 6). However, NB1 and NB2 can also be derived by imposing the adequate restrictions on the parameter κ in a GNB.
9. The maximization was conducted by using AD-model builder C++ interface, using as starting points the maximizers obtained from the MaxLik routine in GAUSS. The algorithms in GAUSS and AD-model builder produced the same maximizers and values of the log-likelihood functions at a maximum, but GAUSS could not invert the final numerical Hessian in some NB models.
10. In this calculation the income parameter δ was scaled to 177.83 to account for the € conversion factor as the original yearly income data was in million of Lire. Also the predicted effect was scaled down by 10 because the travel cost data was in tenths of €.

REFERENCES

Burt, O.R., and Brewer, D. (1971), 'Estimation of net social benefits from outdoor recreation', *Econometrica*, **39**: 813–27.

Cameron, A.C. and P.K. Trivedi (1998), *Regression Analysis of Count Data*, Econometrics society monograph n. 30, Cambridge University Press.

Creel, M.D. and J.B. Loomis (1990), 'Theoretical and empirical advantages of truncated count data estimators for analysis of deer hunting in California', *American Journal of Agricultural Economics*, **72**: 434–41.

Englin, J., P. Boxall and D. Watson (1998), 'Modeling recreation demand in a poisson system of equations: an analysis of the impact of international exchange rates', *American Journal of Agricultural Economics*, **80**: 255–63.

Feather, P. and D. Shaw (1999), 'Estimating the cost of leisure time for recreation demand models', *Journal of Environmental Economics and Management*, **38**: 49–65.

Feather, P., D.M. Hellerstein and T. Tomasi (1995), 'A discrete-count model of recreation demand', *Journal of Environmental Economics and Management*, **29**: 214–27.

Greene, W.H. (1993), *Econometric Analysis*, New York: Macmillan.

Greene, W.H. (1997), *FIML Estimation of Sample Selection Models for Count Data*, Stern School of Business, New York University, July.

Grijalva, T.C., R.P. Berrens, A.K. Bohara and W.D. Shaw (2002), 'Testing the validity of contingent behaviour trip responses', *American Journal of Agricultural Economics*, **84**: 401–14.

Gurmu, S. and P.K. Trivedi (1996), 'Excess zero count models for recreational trips', *Journal of Business and Economic Statistics*, **14**: 469–77.

Haab, T.C. and K. McConnell (1996), 'Count data models and the problem of zeros in recreation demand', *American Journal of Agricultural Economics*, **78**: 89–102.

Hellerstein, D.M. (1991), 'Using count data models in travel cost analysis with aggregate data', *American Journal of Agricultural Economics*, **73**: 860–66.

Hellerstein, D. and R. Mendelsohn (1993), 'A theoretical foundation for count data models, with an application to a travel cost model', *American Journal of Agricultural Economics*, **75**: 604–11.

LaFrance, J. (1990), 'Incomplete demand systems and semi-logarithmic demand models', *Australian Journal of Agricultural Economics*, **34**: 118–31.

LaFrance, J. and W.M. Hanemann (1989), 'The dual structure of incomplete demand systems', *American Journal of Agricultural Economics*, **71**: 262–74.

Mas-Colell A., M. Whinston and J.R. Green (1995), *Microeconomic Theory*, Oxford University Press.

Morey, E.R., R.D. Rowe and M. Watson (1993), 'A repeated nested-logit model of Atlantic salmon fishing', *American Journal of Agricultural Economics*, **75**: 578–92.

Morey, E.R., D.M. Waldman, D. Assane and D. Shaw (1995), 'Searching for a model of multiple-site recreation demand that admits interior and boundary solutions', *American Journal of Agricultural Economics*, February, **77**: 129–40.

Moroder, H. (2000), 'Qualità economica, qualità ambientale: la sfida del turismo nelle Alpi', in Cipra, *Turismo nelle Alpi. Qualità economica. Qualità ambientale*, **18**: 31–6.

Ozuna, T. and I. Gomez (1994), 'Estimating a system of recreation demand functions using a seemingly unrelated Poisson regression approach', *Review of Economic and Statistics*, **76**: 356–60.

Parsons, G.R., P.M. Jakus and T. Tomasi (1999), 'A comparison of welfare estimates from four models for linking seasonal recreational trips to multinomial logit models of site choice', *Journal of Environmental Economics and Management*, **38**: 143–57.

Phaneuf, D.J., C.L. Kling and J.A. Herriges (2000), 'Estimation and welfare calculations in a generalized corner solution model with an application to recreation demand', *Review of Economics and Statistics*, **82**: 83–92.

Romano, D., R. Scarpa, F. Spalatro and L. Viganò (2000), 'Modeling determinants of participation, number of trips and site choice for outdoor recreation in protected areas', *Journal of Agricultural Economics*, **51**: 224–38.

Shaw, D.W. (1992), 'Searching for the opportunity cost of an individual's time', *Land Economics*, **68**: 107–15.

Shonkwiler, J.S. (1995), *Systems of Travel Cost Models of Recreation Demand*, W-133, 8th Interim Report.

Shonkwiler, J.S. (1999), 'Recreation demand systems for multiple site count data travel cost models', Chapter 9 in J.A. Herriges and C.L. Kling (eds), *Valuing Recreation and the Environment: Revealed Preference Methods in Theory and Practice*, Cheltenham: Edward Elgar.

Shonkwiler, J.S. and W.D. Shaw (1996), 'Hurdle count-data models in recreation demand analysis', *Journal of Agricultural and Resource Economics*, **21**: 210–19.

Tschurtschenthaler, P. (2000), 'La creazione del valore aggiunto quale indicatore per la valutazione del significato economico del turismo', in Cipra, *Turismo nelle Alpi. Qualità economica. Qualità ambientale*, **18**: 61–4.

Von Haefen, Roger (2000), 'A Complete Characterization of the Implications of Slutsky Symmetry for the Linear, Log-Linear, and Semi-Log Incomplete Demand System Models', Manuscript, U.S. Bureau of Labour Statistics, Washington D.C.

7. Modelling choice and switching behaviour between Scottish ski centres

Geoff Riddington, Colin Sinclair and Nicola Milne

1. INTRODUCTION

A key element in appraising an investment is a forecast of the demand for the product or service. Often, when the market is relatively static, then the forecast revolves around the market share and particularly the way customers will switch from current purchase patterns to the new product or service. In turn this means that we need to develop an understanding of the way consumers choose their consumption patterns and to model the effect of the factors underlying the choice.

Over the last few years there has been considerable investment in the ski centres in Scotland and more, rather contentious, developments are planned. This chapter tries to identify the factors that determine the effects of expenditure at a site by developing a model that quantifies the relationship between the quality of the facilities, prices and the choice of individual skiers. The layout of the chapter is as follows. First, we briefly examine the market for skiing in Scotland. Secondly, we look at the specification and estimation of the chosen model, the Nested Multinomial Logit. Thirdly, we discuss the data, and specifically the estimation of potential expenditures for non-chosen sites. Fourthly, we examine the final estimated models and the resultant implications for ski investment. Finally we discuss the role and limitations of the approach to investment in leisure activities.

2. THE MARKET FOR SKIING IN SCOTLAND

Scotland has five ski centres; Glencoe, Nevis Range, Cairngorm, Glenshee and The Lecht. As Figure 7.1 shows these are geographically dispersed but are within driving distance of the densely populated central belt. The

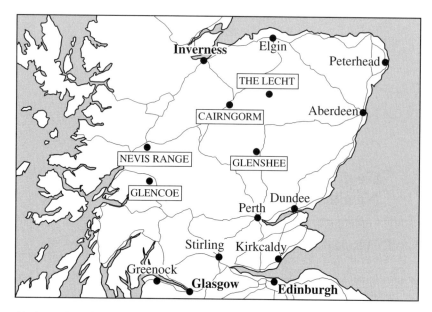

Figure 7.1   The ski centres of Scotland

demand for Scottish skiing is predominantly from a Scottish market, with over 90 per cent being either day or weekend trips (Milne, et al. 1998). Mackay Consultants (1995) estimate that there were 504000 skier days in the 1994/1995 season at all five Scottish ski sites. Data on trip frequency gathered in the present study suggested that there were around 200000 skiers making trips to Scottish ski centres in the 1995/1996 season.

Central to the variation in the number of skier days are the snow and weather conditions. Figure 7.2 shows the total number of skier days each year in Scotland between 1981 and 1995. In this context one skier visiting three times would generate three skier days, no matter how short the day. In good seasons up to 680000 skier days may be recorded, in poor as little as 190000. With high fixed costs, overall the industry will only break-even at around half a million skier days. A series of bad winters makes investment extremely risky. Despite this, over the years there has been considerable extension and upgrading of facilities, largely made possible by public subsidy of up to 70 per cent of capital costs.

Milne et al. (1998) estimated that skiers spent a total of £17665224 in the Highlands Enterprise area and that this level of spending supports directly and indirectly 1500 jobs during the winter months. The industry is thus generally regarded as making an extremely important contribution to the rural highland economy. However, overall demand and real prices are static and

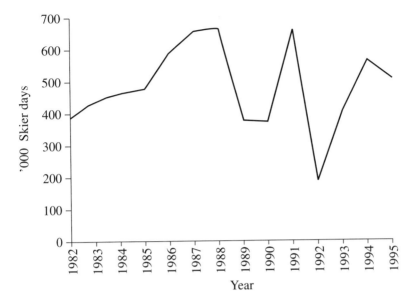

Figure 7.2   Skier days in Scottish centres

thus the investment in Scotland can best be viewed as an attempt to maintain market share through quality improvement in the face of increasing competition from overseas (Milne et al., 1998).

3.   NESTED MULTINOMIAL LOGIT MODELS

Choice models are used to explore and explain economic choices in a wide variety of areas ranging from labour force participation (for example Cogan, 1980) through brand preference (Baltas et al., 1997) to church attendance (Sawkins et al., 1997). Most commonly these are binary choice models using either a probit or logit specification. Multinomial models are concerned with situations where there are a number of choices available. Successful models can be found in many fields such as marketing (Bucklin et al., 1995; Kamakura and Kim, 1996) evaluating environmental quality (Kling and Thomson, 1996), modal transport choice (Sinclair, 1998) and quantifying recreational demand (Haab and Hicks, 1997). All can be dated back to Luce (1959) with the theory best developed and explained in Ben-Akiva and Lerman (1985).

The models assume that individuals seek to maximise their utility when choosing from a finite set of discrete alternatives (brands of commodities, transportation mode, ski sites and so on). Individuals are assumed to act within a framework of bounded rationality so that the utility of the alternative chosen exceeds the utility of all other feasible alternatives. If an individual chooses alternative k then

$$U_{ik} > \max (U_{ij}) \quad \text{for all } j \neq k.$$

Of course utility cannot be observed, only the results. Utility is assumed to be a linear function generated by a set of known and unknown factors that relate to the characteristics of the individual, of the products, or of both. Thus if a skier from Aberdeen chooses to ski at the Lecht then for this customer at this time,

(a) the snow might be satisfactory (a feature of the choice);
(b) the day pass cheapest (again a feature of choice);
(c) suits the level of expertise (a feature of the individual);
(d) the road distance shortest (a function of both choice and individual).

These identifiable factors together with a number of 'other' unidentified factors (for example a friend from England is staying close to the centre) generates a higher utility for skiing at the Lecht than anywhere else for that particular skier/individual.

The unknown factors are represented by a stochastic term and the effects of the characteristics are assumed to be additive. Thus the additive utility model is

$$U_{ij} = \beta X_{ij} + \varepsilon_{ij}$$

where β is a $1*n$ vector of fixed coefficients and X_{ij} an $n*1$ vector of characteristics. The value of the stochastic term is of course unknown, but we can estimate the choice that is most likely given the set of characteristics. For example if, for an individual i, Glencoe is cheaper, nearer, has better snow, more runs, and more accommodation then the probability of choice will be very high but not 100 per cent, because, unknown to us, a partner might have a season ticket for Nevis Range.

Whilst the limited number of factors considered (discussed in the next section) contributes to the uncertainty there are two other elements in the specification that will also generate error. The underlying model implies that overall satisfaction (or dissatisfaction) is the sum of a number of smaller satisfactions generated by the factors. This is unlikely to be completely valid (for example snow conditions and weather might combine in a multiplicative fashion) and will lead to error. Possibly even more importantly the effect of each factor on the satisfaction of the individual is assumed to be constant; everyone responds to the sun in the same way. The obvious invalidity of such a model has led to the assumption that the parameter coefficient represents some 'average' effect and that individual variance from the mean is independent of factor size, appropriately distributed and simply forms part of the stochastic term. However, as we discuss in the final section, economic logic leads one to hypothesise that the variances are not independent, for example the least cost conscious will gravitate towards the most expensive sites. This will thus introduce a downward bias when assessing the effects of the factors on the choice.

Assumptions about the size, distribution and independence of these unknown effects (the stochastic term) are critical to the estimation of the effects of the known factors. Consider firstly the simple binary model where the stochastic terms are assumed to be zero-mean normally distributed. For simplicity we term the known element βX_{ij} the systematic component and label it V_{ij}. If individual i chooses product 1 rather than 0

$$U_{i1} > U_{i0} \text{ i.e. } V_{i1} + \varepsilon_{i1} > V_{i0} + \varepsilon_{i0} \text{ or } \varepsilon_{i1} - \varepsilon_{i0} > V_{i0} - V_{i1}$$

Since the stochastic terms are zero-mean normally distributed the difference will also be zero-mean normally distributed. The variance of the stochastic term will depend upon the scale of the utility measure or alternatively we can make the scale consistent with unit variance. If we assume that the difference is standard normal then, if we have estimates of β and values for X_{ij} and consequently $V_{i0} - V_{i1}$, we can establish the probability that $U_{i1} > U_{i0}$. For estimation purposes we choose values of β that maximise the product of the probabilities for all individuals in the sample.

The multinomial case is similar in theory but much more complex in practice. Consider the three-choice case where product 2 has been chosen over 1 and 0. In this case we need to establish the joint probability that $U_{i2} > U_{i1}$ and $U_{i2} > U_{i0}$. Since these are normally distributed this is theoretically possible but we need, in addition to β, the variance of each of the stochastic terms and, importantly, the relationship between the stochastic terms. Even if we assume independent, identically distributed standard normal distributions we still have to calculate by integration the joint probability for each observation at each set of potential values of β. This generates a significant computing cost. When we have five choices and we allow for different variances and non-independence, the model is currently too difficult to estimate.

An alternative is based on the use of the Gumbel distribution. The Gumbel has a similar shape to the normal, logistic and Weibull distributions, but has one extremely useful feature. If the stochastic terms are independent identically distributed with a Gumbel distribution with scale μ then

$$\text{Max}(V_{1i}+\varepsilon_{1i},\ V_{2i}+\varepsilon_{2i},\ V_{3i}+\varepsilon_{3i}, V_{4i}+\varepsilon_{4i},\ ....,V_{mi}+\varepsilon_{mi})= V_i^* + \varepsilon_i^*$$

where $V_i^* = (\log(\Sigma\exp(\mu V_{ki})/\mu)$ and ε_i^* is Gumbel with zero mean and scale μ.

If the scale is set to unity then we obtain the multinomial logit model.

$$\Pr(y=j)=\frac{e^{\beta_j x_i}}{\displaystyle\sum_{j=1}^{J}e^{\beta_j x_i}} \qquad \text{for } j=1,2,...,J$$

The above model is based on the concept of cardinal utility. There are, however, two areas of indeterminacy. First, utility can only be assessed in terms of other products; there is no agreed base value. Secondly, there is no scale. To meet these problems we normalise on one particular product (that is give the utility of that product the base value of zero) and scale the utility measures so that the stochastic term has a variance (scale) that makes estimation easier.

The assumption that disturbances are independently and identically distributed introduces an important restriction in the model known as the independence of irrelevant alternatives (IIA) property. 'The IIA property holds that for a specific individual the ratio of the choice probabilities of any two alternatives is entirely unaffected by the systematic utilities of any other alternatives' (Ben-Akiva and Lerman, 1985, p. 108). This assumption may in some instances lead to paradoxical results. Under this structural restriction the cross elasticities of any response l with respect to any of the independent variables for choice k will be the same for all $l \neq k$. The probability of the individual choosing l over k thus remains constant irrespective of the composition of the choice set. In marketing, for example, a new brand would draw proportionately equal shares from every existing brand. The IIA property assumes all brands to be perceived as distinct and independent so that errors in estimating the utility associated with each alternative (which could arise for example, from a perception of similarities among the brands unobserved by the model) are not correlated.

This is unfortunately unlikely in the context of geographic variables. Unknown factors, such as the presence of family or friends in an area, will apply to all sites close to that area. Similarly poor road conditions make the assumption of independent stochastic terms unlikely. A partial solution is to apply a nested logit model, where similar alternatives are clustered together in a manner reflecting their correlated utilities. The nested model has a hierarchical structure like a tree with branches showing choices among elemental alternatives such as East or West and twigs representing choices among the various branches (Glencoe Nevis Range, Glenshee The Lecht). Figure 7.3 shows the nest used in our problem. In this case a change in the price at Nevis Range is assumed to have more effect on Glencoe than on the other centres, whilst a change at Cairngorm would have equal effects on all the other sites. The equal effects simplification is undesirable although not, we believe, untenable. As with the assumption of the Gumbel, it is simply necessary to allow estimation.

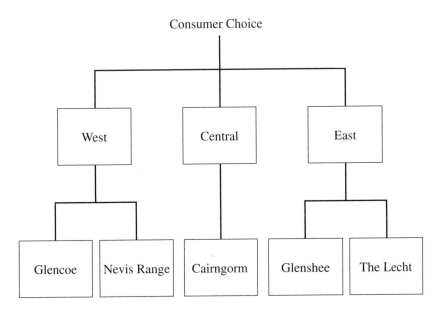

Figure 7.3   Tree structure for ski centre choice

Originally estimation was sequential. Firstly for a given β the utilities of the choices at the base (twig) level are established (relative to all the choices). The aggregate of these utilities in a branch is termed the inclusive value. This value is then compared to the aggregate values from the other branches and the 'inclusive value parameters' μ. that scale the inclusive values to reflect the likelihood of choice of each branch.

Maximum likelihood techniques now allow nesting up to four deep (for example in Limdep, 1998) and are relatively robust if the model has been specified correctly. The problem of the IIA is not, however, completely resolved through the nesting structure; cross elasticities will still be identical within a branch.

An alternative approach is to drop the assumption of identical distributions, replacing them with normal distributions with different variances for each choice, and with errors that may be correlated. However, unless we applied a priori values to the correlation matrix we could not find a solution to our five choice problem. Work presented elsewhere (McFadden, 1984; Riddington, 1998) suggests that differences between this multinomial probit model and the nested logit would be slight and possibly more biased. We present here, therefore, only results from the nested model.

4. THE DATA SET AND MODIFICATIONS

During February and March 1996, a total of 670 adults took part in face-to-face interviews conducted at the five Scottish ski centres over ten days. The responses of 340 children were gained indirectly through the responses of the adult in their party. In an attempt to avoid biased results all interviews took place over one weekend day and one quieter weekday at each site. The spread of responses is shown in Table 7.1.

Table 7.1   The survey

Sites	No. skiers at each site in sample	% of skiers at each site in sample	Population skier days at each site	% of population skier days at each site
Glencoe	212	21	34000	7
Glenshee	193	19	129000	26
Cairngorm	254	25	211000	42
Nevis	218	22	87000	17
The Lecht	133	13	43000	8
Total	1010	100	504000	100

Of the 670 adults in the sample 62 per cent were male and 38 per cent female. These proportions are in line with those reported in the System Three Scotland (1994) and Mackay (1986) studies.

The utility of a ski centre for an individual skier is determined by a combination of centre characteristics; snow cover, type of runs, availability of accommodation and individual specific characteristics, such as distance between the site and the individual's place of residence and expenditure per person per day.

The snow coverage at the site at which interviews took place on any particular day was known but not the coverage at the other four sites. Details of snow coverage, weather conditions and the number of runs which were open were kindly provided by the historic logs of ski companies. This allowed a ranking for quality of snow at the five sites to be calculated. The percentage of hard (black and red) runs was calculated from the piste maps of the ski sites and included as a variable.

The availability of accommodation around the locality of each ski site was determined by a simple count of the number of beds reported to be near each site in the Ski Scotland Brochure (1995). This brochure could reasonably be expected to act as a point of reference for skiers wishing to make an overnight stop near their chosen ski centre.

The total expenditure of each individual at the site they visited was known. This figure covered all costs that had been incurred in the area, including price of the tow ticket, ski hire, tuition, accommodation and food and entertainment. It did not include costs such as petrol purchased outside the area although this may have been used in order to go skiing nor, more importantly, was any cost placed against journey time.

The cost that would have been incurred elsewhere was obviously unknown but it is possible to infer the expected expenditure by using regression analysis. This was the method employed by Eymann and Ronning (1997) and involves relating actual expenditure by individuals at each site to known costs such as tow prices and local expenditure and characteristics of the individual such as age and whether they were hiring skis, taking tuition and staying overnight. These models explained between 44 per cent (Glencoe) and 68 per cent (Glenshee) of the variance. The characteristics of the individual was then substituted in the models for those centres that had not been chosen, and projected expenditures for that individual at that site estimated.

The distance travelled was simply calculated on the basis of the hometown of the respondent. They were used because it was believed that, for day-trippers, journey times are of critical importance because they reduce skiing time.

5. RESULTS

Initially the variables shown in Table 7.2 were specified in a simple multinomial logit model. Distance was surprisingly found to have both the wrong sign and be insignificant and was dropped from the model. The model was then tested for the IIA property using the Hausmann and McFadden (1984) specification test. Effectively if the IIA property holds, modelling the system with four or five choices should yield roughly the same parameter coefficients. In our experience it is difficult to find situations where there is little parameter change, even if there is no reason to

Table 7.2   Variables used in the models

Variable	Description
EXPEST	Expected expenditure at each site
HARD	% proportion of ski runs which were hard at each site
BEDS	Amount of accommodation in locality of each site
COVER	Relative quality of snow cover at each site
DISTANCE	Distance of site from home of individual

suppose correlation of the stochastic terms. Instead we tend to look for situations of very clear change. In this case the model showed chi squared statistics with significance values >0.97 suggesting there was a serious problem and a nesting structure ought to be applied to the model.

The nesting structure chosen was to split the sites into a West branch which contained Glencoe and Nevis Range – the sites on the West coast; an East branch which contained Glenshee and the Lecht – sites on the Eastern side of Scotland and a final branch with Cairngorm on its own. Nesting on a geographical basis was justified by an *a priori* belief that undefined geographical features would exert influence on skier choice. Cairngorm, which is closest to the sites in the East branch geographically, was kept in a separate branch on its own. In part this reflects the fact that Cairngorm, with its dominance of the overnight and long stay markets, would have unknown factors that were very different from all other sites.

Again the model was unsatisfactory in terms of the distance variable. After some discussion it was agreed that the result reflected the fact that there existed two markets for skiers, the day trip market where journey time was critical and the overnight market where journeys normally took place during the hours of darkness (Friday nights and Sunday evenings). Two nested models were then estimated, one for day-tripper and one for skiers staying overnight in the locality. Not surprisingly accommodation was totally insignificant for day-trippers whilst distance and snow cover was unimportant for the overnight market. Table 7.3 gives the resulting coefficients and their Z statistics.

Apart from the signs, the coefficients themselves are difficult to interpret being dependent upon the scale of the variable, the choice used for normalisation and the scale of the utility measure (which has been chosen to give unit variance). The Z scores, however, still indicate the significance of the variable and in this case strongly indicate the critical role of the cost on consumer choice.

It is also difficult to obtain meaningful fit statistics. First, we can examine the proportion predicted correctly, the 'count R^2'. These have been strongly

Table 7.3   Coefficients and Z statistics of the two models

	Day Trippers		Weekenders	
Factor	Coefficient	Z statistic	Coefficient	Z statisitic
Cost (Expest)	−0.149	11.48	−0.0203	7.64
Difficulty	0.017	3.28	0.0003	0.06
Accomodation	–	–	0.0024	4.81
Snow Cover	−1.17	6.04	–	–
Distance	−0.0019	0.56	–	–

Table 7.4   Measures of goodness of fit

	Count R^2	McFadden's R^2
Day Tripper	49.7%	16.7%
Weekender	35.5%	0.49%

criticised because applying a simple constant proportion can also lead to significant explanation. For example in a binary model with a 50:50 split, assuming only one will ever be chosen will yield a count R^2 of 50 per cent. In this case, however, the count R^2 values are substantially in excess of the 'Monkey Score' of 20 per cent. As an alternative we can use a Likelihood Ratio or Lagrangian Multiplier Test to ascertain if there has been a significant increase in the log likelihood over the constant only (proportions) model. The chi-squared test on the log likelihood ratio gave highly significant results for both models. McFadden's R^2 (which is effectively the LM ratio) is presented, along with the count R^2, in Table 7.4. Whilst both models are significant, the impact of the identified characteristics is much less strong on the weekend market. Customers staying for the week or weekend would appear to choose their location some time before the departure date and on the basis of what might generate a good holiday rather than a cost-effective skiing experience. In contrast day-trippers will only travel if there is a good chance of good skiing.

Tables 7.5 and 7.6 give both the own and cross elasticities derived by applying the models to changes around the mean values of the parameters and examining the change in likelihoods. Table 7.5 clearly distinguishes the different cost elasticities between day-trippers and weekenders. In the case of Cairngorm we believe that the true figure is probably around zero. Aviemore is the only ski centre with recognisable 'apres ski' which attracts a young clientele with little cost consciousness.

Table 7.5   Cost elasticities

From\To		Cairngorm	Nevis Range	Glencoe	Glenshee	The Lecht
Cairngorm	Day	**−1.353**	0.367	0.367	0.367	0.367
	Ont	**0.372**	−0.21	−0.21	−0.21	−0.21
Nevis Range	Day	0.390	**−3.76**	2.14	0.392	0.392
	Ont	0.321	**−1.116**	0	0.321	0.321
Glencoe	Day	0.411	2.246	**−3.24**	0.411	0.411
	Ont	0.199	0	**−1.07**	0.199	0.199
Glenshee	Day	0.22	0.22	0.22	**−4.126**	1.051
	Ont	0.087	0.087	0.087	**−0.544**	0.415
The Lecht	Day	0.317	0.317	0.317	1.737	**−2.285**
	Ont	0.049	0.049	0.049	0.235	**−0.626**

Table 7.6   The effect of accommodation

From\To	Cairngorm	Nevis Range	Glencoe	Glenshee	The Lecht
Cairngorm	**−0.473**	0.204	0.204	0.204	0.204
Nevis Range	−0.214	**0.644**	−0.018	−0.214	−0.214
Glencoe	−0.04	−0.04	**0.184**	−0.039	−0.039
Glenshee	−0.065	−0.065	−0.065	**0.393**	−0.308
The Lecht	−0.007	−0.007	−0.007	−0.033	**0.089**

The second feature is the very high cross elasticity between Glencoe and Nevis Range for day-trippers, which disappears completely for weekenders. For the latter they are largely complementary.

Table 7.6 shows the suggested effect of an increase in accommodation on the choice of a particular centre. The result for Nevis Range suggests that there is a clear shortage of appropriate accommodation in the immediate vicinity. The Cairngorm result, if it is anything more than a statistical illusion, possibly indicates an over supply. Given the cost inelasticity the two together may indicate a shortage of quality accommodation. For day-trippers the average elasticity for the distance was low at around 0.2. This is a relatively surprising and important result as the outstanding characteristic of the next projected ski centre at Drumochter is its closeness to the central belt.

The only choice where the range and difficulty of the site is important is Nevis Range, where the model predicts that an increase in the number of difficult runs would significantly increase the likelihood of a skier choosing the centre. The extra skiers would predominantly come from Glencoe.

Interestingly, after the surveys which underlie this work were undertaken Nevis Range opened a new area of difficult runs.

6. CONCLUSION

When undertaking new projects most analysts will tend to use the stated preferences of consumers. As is well known stated preferences always tend to overstate the effect of a change, for example many individuals would seriously believe (and state) that they would go skiing if prices were lower and slopes closer. In reality, however, existing social and recreational patterns would act as a strong but unrecognised deterrent and there would be substantially less change than predicted. The alternative therefore is to examine the revealed preferences and try to model their choices in the past. As this chapter shows this is possible but is by no means an easy task.

The results presented here almost certainly underestimate change, largely because of sample bias. If you ask individuals at a meeting on a Monday evening if Monday evenings are a good time for the meeting then most will agree. If it is a poor time then they are unlikely to be present. In the models we assume that the parameter linking utility and journey time is constant for all individuals with individual variations from the mean being part of the stochastic term. Since those who place least cost on journey time will be sampled at the sites furthest away, the stochastic term will be correlated with the distance which will, in turn, bias the coefficient downwards. A similar effect is apparent with cost elasticity where the least cost conscious will be sampled at the location with the highest cost.

How useful, then, are these models and results? First, in general terms, they act as an important counterbalance to stated preference. Secondly in this case they do reveal quite vividly the importance of cost to the daytripper and the significant competition that does exist between centres (suggesting the sense in pursuing strategies that tie individuals to a centre). Finally they do provide site owners and Local Development Agencies with guides to the most effective development strategies.

Our final conclusion, therefore, is that modelling choice is both difficult and potentially rewarding.

REFERENCES

Baltas, G., P. Doyle and P. Dyson (1997), 'A model of consumer choice for national versus private label brands', *Journal of Operational Research Society*, **48**: 988–95.

Ben-Akiva, M. and S.R. Lerman (1985), *Discrete Choice Analysis*, Cambridge, MA: MIT Press.

Bucklin R.E., S. Gupta and S. Han (1995), 'A brands eye view of response segmentation in consumer choice behaviour', *Journal of Marketing Research*, February, 66–74.

Cogan, J.F. (1980), 'Married Women's Labor Supply: A Comparison of Alternative Estimation Techniques', in J. Smith (ed.), *Female Labor Supply: Theory and Estimation*, Princeton University Press

Eymann, A. and G. Ronning (1997), 'Microeconometric models of tourist destination choice', *Regional Science and Urban Economics*, **27**: 735–61.

Haab, T.C. and R.L. Hicks (1997), 'Accounting for choice set endogenity in random choice models of recreation demand', *Journal of Environmental Economics and Management*, **34**: 127–47.

Hausmann J. and D.L. McFadden (1984), 'A specification test for the multinomial logit model', *Econometrica*, **52**: 1219–40.

Kamakura, W.A. and B.D. Kim (1996), 'Modelling preference and structural heterogeneity in consumer choice', *Marketing Science*, **15**(2): 152–72.

Kling, C.L. and C.J. Thomson (1996), 'The implications of model specification for welfare estimation in nested logit models', *American Journal of Agricultural Economics*, February, 103–17.

Limdep (1998), *Limdep V7 and Nlogit 1*, Econometric Software Inc., Plainfield, New York.

Luce, R. (1959), *Individual Choice Behaviour: A Theoretical Analysis*, New York: John Wiley and Sons.

McFadden, D.L. (1984), 'Econometric Analysis of Qualitative Response Models', in *Handbook of Econometrics*, Elsevier.

Mackay Consultants (1986), *Expenditure of Skiers at Cairngorm and Glencoe*, Final Report for the Highlands and Islands Development Board, August.

Mackay Consultants (1995), *Scottish Tourism Commentary*.

Milne, N. (1997), '*The Appropriate Specification of the Multiplicand and the Incorporation of Displacement Effects within Economic Impact Assessments; A Study of the Net Additionality of Individual Scottish Ski Centres*', MPhil Thesis, GCU November 1997.

Milne N., A. Radford and G. Riddington (1998), 'The Economic Impact of Scottish Ski Centres on the HIE Region', *Fraser of Allendar Quarterly Review*, Spring.

Riddington, G.L. (1998), 'Monte Carlo Experiments with Probit and Nested Logit Models', Working Paper, Glasgow Caledonian University (August 1998).

Sinclair, C. (1998), 'Discrete Choice Analysis and Modal Choice in Scottish Passenger Transport Corridors', Faculty of Business Working Paper 12, Glasgow Caledonian University July 1998

Sawkins, J., P. Seaman and H. Williams (1997), 'Church attendance in Great Britain: an ordered logit approach', *Applied Economics*, **29**: 125–34.

System Three Scotland (1994), *Scottish Ski Holiday Survey*, Highlands and Islands Enterprise, Inverness, Scotland.

PART II

Forests

8. Spatial distribution versus efficiency effects of forest recreation policies using a regional travel cost model

W. George Hutchinson, Riccardo Scarpa, Susan M. Chilton and Trevor McCallion

1. INTRODUCTION

While efficiency concerns dominate and have motivated much of the valuation literature based on travel cost modelling, distribution issues are often ignored. However, depending on management objectives, distribution issues may be deemed of similar relevance to, or even greater relevance than, total benefit estimation. The objective of this chapter is to explore the equity effects of a set of management policies for forest recreation using a conventional individual travel cost approach. In particular, we explore distribution issues of welfare changes derived from a stylised travel cost model of participation and site choice for forest recreation.

Since the seminal work by Bockstael et al. (1987) a variety of specifications for individual travel cost models (TCM) have been developed. Destination choices decisions are often analysed by means of models based on the well established random utility interpretation of McFadden's (1974) multinomial (conditional) logit model (MNL). Typically, these are employed to estimate the probability of the individual choosing a given destination conditional on socio-economic variables of the visiting party, and on a set of site choice attributes, including the cost of the trip. For this category of models the effects of changes in the choice set attributes on population welfare measures are well understood. The spatial distribution of benefits across trip origin districts can also be predicted by these models and is developed for the first time in this chapter. In the study we use a TCM based on choice probability and count modelling to address spatial distribution of benefits. Namely, we investigate the distributional implications of alternative policy options in forest recreation management for the 14 forest recreation sites in Northern Ireland which provide 90 per cent of the estimated market for forest visits.

Drawing conclusions on distribution effects requires a fine-grid spatial sampling of the population of users. Starting from a general population sample is risky as many households are not in the recreational market of interest. Data from on-site interceptions appear to offer a more effective sampling technique. However, in using such data to predict the geographic distribution of benefits, one must be confident that all sites in the relevant market are included and that the observed data on trips are representative of the spatial distribution of trips across trip origins. We surveyed on-site and face-to-face the heads of 5048 recreational parties comprising 16600 visitors at the 14 major forest parks which receive an estimated 90 per cent of all such visits in Northern Ireland. In the estimation, our sample is weighted using the Manski-Lerman (1977) transformation for choice-based sampling to reflect the total number of visitors to each site. The sample is large enough to reflect adequately the proportion of trips from each of the 26 trip origins which in our data coincide with the region's administrative districts (see Figure 8.1). This data set allows us to exploit the fundamental geo-spatial nature of a linked discrete-choice/count-data model (Parsons et al., 1999) not previously explored in the literature. We use maximum likelihood parameter estimates to predict the spatial distribution of welfare changes arising from a set of policies and examine several aspects of the distribution of environmental benefits. We then compare these findings with the less informative aggregate efficiency effects produced by conventional modelling.

Many TCM studies estimate the welfare effect of an identical policy change introduced uniformly across all sites. For example, Kaoru et al. (1995) investigate the effect of a 5 per cent increase in total fish catch at each site and a 36 per cent decrease in nitrogen loading, while Romano et al. (1999) investigate a 10 per cent increase in the size of all Environmentally Protected Areas and Bockstael et al. – in their seminal work – (1987) a 30 per cent reduction of pollutants at all sites. In some cases, this uniform change may represent a policy-relevant subject of investigation. In many real world situations, however, significant changes may be introduced at a single site or subset of sites, while the management status remains unchanged in the remainder of sites.

It is frequently the case that policy changes affecting site-specific attributes may be restricted to a subset of the recreational choice set. Examples of TCM analyses used to model these types of changes include a 30 per cent reduction of pollutants at downtown Boston beaches (Bockstael et al., 1987), welfare loss from forest burning along the most popular Tulabi Lake route (Englin et al., 1996), and loss of 10 fishing sites from a 35 site model (Kaoru et al., 1995). In general, it is expected that uniform changes across sites produce benefit changes that are spatially widely distributed, broadly

Forest Parks:

1	Tollymore	8	Glenariff
2	Castlewellan	9	Ballypatrick
3	Hillsborough	10	Somerset
4	Belvoir	11	Florencecourt
5	Gosford	12	Lough Navar
6	Drum Manor	13	Castle Archdale
7	Gortin Glen	14	Crawfordsburn

Figure 8.1   Forest parks and district trip origins in Northern Ireland

reflecting the distribution of visits across district origins. This is certainly confirmed in our simulations. We also show that the benefit effect of changes introduced at single sites, or at a subset of sites, may often be spatially concentrated in the trip-origin districts where the sites (or site) in question hold(s) a significant 'market share' of visits. Combining this information with that concerning the socio-economic characteristics of these districts, or the state of local provision of substitutes for recreation, may provide more insightful welfare change estimates and policy guidance than merely focussing on total efficiency.

Our study considers a third class of welfare change which can be predicted by our regional TCM framework. These changes arise when – for example – forest management seeks to selectively change the pattern of recreation at the regional level by targeting segments of the population of visitors by tailored interventions at selected forests. For example, visitors may be encouraged to make greater use of an underdeveloped park by site quality improvements and discouraged from visiting a congested forest by an increase in entry charges. Adjustments of this nature will increase benefits to those using the improved site and reduce benefits to those using the site with increased charges. While at the regional level there will be either an aggregate efficiency gain or loss, we use the model to predict the distribution of gains and losses at the trip origin or administrative district level.

The rest of this chapter is organised as follows. In Section 2 we discuss the relevance of distribution versus efficiency issues in recreational benefits. In Section 3 we deal with the survey data and details of the regional TCM. In the fourth section we provide details of model estimation and the method of policy simulation. In Section 5 we illustrate our results on the aggregate efficiency effects and benefit distributions obtained from the six policy scenarios. Finally, Section 6 offers a discussion of our findings with some conclusions.

2. EQUITY VERSUS EFFICIENCY IN RECREATION BENEFITS

Much of the existing valuation literature has approached the evaluation of alternative policies for outdoor recreation by uncritically embracing Potential Pareto Improvement (PPI) as an all sufficient measure of welfare change. Hence, the distribution of benefits and losses are not an issue and the only information provided for decision making is the aggregate net benefit, properly termed the 'efficiency effect' (Mishan, 1973).

The efficiency effect is the aggregate net gain or loss resulting from an economic change. The *distribution* or *equity* effect is the non-aggregated values of gains and losses, which are distributed between individuals and groups as a result of the economic change. In the case of a potentially beneficial change, the distribution effect is easily measured by adding up the losses incurred by individuals and groups as a result of the economic change; these losses will be more than offset by benefits. In the case of a 'potentially' detrimental environmental change, the efficiency effect will be negative and the distribution effect will be calculated by aggregating any gains experienced by individuals and groups as a result of the change. These gains will be more than offset by losses incurred by others.

Some economic and environmental changes may produce benefits to some without losses to any, and these cases will constitute Pareto improvement in its original sense – examples of these are shown in scenarios 1b and 2a, in Table 8.7. Nevertheless, many types of environmental change will produce definite distribution effects, with some losers and some gainers. Examples of these are shown in scenarios 3a and 3b. Distribution effects calculated in the manner suggested above can usefully be expressed as a percentage of the efficiency effect and can exceed 100 per cent of the efficiency effect (for example scenario 3b in Table 8.7).

Johansson et al. (1989), Hanemann (1989) and Hanemann and Kanninen (1999) have all discussed the theoretical possibility of trading-off simultaneous non-market costs and benefits of a single programme using the Contingent Valuation Method (CVM). They have done so only in the context of establishing the appropriate efficiency effect. To the authors' knowledge, this is the first study in the environmental valuation literature which attempts a separation of gains and losses into the, theoretically correct, distribution and efficiency effect based on Mishan (1973 and 1988). In TCM modelling, gainers and losers are not self-declared, as in CVM, but may be identified by changes in predicted choice probabilities. Gainers tend to be those who make frequent visits to sites where the expected benefits from recreation are improved by the proposed change, while losers are prevalently visitors who make heavy use of sites whose recreational potential is reduced. The method employed, of aggregating the economic effect of change for each individual's choice occasion to the district council area, allows these gains and losses to be simultaneously explored at the level of the district of origin of each visit.

A theoretical issue which is not fully elaborated in CVM literature concerns the trade-off of non-market cost against the benefits of the same programme, and whether costs and benefits should be simultaneously valued in theoretically consistent Hicksian compensating terms. If so, then – in the CVM context – a willingness to accept (WTA) measure should be used for valuing costs. This may be subject to the known WTA upward bias, found to produce estimates two to five times greater than a corresponding willingness to pay (WTP) measure (see Cummings et al., 1986). A solution is to measure benefits in compensating terms and compare these to non-market costs measured in equivalent terms using in both cases a WTP measure, as in Brookshire et al. (1980). Whilst overcoming any inherent upward bias in the WTA measure, the lack of theoretical rigour in this solution is overlooked. Mishan (1976 and 1988), demonstrates the potential for intransitivity in a compensating variation/equivalent variation (CV, EV) test. A change measured in CV terms may pass a cost–benefit test. Reversing the change, measured in EV terms, may also pass. An inconsistent ordering of the two states results using different Hicksian measures. Valuations which mix compensating and equivalent measures, of positive and negative willingness to pay, may produce results inconsistent with valuations using other Hicksian measures. To test for this, a consistent ordering of before and after change states should result from compensating, equivalent and mixed measures. If so, divergent estimates could be treated as bounding the actual value. If not, economists have no mandate to recommend a course of action (Mishan, 1988).

By contrast with the conceptual problems of valuing gains and losses using CVM, the TCM method employed here is theoretically consistent. Non-market gains and losses from proposed changes within the choice set are simultaneously estimated in the same valuation exercise at each district council area, and are presented in consistent Hicksian compensating variation terms.

3.   SURVEY DATA

The fourteen forest parks surveyed are all well developed recreational facilities with a number of estimated annual visits ranging from 15 000 to 1 000 000. Visit origins and destinations are well spread out throughout the region (see Figure 8.1 for locations). The system includes twelve forest service parks, all of which are managed for both recreation and timber production and two heavily wooded country parks run by the Department of the Environment (DOE). One of the two DOE country parks (Crawfordsburn) is managed purely for recreation and the other park (Castle Archdale) is multi-purpose.

Site size ranges from 94 to 2609 hectares. These fourteen sites receive over 90 per cent of all forest recreation trips in Northern Ireland and constitute 13 per cent of the forested area in the region. Northern Ireland is a self-contained territory and trips to the Republic of Ireland for the exclusive purpose of forest recreation can safely be assumed to be negligible. So, the system forms a closed market area with less than 1.3 per cent of the trips in this survey originating from outside the region (virtually all of these from the Republic of Ireland). Northern Ireland therefore makes an ideal setting for a regional TCM study concerned with the distribution aspects of recreational benefits.

Data were collected by surveys conducted by on-site sampling, on a face-to-face basis using trained interviewers from Queens University Belfast.

The administration took place over a three week period at the height of the recreation season in July and August 1992. Some 5048 parties of forest visitors were surveyed with a maximum of 500 parties interviewed at major sites, down to less than 200 at two of the least used sites. The sampling proportions derived from this survey strategy do not reflect the known population proportions of visits at sites. To account for this, in estimating the discrete choice model parameters, adjustments were made to reflect population proportions using the Manski and Lerman (1977) transformation, a procedure easily conducted using LIMDEP 7® (Green, 1995).

In our survey, respondents were questioned on the origin and destination of each day trip, on subjective estimates of travel distance, on the number of people in the party, on the mode of transport and total number of trips taken in the last twelve months to Northern Ireland forest parks, along with conventional socio-economic data. Travel distances entered in the DC model were objectively measured from the major population centre in each district area to each site using Auto Route® Software and are summarised in Table 8.1. In computing travel cost values we followed a conventional approach of charging travel at direct cost per person in the vehicle plus travel time costed at 1/3 of the wage rate. The arbitrary nature of all such calculations is one of the most unsatisfactory aspects of the travel cost method (see Randall, 1994).

The recreational quality of a forest site cannot be entirely represented by measurable forest attributes such as data on species mix, tree age structure, length of trails, parking spaces and so on. Site quality depends on both these objective measures and subjectively assessed factors such as the quality of landscape design and aesthetic appeal of the terrain in which the forest is located (see Hanley and Ruffel, 1993). As the intention of this study is to model a considerable number of policy scenarios showing the interactions of site quality, travel cost and charging strategies, we use a single continuous index of site recreational quality. A single index of destination attractiveness is a modelling technique conventionally used in discrete choice analysis. Our index was compiled by landscape architects (McCormack and O'Leary, 1993) who visited and appraised each forest in the choice set by using a predefined methodology for quantitative aesthetic assessment, hence producing a quasi-objective index. Following the principles of landscape design and aesthetic resource assessment (Bell, 1993) these experts used a checklist to score each site out of a possible 246 points. Under 37 subheadings, points were awarded with ascending weights, for approach to site, entrance drive and car park, site layout and *genus loci* of the site and its context. Total site scores are summarised in Table 8.1 and vary from 70 to 216. Management can implement specific policies to improve a site's index total score by increasing scores of subheadings

Table 8.1 Forest site quality scores, distance to the 26 districts from each forest and forests' share of total trips

Forest site	Tollymore	Castlewellan	Hillsborough	Belvoir	Gosford	Drum Manor	Gortin Glen	Glenariff	Ballypatrick	Somerset	Florence Court	Lough Navar	Castle Archdale	Crawfordsburn
Site quality index score	167	144	92	82	89	116	112	181	56	50	190	158	147	164
Autoroute distances (return miles) Mean distance from site to each of the 26 districts	113	113	83	77	95	85	120	103	116	105	158	169	153	83
Shortest distance from site to Population Centre of nearest district	26	24	8	2	16	4	20	30	4	4	10	20	24	14
Longest distance from site to furthest district	216	212	176	180	160	140	194	206	228	188	232	244	218	190
Existing share of trips (%)	10.5	4.2	11.7	16.1	2.4	1.2	1.7	3.0	1.1	0.4	0.8	0.3	2.0	44.5

currently with low scores. Scores can also deteriorate if management fails to protect and maintain high scoring features of the site. We will use a variety of operationally feasible management adjustments to the price and product quality of sites within each modelling context.

4. MODEL SPECIFICATION AND ESTIMATION

Since the seminal work by Bockstael et al. (1987) on household production functions and recreation decisions, a number of multi-stage decision models have been proposed to jointly account for the participation and demand intensity decision observed in outdoor recreation. Repeated choice models (Morey et al., 1993) approaches have been combined with count models (Creel and Loomis, 1992; Hellerstein and Mendelsohn, 1993) and evolved into various forms of linked model (Feather et al., 1995; Parsons and Kealy, 1995; Hausman et al., 1995). Thanks to the limiting behaviour of binomial probabilities, Poisson counts and negative binomial counts can be used where heterogeneity and overdispersion are accounted for.

4.1 MNL Model

In this family of models the destination choice decision is modelled by an MNL model, where individuals choose sites on the basis of their perceived indirect utility from the visit, which in turn depends on site attributes and cost of access. Following McFadden (1974), choice probabilities are a function of the characteristics of alternative sites. Recreationist i receives utility visiting a site j $U_{ij} = V(X_{ij})$ where X_{ij} are characteristics of site j and $U_{ij} = V_{ij} + u_{ij}$ where $V_{ij} = f(X_{ij}; \theta)$ is the deterministic component and the u_{ij} the *unobserved* random component of utility. The probability π that site j be visited out of a choice set of K is:

$$\pi(j) = \text{Prob}\, [V_{ij} + \varepsilon_{ij} \geq V_{ik} + \varepsilon_{ik} \, ; \, V_k \, \varepsilon \, C] \qquad (8.1)$$

Where u is independently distributed Type I Extreme Value Variables (Weibull) then according to McFadden (1974).

$$\pi_i(j) = \frac{\exp(V_{ij})}{\Sigma_{k \in c} \exp(V_{ik})} \qquad (8.2)$$

Assuming a linear functional form the utility function gives:

$$V_{ij} = \beta_1 + \beta_2 X_{ij2} + \beta_3 X_{ij3} + \beta_n X_{jn} + \mu\,(Y_I - P_{ij}) \qquad (8.3)$$

Where X_{ijn} are n site attributes, Y_i is income, P_{ij} travel cost and the β_s and μ parameters to estimate. Y_i drops out of the formulation as do all other visitor's characteristics as they do not vary across sites.

A formal property of the MNL model is that the relative probabilities of choice alternative are unaffected by alternatives excluded from the set. This property, known as the independence of irrelevant alternatives (IIA), is discussed in Maddala (1994). A specification test for this property is proposed by Hausman and McFadden (1984). The test statistic is:

$$S = (\beta_v - \beta_r)' \, (V_v - V_r)^{-1} \, (\beta_v - \beta_r) \qquad (8.4)$$

Where β_v^1 and β_r^1 indicate parameter estimates for unrestricted and restricted (smaller choice set) models and $V_v - V_r$ a corresponding covariance matrix for the estimates. The S statistic is asymptotically chi-square distributed with degrees of freedom equal to the rank of $V_v - V_r$. Under the null hypothesis that the IIA property holds, $\beta_v - \beta_r$ is a consistent estimator of zero. Results of this test for our model are shown in Table 8.2 (bottom line).

Table 8.2   Discrete choice model for site selection – NI

Variable	Coefficient	Asymmetric z values
Site quality	0.014091	35.316
Distance	−0.045008	−44.345
Castlewellan	−0.79049	−10.738
Gosford	−0.61827	−6.325
Drum Manor	−1.4894	−10.470
Glenariff	−0.6769	−6.624
Somerset	−2.0358	−7.781
Florence Court	−1.9724	−10.605
Lough Navar	−2.0458	−7.443
PSEUDO R[2a]	0.513	
Log-likelihood	−6493	
HM test[b]	0.782946	
	(0.0002)	

Notes:
[a] The pseudo R^2 is a measure for goodness of fit of logit models defined as $1 - [\log(L_{R0}/\log L_{R1})]$ where L_{R0} is the maximum value of the likelihood function maximised with respect to all parameters and L_{R1} is the maximum value maximised with respect to the intercept only and all other parameters set to zero.
[b] HM test is the Hausman–McFadden (1984) test statistic for removal of Crawfordsburn from the choice set (0.0002). The number in parenthesis is the p value for violations in the IIA assumption.

Following Small and Rosen (1981) and Hanemann (1984) the compensating variation amount the individual must be compensated to remain at the same utility level following a change in price or site quality is:

$$CV = -\frac{1}{\mu}\{\ln[\Sigma_{j\in c}\exp(V_{jo})] - \ln[\Sigma_{j\in c}\exp(V_{ji})]\} \qquad (8.5)$$

Using the site quality and distance data summarised in Table 8.1 and our sample of 5048 on site observations the DC estimates in Table 8.2 were obtained using the Manski–Lerman approach in LIMDEP 7® (Green, 1995). Variables include significant alternative (site) specific constants, to account for differences in utility not accounted for by site quality and distance variables in Table 8.1 (Ben Akiva and Lerman, 1994; Coyne and Adamowicz, 1993 and Englin et al., 1996). The MNL maximum likelihood parameters estimates for distance and quality are found to be significant and of expected sign, while the McFadden pseudo R^2 indicates goodness of fit (Table 8.2).

4.2 Count Model of Trip Frequency

The site-choice decision is linked to a count model explaining demand intensity. For each visitor this is observed as a non-negative integer value equal to the number of trips over the time interval at hand, and hence modelled as a count. Parsons et al. (1999) review the various linking functions proposed so far in the literature, and find little practical difference between them. In our count model the number of trips taken in a year is assumed to be a function of the individuals' characteristics and the 'inclusive value' associated with each visit, computed from the MNL model estimates. The inclusive value (log-sum of the exponentials) can be interpreted as an expected preference measure of a trip's utility conditional on sites' attributes, including the costs of reaching these sites. The better the access a district area has to sites with good quality attributes, the larger the inclusive value available to individuals resident in that district.

The computed value is then used as an explanatory variable in the zero-truncated negative binomial count model which explains trips demand in the usual semi-log fashion:

$$E(y|\mathbf{\theta},\mathbf{x}) = \lambda = \exp(\mathbf{x}\mathbf{\theta}), \qquad (8.6)$$

where y is the number of trips, $\mathbf{x}$ is an n by h matrix of data with the explanatory variables of trip counts, including the inclusive value and constant, and $\mathbf{\theta}$ is an h by 1 parameter vector. It is useful to remember that the negative binomial is consistent with a process with Poisson marginal probabilities mixed with a gamma-distributed multiplicative error term v, with mean 1 and variance >0:

$$E(y|\mathbf{\theta},\mathbf{x}) = \lambda v = \exp(\mathbf{x\theta})\exp(\varepsilon) = \exp(\mathbf{x\theta} + \varepsilon). \qquad (8.7)$$

This is conceptually convenient as it allows for omitted variables and individual idiosyncratic behaviour unobservable to the researcher and potentially causing the heterogeneity observed in the data.

The compensating variation in equation (8.5) is a *per trip* measure of the value of improvement in site characteristics. Morey (1994) shows this to be an inadequate measure as an individual changes the number of seasonal trips taken in response to the environmental change. We model the individual number of trips per year using a truncated negative binomial estimator to account for the positive integer value of trips taken given participation, as well as to allow for overdispersion through log-gamma errors in the linear semi-log index.

The values in Table 8.3 support the existence of overdispersion in our data set with a significant dispersion parameter estimate α. The link variable – the inclusive value – has a highly significant positive coefficient, as expected, while income has a positive but non-significant coefficient.

Table 8.3   Count data trip frequency models – NI

	Coefficients	(t stats)
Variable	Truncated negative binomial model (left truncated at Y = 0)	
Constant	2.6399	(30.731)
Inclusive value	0.22208	(10.354)
Household income	0.00192	(0.190)
Male respondent	0.08753	(2.013)
Friday or Saturday Trip	0.41747	(7.903)
α	4.1840	(13.733)
PSEUDO R^2	0.888	
Log-likelihood	-18794	

5.   POLICY SIMULATION

To simulate the effects of the six policy scenarios discussed earlier we use the estimates for the linked MNL count data models presented in Tables 8.2 and 8.3 above.

Conventionally, an MNL model based on a random sample of the population could be used to sum individuals' choice probabilities to produce population estimates for the choice probabilities for each site in Northern Ireland. As our sample is choice-based, we produce individual site choice probabilities for the trips from each district council area. We then weight these shares by the population of trips known to originate from that district area. This produces the overall estimated share of trips to each of the fourteen sites in Northern Ireland. Such an estimated share coincides very closely to the observed shares in Table 8.1. From the econometric viewpoint the process is formally identical to the conventional process of aggregating at the regional level.

In Table 8.4 we present the forecast share of trips for each site and for each of the six management policy scenarios. The estimated effect of the scenarios on welfare is given in Tables 8.5, 8.6 and 8.7. The process of summing individual choice probabilities and measures of utility change at a district area level offers interesting insights for policy analysis. In practice we partition the n individuals in the sample into their respective K districts of origin for the trips. At the kth district level, which is our geographical unit of analysis, the predicted total change in welfare for each simulation scenario is found by adding up the product of the (per choice occasion) predicted compensating variation and the predicted number of trips across all the visitors from the district using equation (8.5) as follows:

$$CV_k = \sum_i \hat{y}_i CV_i, \qquad \forall i \in K. \qquad (8.8)$$

The value is based on the estimates from the MNL and NB model of the status of the individual visitor and the changes representing the policy change from the status quo.

In particular, simulated changes in forest management are assumed to translate themselves either into changes in the site quality indices or into site-specific entry charges. These changes are the equivalent of changes in product quality or price for market goods. To simulate the effect of a change in charging at a site we take the estimated parameters of the linked models in Tables 8.2 and 8.3 and input an amended data set which makes an appropriate adjustment in distance to the site to simulate the adjustment to the entry charge. Following our strategy for costing travel distance we add or subtract 11 miles per trip for each adjustment of £1 to a site's entry charge. Table 8.4 gives the estimated share of trips to each site after a £1.50 charge per visit is imposed at Crawfordsburn. The inclusive values derived from the choice model before and after the charge adjustment are entered in the count data model. The estimated effect on participation is given as

Table 8.4 Effect of policy scenarios on site share and number of trips taken

Policy Scenario Number	Description of policy scenario	% share of visits														Total visits
		Tollymore	Castlewellan	Hillsborough	Belvoir	Gosford	Drum Manor	Gortin Glen	Glenariff	Ballypatrick	Somerset	Florence Court	Lough Navar	Castle Archdale	Crawfordsburn	
	Original pre change position	10.5	4.2	11.7	16.1	2.4	1.2	1.7	3.0	1.1	0.4	0.8	0.3	2.0	44.5	2225828
1a	Charge £1.50 at Crawfordsburn	13.1	5.2	15.2	22.0	2.8	1.4	1.9	3.7	1.3	0.5	0.9	0.3	2.2	29.7	2091730
1b	Improve site quality to 150 at Hillsborough	9.1	3.6	21.9	14.0	2.0	1.1	1.6	2.8	1.1	0.4	0.8	0.3	2.0	39.3	2294739
2a	Abolish charging	12.3	5.1	10.9	15.3	2.6	1.3	1.9	3.6	1.2	0.4	0.8	0.3	1.8	42.5	2265681
2b	Decrease of 20% in site quality	9.7	4.1	13.1	18.7	2.7	1.2	1.8	2.6	1.4	0.5	0.7	0.3	2.0	41.3	2046499
3a	Charge £0.50 at Crawfordsburn and cease charging (£0.65) at Glenariff, Tollymore and Castlewellan	14.1	5.6	12.2	17.2	2.3	1.2	1.7	4.0	1.1	0.4	0.8	0.3	2.0	37.1	2204302
3b	Charge £0.50 at Belvoir, cease charging (£0.45) at Gosford while improving Quality to 140 and Improve Quality to 120 at Somerset	10.4	4.1	11.7	12.6	5.0	1.1	1.6	2.9	1.1	0.9	0.8	0.3	2.0	45.6	2222107

an adjustment to the total number of annual trips taken by visitors in the outer columns of Table 8.4. The effect of site quality changes are simulated by directly changing the quality index and imputing the new data set in the linked models in Tables 8.2 and 8.3.

6.   EFFICIENCY AND SPATIAL DISTRIBUTIONS OF SELECTED POLICY SCENARIOS

The results for the six simulated policy scenarios in Table 8.4, column two, illustrate the potential of the method. These link the site choice model estimates in Table 8.2 and the demand model estimates in Table 8.3 to estimate the effects of a variety of realistic managerial actions such as entry charges and changes in site recreational quality, which are within the range of extrapolation values supported by the sample and hence by the models. Policy simulations are chosen to illustrate the diversity of distributional effects on economic welfare. Changes in site management are divided into three pairs of two scenarios each.

The first pair introduces significant changes at *single sites*. The prediction is of a net benefit change, largely concentrated in a few district areas.

The second pair introduces changes *broadly spread across sites*. The prediction is of widespread effects on economic welfare throughout the region. The distributions for each type of welfare change is presented and compared graphically in Figure 8.2.

The third pair of scenarios concern cases where managers *decide on a regional restructuring*. This is achieved by increasing the attraction of one or several sites (by improving site quality or reducing charging) and reducing the attraction of another site or sites (by increased charging or reducing site quality). Such strategic adjustments may be made to meet specific site revenue targets, to minimise site overcrowding or underuse, or to meet goals of equitable access to such facilities throughout a region.

Simultaneous changes within the regional model are particularly interesting if the recreational attraction of some sites is increased while others is reduced. Two plausible examples of this type are shown in the final scenario group. In this case the regional model predicts welfare gains at some districts and losses at others. In at least one case we anticipate the net efficiency effect will be small relative to the gains and losses at several districts. Both the spatial distribution and aggregate effects of scenarios 3a and 3b are presented in Table 8.7.

6.1   Management Changes at Single Sites: Policy Scenarios 1a and 1b

In the presentation of results we endeavoured to reduce a voluminous output to a compact easily readable one. While all results are obtained with the method illustrated for the first scenario in Table 8.5, the results for all scenarios are recorded in Tables 8.6 and 8.7. The first scenario looks at the introduction of a charge of £1.50 per person entering the heavily used site at Crawfordsburn, located on Belfast Lough approximately 6 miles from Belfast. The 'no-charging' policy currently applied at this major recreational woodland is inconsistent with the charging policy at many Forest Service parks. This policy is due to the site being run, as a country park, by the Department of the Environment.

6.1.1   Scenario 1a   Imposing a £1.50 entry charge at Crawfordsburn

The effect of the £1.50 charge appears in Table 8.4. The Crawfordsburn share of visits falls to 30 per cent while the share of other sites rises accordingly but the annual total trips taken in the region falls to 2 091 730. The loss of compensating variation (CV) per trip and measures of total welfare loss are illustrated in detail in Table 8.5. The spatial distribution of total welfare loss across the region shows that this is largely concentrated in the North Down, Belfast, Castlereagh, Newtownards and Lisburn districts. These findings are consistent with our theoretical predictions for the effects of environmental change concentrated at a single site. The considerable variation in welfare loss across districts is shown by the inter-quartile range of individual losses in Figure 8.2.

6.1.2   Scenario 1b   Improving the site quality of Hillsborough to an index value of 150

Hillsborough is a small attractive and heavily visited forest located close to a picturesque village some thirteen miles South West of Belfast in the heavily populated Lisburn district.

The present site area of 95 hectares could be extended to incorporate parkland and ornamental gardens in the vicinity. Improvements could be made in built amenities to provide a visitor centre and a better car park. Considerable improvements could also be made in forest trails and forest landscaping. This scenario estimates the effect of an increase in the overall site quality index from the present low value of 92 (out of 246) to a high scoring 150. This would effectively raise the site quality ranking from 10th to 5th out of the 14 sites in the choice set.

The result is that market share would practically double from 11.7 per cent to 21.9 per cent. The welfare gains shown in Table 8.6 and Figure 8.2 are largely concentrated in districts close to the site, namely Lisburn,

Table 8.5   Compensating variation (CV) by trip origin arising from £1.50 charge at Crawfordsburn

Trip origin	(£/trip)	Multiplied by existing number of trips	Multiplied by revised number of trips (CV)
All trips	−0.57	−1 270 820	−1 168 951
Belfast	−0.72	−262 478	−242 170
Cookstown	−0.04	−694	−672
Banbridge	−0.15	−6 861	−6 536
Antrim	−0.54	−11 229	−10 545
Castlereagh	−0.60	−218 803	−204 949
Limavady	−0.05	−107	−105
N. Down	−1.07	−430 447	−384 258
Omagh	−0.00	–	–
Craigavon	−0.21	−11 001	−10 979
Ballymena	−0.21	−5 865	−5 727
Armagh	−0.08	−3 333	−3 493
Newtownards	−0.79	−117 165	−107 798
Magherafelt	−0.22	−2 155	−2 101
Lisburn	−0.39	−112 786	−107 039
Larne	−0.36	−4 384	−4 252
Ballymoney	−0.06	−273	−294
Dungannon	−0.12	−2 305	−2 340
Moyle	−0.01	−237	−219
Carrickfergus	−0.66	−16 227	−14 918
Derry	−0.01	−73	−88
Strabane	0.00	–	–
Newry	−0.07	−2 770	−2 783
Fermanagh	0.00	–	–
Coleraine	−0.05	−1 208	−1 115
Downpatrick	−0.14	−19 679	−18 736
Newtownabbey	−0.71	−40 740	−37 698

Belfast, Castlereagh, North Down and Craigavon. The interquartile range on individual benefit is somewhat smaller than the previous scenario because the greatest benefit per visit to visitors from the Lisburn district applies to less than 12.5 per cent of total visits and therefore appears as an outlier outside the interquartile range.

Overall the prediction that the welfare effect of changes introduced at a single site are for the most part concentrated in several districts is supported by the results in Table 8.7.

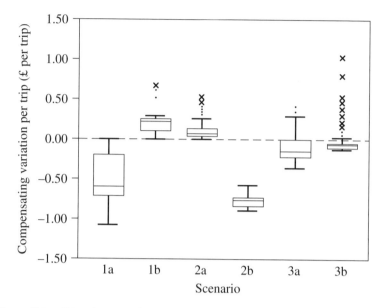

Figure 8.2   Distribution of gains and losses arising from the six scenarios

6.2   Uniform Management Changes Spread Across All Sites: Policy Scenarios 2a and 2b

6.2.1   Scenario 2a   Remove entry charges at all charging sites

Charging currently takes place at eleven of the fourteen Northern Ireland parks. Only one quarter of visits are to these parks and the most heavily visited parks, Crawfordsburn, Belvoir and Hillsborough apply no entry charge. The two Department of the Environment Country parks, Crawfordsburn and Castle Archdale, also have no charge, while all charging parks are managed by the Forest Service.

Here, visitors are charged at the gate a flat rate of £1, £1.50 or £2 per car, irrespective of the number of occupants. Our survey found a fairly high, average car occupancy rate of 3.3 people. Charging therefore works out at a very reasonable rate per visitor. The effect of ending it can be simulated by using the assumptions on travel costs previously explained and thereby making equivalent reductions in the data for distance to each charging site by 7, 5 and 3 miles return distance according to whether charging was £1, £1.50 or £2 per car. As there are 11 charging sites the following reductions in distance from all districts to these sites are made as follows: Tollymore (7miles), Castlewellan (7miles), Gosford (5miles), Drum Manor (5miles),

Table 8.6 Effect of policy scenarios on WTP per trip from each district (£/trip)

| Trip origin | Policy scenario number | | | | | |
	1a	1b	2a	2b	3a	3b
Belfast	−0.72	0.26	0.00	−0.76	−0.22	−0.10
Cookstown	−0.04	0.09	0.35	−0.68	0.04	0.18
Banbridge	−0.15	0.53	0.36	−0.74	0.27	0.23
Antrim	−0.54	0.24	0.18	−0.77	−0.06	−0.04
Castlereagh	−0.60	0.24	0.09	−0.73	−0.15	−0.12
Limavady	−0.05	0.02	0.36	−0.57	0.09	0.55
North Down	−1.07	0.12	0.05	−0.85	−0.35	−0.04
Omagh	0.00	0.01	0.32	−0.71	0.00	0.03
Craigavon	−0.21	0.63	0.27	−0.68	0.10	0.40
Ballymena	−0.21	0.09	0.43	−0.85	0.31	0.01
Armagh	−0.08	0.30	0.38	−0.63	0.11	1.05
Newtownards	−0.79	0.17	0.09	−0.79	−0.21	−0.08
Magherafelt	−0.22	0.09	0.34	−0.74	0.06	0.12
Lisburn	−0.39	0.68	0.12	−0.69	−0.04	−0.05
Larne	−0.36	0.13	0.33	−0.84	0.18	−0.05
Ballymoney	−0.06	0.03	0.44	−0.60	0.23	0.30
Dungannon	−0.12	0.24	0.34	−0.67	0.05	0.49
Moyle	−0.01	0.00	0.53	−0.62	0.31	0.03
Carrickfergus	−0.66	0.24	0.11	−0.77	−0.15	−0.09
Derry	−0.01	0.01	0.41	−0.64	0.01	0.07
Strabane	0.00	0.00	0.41	−0.65	0.00	0.02
Newry	−0.07	0.28	0.47	−0.75	0.36	0.53
Fermanagh	0.00	0.00	0.15	0.89	0.00	0.01
Coleraine	−0.05	0.02	0.35	−0.53	0.17	0.82
Downpatrick	−0.14	0.14	0.48	−0.84	0.43	−0.02
Newtownabbey	−0.71	0.24	0.09	−0.77	−0.19	−0.09
All trips	−0.57	+0.27	+0.14	−0.76	−0.09	0.00

Gortin Glen (5miles), Glenariff (7miles) Ballypatrick (5miles) Florence-court (3miles) and Lough Navar (5miles). The simulation was computed with the estimates in Tables 8.2 and 8.3. The results are in Table 8.4. They show that stopping charges would result in an increase of the share of visits to former charging sites (especially Tollymore and Castlewellan), with an overall increase of 40000 visits per year.

Estimate of welfare change show a benefit of £333322 for Northern Ireland as a whole in Table 8.7. Unlike changes at single sites, this benefit is widespread in its spatial distribution across most districts as the eleven

Table 8.7   Effect of policy scenarios on WTP at each district (£)

Trip origin	Policy scenario number					
	1a	1b	2a	2b	3a	3b
Belfast	−242170	96977	21	−253773	−76815	−35352
Cookstown	−672	1527	6299	−10859	780	3180
Banbridge	−6536	25728	17142	−31062	12557	10588
Antrim	−10545	5182	3751	−14732	−1167	−742
Castlereagh	−204949	91481	32743	−246977	−53077	−44855
Limavady	−105	47	810	−1155	196	1255
North Down	−384258	51018	20975	−311038	−133777	−16286
Omagh	−88	184	7647	−15207	61	710
Craigavon	−10979	35208	14338	−33247	5335	21403
Ballymena	−5727	2509	12727	−21686	9112	193
Armagh	−3493	13081	16378	−24339	4449	47303
Newtownards	−107798	25253	13528	−107909	−30546	−12168
Magherafelt	−2101	917	3455	−6648	585	1139
Lisburn	−107039	212127	35319	−185575	−11520	−13230
Larne	−4252	1658	4199	−9274	2221	−601
Ballymoney	−294	121	2119	−2560	1093	1420
Dungannon	−2340	4690	6835	−11983	899	9716
Moyle	−219	91	11932	−12393	6975	581
Carrickfergus	−14918	6046	2689	−17200	−3595	−2181
Derry	−88	37	3122	−4338	49	525
Strabane	−9	19	3505	−4936	22	132
Newry	−2783	11460	19531	−27272	14722	21860
Fermanagh	−40	84	8533	−45918	16	421
Coleraine	−1115	462	8764	−11978	4199	21532
Downpatrick	−18736	20210	71678	−107875	64178	−2637
Newtownabbey	−37698	13849	5282	−40693	−10564	−4892
All trips	−1168951	619968	333322	−1560628	−193610	9011

charging sites are geographically dispersed throughout the region (see Figure 8.1). The results show major benefits in districts where a high proportion of trips were to former charging sites for example Moyle, Downpatrick and Newry benefiting by £0.53, £0.48 and £0.47 per trip respectively. A noteworthy finding is that the Belfast area received little benefit from an end to charging in Tables 8.6 and 8.7. Although Belfast alone accounts for 16.4 per cent of all trips in the sample a high proportion of these trips were observed to take place at the three major non-charging sites, Crawfordsburn, Belvoir and Hillsborough. Figure 8.2 shows that the distribution of benefits produced by dropping entrance charges are heavily concentrated around a median value of £0.14 per trip with a smaller inter-quartile range than for changes introduced at single sites.

6.2.2 Scenario 2b Decrease the index value of site quality by 20 per cent at all sites

The next scenario is typical of the type of change normally estimated by this sort of modelling. It looks at uniform decrease in site quality. With seven of the fourteen Northern Ireland sites rated between 89 and 158 on a site quality index, a 20 per cent decrease could reduce a site to a compar-able ranking to other sites currently widely accepted as of inferior quality. A 20 per cent movement up or down the quality scale, singly or simultane-ously with other sites represents a considerable movement in this parame-ter. The type of travel cost modelling in this study also demonstrates a considerable sensitivity of willingness to pay estimates to the quasi-objective site quality rating. The effect of a simultaneous 20 per cent decline at all sites is estimated to reduce participation by just under 10 per cent to 2 046 499 annual visits. The predicted changes in the share of visits across sites are small and tend towards a reduction in the share held by distant above average quality sites, with a corresponding increase in the share held by lower quality sites at convenient distances (see Table 8.4). Average loss in benefit is a substantial £0.76 per trip and this varies little between dis-tricts, from a minimum of £0.53 in Coleraine district to a maximum of £0.89 in Fermanagh. The overall estimated loss of economic welfare is a substantial £1 560 628 per year, reinforcing the relevance and sensitivity of the quality index in this type of modelling. Consistent with theoretical pre-dictions, this welfare change is broadly spread across all districts. The difference in absolute amounts in Table 8.7 largely reflects population dis-tribution and number of trips originating in each district. It is interesting to compare the spatial distribution of loss from this uniformly spread quality decline with the loss from the £1.50 charge introduced only at Crawfordsburn country park in scenario 1a. The uniform change shows a much smaller inter-quartile range in loss per trip across district council areas with little difference between the mean (£0.76) and median (£0.75) loss per trip in Figure 8.2.

6.3 Increase in Recreational Potential at Some Sites and Decrease at Others: Policy Scenarios 3a and 3b

The type of regional TCM presented here allows the analyst to consider restructuring policies which reduce differences in charging strategies between several providers (for example Forest Service and Department of the Environment parks). It also permits investigation of equity issues, such as providing more equitable charging and access to this type of recreation across the region, and the option of combining several policy instruments.

In Northern Ireland the Forest Service manages twelve of the fourteen parks and simultaneously operates a charging and no-charging policy at different sites. It is therefore possible for the Forest Service to act independently or jointly with the Department of the Environment to restructure regional provision. In the following two scenarios we predict the effects of a more equitable charging and provision strategy across the region. The general tendency in both strategies is to introduce charges at high demand sites in the Greater Belfast area (see Figure 8.2) to fund the increase of recreational potential at several other sites throughout the region.

6.3.1   Scenario 3a   Imposing a £0.50 entry charge at Crawfordsburn and removing entry charges of £0.65 at Glenariff, Tollymore and Castlewellan

In the first of these two scenarios we assume that if a harmonised management strategy for forest recreation were introduced by the Department of the Environment and the Forest Service, then consideration might be given to charging at major sites close to Belfast. Crawfordsburn could be the most obvious site at which to introduce charges as it receives the highest number of visitors of any forest park in Ireland (approximately 1 million per annum).

A moderate charge (£0.50 per person) could help reduce undesirable congestion at peak times. The predicted substitution effects show that visitor numbers could be increased at the three high quality but less heavily used sites Tollymore, Castlewellan and Glenariff, all of which are within a 42 mile (one way) trip from Belfast. These increases could be encouraged by removing the entry charges of approximately £0.65 per person at these sites. By simultaneously introducing these changes our modelling suggests that the share of total trips which visit Crawfordsburn would fall by approximately 6 per cent in Table 8.4. The net effect of this restructuring is estimated to be a £193610 economic efficiency loss made up as predicted by substantial gains at the Downpatrick and Newry districts offset by larger losses at North Down, Belfast, Castlereagh and Newtownards (see Tables 8.6 and 8.7). As the four sites affected by this scenario are among the most heavily visited in the region, and are geographically well dispersed, the changes introduced in charging affect economic welfare significantly at most districts in the region. The inter-quartile range on loss per trip extends from zero to £−0.25 approximately with significant benefits located in the positive outlier, as shown in Figure 8.2.

6.3.2 Scenario 3b   Imposing a £0.50 entry charge at Belvoir, removing the charge of £0.45 at Gosford while improving the site quality index of Gosford to 140 and of Somerset to 120

In this final scenario the Forest Service could unilaterally re-align its management strategy by introducing a low (£0.50) charge at Belvoir, a small, heavily used site (330 000 annual visits) on the edge of Belfast. This change would address the current inequitable availability of non-charging facilities to residents of Belfast and adjoining districts.

Correspondingly the Forest Service could increase provision in underprovided areas of the region such as Mid Ulster and the North West. This scenario removes charging and introduces major site quality improvement (to an index value of 140) at Gosford Forest Park in Mid Ulster. The scenario would also create a good quality Forest Park for the North West (with an index score of 120). This would be located at Somerset Forest Park which is currently a low quality facility (with an index score of 50). Using the usual TCM point estimates, the net effect of this restructuring would result in a negligible economic efficiency gain of £9011 at the regional level. This is made up, as one would expect, of sizeable gains in Armagh, Newry, Craigavon and Coleraine districts, offset by large losses in Castlereagh and Belfast (see Table 8.7).

Although this last restructuring scenario has fairly widespread spatial effects throughout the region the most significant effects per trip are experienced at districts such as Armagh, Coleraine and Limavady (see Table 8.6). These districts do not account for a high proportion of total visits while the districts providing most visits are less affected. Figure 8.2 illustrates how most of these high level gains fall in the outliers and extremes, well outside the inter-quartile range where most individual visitors gains and losses are located. As predicted this scenario also demonstrates the interesting case where the point estimates of the distribution of welfare between districts is more convincingly demonstrated and is of much greater economic significance than the very small net efficiency gain of £9011 at the regional level.

When summed up the losses across various districts amounts to £132 944 and produce a distribution effect from this 'potentially beneficial environmental change' which amounts to almost 15 times the value of the net efficiency gain.

7. DISCUSSION AND CONCLUSIONS

The large number of previously published TCM studies use a variety of econometric specifications to provide estimates of what we term *aggregate efficiency effects* (following the definition in Mishan, 1973 and 1988). We attempt an extension of this ongoing concern in the mainstream literature, by addressing previously neglected distribution issues. We use a large on-site survey of forest visitors conducted at all major forest parks in Northern Ireland to provide a fine grid spatial sampling of the population of visitors. Using a simple and stylised linked MNL-count model, we exploit the comprehensiveness of our data and the nature of our self contained recreation market to disaggregate the welfare change predictions to the district trip origin level, as well as to the conventional regional level. Empirically this exercise is based on the predicted market shares which each recreational site holds, in terms of trips from each district.

Our model predicts that policy changes induce significant distributional changes in forest recreation benefit once these are disaggregated at the district level, depending on whether the site undergoing the change originally held a sizeable market share of trips from that district. As some sites receive most trips from only some of the 26 trip origins in the region, the CV effect of change at these sites will be geographically concentrated at the districts in question and will have little or no effect at districts with few recorded visits to the sites. We validate our theoretical predictions by specifying and running three classes of policy scenarios each with two specific policy proposals. The empirical outcomes of these simulations closely coincide with theoretical expectations.

The key empirical findings are as follows. Management change at a single site can produce effects largely concentrated at a few district areas, while a uniform change across all sites tends to produce widespread effects across the region. Managing a regional recreational resource equitably and efficiently may also involve simultaneous changes introducing recreational improvements at some sites while restricting recreation at others. This may result in CV gains at some districts offset by losses at others. We argue that this information may be combined with knowledge of the different socio-economic characteristics of the affected districts to identify the extent of regressive and progressive equity effects of policies for management of these recreational resources.

These empirical findings should not be trivialised as they introduce additional information on the distribution effect of welfare change. In many cases this is as relevant to decision making as the efficiency effect of welfare change which has until now represented practically the sole preoccupation of the environmental valuation literature.

ACKNOWLEDGEMENTS

The authors gratefully acknowledge the assistance and advice of Mr David Matthews of the Biometrics Division of the Department of Agriculture and Rural Development.

REFERENCES

Bell, S. (1993), *Elements of Visual Design in the Landscape*, London: E. and F.N. Spon.

Ben Akiva, M. and S.R. Lerman (1994), *Discrete Choice Analysis*, Cambridge MA: The MIT Press.

Brockstael, N.E., W.M. Hanneman and C.L. Kling (1987), 'Estimating the value of water quality improvements in a recreational demand framework', *Water Resources Research*, 23(5): 951–60.

Brookshire, D.S., A. Randall and J.R. Stoll (1980), 'Valuing increments and decrements in natural resource service flows', *American Journal of Agricultural Economics*, 62(3): 478–88.

Creel, M. and J. Loomis (1992), 'Recreation value of water to wetlands in the San Joaquin valley: linked multinomial logit and count data trip frequency models', *Water Resource Research*, 28(10): 2597–606.

Coyne, A.G. and W. Adamowicz (1993), 'Modelling choice of site for hunting Bighorn sheep', *Wildlife Society Bulletin*, 20: 26–33.

Cummings, R.G., D.S. Brookshire and W.D. Schulze (1986), *Valuing Environmental Goods: an Assessment of the Contingent Valuation Method*, USA: Rowman & Littlefield Publishers, Inc.

Englin, J., P.C. Boxall, C. Kalyan and D.O. Watson (1996), 'Valuing the impact of forest fires on backcountry forest recreation', *Forest Science*, 42(4): 450–55.

Feather, P., D. Hellerstein and T. Tomasi (1995), 'A discrete count model of recreational demand', *Journal of Environmental Economics and Management*, 29: 214–27.

Green, W.H. (1995), *LIMDEP ® Version 7.0 User's Manual*, Econometric Software Inc. Bellport N.Y.

Hanemann, W.M. (1984), 'Welfare evaluations in contingent valuation experiments with discrete responses', *American Journal of Agricultural Economics*, 66: 332–41.

Hanemann, W.M. (1989), 'Welfare evaluations in contingent valuation experiments with discrete responses data: reply', *American Journal of Agricultural Economics*, 71: 1057–61.

Hanemann, W.M. and B. Kanninen (1999), 'The Statistical Analysis of Discrete Response CV Data', in I.J. Bateman and K.G. Willis, (eds), Valuing Environmental Preferences, Oxford University Press.

Hanley, N.D. and R.J. Ruffel (1993), 'The contingent valuation of forest characteristics: two experiments', *Journal of Agricultural Economics*, 44: 218–29.

Hausman, J. and D. McFadden (1984), 'Specification tests for the multinomial logit model', *Econometrica*, 25(5): 1219–40.

Hausman, J., G. Leonard and D. McFadden (1995), 'A utility consistent, combined discrete choice and count model: assessing recreational use losses due to natural resource damage', *Journal of Public Economics*, 56: 1–30.

Hellerstein, D. and R. Mendelsohn (1993), 'A theoretical foundation for count data models, with an application to a travel cost model', *American Journal of Agricultural Economics*, **75**: 604–11.

Johansson, P.O., B. Kriström and K.G. Mäler (1989), 'Welfare evaluation in contingent valuation experiments with discrete response data: connect', *American Journal of Agricultural Economics*, **71**: 1054–6.

Kaoru,Y., V.K. Smith and L.J. Long (1995), 'Using RUM to estimate the recreation value of estuarine resources', *American Journal of Agricultural Economics*, **77**: 141–51.

Maddala, G.S. (1994), *Limited Dependent and Qualitative Variables Econometrics: Econometric Society Monographs*, Cambridge University Press.

Manski, C.S. and S.R. Lerman (1977), 'The estimation of choice probabilities from choice based samples', *Econometrica*, **45**(8): 1977–88.

McCormack, A. and T. O'Leary (1993), 'Aesthetic Resource Assessment – Forest Parks – Northern Ireland, Republic of Ireland and Scotland', Department of Forestry Working Paper. University College Dublin.

McFadden, D. (1974), 'Conditional Logit Analysis of Qualitative Choice Behaviour', in P. Zarembka (ed.), *Frontiers in Economics*, New York: Academic Press.

Mishan, E.J. (1973), 'Welfare criteria resolution of a paradox', *Economic Journal*, **83**: 747–67.

Mishan, E.J. (1976), 'The use of compensating and equivalent variation in cost–benefit analysis', *Economic Letters*, **43**: 185–97.

Mishan, E.J. (1988), *Cost Benefit Analysis*, 4th edn. London: Routledge.

Morey, E.R. (1994), 'What is consumer surplus per day, when it is a constant independent of the number of days of use and what does it tell us about consumer surplus?', *Journal of Environmental Economics and Management*, **26**: 257–70.

Morey, E.R., R.D. Rowe and M. Watson (1993), 'A repeated nested-logit model of Atlantic salmon fishing', *American Journal of Agricultural Economics*, **75**: 578–92.

Parsons, George R. and Mary Jo Kealy (1995), 'A demand theory for number of trips in a random utility model of recreation', *Journal of Environmental Economics and Management*, **29**(30): 418–33.

Parsons, G.R., P.M. Jakus and T. Tomasi (1999), 'A comparison of welfare estimates from four models linking recreation trips to multinomial logit models of site choice', *Journal of Environmental Economics and Management*, **38**: 143–57.

Randall, A. (1994), 'A difficulty with the travel cost method', *Land Economics*, **70**(1): 88–96.

Romano, D., R. Scarpa, F. Spalatro and L. Viganò, (1999), 'Modelling determinants of participation, number of trips and site choice for outdoor recreation in protected areas', *Journal of Agricultural Economics*, **51**(2): 224–38.

Small, K.A. and H.S. Rosen (1981), 'Applied welfare economics with discrete choice models', *Econometrica*, **49**(1): 105–29.

9. Perceptions versus objective measures of environmental quality in combined revealed and stated preference models of environmental valuation

**Wiktor Adamowicz, Joffre Swait,
Peter C. Boxall, Jordan Louviere and
Michael Williams**

1. INTRODUCTION

Interest in combining revealed preference (RP) and stated preference (SP) data has risen in transportation (Ben Akiva and Morikawa, 1990) and marketing (Swait and Louviere, 1993; Swait et al., 1994). There are few studies in environmental economics, however, that have combined these data sources to examine effects of environmental quality change (Adamowicz et al., 1994; Cameron, 1992; Louviere, 1994). The advantages of combining RP and SP data include an increase in the amount of information available, the possibility of modelling 'new goods' (or goods with attribute levels outside the range of current levels), and the reduction in collinearity offered by the SP statistical designs (Adamowicz et al., 1994). While these features represent significant advantages in modelling the effects of environmental quality changes on recreation demands, a number of important issues remain to be examined. One of the major issues is the use of objective versus perceptual measures of environmental quality.

In this chapter we examine a set of RP, SP and combined models of recreational site choice in a random utility framework. In these models the choices are assumed to be independent and are based on the respective utilities an individual receives from sites in a set of available alternatives (the choice set). The utility associated with alternative i is:

$$U_i = V_i + \varepsilon_i \qquad (9.1)$$

where (V_i) is the deterministic component and (ε_i) is an error component. While most economic analysis employing this structure relies on the use of objective measures of attributes (prices, environmental quality, and so on) to form V_i there are actually many ways to 'generate' the deterministic component. Table 9.1 provides an overview of three possible dimensions that describe data that could generate V_i. The first is the form of attribute data. These include objective measures of attributes, respondent perceptions of attributes, or descriptions of sites constructed by combinations of researcher generated attributes. A second dimension is the manner in which choice data is generated by the respondent. These include choices that individuals reveal in their actual behaviour (RP), or responses to a designed stated preference task. Finally, the RP choices may be based on a choice set[1] defined by the researcher or based on a choice set defined by the individual.[2]

Table 9.1   Data structures for examining choice behaviour

| | Choice data | | |
| | Revealed choices Choice set definition | | Stated choices Choice set definition |
Attribute data	Researcher defined	Respondent defined	Researcher defined
Objective	1 (RPo)[a]	2	X
Perceived	3	4 (RPp)	X
Constructed	X	X	5 (SP)

Note: [a] RPo, RPp and SP are acronyms for Revealed Preference objective data, Revealed Preference perceptions data and Stated Preference respectively.

These alternate structures generate five possible models representing choice. It is also possible to combine the various models. In this chapter we focus on a subset of the possible choice structures and examine the elements on the diagonal in Table 9.1, and combinations of these three structures. This provides us with a cross-section of the possible models, and allows us to focus on the issue of using perceptions versus objective measures in site choice models.[3] These alternate structures are labelled RPo (RP objective), RPp (RP perceptions) and SP (stated preference).

In our examination of the attribute data structures in site choice models we utilized two new features in the estimation of the joint RP–SP models. These joint models are only meaningful if the null hypothesis of parameter equality, after accounting for relative scale differences, is accepted (Swait and Louviere, 1993). We examine these relative scale factors, and test hypotheses of parameter equality for RP and SP models using both objective and perceived data. In doing this we employ a FIML approach to the estimation of the relative scale parameter rather than grid search procedures which were used by previous researchers (for example Adamowicz et al., 1994). The likelihood function we use is also different than those used in previous studies in that it examines the weighting of choices versus choice sets. This issue arises in joint RP–SP models because in the RP data an individual provides information on the number of choices of each alternative from a specified choice set, while in the SP data an individual provides one choice from a series of different choice sets. The likelihood function employed here addresses this problem through the weighting and transformation of the two types of choice data.[4]

This chapter employs data collected from recreational moose hunters in Alberta Canada. These individuals were asked about their hunting trips, their perceptions of hunting site attributes and they were asked a series of stated preference questions about hunting site choice. The perceptions data were measured in the same units as the objective measures and the attributes presented in the stated preference design, allowing a direct comparison between the measures and models. The results show that the RP (objective) and RP (perceptions) models appear to suffer from collinearity and missing attribute levels. The joint model results show that RP models can be combined with SP data and, after accounting for variance effects, there is no significant difference between the parameters of these two data structures. However, it is difficult to choose between the specific joint RP–SP models using measures of fit and other descriptive model performance indicators. We examine various methods of model selection to determine the 'best' model and find that the joint RP–SP model based on perceptions moderately outperforms the other models. However, welfare measurement with models based on perceptions of quality attribute can be problematic. Can welfare be affected by altering perceptions and not actual ('objective') conditions? Will perceptions converge towards objective attribute values? We conclude the chapter with a discussion of these issues.

2. MODELLING AND DESIGN ISSUES

2.1 Random Utility Model

As described above, we examine models of recreational site choice in which the individual chooses one site from a set of available alternatives. Selection of one alternative over another implies that the utility (U_i) of that object is greater than the utility of another (U_j). Since overall utility is random one can only analyse the probability of choice of one alternative over another, or:

$$Pr\{i\} = Pr\{V_i + \varepsilon_i > V_j + \varepsilon_j; \forall\, j \in C_n\}, \qquad (9.2)$$

where C_n is the choice set of individual n. Assuming a Type I extreme value error distribution with scale parameter μ, (9.2) produces the conditional logit specification of the probability of choice (McFadden, 1974):

$$Pr\{i\} = \frac{e^{\mu V_i}}{\displaystyle\sum_{j \in C_n} e^{\mu V_j}} \qquad (9.3)$$

In a single data set identification of μ is not possible. However, in cases where two or more data sets are being combined, estimation of the relative scale parameter (capturing the ratio of the variances between the various data sets) is possible (Swait and Louviere, 1993).

3. DATA COLLECTION AND EXPERIMENTAL DESIGN

The particular form of recreation we investigate is moose hunting in Alberta, Canada. Moose hunting is a popular form of recreational activity in the province. There is also considerable concern that changes in habitat caused by forestry activity and other industrial uses of wildlands will have a significant effect on recreational hunting values. Thus, this research is focused on the effects of changes in wildland habitats as a result of forestry activity.

The study area consists of 14 Wildlife Management Units (WMU) in west central Alberta. This region is also a centre for forestry activity in the province. A survey designed to collect SP choices, RP information, attribute perceptions, and demographic information was constructed (see McLeod et al. (1993) for a more detailed description of the survey approach). The survey also included a contingent valuation question about a management change at a particular WMU. Focus groups were held to aid in questionnaire design and issue definition. A sample of 422 moose hunters from rural towns in the study area and one nearby major urban centre were drawn from the set of provincial moose hunting licence holders.

An important data collection issue was to obtain SP, RP, attribute perception, and demographic information from *each* respondent. Since the survey was considerably long and complex, telephone and mail surveys were ruled out as options. Instead, in-person interviews in group meetings were used. Our survey strategy involved attracting respondents to meetings at one of five towns or cities within the study region. Each potential respondent was sent a letter explaining the project. They were then telephoned and asked to attend one of the meetings in their local area. After accepting an invitation to attend a session, the respondent was then telephoned again the day before the meeting. Of the 422 hunters in the sample, 312 (74 per cent) agreed to participate in a meeting. Of these 312, 271 (64 per cent of the entire sample and 87 per cent of those who agreed to participate) actually attended one of the meetings. The meetings ranged in size from 20 to 60 respondents. The meetings were structured such that the initial portion of the session involved the completion of the questionnaire and the final portion was a discussion on wildlife management issues. Each individual completed a questionnaire within the group setting. The order of the sections of the questionnaire was randomized across respondents in order to avoid ordering effects.

3.1   Stated Preference Design

The particular design strategy we employed involved initially determining a set of decision attributes and levels to represent recreational hunting site choice (in this case, choice of a particular Wildlife Management Unit, or WMU, described as a *generic bundle of attribute levels*; thus, there is no association of these alternatives with actual WMUs). We conceptualized the hunters' decision problem as one in which we would offer them a choice between pairs of competing WMU descriptions, and give them the option of choosing to hunt in one of the described WMUs or to not go moose hunting at all. Each WMU description was based on attributes and levels that were determined from focus group discussions with hunters and from previous research on site choice. These attributes are displayed in Table 9.2. The design problem involves selecting a sample of WMU profile pairs from the universe of pairs given by a $(2^2 \times 4^4) \times (2^2 \times 4^4) \times (2$ versions) factorial, in other words, treating left- and right-hand pairs as a composite set of attributes and levels. As discussed by Louviere and Woodworth (1983), the necessary and sufficient conditions to estimate the parameters of a broad class of multinomial logit models can be satisfied by selecting the smallest orthogonal main effects design from this larger factorial to create the WMU profiles and pairs simultaneously. The smallest orthogonal main effects design consists of 32 pairs, which were blocked into two sets of 16 pairs each using a two-level blocking factor.

This design strategy produced a survey in which hunters were shown 16 pairs of WMU profiles and asked what they would most likely do if their

CHOICE OF MOOSE HUNTING SITE

In this section you will examine 16 different scenarios which offer you the choice of hunting moose at two different sites or not hunting, Please assume that the two sites presented in each scenario are the only sites that you can choose from for your next hunting trip. We want you to indicate for each scenario which site you would choose, if either.

The enclosed information sheet entitled 'Glossary of Terms' provides detailed information about the terms used in this section of the survey.

1. Assuming that the following areas were the **ONLY** areas available, which one would you choose on your next hunting trip, if either?

Features of Hunting Area	Site A	Site B	
Distance from home to hunting area	50 kilometres	50 kilometres	
Quality of road from home to hunting area	Mostly gravel or dirt, some paved	Mostly paved, some gravel or dirt	
Access within hunting area	Newer trails, cutlines or seismic lines, passable with a 2WD vehicle	Newer trails, cutlines or seismic lines passable with a 4WD truck	Neither Site A or Site B
Encounters with other hunters	No hunters, other than those in my hunting party, are encountered	Other hunters, on ATVs, are encountered	I will NOT go moose hunting
Forestry activity	Some evidence of recent logging found in the area	No evidence of logging	
Moose population	Evidence of less than 1 moose per day	Evidence of less than 1 moose per day	

Check ONE and only one box   ❑   ❑   ❑

Please complete all 16 of the scenarios that follow. *Missing any of these questions will not allow us to properly analyze your choices!*

Figure 9.1   Example of the instrument used to gather stated preference data

choices were restricted to only the left- and right-hand WMUs and the choice of not moose hunting in the region at all (see Figure 9.1 for an example of the choice question).[5] Logical reasons why such choice restrictions might occur were suggested, such as floods, wildlife management decisions to close areas to hunting, blocking of access by timber companies, and so on. Such occurrences are realistic and had occasionally happened in the past; hence, they provide hunters with rational reasons why choices might be restricted. Thus, the data for analysis consists of the single choice from a trinary set of options observed in each of the 16 sets for each hunter in the sample.

3.2 Revealed Preference Data

In contrast to the SP approach, RP models arise from information on actual hunting trips. Each hunter was asked to complete a 'trip log' that elicited information on the hunting trips for the 1992 season. Information collected included destination (WMU), distance, dates of trip, party size, length of trip and harvest.

3.3 Objective Quality Attributes

Objective measures of site attributes were collected from Alberta Fish and Wildlife managers who were familiar with the study area. The attributes were moose population levels, access levels, congestion levels, road quality, and presence of forestry activity. Attributes were collected using exactly the same categories as the attributes in the SP task (see Table 9.2). This provides a direct correspondence between the SP task and the objective RP measures. Objective distance measures were calculated by measuring (using a rotary planimeter and a 1:250 000 map of roadways to the areas) the distance between each hunter's residence and a point nearest the centre of each WMU that could be reached by road or truck trail. This distance measure was translated into travel cost using an estimated out-of-pocket cost of $0.27/km plus the value of travel time. Travel time value estimates were based on individually reported full wage rates for those individuals who indicated that they could have been working during the time they were hunting, and a zero value for those who indicated that they could not have been working during this period.

3.4 Perceptions of Quality Attributes

Each individual was asked to provide his perceptions of quality attributes in each WMU in the study region. The respondents were asked to check off the level of each attribute that they felt best represented the conditions in each hunting zone. They were also allowed to choose 'I don't know' for each zone. These attributes were exactly the same as those used in the SP task and the RP objective measures (Table 9.2).

In summary, we model three different characterizations of choice (SP, RPo and RPp) that are illustrated by the following equations:

$$RPo: U_i = X_o \beta_{RPo} + \varepsilon_i; \ C_n = 1, 14 \ (researcher \ defined)$$
$$RPp: U_i = X_p \beta_{RPp} + \varepsilon_i; \ C_n = (set \ defined \ by \ respondent,$$
$$maximum \ size = 14)$$
$$SP: U_i = X_{sp} \beta_{SP} + \varepsilon_i; \ C_n = 1, 3 \ (site \ A, \ site \ B, \ neither)$$

Table 9.2   Attributes used in the stated preference experiment

Attribute	Level
Moose populations	Evidence of <1 moose per day
	Evidence of 1–2 moose per day
	Evidence of 3–4 moose per day
	Evidence of more than 4 moose per day
Hunter congestion	Encounters with no other hunters
	Encounters with other hunters on foot
	Encounters with other hunters on ATVs
	Encounters with other hunters in trucks
Hunter access	No trails, cutlines or seismic lines
	Old trails, passable with ATV
	Newer trails, passable with 4 wheel drive vehicle
	Newer trails, passable with 2 wheel drive vehicle
Forestry activity	Evidence of recent forestry activity
	No evidence of recent forestry activity
Road quality	Mostly paved, some gravel or dirt
	Mostly gravel or dirt, some paved
Distance to site	50 Km
	150 Km
	250 Km
	350 Km

where X_o indicates the use of objective measures of the attributes, X_p indicates use of individual specific perceptions measures, X_{sp} indicates the use of attributes defined in the stated preference task, and C_n is the choice set. These three models form the basis for the econometric analysis in which we examine the models separately and in combination.

4.   MODEL ESTIMATION

4.1   Stated Preference Model

A stated preference model was estimated using maximum likelihood. All attributes were included in the model as were two alternative specific constants (ASCs) (one for each hunting alternative).[6] The alternative of not hunting (non-participation) is the third alternative and attribute levels are assumed to be zero for this choice. Attributes (except travel cost) are effects coded rather than dummy coded because dummy coding incorporates the base category into the intercept while effects coding avoids this by making the parameter value for the base equal to the negative sum of the parameter values for the other three categories.[7] In testing specifications it became clear that there were two distinct groups in the sample, hunters residing in rural areas and hunters residing in the major city in the region (Edmonton). Therefore, interactions between urban residence (urban = 1, non-urban = − 1) and all attributes were included in the model.

The model is highly significant and most of the main parameters are significant (Table 9.3). Travel cost is negative and significant as expected. Respondents from urban areas have a significantly different travel cost parameter, reflecting their willingness to travel further for hunting experiences. The ASCs[8] associated with each site (Site A and Site B) are significant and reflect the higher utility, all else held constant, associated with hunting. The use of ASCs to model non-participation is relatively crude as it does not include any attributes for the non-participation alternative. However, it is a simple and useful approach that should reduce bias associated with models that force participation (Morey et al., 1993).[9]

An access level with Old Trails is the most appealing to the hunters as is hunting in areas with low congestion (No Hunters). Somewhat surprisingly, forestry activity is not a significant factor in predicting site choice. We surmise that once factors such as access and congestion are accounted for, forestry activity does little to explain choice. In other words forestry activity is correlated with access, congestion, and probably moose populations because the activity provides access and often improves habitat for moose. Moose population levels, as expected, are highly significant with the lowest level of moose population having a strong negative coefficient. Many of the interaction effects are not significant but are retained in the model to maintain a consistent specification between model structures.

4.2 Revealed Preference Models

4.2.1 Objective measures model

A revealed preference model employing the objective measures of the attributes was estimated using the actual choices made by the hunters (RPo; Table 9.3). The rural–urban interaction effects were also estimated (but not reported in Table 9.3) as was a set of ASCs (eight total ASCs, six unique ASCs) to account for characteristics not included in the set of attributes. A full set of ASCs could not be included in the model because of poor conditioning of the design matrix. The four ASCs reflect the maximum number that could be estimated after incorporating equality restrictions for sites assumed to have similar characteristics.[10]

The parameters for several attribute levels could not be estimated in this model, either because the level did not exist in reality or because of

Table 9.3 Parameters of site choice models

	RP-Objective	RP-Perceived	SP	RPo-SP	RPp-SP	RPo-RPp	RPo-RPp-SP
Travel Cost	-0.0098	-0.0053	-0.0047	-0.0127	-0.0043	-0.0096	-0.0058
	(-5.4)	(-2.8)	(-17.8)	(-6.4)	(-4.7)	(-4.6)	(-6.1)
Road Quality							
UnPaved	0.1303	-0.0295	-0.0494	-0.0627	-0.0295	-0.0180	-0.0115
	(0.6)	(-0.1)	(-1.5)	(-0.8)	(-1.0)	(-0.1)	(-0.3)
Access							
NoTrail	—	—	-0.1082	-0.2913	-0.1005	—	-0.1348
			(-1.8)	(-1.7)	(-1.7)		(-1.8)
OldTrail	1.4911	0.1037	0.3301	0.7078	0.2808	0.4095	0.3341
	(1.5)	(0.5)	(5.3)	(3.7)	(3.7)	(2.4)	(4.1)
4WDTrail	—	0.1540	0.0624	0.2055	0.0628	-0.1257	0.0609
		(0.9)	(1.1)	(1.5)	(1.3)	(-0.7)	(1.1)
Congestion							
NoHunters	-2.8610	0.3206	0.5967	1.6297	0.5327	—	0.6750
	(-2.5)	(0.7)	(10.6)	(5.2)	(4.4)		(5.4)
OnFoot	—	-0.6137	0.0044	-0.0048	-0.0380	-0.6074	-0.0526
		(-2.1)	(0.1)	(-0.0)	(-0.7)	(-1.7)	(-0.7)
OnATV	—	0.1948	-0.2677	-0.7550	-0.2290	0.1582	-0.3026
		(0.8)	(-4.5)	(-4.1)	(-3.3)	(0.7)	(-4.0)
Logging	0.0726	0.1483	0.0370	0.0316	0.0329	0.0807	0.0357
	(0.1)	(1.0)	(1.1)	(0.4)	(1.1)	(0.5)	(1.0)
Moose Pop.							
Moose1	0.0023	-1.0378	-1.2218	-3.2069	-1.0388	-0.8539	-1.2470
	(0.0)	(-3.9)	(-18.5)	(-5.6)	(-4.9)	(-3.1)	(-6.1)

Moose2	-0.0900	0.1956	0.0040	-0.2534	-0.0064	0.1239	-0.0672
	(-0.2)	(1.0)	(0.1)	(-1.9)	(-0.1)	(0.6)	(-1.2)
Moose3	-1.3721	0.0530	0.4447	1.2469	0.3577	-0.0087	0.4277
	(-1.5)	(-0.2)	(7.8)	(5.1)	(4.1)	(-0.0)	(5.0)
$\theta_1 = \ln\tau_1$				-0.9840	0.1247	-0.2744	-0.1280
				(-5.8)	(0.6)	(-1.5)	(-0.8)
$\theta_2 = \ln\tau_2$							-0.0678
							(-0.3)
ρ^2	0.2437	0.1834	0.2581	0.2566	0.2740	0.2143	0.2445
Number of Choice Sets	199	190	4256	4455	4446	389	4645
Number of Observations (Choice Sets x Alternatives per Choice Set)	2786	1315	12768	15554	14083	4101	16869

Notes:

Asymptotic t-statistics are in parentheses. For variable definitions see Table 9.2, SP = stated preference, RPo = revealed preference, objective attribute measures, RPp = revealed preference, perceived attribute measures. Coefficients on alternative specific constants (ASCs) and interactions of attributes with 'urban' characteristics are not included in this table but are available from the authors upon request.

collinearity between attributes. For example, only one of the three parameters for access (Old Trail) and for congestion (No other hunters) could be estimated. This problem arises because of lack of variation in the data on these attributes.

Using these objective measures of attributes, utility is significantly affected by travel costs and encountering no other hunters (relative to encountering other hunters in trucks). Interacting the attributes with a dummy variable representing urban residence suggests that urbanites are significantly less affected by the disutility of travel and have significantly different preferences over access levels (Old Trails) and moose populations. Some of the signs of these parameters are somewhat counterintuitive. For example, encountering no other hunters has significantly lower utility than encountering other hunters in trucks.

4.2.2 Perceptions model

A second revealed preference model (RPp) employing the perceptions of the attributes by each respondent was estimated using the actual site choices made by the hunters (RPp; Table 9.3). Perceptual information was used for the access, forestry, moose population and congestion attributes, while objective measures of distance and road quality were used. The rural–urban interaction effects were also included in this model, as were the ASCs.

An issue that arises here is the treatment of missing perceptions information. Missing perceptions could be replaced with the modal response from the sample (since the attributes are categorical the modal response seems most appropriate). Alternatively, if an individual stated that they did not know anything about a particular site, it could be removed from their choice set. In this case a site was excluded from an individual's choice set if the individual responded 'I don't know' to *all* of the attribute perception categories for that site (except distance and road quality). If they responded 'I don't know' to any individual attribute perception, their response was replaced with the modal response of the sample points from the same town of residence as the respondent. Thus, the resulting data contain individual specific choice sets where the choice sets comprise sites that the individual reported at least some perception of quality attributes.

The results from the perceptions model are different from the objective measures RP model. First, the ρ^2 value ($1 - \log$-likelihood $(0)/\log$-likelihood (β)) for the RPp model is lower than the RPo (0.1834 versus 0.2437). Second, more attribute parameters could be estimated because there was more variation in the perception attribute data than in the objective data. Two levels of the access attribute and all three levels of the congestion attribute could be estimated. Site choice is significantly affected by travel cost, one level of the congestion attribute, and moose populations. As expected, low moose populations reduce utility. Urban hunters experience less disutility from travel (as in the RPo model). However, the congestion results still appear to be counterintuitive with low congestion levels having high disutility.[11] A final difference between the RPp model and the RPo model is that in the former a larger set of ASCs could be identified without placing restrictions on them. In the RPp model, 12 ASCs were identified whereas in the RPo model only 6 unique ASCs were estimable.

4.2.3 Joint models

Joint models were estimated using either the RP-objective measures data and/or the RP-perceptions data and/or the SP data. These models were estimated by 'stacking' the data matrices from the individual models (RP and/or SP) and estimating a single set of parameters. We estimated four models: SP in combination with RPp, SP with RPo, SP with RPp and RPo, and RPp with RPo. Tests of significance of parameter equality between the individual components (SP, RPo, RPp) and accompanying tests of scale parameter differences were accomplished using the methods outlined by Swait and Louviere (1993). The design matrix of one data set is multiplied by a relative scale factor. This scale factor is estimated as a parameter using FIML methods. The resulting joint model incorporates the difference in scale (variance) between the data series. Hypothesis tests of parameter equality, conditional on different scale, are carried out using a likelihood ratio test of the restricted (joint) and unrestricted models.

An important element in this joint model estimation was the appropriate weighting of the likelihoods from model components. For example, consider the case of combining SP and RP data. In the SP task, each triple of alternatives is considered a choice set and each person provides one response (choice) in this set. In the RP data sets, however, the choice set is fixed for the individual and each individual may make several trips to each of the sites. The RP data can be modelled on a trip frequency basis (each trip comprises a choice within the choice set) or it can be modelled in terms of proportions of trips to each of the sites.[12] This equivalence is premised on the total number of trips being fixed for each individual, which is the case here since the trips were made in the past and cannot be altered.

Assuming that the SP and RP data are independent, and that there is independence among the SP replications of an individual respondent, the likelihood function for the joint conditional logit model can be written as:

$$L(\beta,\tau) = \sum_{n=1}^{N^{RP}} \sum_{i \in C_n} f_{in}^{RP} \ln \Pr\{i|\beta\} + \sum_{n=1}^{N^{SP}} \sum_{i \in C_n} f_{in}^{SP} \ln \Pr\{i|\beta,\tau\}$$

where n indexes individuals from the RP and SP samples; I indexes alternatives (sites); f_{in}^{RP}, f_{in}^{SP} are the frequencies of choice in the RP and SP observations respectively; $\Pr\{i|\beta\}$ and $\Pr\{i|\beta,\tau\}$ are the probabilities of individual n choosing alternative i (as in equation (9.3)) in the RP and SP samples respectively; β is the parameter vector for a linear-in-parameters deterministic component of the utility function and is assumed to be the same in both the RP and SP models; and τ is the ratio of the scale parameter of the SP data to the scale parameter of the RP data (or equivalently, τ can be thought of as the ratio of the square root of the variances of the RP and SP error terms). In the RP data, f_{in}^{RP} will weight the observations according to their frequency; hence, if some individuals took many trips, that observation will receive considerably more weight than other observations. In the SP choices, f_{in}^{SP} will be either 1 or 0 and will sum to 1 over all alternatives in each choice set. Therefore, we specify f_{in}^{RP} as *proportions* so that these also add up to 1 over each RP choice set. The use of proportions rather than frequencies for the RP data eliminates overweighting of each RP observation more than any individual SP observation. Thus, by making the total of the dependent variable sum to 1 within each choice set, whether of RP or SP origin, we have given each RP and SP observation equal weight.

The parameter estimates from the joint models are presented in Table 9.3. The results of hypothesis tests of parameter equality and scale variability are presented in Table 9.4. At a 5 per cent level of significance, the hypothesis of parameter equality between SP and RPo must be accepted. This means that these two models share the same preference structures, after allowing for error variance heterogeneity. At a 5 per cent level this hypothesis is also not rejected for the RPp–SP model. The RP model with perceptions of attributes is not significantly different from the stated preference model. However, the model combining all three sets of data strongly rejects parameter equality. Finally, the RPo and RPp models are not

Table 9.4   Tests of scaling and parameter equality

Model	Log-Likelihood	No. of Parameters	Chi-Squared Value	Degrees of Freedom	P-Value
RP-Objective	−397.2	21			
RP-Perceived	−261.4	33			
SP	−3468.7	28			
RP-Objective + SP	−3871.7	41	11.6	8	0.170
RP-Perceived + SP	−3745.7	41	31.2	20	0.052
RP-Obj. + RP-Per.	−664.1	33	11.0	21	0.963
RP-Obj. + RP-Per. + SP	−4171.0	42	87.4	40	0.000

significantly different in terms of parameter values, once difference in scale is accounted for (as evidenced by the acceptance of the null hypothesis).

The scale parameters estimated are actually for the exponential of the relative scale factor, that is $\tau = \exp(\theta)$, where θ is the parameter shown in Table 9.3. In the RPp–SP model, θ is estimated as 0.1247 with a t-statistic of 0.6. This suggests that the actual scale factor (not the exponential of the scale factor) is not significantly different from unity, implying that not only are the parameters in these two models not different but, in addition, the variances are not different. However, in the RPo–SP model θ is -0.984, and is significantly different from zero (t-statistic $= 5.8$). This implies that the variances of RPo and SP are significantly different and that the variance in the RPo model is higher than the variance in the SP model.

The parameters of the RPo–RPp–SP model should be interpreted with caution since they involve restrictions that are not supported by the hypothesis test. However, the joint models, RPo–SP and RPp–SP, can be interpreted as typical conditional logit models. Note that in this case the elements that were missing in the two RP models (coefficients on some of the attributes) are estimable (Table 9.3). There are more significant attributes in the joint model (relative to the RPo model) and most of the signs are as expected. In contrast to the RPo model, the moose population coefficients in the RPo–SP model reflect increasing preference as moose populations rise; a factor expected in this type of activity. It is interesting to note that this pattern is observed in all models except the RPo model, which is the type of model most commonly estimated by researchers. Finally, it is possible in the joint models to estimate a larger set of ASCs. This was not possible using the RP data alone.

Given these results, which model is preferred? Based upon the tests of scaling (Table 9.4), the RPo–RPp–SP model can be rejected. We reject three other models based upon examination of estimated parameters (Table 9.3): the RPo model is rejected based upon missing attribute levels and the counterintuitive results with some attributes such as moose populations, and the RPp and RPo–RPp models are rejected due to missing attribute levels and similar counterintuitive results. Although the moose population parameters perform as expected in these latter models, the congestion parameters do not conform with our expectations.[13] They also have the lowest ρ^2 of all of the models.

Since our version of the SP model is based on generic sites (rather than specific WMUs) it does not contain ASCs for actual moose hunting sites. Therefore, the performance of this model is also relatively poor using the criteria described above. However, since we are interested in evaluating SP methods by themselves as well as in joint models, we continue to consider this model.

We are left with the two joint models, RPo–SP and RPp–SP and the SP model. The parameters for the moose populations, congestion, and access attributes perform as expected; their ρ^2 values are similar; and all attributes and WMU ASCs are estimable where possible. In order to choose between these models, we examine their performance in simulations of actual site choices. We do not have a holdout sample, but the models we are interested in have been estimated on either joint RP–SP data or SP data alone. Thus, none of them have been examined in terms of their power in predicting RP choices only. Furthermore, we examine how well the model based on objective measures (RPo–SP) performs when perception data are the basis of the simulation and vice versa. More specifically, we examine predictions from the following models:

Predictions using Objective Data (X_o):

$$U_i = X_o \beta_{(SP)}$$
$$U_i = X_o \beta_{(RPo-SP)}$$
$$U_i = X_o \beta_{(RPp-SP)}$$

Predictions using Perceptions Data (X_p):

$$U_i = X_p \beta_{(SP)}$$
$$U_i = X_p \beta_{(RPo-SP)}$$
$$U_i = X_p \beta_{(RPp-SP)}$$

The simulation exercises produce three measures of model performance, a simulated ρ^2, a Pearson ratio test, and comparisons of predicted versus actual frequencies of choice. The ρ^2 comparison is based on the notion that in models of this size a small (>0.01) improvement in the ρ^2 can be interpreted as a superior model in a non-nested test sense (Horowitz, 1982).[14] The Pearson ratio examines the standardized residuals from the model and in a well specified model approaches 1 asymptotically. The difference between simulated and observed frequencies of choice are examined using both a sum of absolute errors and a sum of squared errors.

The results of our simulation exercises are presented in Table 9.5. In the simulations using objective data, the RPo–SP model performs best (highest ρ^2, lowest sum of squared errors). This is not surprising given that the objective model is based on objective (and stated) data. However, the RPp–SP model performs quite well also, with sum of squared errors results comparable to the RPo–SP model and much lower errors than the SP model exhibits. The simulations using the perceptions data are different.

Table 9.5 *Results of tests of model performance*

Data used	Objective data			Perceptions data		
Coefficient set used	SP	RPo–SP	RPp–SP	SP	RPo–SP	RPp–SP
Simulated[a] ρ^2	0.071	0.246	0.157	0.106	0.083	0.178
Pearson ratio[b]	0.71	0.973	0.672	0.66	0.65	0.626
Sum of abs. errors in choice prediction[c]	3.31	2.49	2.43	2.61	3.30	2.56
Sum of squared errors in choice prediction[d]	457.46	290.84	293.64	379.59	434.65	315.01

Notes:
[a] Using the RP-objective data and the RP-perceptions data, and the parameter vectors from the SP, RPo–SP and RPp–SP models, likelihood values are simulated and ρ^2 calculated.
[b] The Pearson Ratio is the ratio of the Pearson residual and the degrees of freedom in the model. In a well specified model the Pearson Ratio should asymptotically approach 1(NTELOGIT, 1992). This ratio is calculated using the simulation process described in the footnote above.
[c] For both RP-objective data and RP-perceptions data, choice frequencies are simulated using the parameters from the three models. The sums of absolute value of differences between actual and predicted choice frequencies are presented here.
[d] For both RP-objective data and RP-perceptions data, choice frequencies are simulated using the parameters from the three models. The sums of squared differences between actual and predicted choice frequencies are presented here.

The RPp–SP model performs best while the RPo–SP model is very poor in predicting choice in this case. The ρ^2 is small (0.083) and the errors (absolute and squared) are very high. Based on this information we feel that the RPp–SP model is the most robust and can predict choice well using either objective or perception information. We conclude that in our empirical example the RPp–SP model is the superior model.

5.   IMPLICATIONS OF USING PERCEPTIONS DATA

Researchers have claimed that choices are made on the basis of perceptions (for example, McConnell, 1993). However, there has been relatively little use of perceptions of quality attributes in applied economic modelling probably because the variation in the data may be reduced when perceptions are employed and/or due to the high level of effort involved in collecting individual level perceptions information. Our results suggest that collection of such data may be useful in modelling choice and estimating joint models.

While useful on the surface, however, some problems arise in using perceptions information in modelling recreation site choice. First, when attempting to simulate choices for individuals not in the sample it is not clear what form of attributes should be used in the model unless perceptions have also been collected from these individuals. Second, even if sampled individuals are being used to predict choice or measure welfare impacts, the use of perceptions may be problematic. For example, if an agency wishes to improve the quality of a particular site by improving one attribute, they may believe there is a base level and a particular target level of quality. In a model based on objective measures, the welfare impacts would simply be measured by examining the difference in utility between the base level and target level. When using perceptions information, however, individuals will have their own perceptions of base quality levels and the agency's target level of quality may be different from the individual's base level perceptions.

One approach to measuring the value of quality changes is to measure the impact of changing each individual's perceived quality level by a fixed amount (a percentage for continuous attribute or a level for categorical attributes). An alternative approach is to change perceptions to the agency's objective measure for those individuals who have perceptions that are lower than the target level, and assign zero changes for individuals who have perceptions greater than or equal to the target. This approach assumes that the individual's perception converges to the agency target level over time (or that the agency is essentially 'correct' and individuals converge to these estimates).

We use the second of the two approaches described above to examine the welfare implications of changing moose populations from level 1 (lowest population) to level 2 for WMU 344. This is a site that has been the focus of considerable research on forestry–wildlife interactions and exhibits the lowest populations and density of moose in our study area. We examine a second change which involves closing this WMU to hunters. This involves deleting it as one of the alternative sites in a choice set and is not affected by the use of perceptions data in the same manner as the moose population change since the site is unavailable regardless of the potential differences between agency and individual attribute perceptions. Three models are used to examine these impacts; SP, RPo–SP, and RPp–SP using the two different data sources; objective and perceptual. The measures are expected to differ because of parameter differences between the models and because the sources of data are different. We utilize Hanemann's (1984) estimate of compensating variation per trip.

Results of welfare changes (averages over the sample) are shown in Table 9.6. The lowest welfare measure ($8.93/trip) is for the moose population change results using the SP model. The RPp–SP model provides a welfare measure that is nearly twice as large as the SP measure and the RPo–SP measure is over six times the size of the SP measure. Clearly, the choice of model significantly affects the welfare estimate.

Table 9.6   *Per trip estimates of welfare change associated with some attribute changes for moose hunters in Alberta*

Data source	Model	Environmental quality change	
		Change perception to agency target[a]	Close recreation site[b]
Objective	SP	$8.93	−$5.81
	RPo–SP	$56.35	−$7.73
	RPp–SP	$16.11	−$10.71
Perceptual	SP	$3.63	−$9.61
	RPo–SP	$1.34	−$7.33
	RPp–SP	$7.44	−$20.16

Notes:
[a] Increase moose population in WMU 344 from level 1 to level 2 (agency target). In perceptions data, attribute perceptions are increased to the agency target level if the perception by the individual is below that level.
[b] Close WMU 344.

A somewhat different picture emerges using the same models with the perceptual data. First, the welfare measures are smaller when using the perceptions data. This is probably due to the fact that individuals are only assumed to experience a welfare gain when their perception of the site quality is below the agency target. If they perceive the moose population to currently be greater than or equal to the agency target, they have no welfare gain. Second, the measures from the three models are more similar using the perceptions data. In this case, the RPo–SP model produces the lowest measure while the RPp–SP is highest.

The site closure welfare measures are less variable than the results presented above. However, unlike the moose population change, the welfare changes using the perceptual data are higher (in absolute value) in each model than those using the objective data. The largest welfare changes for closing the site are provided by the SP and RPp–SP models using perceptual data.

In comparing the RPo–SP and RPp–SP models, the model based on perceptions produces higher welfare measures in all cases except the moose population increase using objective data. It seems that individuals in the sample perceive moose populations to be better than the agency does, and this results in a relatively small welfare measure in response to the population improvement. The fact that individuals perceive moose populations to be higher than the agency probably leads to higher 'marginal utility' coefficients in the objective model than the perceptions model. The fact that WMU 344 was not visited very frequently is not explained by moose populations in the perceptions model, while it may be in the objective measures model.

6.   A DISCUSSION ON THE DIFFERENCE BETWEEN PERCEIVED AND OBJECTIVE MEASURES

An issue that arises from the estimation results and welfare measures is how the difference in data source leads to a difference in results. How does the difference between perceived and objective measures of attributes lead to strikingly different parameters and welfare measures? A first response is that the perceptions and actual measures are not always strongly correlated. There is a significant positive correlation between moose population perceptions and objective measures. Examining the objective assessment versus the modal perceived response by hunters provides a correlation of 0.64. However, similar correlations for access and congestion variables are 0.30 and 0.11 respectively, and the latter correlation is not statistically significant. The underlying reasons for these divergences between perceptions and objective measures is itself an interesting topic for further research. The impact of such divergences on statistical models is also worthy of further study. However, at a minimum, this correlation information suggests that the agency and the hunters differ significantly in their views of access to the sites. Thus, it is not surprising that coefficients, at least for these factors, will be different between the models.

In terms of the difference in welfare measures, hunters generally perceived sites to have higher (on average) moose populations than were suggested by the objective measures. Thus, using the perceptions data in the manner we have, the welfare measures for a population increase are expected to be smaller when perceptions are used. When closing a site, however, the fact that perceptions are generally higher for moose populations suggests that the welfare losses under perceptions will be larger than those under objective measures. These general trends are illustrated in Table 9.6 except that the loss associated with closing site 344 is slightly larger in the objective case than in the perceptions case when the RPo–SP parameters are employed. This may be a result of the relatively large ASC for site 344 in the RPo–SP model (which may result from the lower amount of individual specific variation and lower explanatory power associated with attributes).

There is also very little variation across sites in the objective measures of access and congestion, suggesting that parameter estimation using these data will be difficult. In the objective data there is also no variation in the attributes between hunters. In the perceptions data there is considerably more variation across sites and variation between hunters. This difference in variation can be interpreted as the reason for the differences in scale effects between the models. For example, in the RPo–SP the RPo variance is significantly higher than the SP variance, while in the RPp–SP model, the RPp and SP variances are not significantly different. The variation in the attributes in the perceptions data may capture more of the variation in the observed component of the random utility model rather than the error term. Thus, the lack of variation in the objective data may lead to the higher error variance in the RPo data. This is also supported by the fact that the scale parameter in the RPo–RPp model shows a higher variance in the RPo component (Table 9.3).

7.   CONCLUSIONS

What does our chapter contribute to the methodology of environmental valuation? First it replicates Adamowicz et al.'s (1994) finding of RP–SP parameter equality, once variance heterogeneity is accounted for, and shows that joint RP–SP models are superior to RP models alone. Even combining objective and perceived measures within an RP model appears to improve the model performance, at least relative to using an objective measures model alone. Our study also presents an attempt to scale three data sets. Although the null hypothesis for equal parameters was not accepted in this case, the attempt illustrates the possibility of combining more than two data sources and accounting for variance heterogeneity.

Second, our study is the first (to our knowledge) to examine both perceptions and objective attribute measures within the same general model in a nonmarket valuation context. Researchers have been claiming that choices are made on the basis of perceptions of attributes. Our results on this matter suggest that this is the case, but in our empirical example this result was not overwhelming. The perceptual models performed slightly better than those based on objective data. However, welfare analysis using perceptions data remains a significant challenge. The divergence between objective and perceived measures suggests that a dynamic and/or stochastic model is required. This model should incorporate a mechanism for the movement of perceptions toward objective measures as quality signals are observed by the individual. The model should also consider the impact of attribute uncertainty on decisions and welfare. Clearly, the treatment of perceptions is an issue that requires further investigation.

The one case where a 'fair' comparison between perceptual and objective welfare measures can be made is a change involving recreational site closure. Here there is no question about which quality levels to choose for the base and altered situations; the site is simply removed from the choice set. Table 9.6 provides welfare measures for the closure of one of the sites (WMU 344). Other site closures can be examined but we expect the results to be qualitatively similar. In this case the perceptual welfare measures were larger than the objective ones. This result is in part due to the fact that the perceptions of site quality at the site we closed are, in general, higher than the objective measures. It is tempting to suggest that previous attempts to model environmental changes using objective data may have underestimated the value of those changes. However, further comparative studies must be conducted before this result can be considered general.

Although our model selection tests support the use of a joint SP–RPp model one must question whether the benefits of employing perceptions data outweigh the costs. In our empirical example, the benefits of perceptions information seem to be modest, while the costs (survey time, explanation, and so on) were significant. Also, given the difficulty in measuring changes in welfare with perceptions data, one would need to find significant benefits associated with this type of data to outweigh the costs. While in our sample the gains from using perceptions are modest, it could be that gains in other samples are significant. Our case involves relatively active, intense recreationists. In a less intense activity such gains may be significant.

Third, given the development of new techniques in the literature (discrete choice models and multi-model estimation with scaling) it is important to determine what constitutes the best model. In our study, we used a variety of in-sample tests to support the selection of the joint RPp–SP model as the preferred one. Better techniques, such as out-of-sample tests and approaches where each type of model is used to predict the choices from the other models (Swait et al., 1994), should be examined.

Finally, the issue of choice set determination is a key topic for future research. The size of the choice sets may differ dramatically depending on the assumptions used to construct these sets. Our use of perceptual data to develop individual specific choice sets produced choice sets that were approximately half the size (on average) of the overall choice set. Other methods have also been used to determine choice sets (for example Karou et al., 1995; Peters et al., 1995). We believe this is a critical issue in environmental valuation that has received relatively little attention in the literature.

ACKNOWLEDGEMENTS

The authors would like to thank three anonymous reviewers, the participants of the Fourth Annual Meeting of the Canadian Resource and Environmental Economics Study Group and Forestry and the Environment: Economic Perspectives II for comments on this paper. The research assistance of Kristy McLeod and Bonnie McFarlane is also gratefully acknowledged. Funding was provided by the Science and Technology Opportunities fund of the Canadian Forest Service, the Canada-Alberta Partnership Agreement in Forestry and the NCE program in Sustainable Forest Management. This chapter was originally published in the *Journal of Environmental Economics and Management* (1997), **32**: 65–84. We thank Academic Press for permission to reproduce it here.

NOTES

1. An important aspect of modelling recreation site choice is the determination of the choice set (for example Kaoru et al., 1995; Peters et al., 1995). In the case of attributes measured by an agency, the choice set can be defined as all available sites if attribute data are available for these sites. When using perceptions data, the individuals may report that they are unaware of certain sites or they do not have any information to base perceptions on. These missing perceptions observations could be replaced with some other values

(for example means or modal responses from other recreationists) or individuals who do not complete the entire set of questions could be deleted from the analysis. The latter is probably unwise since considerable information will be lost. However, this approach is often used in applied analysis. As an alternative, one could adjust the choice set of the individual to reflect the fact that if the individual is not aware of the attributes of a site, it is unlikely that the site is part of the individual's choice set. Note that in SP experiments, the choice set is based on site descriptions constructed from the set of site attributes and becomes part of the design of the experiment under researcher control.

2.   Note also that RP models are *ex-post* in nature since the model is constructed on trips already taken, while SP models are based on *ex-ante* information since the individual is indicating which site they will choose on the next choice occasion.

3.   While we use researcher defined choice sets in the objective measures models and respondent defined choice sets in the perceptions models, it is worth noting that these two forms of choice set definition made relatively little difference in terms of predictive ability, at least for these data (McLeod, 1995).

4.   An additional issue that arises in models of this type is the existence of non-participation as part of the choice set. RP applications tend not to include non-participation because data on this 'choice' are generally not collected and because modelling non-participation generally requires some form of time series or panel data structure (that is one must observe non-participation choice occasions). As Morey et al. (1993) point out, excluding non-participation can result in significantly biased welfare measures. In our application, the SP component includes non-participation as one of three options available to the individual. Thus, non-participation is built directly into the choice set and the issue of hunters leaving the activity can be examined. Of course, since the sample was based on hunters, the situation of individuals becoming active as hunters is still problematic as data on the non-hunting public are required.

5.   This stated preference structure has been examined in terms of its performance and consistency with other stated preference protocols. It appears to be a very reliable structure, at least within the context of marketing and transportation research (see Carson et al. 1994; Louviere, 1994).

6.   In order to save space, the table reports the coefficient estimates for the direct effects of attributes only. Coefficients on alternative specific constants (ASCs) and interactions between attribute levels and the 'urban' characteristics of individuals are not reported but are available from the authors upon request.

7.   Categorical attributes are commonly structured in models as sets of dummy variables where one category is designated as the 'base' and its effect is captured in the model intercept. Thus, a four level categorical variable would have 3 columns in the matrix of explanatory variables that are either (1,0,0), (0,1,0), (0,0,1) or (0,0,0) corresponding to the 1st, 2nd, 3rd and 4th categories. The 4th category in this case is captured in the intercept. Effects coding avoids incorporating the base category in the intercept by making the parameter value for the base equal to the negative sum of the parameter values for the other three categories. The columns in the design matrix are (1,0,0), (0,1,0), (0,0,1) or $(-1,-1,-1)$ corresponding to the 1st, 2nd, 3rd and 4th categories. Adamowicz et al. (1994) discuss the rationale for using effects codes rather than dummy codes in discrete choice models.

8.   Alternative specific constants (ASC) capture the 'utility' of an alternative that is not captured by the attributes in the model. For example, the utility of site i may be modelled as a function of an attribute X and an ASC as: $V_i = a_i + bX_i$ where a_i is the ASC. However, since ASCs are not related to specific attributes, they do not explain choice in terms of observable attributes. Thus, ASCs improve model performance, but they cannot easily be used in predicting the effect of changes due to attribute changes. Ideally, one would want to use attributes to thoroughly explain choice.

9.   In a case where the choice set involves distinct groups (sets of sites and non-participation for example) it is necessary to test for violations of the IIA property of the logit model. We examined a nested logit model in which the individual first chooses to participate or not, and then chooses one of the two available sites. We found that the nested

model was not significantly different from the simple conditional logit model for our data set. Therefore, we use conditional logit estimators throughout the remainder of the chapter.

10. For example, WMU 338 and 348 are assumed to have the same ASC since both do not have a lottery rationed bull moose hunt during the rut.

11. Modelling congestion as an attribute is often a troublesome task. Sites are often congested because they are attractive, thus congestion variables may be confounded with other attributes. Congestion may be associated with good access, high moose populations or other attributes.

12. In a data set where each individual has the same total number of choices, either approach will produce identical coefficients. However, the standard errors in the latter approach must be adjusted by the square root of the number of trips to be consistent with the former approach (assuming that the total number of trips is constant across observations).

13. Congestion effects are quite complex and are often non-linear in nature (see Shelby, 1980). That is, encounters with a few people may be desirable while encounters with many may be very undesirable. Our categorization of the congestion variable may not be able to capture all of the complexity of this issue.

14. This 'test' is discussed in Ben-Akiva and Lerman (1985, p. 172).

REFERENCES

Adamowicz, W.L., J. Louviere and M. Williams (1994), 'Combining stated and revealed preference methods for valuing environmental amenities', *Journal of Environmental Economics and Management*, **26**: 271–92.

Ben-Akiva, M. and S. Lerman (1985), *Discrete Choice Analysis: Theory and Application to Travel Demand*, Cambridge, MA: MIT Press.

Ben-Akiva, M. and T. Morikawa (1990), 'Estimation of switching models from revealed preferences and stated intentions', *Transportation Research A*, **24A**: 485–95.

Cameron, T.A. (1992), Combining contingent valuation and travel cost data for the valuation of nonmarket goods', *Land Economics*, **68**: 302–17.

Carson, R.T., J.J. Louviere, D. Anderson, P. Arabie, D.S. Bunch, D.A. Hensher, R.M. Johnson, W.F. Kuhfeld, D. Steinberg, J. Swait, H. Timmermans and J.B. Wiley (1994), 'Experimental Analysis of Choice', in D. Lehmann (ed.), *Marketing Letters: Special Issue on the Duke Invitational Conference On Consumer Decision Making and Choice Behaviour*.

Hanemann, W.M. (1984), 'Applied welfare analysis with quantitative response models', Working Paper no. 241, University of California, Berkeley.

Horowitz, J. (1982), 'Statistical comparison of non-nested probabilistic discrete choice models', *Transportation Science*, **17**: 319–50.

Kaoru, Y., V.K. Smith and J.L. Liu (1955), 'Using random utility models to estimate the recreational value of estuarine resources', *American Journal of Agricultural Economics*, **77**: 141–51.

Louviere, J.J. (1994), 'Relating stated preference measures and models to choices in real markets: calibration of CV responses', Paper presented at the DOE/EPA workshop on Using Contingent Valuation to Measure Non-Market Values, Herndon, VA, May 19–20.

Louviere, J.J. and G.G. Woodworth (1983), 'Design and analysis of simulated consumer choice or allocation experiments: an approach based on aggregate data', *Journal of Marketing Research*, **20**: 350–67.

McConnell, K.E. (1993), 'Indirect Methods for Assessing Natural Resource Damages Under CERCLA', in J. Kopp and V.K. Smith (eds), *Valuing Natural Assets*, pp. 153–96.

McLeod, K., P.C. Boxall, W.L. Adamowicz, M. Williams and J.J. Louviere (1993), 'The incorporation of non-timber goods and services in integrated resource management', Project Report 93–12, Department of Rural Economy, University of Alberta, Edmonton, Alberta.

McLeod, K. (1995), 'Perceived site quality in random utility models', Unpublished M.Sc. Thesis, Department of Rural Economy, University of Alberta.

Morey, E.R., R.D. Rowe and M. Watson (1993), 'A repeated nested-logit model of Atlantic salmon fishing with comparisons to six other travel-cost models', *American Journal of Agricultural Economics*, **75**: 578–92.

NTELOGIT (1992), *Multinomial Logistic Regression Software, Intelligent Marketing Systems*, Edmonton, Alberta.

Peters, T., W. Adamowicz and P. Boxall (1995), 'The influence of choice set considerations in modelling the benefits of improved water quality', *Water Resources Research*, **613**: 1781–7.

Shelby, B. (1980), 'Crowding models for backcountry recreation', *Land Economics*, **56**: 43–55.

Swait, J. and J.J. Louviere (1993), 'The role of the scale parameter in the estimation and comparison of multinomial logit models', *Journal of Marketing Research*, **30**: 305–14.

Swait, J., J.J. Louviere and M. Williams (1994), 'A sequential approach to exploiting the combined strength of SP and RP data: application to freight shipper choice', *Transportation*, **21**: 135–52.

10. Using Geographical Information Systems (GIS) to estimate and transfer recreational demand functions

**Ian J. Bateman, Andrew A. Lovett,
Julie S. Brainard and Andrew P. Jones**

1. INTRODUCTION

Spatial variation, as a key concept underlying much of economics, has been discovered (Hotelling, 1929) and frequently rediscovered in mainstream economics (for example Case, 1991; Fujita et al., 1999). Indeed, economic analyses of recreational demand are, by their very nature, intimately concerned with space. However, these analyses are frequently naïve regarding the incorporation of the spatial dimension within studies. This chapter examines the contribution which Geographical Information Systems, or GIS as they are more usually known, can make in assisting economists to consider the true complexities of space within travel cost analyses of both the value of outdoor, open-access recreation, and in estimating and transferring functions predicting such values and the number of people likely to arrive at any given set of recreational sites.

Because many readers may be unfamiliar with GIS the chapter begins by presenting an introductory overview of such systems and their functionality, focussing in particular upon their applicability to studies of recreation demand. We then discuss the usefulness of GIS in estimating economic measures of the unpriced benefits of open-access recreation. This consideration is then extended to consider the potentially substantial improvements which GIS may afford to benefit transfer analyses. Here we develop a methodology for transferring both valuation and 'arrivals functions'. Finally our concluding remarks highlight certain limitations of this approach.

2.   GIS: DEFINITION, DATA AND FUNCTIONALITY

A GIS can be defined as 'a system for capturing, storing, checking, integrating, manipulating, analysing, and displaying data that are spatially referenced to the earth' (Department of the Environment, 1987, p.132). However, use of the term GIS can be confusing. At one extreme it may be employed to describe a piece of software, examples being Arc-Info, MapInfo, or SPANS (Fotheringham et al., 2000). At the other extreme, GIS is sometimes used to refer to specially tailored systems designed to support activities such as traffic management or automated mapping. Within the context of the research environment, the former description is normally more appropriate, and the term is typically taken to comprise a commercially developed software application, along with the data and computer hardware used to run it. In this respect, GIS are the analogue of the numerous other software applications that are available for the analysis of quantitative data. However, in terms of their functionality, the key factor that separates a GIS from these more traditional applications is encapsulated by the final five words of the above definition; GIS are specifically designed for the analysis of data that are *spatially referenced to the earth*. Hence their real utility in the research environment arises when *geographical* or *spatial* relationships form significant elements in the problem being investigated. Such relationships, of course, provide the physical underpinnings of any successful analysis of recreational demand.

The physical data model used to represent the locations of entities in a GIS generally conforms to one of two types, namely *raster* or *vector* structures (Zeiler, 1999). Figure 10.1 illustrates these two main approaches. In the *raster* data model, an array of cells, or pixels, are used to represent real-world objects. The cells can hold attribute values based on one or more encoding schemes including categories, integers, or floating point values. The raster model is particularly suitable for representing information that has been collected from imaging sources such as aerial photography or satellite remote sensing. It is also an especially appropriate way for depicting phenomena such as temperature, soil type or land-cover that vary continuously throughout space. In contrast, the *vector* data model is closely linked with a view of objects that possess discrete boundaries. Here the position of entities such as points (for example wells, soil pits, houses), lines (for example rivers, roads, power-cables) and areas (for example census tracts, county boundaries, groundwater protection zones) are defined by sets of co-ordinates which may be separated in the case of points, or joined to form linear or polygonal features. The vector data model is appropriate for the representation of data that has been digitised from paper maps, and has been widely implemented in GIS because of the precise nature of its

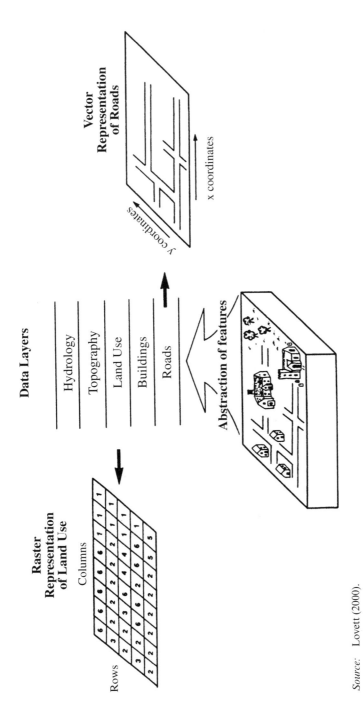

Source: Lovett (2000).

Figure 10.1 Representing real-world phenomena as raster or vector layers

representation method, its storage efficiency, the quality of its cartographic output, and the wide range of functional tools that may be employed in its analysis.

The specific range of analytical tools that are available in any GIS environment will be somewhat dependent upon both the characteristics of the software package and the data model being used. However, most GIS offer the functionality required to answer a diverse range of spatially grounded questions that are commonly of interest to economists. This diversity is clearly illustrated by the research examples discussed later in this chapter. Nevertheless, for the purpose of simplification, the functional attributes of GIS that make them particularly useful in this field can be grouped into the seven key categories outlined in Table 10.1. The ability to *identify* the presence of features at a specified spatial location is of obvious application to recreational analyses where, for example, the presence of broadleaved trees or water features might be a significant determinant of demand. Similarly, determination of the *location* of a certain type of feature also has a wide range of uses, such as the identification of the spatial distribution of neighbourhoods with certain socio-economic characteristics may influence demand patterns for differing recreational assets. This facility can be combined with the *buffering* abilities of a GIS to examine catchments around recreational sites and, for example, identify which populations are most likely to benefit from a given site improvement.

Table 10.1   Typical questions that a GIS can be used to answer

Type of question	Example
Identification	What is at a particular location?
Location	Where does a certain type of feature occur?
Buffer	What features fall within a selected distance from a specified feature?
Pattern	Is there a spatial association between two types of features?
Trend	Which features have changed over time?
What if	What will happen if a particular change takes place?
Routing	What is the best way to travel between two points?

Source: Based on Rhind (1990); Kraak and Ormeling (1996).

A number of GIS features can also inform analyses of temporal change to the environment within and around recreational sites. The identification of *patterns* in spatial data has important applications in landscape ecology models, where the mosaic of different habitats in an area may be a key predictor of biodiversity. Here, GIS can assist with the calculation of configuration measures such as fragmentation indices (Bockstael, 1996). Changes in such indices may provide insight regarding the predicted long-term quality characteristics of sites and their likely recreational potential. Similarly, the ability of GIS packages to quantify spatio-temporal *trends* in data may be useful in a number of applications, such as those concerned with the modelling and prediction of urban growth patterns (Irwin, 2000) and their possible long-term impact upon recreational demand (Longley et al., 2001 and Bateman et al., 2002 provide selections of web-based sites containing information relevant to a variety of GIS applications).

The capacity to ask *what if* types of question can enhance the functionality of virtually any application, from the determination of the likely increase in visitation rate associated with the upgrading of a recreational facility, to the identification of the optimal location for a new facility in order to minimise environmental disamenity from commuting activities (Carr, 1998, applies such techniques to the location of industrial parks). Solutions to such location-allocation problems, where the requirement is for the identification of optimal sites based around user specified criteria, are provided by the majority of GIS.

While all of the above facilities have some bearing upon the modelling of recreational demand, it is the *routing* capabilities of a GIS, permitting the identification of optimal *routes* through road and footpath networks, which has the most obvious application to such studies (Brainard et al., 1997). Here GIS can be used to supply measures of travel times and distances that may be converted into predictors of travel cost. It is the ability of a GIS to enhance the accuracy of these basic measurement exercises and to repeat them for huge matrices of potential visitors and existing or planned recreational facilities which underpins the contribution of these systems to economic analyses of recreation.

Empirical illustration of such functionality is provided in the following two sections. These applications highlight how GIS may be used to combine a variety of spatially referenced data in the form of digital maps and satellite imagery with more conventional variables to enhance economic models. These examples also illustrate how GIS provides an ideal medium through which functions describing recreational values and quantity demand may be transferred from studied 'survey' sites to policy relevant 'target' sites. We also show how the technology may be used to query and visualise model output, for example in the form of maps. It is this capacity to improve modelling, facilitate transfers and display findings that we feel establishes the potential for GIS to significantly enhance economic analysis and decision making.

3.   MODELLING RECREATIONAL VALUES[1]

The spatial analytic capabilities of a GIS make it the ideal medium for conducting travel cost assessments of recreational values. GIS routines for measuring distance and consequent travel time from multiple precise outset origins to a variety of potential visit destinations have greatly enhanced the ability of researchers to introduce much needed real-world complexities into their analyses. Initial applications of GIS to travel cost exercises were primarily concerned with improving the base measurements of travel time and distance which underpin the method, and in assessing the impact upon consumer surplus estimates of such improvement.

The precise derivation of the base data underpinning many travel cost studies is rarely discussed in published papers despite this being initially the most fundamental problem facing the researcher. An illuminating quote from Rosenthal et al. (1986, p. 3) underscores this importance and goes some way to explaining the coincident reticence: 'there is only one primary and essential piece of data: the city and/or county where the recreationalists who visited the site began their trip'.

Visit origin is therefore defined as being some central point of an area (usually just the simple geometric centre, rather than even some population weighted measure). Given the extent of the average city, let alone the size of a county, this lack of precision in such 'essential' and most basic data is disturbing. Some might argue that the above reference is relatively dated. However, a brief inspection of more recent papers, even in the most prestigious journals, indicates that little has changed; as Mendelsohn et al. (1992, p. 931) state in a more recent travel cost analysis: 'In this study, each county is an origin'. Another line of defence might be that, on average, the centre of a city/county might be a reasonable approximation of trip origin. However, living on the side of a city closest to, as opposed to furthest, from a site might well be a very major reason as to why the trip in question occurred. A further problem arises from the fact that site locations themselves are regularly defined in a similar way, giving rise to the possibility of a systematic bias in measurements.

An even greater degree of silence is apparent with respect to how distances are calculated between these specified origins and the site. Again one of the few willing to commentate upon this mystic art is that by Rosenthal et al. (1986, p. 17) who admit that the use of maps can be 'quite tedious' and so, for major studies, recommend the use of 'airline distances' (that is, straight lines) along with the application of 'road circuity' factors. Even if we ignore the fact that roads are not uniformly circuitous, such an approach assumes that all visitors have an identical availability of roads; a set of circumstances which could in fact only be achieved by laying tarmac for

360° and 800 miles (the outer limit of investigation used in the above paper) around each site.

Computer-based routing applications, such as Autoroute, are becoming much more common as tools for the calculation of travel distances. However, while these packages are quite acceptable for calculating the length of long journeys, some concern remains regarding the estimation of shorter trips along minor roads which may be excluded from the databases of such applications. Given that these may constitute a substantial proportion of overall trips any errors may influence consumer surplus estimates. However, it is to be hoped and expected that the accuracy of what can be regarded as restricted 'mini-GIS' systems will steadily improve with time. Given this, our major concern rests with the calculation of travel time.

It has long been recognised that travel time may be the most important factor determining trips (Knetsch, 1963). Although recent research has highlighted a number of avenues for valuing travel time (Bockstael et al., 1987; Larson, 1993; Shaw and Feather, 1999), many studies adopt relatively simple assumptions for calculating the duration of travel. Rosenthal et al. (1986, p. 8) adopt a common shortcut by assuming a constant road speed, and apply this to travel distance (calculated as above) to obtain travel duration. This further generalises an oversimplification in that it assumes that not only road availability but also road quality is identical from all origins (that is, not only does the tarmac stretch 360° around the site and for 800 miles in every direction, but also traffic congestion and other road conditions are identical from all trip origins).

The introduction of a GIS into this analysis avoids the necessity of making such gross simplifications. Precise grid coordinates can be used for both the site and all origins. The actual availability of roads may be examined along with all the twists and turns of that road network, so that precise travel distances can be measured. Furthermore, the road type for each section of a route is readily incorporated into the analysis so that the GIS can calculate more accurate travel times distances taking into account road speeds on each of those segments.

Bateman et al. (1996) describe an initial GIS-based travel cost study for visits to a single site. Here data was obtained from a survey of visitors to a typical open-access woodland recreation site, located within Thetford Forest, East Anglia. Amongst the usual questions asked of visitors was one concerning their home postcode and outset location if different from this. In subsequent analysis a GIS was used to relate this origin information to a 1km resolution grid reference which defined the journey outset origin.

Digital road network details were then extracted from the Bartholomew

1:250000 scale database for the UK. This source provides information on road classes distinguishing 15 separate categories ranging from minor, single-track country lanes to motorways. Typical speeds can be assigned to the different classes of road defined in the Bartholomew's database so enabling travel times to be calculated for discrete sections of road. From these, travel times can be calculated for routes across the whole network. Data detailing average travel speeds for differing categories of road were obtained from a variety of sources (Department of Transport, 1992, 1993; Gatrell and Naumann, 1992; Bateman et al., 1995) with final estimates as listed in Table 10.2.

Table 10.2   Road speed estimates

Road type	Average road speed (mph)	
	Rural	Urban
Motorway	63	35
A-Road primary dual carriageway	54	28
A-Road other dual carriageway	50	25
A-Road primary single carriageway	45	25
A-Road other single carriageway	32	18
B-Road dual carriageway	36	18
B-Road single carriageway	24	12
Minor road	14	11

Travel times from each road segment in the network were calculated via equation (10.1):

$$\text{travel time} = \frac{\text{length of road segment (in miles)}}{\text{speed (miles per hour)}} \qquad (10.1)$$

The calculation of individuals' travel times and distances using the GIS involved three steps. First, the site was identified on the road network and a GIS algorithm used to identify the minimum sum impedance[2] between a specified point (the site) and each unique segment of road. This determines the minimum cumulative time (in minutes) that it takes to reach the start and end point of each road segment. These times are then stored in an output table. Figure 10.2 maps resultant bands of constant travel time (or 'isochrones') which have been simplified to a few categories for this illustration. The figure clearly reflects the distribution and quality of the available road network and represents a substantial improvement upon the concentric travel time zones implicit in studies based on straight line dis-

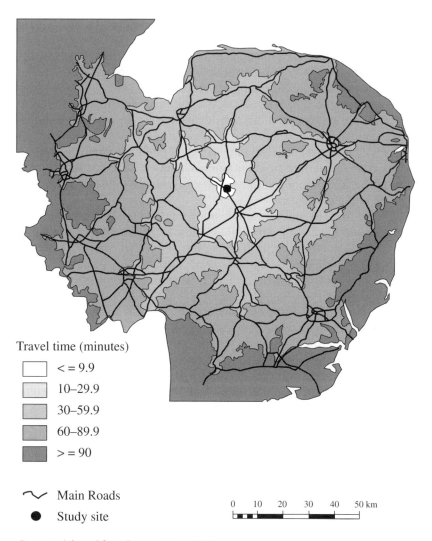

Travel time (minutes)

☐ < = 9.9
▨ 10–29.9
▨ 30–59.9
▨ 60–89.9
▨ > = 90

〰 Main Roads
● Study site

0   10   20   30   40   50 km

Source: Adapted from Bateman et al. (1996).

Figure 10.2   GIS-generated isochrone map for travel cost analysis

tances or which adopt constant travel speeds (with or without 'road circuity factors').[3]

The second step in calculating individual travel times involved matching individual visitor outset origins to the road network. Travel times from each outset origin to the site were then extracted by the GIS.[4] Finally, further

GIS facilities were used to calculate the distance travelled by each visitor along these minimal-impedance routes. Estimates of the travel cost faced by each visitor can then be calculated based upon these travel time and distance elements and the resulting variable added to regressions analyses in the normal manner (see for example, Freeman, 1993).

GIS techniques can therefore be used to automate and improve the accuracy of the basic elements of an individuals' travel cost. In order to investigate the impact which such improved accuracy might have upon resultant estimates of recreational value, Bateman et al. (1999a) compare consumer surplus estimates derived from the approach outlined above with estimates obtained by adopting a number of simplifying assumptions commonly observed in the literature.

An initial focus of interest for this study was the impact upon consumer surplus estimates of using either straight line approximations for calculating travel time and distance from an individuals' outset origin to a recreational site, or adopting the GIS-based methodology outlined above whereby the availability and quality of road networks is incorporated into such calculations.

A further issue investigated by Bateman et al. concerned the simplifying assumptions which analysts frequently adopt regarding definition of the visit outset origin itself. For example, the travel cost studies conducted by both Mendelsohn et al. (1992) and Loomis et al. (1995) use the centre points (or 'centroids') of the US county in which visitors started their journey as trip origin locations rather than the actual address from which the journey began. This can be a substantial and inconsistent simplification. For example, in the Loomis et al. study, median county size ranged from 1181 km^2 to 3925 km^2 (calculated from US Census Bureau, 1995) across the various states considered. In this instance, we would expect that the difference between the actual outset origin and the corresponding centroid would increase with the size of the county.

The use of single outset origins for large areas seems undesirable. However, problems may be exacerbated if the population within a large area is unevenly distributed such as when the majority of people in a coastal county live near the sea.[5] Here a simple geographic centroid may significantly differ from one that is weighted by population.

We can speculate upon the possible consequences of these various assumptions for travel cost estimates of consumer surplus. The impact of using straight lines rather than road distances would seem to be a straightforward reduction in the travel distance and time measures underpinning the travel cost variable. However, it may be that this reduction is not uniform across all visitors, in that the journeys of those coming from nearby origins are likely to be relatively more circuitous than those of individuals travelling from more remote origins. Such factors would result in straight-line approximations giving biased estimates of consumer surplus. The effect of using geographic- rather than population-weighted centroid origins is less deterministic and will vary from case to case depending upon the distribution of population within chosen areas. However, it is the choice of the size of the area for each centroid that is perhaps of most interest. When these are relatively small, centroid origins should provide a good estimate of true journey origin. However, as area size increases, this will only remain correct if true outset origins are randomly distributed across the areas represented by centroids. This is unlikely to be the case even if the population is evenly spread across the area (that is where geographic- and population-weighted centroids coincide). A central tenet of the travel cost method is that, *ceteris paribus*, the lower the cost (that is the closer an individual lives to a site) the more trips will be made. Therefore, in any such surrounding area, more visits will be made from outset origins nearer to the site than from those further away. This means that using centroid origins will systematically overstate the travel cost which visitors from that region are prepared to bear.

Furthermore, in relative terms, this overstatement will be greater for areas nearer to the site than for those further away. This will result in a systematic bias to the estimated demand curve relative to the true relationship (based on actual origins). Here at lower travel costs we substantially over-predict the number of visits, that is the slope of the function becomes steeper and our consumer surplus estimate is biased upwards. The impact of this effect will be directly related to the centroid size used, that is larger areas should lead to larger (more biased) estimates of consumer surplus. Such reasoning seems to be supported by one of the few previous studies to examine this issue. Sutherland (1982) investigated the impact of using circular centroids of either 10 mile or 20 mile width to calculate visitor travel time and distance. Sutherland found that this increase in scale resulted in a substantial rise in resultant consumer surplus estimates.

The above discussion outlines three basic areas for sensitivity analysis:

(i) the impact of using straight line as opposed to road networks (adjusted for road speed) approaches to calculate travel time, distance and hence travel cost;

(ii) whether journey outset origins are precise or based upon centroids of varying size and;

(iii) where centroids are used, whether outset points are taken as simply the geographical centre of that area or whether account is taken of the distribution of population within that centroid.

Empirical analysis of these issues was conducted using the same data as described previously. The GIS was used to identify 1km resolution grid references for visitors' journey outset origins. As expected these were clustered around the site with roughly 90 per cent of origins within 100km of Thetford Forest. The 1km origins form the base and most accurate estimates of journey outset from which welfare measures can be calculated. However, to address the issues under consideration we also defined a series of alternative centroid origins based on progressively larger areas. The smallest of these was the ward – a basic reporting unit of the UK Census. This varies in size according to population density with rural wards generally more extensive in area than their urban counterparts.[6] However, wards are, typically, relatively small areas of between 2–4km width. A set of larger zones was provided by UK district boundaries. These are substantial administrative areas which are generally of the order of the smallest of the US counties considered in the Loomis et al. (1995) study discussed above. Finally, we also used the regions represented by UK counties, which compare with the largest US counties considered by Loomis et al.

We therefore have four resolutions of zone: 1km; ward; district; and county. Figure 10.3 illustrates both the visitors' 1km outset origins and the corresponding county centroids. Inspection of those counties in the immediate vicinity of the site clearly shows that the majority of visitors actually set out from points, indicated by the 1km origins (note that in the figure some of these that are very close to each other have been amalgamated to ease inspection) which are closer to the site than the county centroid origins. This is likely to be the case irrespective of the size or location of the area used to simplify the calculation of outset origins. However, the relative error caused by this effect is much greater for zones close to the site than for more distant areas. This systematic bias is likely to result in an overestimate of consumer surplus as discussed previously.

The GIS was then used to calculate both geographic- and population-weighted centroids for all four scales of zone (exceptions here were the 1km origins where data on population distribution were not available at a level of detail that would make weighted adjustments meaningful).

At each of the four resolutions, travel costs were calculated from all journey origins to the site. Two approaches were tested here, the first assuming simple straight line routes and constant speed while the second approach used information on road availability, quality and road speeds. This latter method recognises that site accessibility increases with the availability of high quality, direct road routes to the site, and declines for areas where this is not the case.

The various travel cost measures obtained from these permutations of calculations were then entered into a series of trip generation functions.

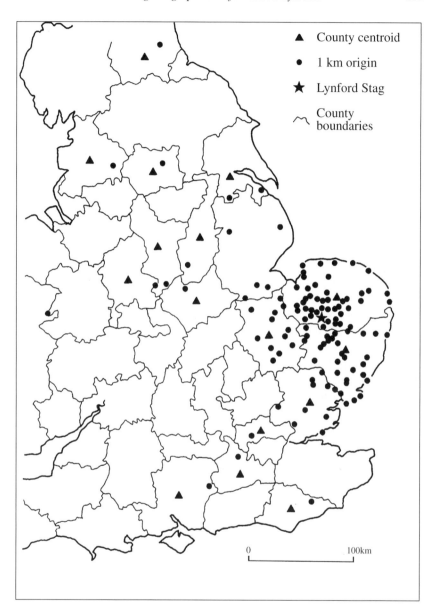

Source: Adapted from Bateman et al. (1999a).

Figure 10.3 *Comparison of 1km resolution journey outset origins with county geographical centroid outset origins*

Statistical tests indicated that defining the dependent variable as the natural logarithm of the number of visits made by a household to the survey site per annum produced the best fit to the data (such a semi-log form is typical of those used throughout the US and UK literature). To ensure comparability across results this functional form and the predictor variables (derived through standard exploratory tests) were kept constant across these analyses so as to ensure that any differences in results were attributable solely to changes in the type of centroid used to derive outset origins. The predictor variables were as follows: travel cost; household size; whether respondent is on holiday;[7] whether respondent is working; whether respondent lives near site; respondents rating of the scenery; whether respondent is a taxpayer; whether respondent is a member of the National Trust; whether the main reason for visit is dog walking. All of these variables were significant at the 5 per cent level.

Following theoretical and empirical arguments (Smith and Desvousges, 1986; Balkan and Kahn, 1988; Willis and Garrod, 1991), trip generation functions were estimated using limited-dependent variable, maximum likelihood techniques (Maddala, 1983). Goodness of fit measures were given by log likelihood values, while consumer surplus estimates were then derived in the usual manner (Willis and Garrod, 1991) and standard errors were used to construct 95 per cent confidence intervals for the travel cost coefficient, upper and lower limits being used to estimate confidence bounds for consumer surplus.

Analyses indicated that comparison of stated travel distance and time with GIS derived measures showed that there was no significant difference (at $p < 0.88$) for our most accurate (1km resolution) origin measures. However, as centroids of progressively larger areas were used as the basis for simplifying individuals' journey outset origins so the resultant measures of distance and travel time began to substantially exceed those stated by visitors during the site survey. Significant differences were found for both district ($p < 0.03$) and county ($p < 0.01$) centroid outset origins. These results in themselves suggest that our central hypothesis may be well founded.

Findings from our analysis are presented in Table 10.3. Here the model highlighted in **bold** is our preferred GIS-based model which uses accurate journey outset origins and takes into account the road network in calculating travel time and distance.

Examining the findings presented in Table 10.3, consider first our assessment of the impact of using straight-line as opposed to road-based measures of travel cost. Here we can see that, irrespective of the type of centroid used to define outset origin, the straight-line measure consistently produces lower estimates of consumer surplus. This is as expected and simply reflects

Table 10.3   Consumer surplus estimates from models with differing specifications of time and distance in the travel-cost variable

Model (see key)					Annual consumer surplus per household (£)	Difference from GIS-based model (bold)	
Area	PWC or GWC	RD or SLD	Travel cost coefficient	t value		(£)	(%)
1km	**GWC**	**RD**	**−0.0281**	**3.08**	**423**	**0**	**0**
		SLD	−0.0343	3.29	347	−76	−18
Ward	PWC	RD	−0.0281	3.03	424	1	0
		SLD	−0.0344	3.26	346	−77	−18
	GWC	RD	−0.0285	3.08	418	−5	−1
		SLD	−0.0338	3.21	352	−71	−17
District	PWC	RD	−0.0236	2.60	505	82	19
		SLD	−0.0269	2.58	443	20	5
	GWC	RD	−0.0236	2.59	504	81	19
		SLD	−0.0281	2.68	424	1	0
County	PWC	RD	−0.0140	1.68	847	424	100
		SLD	−0.0141	1.49	849	426	101
	GWC	RD	−0.0134	1.61	890	467	110
		SLD	−0.0144	1.54	826	403	95

Key:
Area = Indicates the relevant centroid used in each model. Each centroid is to 1 km resolution accuracy.
PWC or GWC = Indicates whether a population weighted centroid (PWC) or geographical centroid (GWC) is used.
RD or SLD = Indicates whether road distance (RD) or straight line distance (SLD) is used.
Bold = GIS-based model using accurate outset origin and road network data.

Note (all models): Petrol costed at 8p/km; Time costed at 43 per cent of wage rate; Identical functional form and variable list (see text). Sensitivity analysis on the 1km model is presented in Bateman et al. (1996).

Source: Abstracted from Bateman et al. (1999a).

the underestimate of true travel cost produced by straight-line approxima-tions. Nevertheless, the degree of difference is substantial, ranging up to 20 per cent for even the most accurate journey outset origins.

As far as the impact of using geographical as opposed to population-weighted centroid origins is concerned we can see that, in this study, there is very little difference in the consumer surplus estimates obtained when accurate outset origins are used, but that non-trivial differences of up to 10 per cent do arise where large centroids are employed.

Finally the effect of changing the size of areas can be examined and here we see the most substantial impacts of the various assumptions that can be made regarding centroid origins, with results fully in line with our prior expectations. The move from defining outset origin by 1km grid reference point to ward level centroid has virtually no impact upon welfare estimates. This is not surprising given that wards often cover just a few square kilometres. However, when we move to using district centroids the biases discussed with respect to Figure 10.3 begin to become noticeable with travel cost coefficients altering as expected and welfare estimates substantially inflated. Holding the method of calculating travel times and distance constant we can see that the move from 1km outset origins to district centroids results in an inflation of roughly 20 per cent in consumer surplus estimates. Notice also that, at the district level, this roughly balances the level of underestimate due to using straight-line assumptions such that consumer surplus estimates appear similar to those derived from our most accurate, GIS-based, model. However, this similarity is merely due to the balancing of these two biases.

The bias caused by adopting centroid assumptions becomes particularly marked when we examine estimates produced from county level centroid origins. Here consumer surplus values increase substantially to the point that those based upon the most accurate outset origins (the 1km and ward centroids) are less than half of the comparable measure obtained using the county level centroids. Notice also that the travel cost coefficient actually becomes statistically insignificant within these county level models, a further indication that such aggregation yields unreliable estimates of consumer surplus.

Given their similarities in functional form and predictor variables, differences in the degree of explanatory power between models were small and confidence intervals on consumer surplus estimates were overlapping (for details see Bateman et al., 1999a). Nevertheless, relative differences suggested that, as expected, models based upon the more accurate outset origins provided by our GIS-based methodology gave a superior prediction of visit numbers. Furthermore, given that most decision makers will be interested in best (central) estimates of consumer surplus, these results do suggest that the use of simplifying assumptions gives some cause for concern and by the same token the use of more accurate GIS-based models seems well justified.

The approach developed above clearly provides a superior method for undertaking travel cost assessments of the recreational value of individual sites. However, GIS techniques also provide an ideal medium for conducting benefit transfer exercises, to which we now turn.

4. TRANSFERRING RECREATIONAL VALUES AND ARRIVALS

Benefit transfer has been defined as 'the transfer of existing estimates of non-market values to a new study which is different from the study for which the values were originally estimated' (Boyle and Bergstrom, 1992, p. 657). GIS provides a ready means for obtaining measures of the underlying determinants of consumer surplus including travel time and distance, travel cost, population distribution and outset origins for potential visitors, the socio-economic characteristics of those populations, the spatial availability of substitutes and complements, and so on. Furthermore, these measures can be obtained in a consistent manner for both surveyed 'study' sites and unsurveyed 'policy' or 'target' sites. It is this consistency, compatibility, availability and richness of measures which provides the quantitative cornerstone which is a vital prerequisite for successful benefit transfer.

The essential assumption required for transfer of travel cost functions is that the coefficient values for predictors, as estimated from survey sites, are assumed to be valid for target sites. Note that only the coefficient is assumed to be constant, not the value of the predictor itself. In this manner we assume that the *relationship* between, say, substitute availability and visits is constant, but allow for the fact that the *level* of substitute availability will vary between sites.

Our initial investigations of the potential for GIS-based benefits transfer is given in Bateman et al. (1999b) which transfers a simple visitor arrival function obtained from the survey of single woodland site described above to five other similar sites located in various parts of Wales. The travel cost variable incorporated into this function used the accurate outset origins and road network data discussed previously. However, in this initial application other predictors, such as substitute availability, variables describing socio-economic variations amongst potential visitor populations, site quality, and so on were omitted from this essentially developmental study. Nevertheless, despite the reduced nature of this function, the GIS allowed the transfer process to incorporate digital map data concerning the available road network (and its quality) and the population distribution (both of Wales and much of England) from which potential visitors might originate. In a test of the validity of this approach, predicted numbers of arrivals for the five Welsh sites were compared with the actual numbers of arrivals as calculated by the Forestry Commission who operate those sites. This comparison indicated that estimated visitors were a good predictor of actual arrivals.

This initial study also demonstrated the ability of a GIS system to readily extrapolate predictions for large study areas. Given the reasonable ability of even this simple function in predicting arrivals at existing sites, the function was then applied to identify the optimal location for establishing a new woodland. To facilitate such an analysis, the GIS was first used to create a regular grid of points across Wales. The transferable function was then used to estimate the number of visitors which would be expected if a new woodland were to be established at the first intersection of this grid. This operation was then repeated in turn for all other points across the grid. The resultant visitor arrivals map is reproduced as the left-hand panel of Figure 10.4. Note that this considers only the impact of creating one new forest, not (as might be thought at first) the impact of afforesting the whole of Wales (an unfeasible proposition).

The visitor arrivals map in Figure 10.4 strongly reflects population distribution in the prediction of recreational woodland visits. In south Wales the influence of cities such as Swansea and Cardiff and the densely populated 'valleys' area results in relatively high visitor predictions. Similarly, in the north-east, the influence of nearby English cities such as Manchester and Liverpool is very clear. Conversely, in mid Wales and western coastal areas, the low population density results in severely depressed visitor arrival estimates. Population impacts tend to be compounded by the distribution of higher quality transport infrastructure. This inflates the already high arrivals numbers generated by the proximity of large centres of population.

The right-hand map of Figure 10.4 translates visitor arrivals into recreational values. Here a meta-analysis of previous valuation studies (detailed in Bateman et al., 1999b) was employed to obtain per visit values which where directly compatible with the arrival numbers predicted in the left hand panel of the figure. The pattern of values is therefore similar to that shown in the latter panel.

The methodology set out above was substantially extended by Brainard et al. (1999). Starting with the basic visitor outset data provided by Bateman et al. (1996), road network and population distribution data were again used to define travel time and distance variables. However, these were also enhanced with measures of the availability of other, substitute, woodlands, socio-economic characteristics and site quality. Substitute availability was estimated by first using the GIS to capture data on the location of other woodlands such as the satellite image reproduced as the left-hand panel of Figure 10.5 (note that various different types of woodland were considered including a combined definition of all woodland types). A regular grid of points covering virtually all of England and Wales was then defined and isochrone maps created for each of these intersections, an example being given as the middle panel of Figure 10.5. By combining these isochrones with the data on woodland location and using empirically derived weights which gave additional emphasis to more local sites, maps

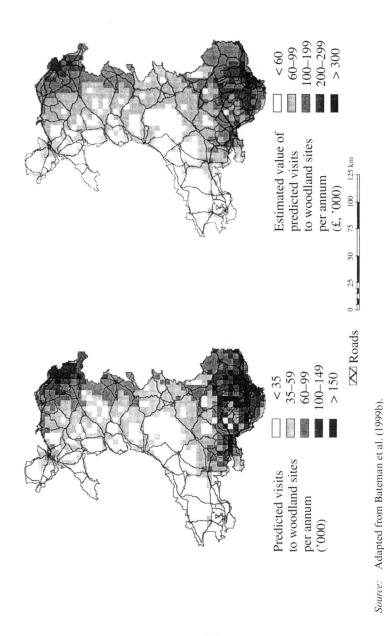

Predicted visits
to woodland sites
per annum
('000)

☐ < 35
▨ 35–59
▨ 60–99
▨ 100–149
■ > 150

▨ Roads

Estimated value of
predicted visits
to woodland sites
per annum
(£, '000)

☐ < 60
▨ 60–99
▨ 100–199
■ 200–299
■ > 300

| 0 | 25 | 50 | 75 | 100 | 125 km |

Source: Adapted from Bateman et al. (1999b).

Figure 10.4   GIS-generated maps of predicted visits to potential woodland sites in Wales and their recreation value

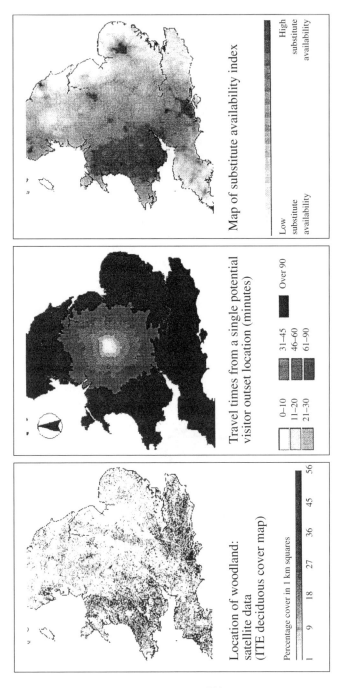

Location of woodland:
satellite data
(ITE deciduous cover map)

Percentage cover in 1 km squares

1   9   18   27   36   45   56

Travel times from a single potential
visitor outset location (minutes)

0–10   31–45   Over 90
11–20   46–60
21–30   61–90

Map of substitute availability index

Low
substitute
availability

High
substitute
availability

0   50 100   200   300 km

Source: Adapted from Brainard et al. (1999).

Figure 10.5   Stages in the generation of a substitute availability map

can be created which indicate the level of woodland substitute availability occurring in every location across this large study area. An example of such a map is given as the right-hand panel of Figure 10.5. This clearly reflects both the location of woodlands and their availability (with major road arteries visible as linear features indicating greater accessibility).[8]

Brainard et al. (1999) also use a GIS to extract data concerning relevant socio-economic characteristics (such as the level of car ownership) for all parts of this large study area. These data were obtained from the UK Census and stored as maps within the GIS. This source also provided details regarding the distribution of population while information on the road network was obtained as before.

Combining the above analyses, Brainard et al. (1999) estimated a transfer model linking arrivals to travel cost, socio-economic variables and the availability of substitute woodlands. Following Lovett et al. (1997), the model was estimated using Poisson regression techniques. This model was then transferred to predict arrivals at a set of English woodlands for which Forestry Commission estimates of arrivals are available. These predictions were refined through an additional analysis taking account of information concerning the quality and facilities available at each site. This information included some 19 binary variables detailing the presence or absence of a variety of site attributes ranging from natural features such as scenic viewpoints and lakes to man-made facilities such as information centres, bicycle hire, cafes and toilets. In addition 6 continuous variables defined items such as the number and length of marked trails, the proportion of broadleaved trees near such trails and the capacity of car parks.

Recreational values were obtained directly from the travel cost functions rather than through meta-analyses and are therefore more likely to capture the characteristics of individual sites. Table 10.4 presents comparisons of Forestry Commission estimates of arrivals with our predictions of visits and recreational values. Given that the Forestry Commission acknowledge that their own estimates are subject to considerable error this comparison cannot be definite, yet the general trend of results seems encouraging with a good correspondence between estimates and predictions in cases other than where models were applied to estimate arrivals at sub-sites within larger woodlands.

The various techniques developed in the above studies have been combined and substantially extended in recent work concerning the demand for informal open-access recreation at inland waterways (Jones et al., 2001).[9] Data for this study were provided from nearly 7000 face-to-face interviews with visitors to 53 British Waterways sites located across Britain. Methodological extensions included the consideration not only of similar resource substitutes (other inland waterways, rivers, lakes, and so on), but

*Table 10.4   Forestry Commission estimates and transfer model predictions
of recreational visits and values for a set of English woodlands*

Site name	Forestry Commission estimate	Predicted visits per annum	Recreational value per party visit (£)	Total recreational value per woodland (£ per annum)
Grizedale	85181	81015**	3.48	281824
Noble Knott	7543	35407	3.51	124149
Whinlatter	55797	60838**	3.36	204571
Blackwater	39338	37518**	5.19	147813
Bolderwood	22963	28503**	4.86	182318
Moors Valley	165552	157561**	4.14	652149
Bucknell	21360	45526	1.63	74117
Salcey	77650	75644**	2.23	168735
Wakerley	51490	42354**	2.06	87456
Dalby	130151	77804*	3.31	257260
Chopwell	42298	54251*	6.36	344846
Hamsterley	76796	71770**	3.50	251462
Simonside	12430	32526	2.94	95462
Blidworth Bottom	54547	41844**	3.15	131776
Blidworth Lane	52754	45103**	3.16	142394
Blidworth Tower	37596	45288**	2.91	131660
Chambers Farm	23605	22808**	1.92	43836
Kielder Castle	24243	56747	3.57	202767
Forest Drive	31641	26200**	3.57	93616
Warksburn	3794	5351*	7.42	39706
Bogle Crag	14924	47475	5.38	255408
Goyt The Street	84279	73400**	2.63	193058
Normans Hill	30936	35975**	2.66	95748
Thieves Wood	72276	45617 *	2.66	121474
Dunwich	18980	15957**	1.56	24828
High Lodge	14940	46925†	1.33	62381
Lynford Arboretum	7101	21356†	2.83	60354
Lynford Stag	42010	14745†	1.91	28098
Two Mile Bottom	22636	22678**	2.72	61676
Sherwood Centre	38919	42325**	1.78	75430

Notes:
** = Predictions within 25 per cent of official estimates.
* = Predictions within 50 per cent of official estimates.
† = Subsites; sites within a larger forest with multiple sites. Excludes three further subsites for which models failed to predict positive visits.
Values are in 1990 pounds.

Source: Adapted from Brainard et al. (1999)

a wide variety of alternative recreational opportunities including other open-access resources (for example National Parks, heathland and moors, woodlands, beaches, and so on), commercial outdoor attractions (wildlife parks, outdoor theme parks, zoos, and so on) and built environment sites (such as historic houses, castles, urban attractions). A further refinement was provided by applying Poisson regression techniques through a series of 'hierarchical' or 'multilevel' models (Bryk and Raudenbush, 1992; Longford, 1993; Goldstein, 1995).

Benefit transfer analysis was conducted by taking subsets of sampled sites from which travel cost functions were estimated and applied to predict arrivals and values at omitted sites. Findings suggested robust relationships determined visit patterns across the country with travel costs to the site being the strongest factor but a host of other determinants proving significant including many of the non-waterway substitutes discussed above. Significant relationships were also identified for a variety of socio-economic and on-site facility predictors. Comparisons of conventional Poisson models and their hierarchical equivalents showed that the latter provided a significant improvement in explaining the data and were useful in identifying omitted variables which in turn provided further gains in overall fit. The spatial analytic capabilities of a GIS meant that transfer of functions to omitted sites was straightforward and resulted in robust estimates of recreation value and visitation which accorded reasonably well with estimates derived from analyses based solely upon data collected at those sites (for example the ratio of observed to predicted visits at the 53 sites considered ranged from 0.63 to 1.72 with a mean value of 1.02 and median of 0.98).

As a further extension to the use of GIS techniques in modelling recreational flows, a simple approach to the transferable prediction of arrival numbers alone is presented by Brainard et al. (2001). Here, rather than modelling the factors which give rise to a particular visit rate from any given potential outset location, the authors switch focus onto the site itself. A model is then constructed relating the number of arrivals at a site to the facilities and activities offered at that site and simple indicators of its accessibility and the surrounding population size. These models are applied to the data on English woodlands described above. As an illustration, the model described in Table 10.5 achieved a high degree of explanation ($R^2 = 0.827$) when applied to the English woodland arrivals data used by Brainard et al. (1999). Here arrivals are simply related to the surrounding population, a measure of accessibility and two measures of site facilities (car park capacity and the length of woodland walks provided).

While useful from the standpoint of a forest manager, simple models such as those presented in Table 10.5 are not readily amenable to the

Table 10.5   A site-based model of arrivals to English woodlands

Variable	Coefficient	t
Constant	+7.561	0.30
Population within 120 minutes	$+5.459e^{-8}$	6.93
Natural log of distance (in km) to nearest main road		
(B class or better)	−0.124	2.25
Natural logarithm of car park capacity	+0.386	5.03
Total length of marked trails (km)	+0.057	4.52

Note: Dependent variable = Natural logarithm of Forestry Commission estimate of the number of vehicles arriving at sites per annum.

Source: Brainard et al. (2001).

estimation and transfer of recreation values. Given this situation, dual development of both simple, site-based models and full benefits transfer models seems the prudent approach for those concerned with both quantity demand and economic efficiency.

5.   CONCLUDING REMARKS

As demonstrated throughout our review of empirical studies, the functionality provided by GIS can considerably enhance the incorporation of a host of spatially defined factors into the modelling of demand for open-access recreation. However, it must be emphasised that a GIS is not a universal panacea for improving data analysis. Indeed, the quality of results obtained depends upon a range of factors common to any quantitative analysis, such as the accuracy of the input information, the appropriateness of the data structures used to store it, and the choice of analytical tools employed.

We have made much of the issues of measurement accuracy (for example, in allowing for road network distribution) and spatial scale (for example, in moving from large area centroids to accurate outset origins). Yet decisions regarding the appropriate spatial data scale and level of data aggregation remain to be made even within a GIS based analysis (Chrisman, 1997). Furthermore, these decisions are not trivial, and indeed may have a significant impact on the manner in which the results ultimately obtained may be interpreted. On a *theoretical* level, the appropriate units for spatial analysis depend upon the questions being asked (Rindfuss and Stern, 1998). Typically, travel decisions are made at the individual or household level. However, this can alter in benefit transfer models where a variety of resolutions may be adopted as the base unit for modelling (for example, regarding the resolution of socio-economic determinants). In *practice*, however, the presence of limitations regarding the availability of data often has at least as great an influence on the choice of aggregation employed as does any theoretical consideration regarding the appropriateness of different scales.

In cases where remotely sensed data is being employed (such as that illustrated in Figure 10.5), the characteristics of the sensing instrument will place the greatest limitations on the spatial scale of analysis, as they will dictate the resolution of the available images and the frequency with which measurements can be made (Ryerson, 1998). However, for travel cost analyses the resolution available from most satellite systems, which typically ranges from 1 to 100 metres, is more than adequate for most analyses. One exception is the modelling of walk-only visits such as those typically made to urban parks and this is a focus of ongoing research within the GIS/environmental economics community.

Notwithstanding the above caveats, there is, we believe, very considerable scope for the continuing development of GIS applications in the field of recreation research. The techniques offered by such an approach directly address many of the limitations in recreation modelling which have restricted previous investigations. As illustrated by the work presented in this chapter, the functionality provided by GIS packages allows the researcher to incorporate spatial complexity directly within applications. The ability to incorporate detailed isochrones into travel cost measurement, to avoid simplifying generalisations regarding journey outset origins, to incorporate and integrate a variety of accessibility, population distribution, socio-economic, substitute availability and site quality variables within valuation and value transfer analyses marks a substantial improvement in the quality of data and analytical possibilities open to the researcher. One of the basic and key implications of this research is, therefore, that researchers should ensure that all future travel cost surveys elicit high quality outset location data, preferably in the form of a postcode or zipcode. Such information is the vital cornerstone of successful GIS analysis contributing not only to a direct improvement in any given application but, perhaps more importantly, to the facilitation of successful benefits transfer across applications and sites.

The applications outlined in this chapter have all concerned revealed preference studies. However, it is our belief that further advances in computing power and functionality of GIS packages will soon permit their useful application to stated preference research. At the moment, new capabilities for Virtual Reality GIS (VRGIS) are beginning to become available. These allow the two-dimensional output of traditional systems to be transformed into three-dimensional 'virtual' environments which can be viewed or explored by users. The development of VRGIS opens up the possibility to convey environmental information in new ways, and may deliver particular benefits to stated preference techniques such as contingent valuation and choice modelling where such systems could be used to deliver scenarios depicting the likely future states of environmental goods being considered.

An obvious VRGIS application concerns the enhancement or provision of recreation sites. The potential for computer manipulated images of landscape change to enhance stakeholder comprehension of competing policy options has already been clearly demonstrated (Simpson et al., 1997). VRGIS offers substantial extensions to this approach affording 3-D, animation and participant interaction such that stakeholders can explore their own preferences for differing landscape options. The explicit link between landscape quality and recreation values clearly opens up avenues for research within this field. Furthermore, a current emphasis on the integration of GIS technologies into World Wide Web sites will increase opportunities for the sharing of both experience and data, and for the design of new survey methodologies that are able to capture much more heterogeneous samples of individuals than it has been possible to include in the past.

This chapter has sought to highlight the great potential which GIS techniques offer for enhancement of studies examining recreational values and quantity demand. This is only one of the many areas in which the application of a GIS can significantly improve the ability of economists to incorporate the complexity of the natural environment within their analyses.[10] The functionality provided by such systems offers the potential to significantly enhance the ability of economists to successfully incorporate the complexity of the real world environment within their empirical analyses of recreation. Indeed the promise of GIS is to turn the spatial dimension from one that is either ignored or inadequately represented, into a key element of empirical economic investigations of the real world.

ACKNOWLEDGEMENTS

The Programme on Environmental Decision-Making at CSERGE is core-funded by the UK Economic and Social Research Council (ESRC). Further funding for the research reported here was provided by British Waterways and the Forestry Commission.

NOTES

1. This section draws extensively upon Bateman et al. (1996) and (1999a). Note that these were primarily methodological developments which did not aim to produce precise value

estimates for the sites under consideration but instead set out to refine the use to GIS techniques for estimating the basic travel time and distance measures fundamental to travel cost analysis. This meant that, in these analyses, we do not consider the impact of substitute sites, this issue being considered in our later analyses as described in the subsequent section.

2. The term 'impedance' is used as the GIS algorithm calculating the difficulty of passing from one point to another. The algorithm used works recursively though the entire road network, keeping information about the minimum-impedance route found so far, until all possible route permutations are exhausted.

3. Further details regarding the definition of these zones and their use within models predicting the number of arrivals at a site are given in Brainard et al. (1997).

4. Comparison of our GIS derived travel times with visitors' stated estimates showed a very strong association between the two (Bateman et al., 1996). While for any surveyed site this would suggest that respondents' estimates are perfectly acceptable as a basis for travel cost analysis, the important advantage of our GIS measures (discussed in detail subsequently) is that they can be prepared for unsurveyed sites to provide the basis for benefit transfer analysis.

5. The Loomis et al. (1995) study considers a number of Californian counties in which this may be the case.

6. This does raise the possibility of heteroscedasticity problems, however, these were not central to the research question in hand.

7. The issue of whether respondents are on holiday raises the problem of how much of the journey cost can be attributed to visiting the site in questions (a less extreme but related problem being that of multi-purpose trips). In Bateman et al. (1996) we address this issue by directly asking survey respondents to state how much of the day's enjoyment is due to visiting that site as opposed to other activities. These responses are then used to scale down trip costs and consequent consumer surplus estimates on an individual basis. A more sophisticated (but demanding) approach is to obtain a mixture of preference and diary-style information including relevant locational (for example holiday postcode) data. Our concern with such a method is the 'Randall's difficulty' problem (Randall, 1994) wherein analysts impute costs which individuals do not even directly observe or react to. Consequently, in more recent work we prefer to estimate separate models for day-trippers and holidaymakers thus reducing if not removing this problem.

8. Note that this model assumes that all woodlands are perfect substitutes for each other. We relax this assumption in ongoing research for the Forestry Commission (mentioned briefly below) by interacting distance to other woodlands with the size of those substitutes such that larger forests are allowed to have a greater impact upon potential visitors than do smaller woodlands.

9. The same authors are currently applying similar techniques within an ongoing study of a larger dataset of nearly 14000 face-to-face party interviews conducted between 1995 and 1998 by the UK Forestry Commission at 159 sites across Great Britain. Results to date confirm the general relationships reported with respect to inland waterways.

10. Bateman et al. (forthcoming) integrates the recreational models presented in this chapter with a variety of related land use change analyses including assessments of the competing agricultural and timber producing value of land, and assessments of the carbon sequestration values of woodland.

REFERENCES

Balkan, E. and J.R. Kahn (1988), 'The value of changes in deer hunting quality: a travel-cost approach', *Applied Economics*, **20**: 533–9.

Bateman, I.J., J.S. Brainard and A.A. Lovett (1995), 'Modelling woodland recreation demand using geographical information systems: A benefit transfers study',

CSERGE Global Environmental Change Working Paper 95–06, Centre for Social and Economic Research on the Global Environment, University of East Anglia and University College London, 65 pp.

Bateman, I.J., G.D. Garrod, J.S. Brainard and A.A. Lovett (1996), 'Measurement, valuation and estimation issues in the travel cost method: A geographical information systems approach', *Journal of Agricultural Economics*, **47**(2): 191–205.

Bateman, I.J., J.S. Brainard, G.D. Garrod and A.A. Lovett (1999a), 'The impact of journey origin specification and other measurement assumptions upon individual travel cost estimates of consumer surplus: a geographical information systems analysis', *Regional Environmental Change*, **1**(1): 24–30.

Bateman, I.J., A.A. Lovett and J.S. Brainard (1999b), 'Developing a methodology for benefit transfers using geographical information systems: modelling demand for woodland recreation', *Regional Studies*, **33**(3): 191–205.

Bateman, I.J., A.P. Jones, A.A. Lovett, I. Lake and B.H. Day (2002), 'Applying geographical information systems (GIS) to environmental and resource economics', *Environmental and Resource Economics*, **22**(1–2): 219–69.

Bateman, I.J., A.A. Lovett and J.S. Brainard (forthcoming), *Applied Environmental Economics: a GIS Approach to Cost-Benefit Analysis*, Cambridge: Cambridge University Press.

Bockstael, N.E. (1996), 'Modelling economics and ecology: The importance of a spatial perspective', *American Journal of Agricultural Economics*, **78** (December): 1168–80.

Bockstael, N.E., I.E. Strand Jr and W.M. Hanemann (1987), 'Time and the recreational demand model', *American Journal of Agricultural Economics*, **69**(2): 293–302.

Boyle, K.J. and J.C. Bergstrom (1992), 'Benefit transfer studies: myths, pragmatism, and idealism', *Water Resources Research*, **28**(3): 657–63.

Brainard, J.S., A.A. Lovett and I.J. Bateman (1997), 'Using isochrone surfaces in travel cost models', *Journal of Transport Geography*, **5**(2): 117–26.

Brainard, J.S., A.A. Lovett and I.J. Bateman (1999), 'Integrating geographical information systems into travel cost analysis and benefit transfer', *International Journal of Geographical Information Systems*, **13**(3): 227–46.

Brainard, J.S., I.J. Bateman and A.A. Lovett (2001), 'Modelling demand for recreation in English woodlands', *Forestry*, **74**(5): 423–38.

Bryk, A.S. and S.W Raudenbush (1992), *Hierarchical Linear Models*, Newbury Park: Sage.

Carr, A.P. (1998), 'Choctaw Eco-Industrial Park: an ecological approach to industrial land-use planning and design', *Landscape and Urban Planning*, **42**(2–4): 239–57.

Case, A.C. (1991), 'Spatial patterns in household demand', *Econometrica*, **59**: 953–65.

Chrisman, N.R. (1997), *Exploring Geographic Information Systems*, New York: John Wiley.

Department of Transport (1992), 'London traffic monitoring report 1992', *Transport Statistics Report*, London: Department of Transport.

Department of Transport (1993), 'Vehicle speeds in Great Britain', *Statistics Bulletin 93(30)*, London: Department of Transport.

Department of the Environment (DoE) (1987), *Handling Geographic Information: Report of the Committee of Enquiry chaired by Lord Chorley*, London: HMSO.

Fotheringham, A.S., C. Brunsdon and M. Charlton (2000), *Quantitative Geography: Perspectives on Spatial Data Analysis*, London: Sage Publications.

Freeman, A.M. III (1993), *The Measurement of Environmental and Resource Values: Theory and Methods*, Washington, DC: Resources for the Future.

Fujita, M., P. Krugman and A. Venables (1999), *The Spatial Economy: Cities, Regions, and International Trade*, Cambridge, MA: The MIT Press.

Gatrell, A.C. and I. Naumann (1992), 'Hospital location planning: a pilot GIS study', *Mapping Awareness '92*, London: Blenheim Online.

Goldstein, H. (1995), *Multilevel Statistical Models*, 2nd edn, London: Edward Arnold.

Irwin, E.G. (2000), 'Using spatial data and methods to study rural–urban change', paper presented at Rural Policy: Issues, Data Needs and Data Access Conference, Washington D.C.

Jones, A.P., I.J. Bateman and J. Wright (2001), *Predicting and Valuing Informal Recreation Use of Inland Waterways: Report to British Waterways*, Centre for Social and Economic Research on the Global Environment, University of East Anglia and University College London, 81 pp.

Knetsch, J.L. (1963), 'Outdoor recreation demands and benefits', *Land Economics*, **39**(4): 387–96.

Kraak, M.J. and F.J. Ormeling (1996), *Cartography: Visualisation of Spatial Data*, Harlow, UK: Longman.

Larson, D.M. (1993), 'Joint recreation choices and the implied values of time', *Land Economics*, **69**(3): 270–86.

Longford, N.T. (1993), *Random Coefficient Models*, Oxford: Clarendon Press.

Longley, P.A., M.F. Goodchild, D.J. Maguire and D.W. Rhind (2001), *Geographic Information Systems and Science*, Chichester, UK: John Wiley & Sons Ltd.

Loomis, J.B., B. Roach, F. Ward and R. Ready (1995), 'Testing transferability of recreation demand models across regions: a study of Corps of Engineers' reservoirs', *Water Resources Research*, **31**(3): 721–30.

Lovett, A.A. (2000), 'GIS and Environmental Management', in T. O'Riordan (ed.), *Environmental Science for Environmental Management*, Harlow: Prentice Hall, pp. 267–85.

Lovett, A.A., J.S. Brainard and I.J. Bateman (1997), 'Improving benefit transfer demand functions: a GIS approach', *Journal of Environmental Management*, **51**: 373–89.

Maddala, G.S. (1983), *Limited-Dependent and Qualitative Variables in Econometrics*, Cambridge: Cambridge University Press.

Mendelsohn, R., J. Hof, G. Peterson and R. Johnson (1992), 'Measuring recreation values with multiple destination trips', *American Journal of Agricultural Economics*, **24**(4): 926–33.

Randall, A. (1994), 'A difficulty with the travel cost method', *Land Economics*, **70**(1): 88–96.

Rhind, D.W. (1990), 'Global Databases and GIS', in M.J. Foster and P.J. Shand (eds), *The Association for Geographical Information Yearbook 1990*, London: Taylor & Francis.

Rindfuss, R.R. and P.C. Stern (1998), 'Linking Remote Sensing and Social Science: The need for challenges', in D. Liverman, E.F. Moran, R.R. Rindfuss and P.C. Stern (eds), *People and Pixels: Linking Remote Sensing and Social Science*, Washington DC: National Academy Press, pp. 1–27.

Rosenthal, D.H., D.M. Donnelly, M.B. Schiffhauer and G.E. Brink (1986), 'User's guide to RMTCM: software for travel cost analysis', *General Technical Report RM-132*, United States Department of Agriculture: Forest Service, Rocky Mountain Forest and Range Experiment Station, Fort Collins, Colorado.

Ryerson, R.A. (ed.) (1998), *Manual of Remote Sensing*, New York: John Wiley.

Simpson, I.A., D. Parsisson, N. Hanley and C.H. Bullock (1997), 'Envisioning future landscapes in the Environmentally Sensitive Areas of Scotland', *Transactions of the Institute of British Geographers*, **22**(3): 307–20.

Shaw, W.D. and P. Feather (1999), 'Possibilities for including the opportunity cost of time in recreation demand systems', *Land Economics*, **75**(4): 592–602.

Smith, V.K. and W.H. Desvousges (1986), *Measuring Water Quality Benefits*, Boston: Kluwer-Nijhoff.

Sutherland, R.J. (1982), 'The sensitivity of travel cost estimates of recreation demand to the functional form and definition of origin zones', *Western Journal of Agricultural Economics*, **7**(1): 87–98.

U.S. Census Bureau (1995), U.S. Census Bureau, URL: http://www.census.gov/, May 1995.

Willis, K.G. and G.D. Garrod (1991), 'An individual travel cost method of evaluating forest recreation', *Journal of Agricultural Economics*, **42**: 33–42.

Zeiler, M. (1999), *Modelling our World: The ESRI Guide to Geodatabase Design*, Redlands, CA: ESRI Press.

11. Backcountry recreationists' valuation of forest and park management features in wilderness parks of the Western Canadian Shield

Peter C. Boxall, David O. Watson and Jeffrey Englin

1. INTRODUCTION

Few studies of the recreational value of Canadian forest ecosystems have been undertaken. The expansion of the forest industry, agriculture, and urban development is making an understanding of these values more important. As industrial uses of the forest continue, knowledge of the relationship between the market and non-market values of goods and services provided by forests will become more important. Consequently, a major research effort was initiated in 1992 to estimate the non-market values associated with backcountry recreation in a system of five wilderness parks in Manitoba and Ontario (see Watson et al., 1994; Englin et al., 1996; Boxall et al., 1995). This chapter reports on one aspect of this effort – the influence of forest characteristics, levels of development, and recreation management features on recreation site choice and valuation. For this analysis one Manitoba park, Nopiming Provincial Park, was chosen as a case study. This park was selected because its management involved an ongoing registration system for backcountry visitors, it has no entrance fees or access restrictions, and because nearly all visitors drove to the park, making travel cost analyses attractive. The ecosystem types and diversity found in Nopiming are similar to those in the other four parks. These features, along with the fact that many backcountry recreationists visit more than one park in this system (Watson et al. in prep.), make studies of their activities in Nopiming representative of the five parks.

The analysis utilizes a multinomial logit version of the travel cost random utility model. The random utility model (RUM) was chosen because it allows the direct valuation of forest attributes, a key objective of the study.[1] The RUM, as applied in this analysis, focuses on the values associated with a number of attributes of backcountry canoeing routes. These include four ecosystem variables and three park management-related variables. The effect of relatively recent forest fires, which are an important historical influence on Canadian Shield forested landscapes, is also examined. Per trip values for hectares of different forest ecosystems and management characteristics are estimated by focusing on them as attributes of recreation site choice. These make comparisons between harvesting and recreational use of forests more straightforward, and provide needed information for assessing fire impacts and multiple use forest planning models. Valuing the management attributes provides justification for park management budgets and helps to prioritize specific management projects.

2. THEORETICAL BACKGROUND

The RUM involves assuming that a recreationist, represented by i, receives utility from visiting a wilderness site, j, which can be represented by U_j. This utility is composed of two parts, a deterministic portion V_j and a random error term ε_j such that:

$$(U_j = V_j + \varepsilon_j), \tag{11.1}$$

This general model can be applied to recreation site choice by considering that an individual faces a choice of one site from a set of C possible sites in a park or wilderness area. Each recreation trip occasion is assumed independent of the others, and site choice is modelled as a function of the characteristics of each alternative site in the park. The probability (π) that site j will be visited is equal to the probability that the utility gained from visiting j is greater than or equal to the utilities of choosing any other site. Thus for individual i:

$$\pi_i(j) = \text{Prob}[V_{ij} + \varepsilon_{ij} \geq V_{ik} + \varepsilon_{ik}; \forall k \in C] \tag{11.2}$$

The conditional logit model estimates these probabilities if the ε's are assumed to be independently distributed Type-I Extreme Value variates (Weibull). McFadden (1974) showed that this assumption allows the site choice probabilities to take the conditional logit form:

$$\pi_i(j) = \frac{\exp(V_{ij})}{\sum_{k \in C} \exp(V_{ik})}. \tag{11.3}$$

Once the variables in the observed or deterministic component of the utility function V are specified and a functional form selected, one can estimate parameters of the utility function using maximum likelihood techniques. The functional form commonly chosen for V is linear (for example, Bockstael et al., 1989; Coyne and Adamowicz, 1992):

$$V_{ij}\beta_1 = \beta_2 X_{ij2} + \beta_3 X_{ij3} + \cdots + \beta_n X_{ijn} + \mu(Y_i - P_{ij}), \qquad (11.4)$$

where X_{ijn} represents n site attribute variables, Y_i is income, P_{ij} is the travel cost of visiting the site, and the βs and μ are parameters to be estimated. Income generally drops out of the formulation because it does not vary by site; in essence site probabilities are assumed to be homogenous of degree zero in income (see Morey et al. (1993) for an alternative approach when individual incomes are available).

Using this model to examine recreation choice behaviour requires a set of recreation sites (C) among which individuals are choosing to visit, as well as actual objective quantitative assessments of the attributes associated with the different sites. This information comprises the values of the various X_ns assumed to be important inputs in a recreationist's indirect utility function (V). This, coupled with a set of data which provides the actual choices or revealed preferences of the recreationists for the sites in C, allows estimation of the conditional logit model using maximum likelihood techniques.

The underlying utility theory allows computation of per trip welfare estimates. Hanemann (1982) showed that the expected utility on any given choice occasion is the sum of utility gained from each choice times its respective probability of being chosen. He used expected utility to estimate the compensating variation associated with a change in prices or quality attributes associated with choices. Thus, measuring a change in welfare associated with decreasing some quality attribute in the indirect utility function involves estimating the amount individuals must be compensated to remain at the same utility level as before the decrease. The following formula from Hanemann (1982) shows this calculation:

$$CV = -\frac{1}{\mu}[\ln(\Sigma_{j \in C}\exp(V_{j0})) - \ln(\Sigma_{j \in C}\exp(V_{j1}))], \qquad (11.5)$$

where CV is the expected compensating variation, μ is the marginal utility of income, V_{j0} is the utility level in the initial state or quality level, V_{j1} is the utility level following a change in quality.

3. DATA DEVELOPMENT

3.1 The Study Area

Nopiming Provincial Park is a 1440 km^2 area located about 145 km east of Winnipeg. It is situated in the Precambrian Shield area and contains numerous rock outcrops and flat hummocky bogs. The rock outcrops can rise as much as 36 metres above the surrounding countryside and are a prominent feature in the park. The park is poorly drained and contains some sedge meadows, bogs, rivers and many lakes of differing sizes. The river systems, which include the Manigotagan, Moose, Black, Oiseau, and Winnipeg Rivers, contain many small rapids and waterfalls and thus are attractive to backcountry recreationists interested in canoeing and kayaking. Nopiming is the only park in a system of three parks in eastern Manitoba in which logging is currently permitted on a limited scale. As a result, the presence of logging in Nopiming is one the significant environmental issues in the province of Manitoba.

3.2 Environmental Characteristics

Most of the land in the park is forested. The rock outcrops are covered with jack pine (*Pinus banksiana Lamb.*) in varying size classes. The bogs contain mostly black spruce (*Picea mariana (Mill.) BSP.*) although tamarack (*Larix laricina (Du Roi) K. Koch*) is also present. Due to a recent history of widespread fires jack pine has gained prevalence and is probably the most abundant tree species in the park, followed by black spruce, trembling aspen (*Populus tremuloides Michx.*), and white spruce (*Picea glauca (moench) Voss*). Other tree species are also present but are not nearly as common as these. The recent fire history coupled with the limited logging has resulted in large areas of regeneration. Rarely does a stand cover more than a 20 hectare area.

The efforts to obtain information about the landscape, forest and recreation features for backcountry waterway routes (hereafter called canoe routes) in the park took several forms. The research team actually travelled along each route and systematically collected information on the quality and quantity of campsites and portages, noteworthy landscape features including the proximity of cutblocks, and the presence of cottages, bridges, waterfalls, rapids and motor boats (see Watson et al., 1994).

In addition, a copy of the provincial forest inventory database was obtained and the forest company (at the time Abitibi-Price Inc.) provided fire history maps and cutblock information for the period 1989–93 for those townships included in the park. The township and base data were loaded into a geographical information system (GIS) where canoe routes were buffered to 200m (including islands), while fires and cutblocks were buffered to 2km in intervals of 200m. Most forest stands were classified into species based upon the inventory classification which was based upon (i) the predominant tree species present in a stand (comprising >40 per cent of the trees) and (ii) two age classes based on cutting class. Species included jack pine, black spruce, white spruce and aspen. For simplicity two age classes were used: 'mature', which included trees of 10m height or greater and/or which have reached rotation age (cutting classes 3, 4 and 5); and 'young' which included the smaller sized trees and disturbed areas that in some cases have been restocked (cutting class 0, 1 and 2).

Overlays among the canoe buffers and forest and other data were performed using a GIS method. This process generated an output map and data table that summarized the information about all input layers. An area analysis on all buffered areas was conducted. In addition, coverages were also measured for the length of the canoe route they comprised. This produced a measure of the lineal length of the shoreline of each ecosystem type along each canoe route.

Forest industry harvest data for the period 1990–93 (hereafter called cutblocks) was incorporated into the GIS database. The area of canoe route 200m buffers that comprised these cutblocks was calculated and used as an environmental attribute. The area of cutblocks in any route was not very large (93 of 5300 ha buffer area was the largest), and the forestry company is required to leave forest buffers along all water routes. This suggests that recent cutblocks are difficult to see while travelling the routes and that most individuals may never know that they are there. In fact observations of recreationists while the authors travelled the routes support this suggestion. Few, if any, individuals were observed to venture more than about 50 metres on land from the water. However, the presence of cutblocks may affect other environmental features that influence canoe route choice behaviour. One of these may be wildlife habitat heterogeneity which could have an impact on wildlife populations and species complexes for viewing.

3.3 Backcountry Recreation Data

Park staff have maintained a voluntary backcountry registration system for at least five years at six designated backcountry entry points. Preliminary analysis of registration records for 1991 and 1992 (Englin et al., 1996) suggest that at least 250 camping parties visit the park in a year for backcountry recreation. Eight different backcountry canoe routes were identified from information on these early registrations. Upon inspection of maps of the park it seemed likely that there are other entry points to the backcountry areas. Following discussions with park visitors and park managers an additional 11 registration stations (for a total of 17) were established throughout the park in the spring of 1993. Each station was located near parking areas and contained a wooden box holding a specially designed registration survey form, maps, and signage attempting to facilitate completion of the registration survey. Voluntary registration systems may not be the ideal method, but given budgetary limitations other methods, such as personal contacts and interviews, were not feasible.[2] Watson et al. (1994) describe the considerable effort used to enhance compliance with the registration survey system.

The survey, shown in Watson et al. (1994), asked for the name and address of the group leader, the number of people in the group, information about the social backgrounds of the group members, type and number of watercraft, the start and completion dates of the trip, the number of times they had visited the route in the last ten years, their awareness of other routes in the park, and they were asked to trace their expected route and camping locations on a map located on the back of the survey.

The registrants' postal or zip code and town or city of residence was used to calculate travel distances between their residence and backcountry entry points in the park. This was done with a planimeter and road maps. For larger cities which contributed a large number of respondents (for example Winnipeg), the postal code system was used to divide the city into smaller regions in order to provide more accurate estimates of distances travelled. An estimate of household income for registrants was determined by linking their postal or zip code with the most recent census data. The resulting income estimate may be inaccurate, but in the absence of other information represents the best available. This type of estimate, however, is common in other travel cost studies (for example Cesario, 1976).

The distance and income measures were used in the following formula to calculate travel costs for each registrant:

travel cost = \$0.22* distance + [1/50*1/3* (income/2040)*distance].

This formula identifies the two components of travel cost: (i) the out-of-pocket expenses for the vehicle, estimated at \$0.22/km (Alberta Motor Association, pers. comm.); and (ii) the opportunity costs of travel time, estimated at one third of the wage rate (Cesario, 1979). Note that in this second term an average speed (including stops) of 50 kph is assumed, and that the hourly wage rate was calculated by dividing income by an estimate of hours worked (2040) during the year. This formula is commonly used to estimate travel costs in the recreation economic literature (for example, McConnell, 1985).

To facilitate preliminary understanding of the importance of various features of the park to backcountry recreationists, a focus group discussion was held with a random sample of 12 individuals drawn from the 1992 registrations. The results suggested that landscape/scenery attributes were rated most important by the recreationists. Other features were rated lower. In order of importance these were: maintained portages, degree of difficulty, diversity of water, wildlife viewing, access, campsites, fishing/hunting potential, and the presence of facilities such as firepits, pit privies and picnic tables. The importance of the landscape attribute was probed further by providing photographic images of vegetation types. Of the predominate vegetation in the area, jack pine stands were rated highest followed by (in order) mixed predominantly coniferous stands, wild berries and bushes, black spruce stands, white spruce stands, mixed predominantly hardwood stands, and areas burned in 1983 fires.

Colour pictures of cutblocks were shown to the participants, but they had difficulty distinguishing them from burned areas. The majority of participants indicated that they had never seen physical evidence of logging in the park and that logging activities had not affected their selection and use of routes. They considered the presence of cottages along canoe routes as detracting from their experience; many indicated they avoid areas where they were found or move through them as quickly as possible. Finally, most participants agreed that power boats negatively influenced their experience and suggested they come to Nopiming largely to get away from power boats which are common in other similar recreation areas in eastern Manitoba.

3.4 Variable and Model Selection

Prior to estimating the economic models, a compilation of the characteristics of the water routes in the park was performed. Variables were constructed based on the route inventories, inspection of maps, and GIS analysis. With respect to the forest variables a number of specifications involving mixed species classes were attempted. This resulted in a high degree of collinearity between forest variables and potential over-specification of the choice model. A set of forest ecosystem variables were finally chosen which worked best and performed according to prior expectations from the focus group and preliminary analysis (Englin et al., 1996).

These forest variables and other recreation and park features were examined for statistical significance in explaining the probability of choosing one of the 20 routes in the park. Each recreationist was assumed to travel along the entire water route so the characteristics found in the buffers along the entire length of the route was used in the analysis. The multinomial logit analysis in LIMDEP was used to estimate the RUM models.

The tree species and fire variables (hereafter called forest variables) were examined in two ways. The first involved their contribution to the *length* of the water route. The second involved their contribution to the *area* of the 200m route buffers developed with the GIS. This second specification was intuitively more appealing due to the likelihood that the length specification would not capture the true magnitude or influence of the forest variables from a visual perspective. Preliminary statistical results using the length specification were also inferior to the area specification.

Alternative specific constants (ASCs) were used to account for some of the differences in utilities not explained by quality attributes. Ideally one would wish to include an ASC for all but one site. However, collinearity among the ASCs and other explanatory variables precluded the use of the entire set. Instead, ASCs were included for sites that had unusual characteristics. While several combinations of ASCs were examined, in most cases the parameters were insignificant. The models presented in this chapter contain two ASCs, one for the Manigotagan River canoe route and another for the Seagrim Lake canoe route. These constants are hypothesized to capture effects that are specific to the particular sites (see below).

The final selection of models for consideration was based on the sign of coefficients based on intuition and theory, focus group results, previous research (Englin et al., 1996), log-likelihood ratio tests, and the size of ρ^2, a statistic analogous to R^2, used to estimate the proportion of variance explained by the model (Ben-Akiva and Lerman, 1985).

4.   RESULTS AND DISCUSSION

4.1   Park Use Results

The registration system resulted in useable information from 388 trips to 20 different canoe routes in the park by backcountry recreationists in 1993. Most registrants took only a single backcountry trip to the park per year. About 80 per cent of the trips were to the six routes formally designated by park staff as routes. The remainder were to undesignated routes. About 65 per cent of the recreationists came from the Winnipeg area, 30 per cent from other parts of Manitoba, and the remainder from other parts of Canada and the US (principally Minnesota). Based upon the routes registrants drew in the survey most people travelled the entire length of a water route, justifying the use of the characteristics found along the entire route as the choice variables. While canoes were the most common watercraft used by the registrants, kayaks and various motorized boats were also utilized (Watson et al., 1994).

4.2 Model Results

Table 11.1 contains the results of four site choice RUM models which performed the best according to the criteria above. In all four, travel costs were a significant negative influence on site choice, suggesting that all things being equal, recreationists prefer to visit sites closer to their homes. This was an expected result, and is a universal feature found in all studies of recreation demand (Fletcher et al., 1990).

The first model (Table 11.1) involves some park management variables and areas of the most recent (1983) forest fires. The presence of the burned areas and cottages have a negative influence on site choice, as expected, as evidenced by the negative signs on their coefficients. The larger number of portages also has a negative influence. The sign of the coefficient on long portages is positive, which is not consistent with prior expectations. It may be, however, that this variable is a proxy for isolation, in which a positive sign would result. Finally ASCs for two routes, the Manigotagan River and Seagrim Lake route, were estimated and are positive. The former is expected given it has some unique features such as the presence of rapids, but it also has historical and symbolic value in the province. Since the Seagrim Lake route is well known for its fishing, the positive coefficient may be capturing the effects of good fishing along that route.

Given the importance of the ten-year fires on route choice, a second model was estimated where the burn measure was replaced with forest ones; in this case the area of immature or regenerating stands of jack pine and black spruce. This second model was estimated to examine the effect of regrowth on route choice. Regrowth variables should conceivably influence choice in the same direction as the burnt areas since they are measuring similar landscape features. The coefficients for the regrowth variables are negative and highly significant in the case of jack pine (Table 11.1). This supports the suggestion that historical fires are a negative influence on backcountry recreation in the Canadian Shield. The park management coefficients remain similar to those in the first model.

The last two models incorporate mature forest variables and cutblock areas. Mature forests add explanatory power to the models as shown by the large increase in ρ^2 (Table 11.1). Mature jack pine and white spruce stands are a positive influence, while mature black spruce and aspen stands are a negative influence on site choice. The remaining variables (fires, cottages, and so on) maintain their significance and signs suggesting that the models are robust. One interesting exception is the longest portage, which becomes negative and more statistically significant than in models 1 and 2. This negative sign is what was originally expected. The last model incorporates the

Forests

Table 11.1   *Estimates of parameters from multinomial logit models*
                explaining choice of water recreation route in Nopiming Park,
                Manitoba in 1993[a]

	Parameters (*t*-ratio)			
Variables	Model 1	Model 2	Model 3	Model 4
Travel cost	−0.1369***	−0.1195***	−0.0600***	−0.0573***
	(−12.010)	(−10.719)	(−4.914)	(−4.651)
Area of recent cutblocks				0.5262
				(1.607)
Burns of 10 years or less	−0.0633***		−0.1016***	−0.0895***
	(−3.723)		(−3.538)	(−2.945)
Mature jack pine			0.6798***	0.6854***
			(9.837)	(9.624)
Young jack pine		−0.3730***		
		(−7.355)		
Mature black spruce			−0.9988***	−0.9311***
			(−6.847)	(−6.047)
Young black spruce		−0.0394		
		(−0.251)		
White spruce of any age			6.2236***	6.2029***
			(5.929)	(5.767)
Aspen of any age			−3.1102***	−3.0299***
			(−5.603)	(−5.246)
Cottages	−1.7962***	−1.7327***	−1.3374***	−1.3498***
	(−11.221)	(−9.968)	(−8.449)	(−8.507)
Longest portage	0.0004***	0.0004***	−0.0018***	−0.0020***
	(2.831)	(2.794)	(−5.126)	(−5.208)
Number of portages	−0.0229***	−0.0268***	−0.0774***	−0.0722***
	(−4.292)	(−5.130)	(−8.007)	(−7.401)
ASC–Manigotagan	2.5517***	2.0857***	3.8477***	3.6939***
	(7.513)	(5.993)	(6.493)	(6.067)
ASC–Seagrim Lake	0.6605***	0.6012***	0.6614***	0.7075***
	(4.059)	(3.695)	(3.256)	(3.421)
Log likelihood at convergence	−946.70	−924.86	−861.23	−858.83
ρ^2 [b]	0.186	0.204	0.259	0.261

Notes:
[a] t statistics in parentheses.
[b]   a statistic analogous to R^2 and is calculated as $[1 - L(\beta)/L(0)]$.
*** significant at the 1% level or beyond.

cutblock variable, and the coefficient is positive and significant at about the 10 per cent level.

The direction of the effects of these factors in influencing backcountry site choices make some sense in explaining actual choices in this park. For example, camp sites are probably better in jack pine and white spruce areas. There may be fewer insects and the ground is likely to be dryer than in black spruce or aspen ecosystems. The density of trees is also more conducive to camping in mature jack pine due to its more dispersed nature on rock outcrops and flat areas. Aspen tends to produce numerous shoots, and is usually associated with shrubs and bushes, which result in greater ground cover in younger stages. There may also be scenic preferences at play which influence route choice – the focus group chose jack pine stands over black spruce, hardwoods and fires. Thus, the revealed preference modelling results closely paralleled the focus group findings in terms of environmental features.

The influence of cutblocks, however, remains problematic. Given the negative public reaction to logging in Nopiming Park reported in the media, it is somewhat surprising to find that cutblocks may have a positive influence on site choice in the park. There are several aspects of the cutblock result that should be considered before reaching any conclusions about this finding. First, the coefficient is significantly different from 0 at about the 11 per cent level. Thus the positive relationship is not strong, and certainly less strong than the other variables in the RUM model. Second, we have little evidence that most recreationists are directly aware of the recent cutblocks along the routes in the park. Evidence on this front involves: (i) extensive field work which suggests that they are not visible unless individuals make significant efforts to travel inland from the water routes (something few recreationists do while they are in backcountry areas in Nopiming); and (ii) the forest company often leaves forest buffers between cutblocks and water routes that are larger than required by regulation. Third, it may be the features associated with cutblocks that are driving the coefficient to be positive. An important one here may be wildlife habitat. It is well known that logging creates habitat for certain wildlife species (for example Stelfox, 1983, 1988). This potential may increase numbers of certain wildlife species which influence visitation in a positive manner through viewing potential. The possibility of spurious correlation between cutblocks and omitted variables led us to utilize the third RUM model in Table 11.1 for the estimation of welfare measures.

4.3 Welfare Measures

The formula in equation (11.5) was used to simulate the CV associated with various quality changes in the park. First, welfare measures associated with

marginal values in the forest and some park management variables are calculated. These appear in Table 11.2 for the five most commonly visited
routes in the park. Jack pine values range from $0.241/ha/trip to less than
$0.001/ha/trip. These values are positive because the simulation involved an
increase by one hectare along each route. Increasing black spruce ranges
from a loss of $0.020/ha/trip to $0.002/ha/trip. Adding cottage developments along Tulabi result in a loss of welfare valued at $4.752/trip while
adding them at Seagrim Lake causes a loss of $1.745/trip. Removing exist-
ing cottage developments at Beresford or portions of the Manigotagan
River (where they currently exist) would result in gains of $0.557 and
$0.733/trip respectively.

The current welfare impacts of the two 1983 severe fires, the Maskwa
Lake and Long Lake burns were also simulated. These fires affected large
areas of the park and involved specific forest damage along 2 routes and 5
routes respectively of the 20 routes 1993 visitors were found using. The
current welfare impacts of these fires were simulated in two ways. The first
involved simply changing the buffer area affected by burns to zero. This
means that the affected buffer area is now included as forest types NOT
modelled in the RUM. This involved mixed pine spruce and aspen ecosystems, Balsam fir and other species not captured in the RUM variables. Table
11.3 provides the results of these changes. The Maskwa Lake burn, which
affected portions of the Tulabi and Rabbit routes, resulted in losses during
1993 to recreationists of about $3.435/trip. The Long Lake fire, which
affected five other routes, resulted in 1993 losses of $2.905/trip. The second,
and probably more accurate way to estimate current losses is to convert the
burn area to a mixture of forest types not included in the RUM model and
those types that are included. This was simulated by estimating the portion
of the buffer that currently comprises the forest types included in the RUM
model (for example mature jack pine, black spruce and so on) and converting the burn areas to a similar proportion of these forest types. The remainder of the buffer area currently affected by fire is converted to the forest
types not included in the model. These results are somewhat different. The
Maskwa burn now caused 1993 damages of $5.878/trip and the Long Lake
burn caused current damages of $21.761/trip.

5.   CONCLUSIONS AND LIMITATIONS

This analysis suggests that mature jack pine ecosystems are a highly valued
forest characteristic for backcountry recreationists using water routes in
wilderness areas in the western Canadian Shield. Estimates of the per trip
recreational value of a hectare of mature jack pine was found to be between

Table 11.2 Estimates of mean per trip welfare measures ($/ha) associated with marginal changes in forest and some management conditions for some canoe routes in Nopiming Park, Manitoba

			Marginal environmental changes			
Canoe route	Mature jack pine (ha)	Mature black spruce (ha)	White spruce (all ages) (ha)	Aspen (all ages) (ha)	Cottage developments (pres/abs)	Additional portages (1 portage)
Tulabi Lake	0.241	−0.020	a	−0.021	−4.752	−0.423
Seagrim Lake	0.048	−0.009	a	a	−1.745	−0.197
Rabbit River	0.049	−0.008	0.025	a	−2.059	−0.168
Beresford Lake	>0.001	−0.002	0.006	−0.001	0.557	−0.015
Mangotagan River	0.006	−0.008	a	−0.001	0.733	−0.020

Note: [a] The route did not have any of these forest types within its buffer.

233

Table 11.3   The current (1993) mean per trip welfare impacts of severe fires that occurred in 1983 on backcountry recreationists in Nopiming Park, Manitoba

	Number of routes affected	Hectares of canoe route affected by fire	Welfare measure ($/ha) for a forest improvement	
			Change fire damaged forest to base[a]	Change fire damaged forest to mature forest[b]
Actual fires				
Maskwa Lake Burn	2	929	3.435	5.878
Long Lake Burn	5	1925	2.905	21.761

Notes:
[a] This change involves converting the entire area of the canoe route buffer to forest types not captured in the forest type variables (for example mixed forest types). In other words the hectares of burned area are simply changed to 0, and none of the forest variables are affected.
[b] This change involves converting the area of the canoe route buffer to BOTH mature forest types and the others not captured formally in the RUM model. The conversion of burned area to mature forest is based on the proportion of mature forest (by species) in the unburned portions of the routes. In other words, if a route with a buffer area of 100 ha has 50 ha burned and 25 ha of mature jack pine remaining in the unburned portion, the quality change simulated involves converting half of the burned area (25/50 ha) to mature jack pine, and the rest (25/50 ha) to remaining forest types (that is area of burn=0).

$0.24 and less than $0.0001. The difference depends upon the other characteristics present in the areas used by the individuals. White spruce is also valued, although less than mature jack pine. Aspen and mature black spruce ecosystems are negatively valued. This makes sense since both ecosystems may provide unpleasant externalities to recreationists. Note, however, that these are marginal benefit estimates and apply to environmental changes that may occur to small areas such as certain canoe routes. Care must be used in using these estimates to value large environmental changes over broad geographic areas such as the entire Canadian Shield.

Two burn scenarios are also examined. Both scenarios examine actual fires that occurred in 1983 and affected several canoe routes in the park. The total current (1993) damages from these fires varied from $2.91 to $21.76 per hectare. The differences are driven primarily by the scale and location of the two fires.

These findings suggest a strong influence for fire in Canadian Shield forest ecosystems, not only from the ecological point of view, but also from the view of the values of services and outputs provided by the forests. Since multiple use and integrated management of forests requires optimizing public benefits, managing forests that are at risk from fire requires an understanding of the magnitudes of the economic impacts of fire. Some of these impacts involve changes in the nonmarket economic values that accrue as a result of the fires. These changes can be associated with forest use (for example this study) or nonuse issues (for example Loomis and Gonzales-Caban, 1994). Backcountry recreation in the region of the Canadian Shield examined is particularly important and probably provides one of the most highly valued nonmarket outputs from the forests there. To fully quantify the nonmarket impacts of forest fires one needs the values of forest in both the burned and unburned states. This analysis has focused on the development of a framework to assess the aesthetic impacts of forest fires on recreation in these states.

One of the findings is that there are different ways to measure the values of forested areas that have been burned. One classification scheme is to measure the burn in terms of its age. If burns are the focus of the analysis this is, perhaps, the most natural way to examine the effects of fires on nonmarket service flows. A second way, however, is to classify the damaged areas as young stands of the trees that are growing back in the burned areas. Either measurement scheme is describing identical areas, the difference is merely one of description. In fact it is also noteworthy that mature jack pine ecosystems, which were found to be preferred by recreationists, are simply forests that have not burned for long periods. Jack pine stands in Nopiming have been subjected to sets of severe fires from 1929 to 1983. The mature ones which comprise the variables in the models presented represent stands that were burned 55–65 years in the past. This suggests that recreation site choice in this part of the Canadian Shield may be partially driven by fires in the long run since the age of the forest stands has a strong influence on recreation choices.

Potentially, a key omission from this analysis is the absence of any wild-life or biodiversity measures. If these effects vary from route to route they may not be adequately modelled by the implicit constant terms in the multi-nomial logit models. One of the 'good' things provided by fires is different ecosystems. As part of the natural course of events in the Canadian Shield forest, many fire adapted species would not survive or flourish without these fires. Thus, the values developed in this analysis present only part of the picture.

The analysis may also suffer from the absence of an annual trip genera-tion function. For small changes in environmental quality this is unlikely to be an important issue with activities like backcountry recreation. Since most of the people in the analysis took a single trip per year it is unlikely that they would stop visiting backcountry areas as a result of changes in a single route. In fact preliminary modelling of trip frequency suggests that the environmental characteristics examined in this chapter do not influence the number of trips taken in a year (Boxall et al., 1995). Instead, they would reallocate the trip to another route, something the the random utility model utilized in the analysis handles well. Changes in the quality of a route would merely change the site chosen, not the decision to go at all. Using the welfare estimates presented in this chapter to value broad changes in quality, however, would likely result in an overestimate of damages since some people could chose to do something other than visit backcountry areas under severe enough environmental changes like extensive fires. Conversely, sharp increases in environmental quality may draw more people into wilderness recreation, and so the welfare estimates may provide an underestimate of the value of increasing environmental quality.

ACKNOWLEDGEMENT

Funding from the Canada–Manitoba Partnership Agreement in Forestry, the Northern Ontario Development Agreement, and the Manitoba Model Forest is gratefully acknowledged. We thank Trucia Howard, Kelly Leavesley, Jim Crone of the Manitoba Department of Natural Resources, Grant Williamson of the Canadian Forest Service, and especially Erik Ellehoj of Geowest Environmental Consultants for assistance with this research. This chapter was originally published in the *Canadian Journal of Forest Research* (1996), **26**: 982–90.

NOTES

1. Note that this form of the travel cost model is used to estimate changes in values associated with levels of environmental qualities. It is not used to provide the aggregate value of the backcountry areas for recreational purposes. The traditional travel cost model is commonly used for this purpose. Common and McKenney (1994) describe this model, and some problems associated with its use.
2. Note that total use of the backcountry areas would be required to estimate the aggregate value associated with recreation. This is needed if the model used was the traditional travel cost model. Common and McKenney (1994) describe this model and show that errors in estimating total use have an important effect on the total value estimate.

REFERENCES

Ben-Akiva, M. and S. Lerman (1985), *Discrete Choice Analysis: Theory and Application to Travel Demand*, Cambridge, MA: MIT Press, 390 pp.

Bockstael, N.E., K.E. McConnell and I.E. Strand (1989), 'A random utility model for sportsfishing: Some preliminary results for Florida', *Marine Resource Economics*, **6**: 245–60.

Boxall, P.C., D.O. Watson, J. Englin and E. Ellehoj (1995), 'Analysis of the revealed preferences by backcountry recreationists for forest and park management features in the Canadian Shield region', Canadian Forest Service Report, Canada–Manitoba Partnership Agreement in Forestry, Winnipeg, Manitoba, 34 pp.

Cesario, F.J. (1976), 'Value of time in recreation benefit studies', *Land Economics*, **52**: 32–41.

Common, M.S. and D.W. McKenney (1994), 'Investigating the reliability of a hedonic travel cost model: A Monte Carlo approach', *Canadian Journal of Forest Research*, **24**: 358–63.

Coyne, A.G. and W.L. Adamowicz (1992), 'Modelling choice of site for hunting bighorn sheep', Wildlife Society Bulletin, **20**: 26–33.

Englin, J., P.C. Boxall, K. Chakraborty and D.O. Watson (1996), 'Valuing the impacts of forest fires on backcountry forest recreation', *Forest Science*, **42**: 450–55.

Fletcher, J.J., W.L. Adamowicz and T. Graham-Tomasi (1990), 'The travel cost model of recreation demand: theoretical and empirical issues', *Leisure Sciences*, **12**: 119–47.

Hanemann, W.M. (1982), Applied welfare analysis with qualitative response models. Working Paper 241, California Agricultural Experiment Station, University of California, Berkeley.

Loomis, J. and A. Gonzales-Caban (1994), 'Estimating the value of reducing fire hazards to old growth forests in the Pacific Northwest: A contingent valuation approach', *International Journal of Wildland Fire*, **4**: 209–16.

McConnell, K.E. (1985), 'The Economics of Outdoor Recreation', in A.V. Kneese and J.L. Sweeney (eds), *Handbook of Natural Resource and Energy Economics*, Vol. 2, New York: North Holland Press, pp. 677–722.

McFadden, D. (1974), 'Conditional Logit Analysis of Qualitative Choice Behavior', in P. Zarembka (ed.), *Frontiers in Econometrics*, New York: Academic Press.

Morey, E., R. Rowe and M. Watson (1993), 'A repeated nested-logit model of Atlantic salmon fishing', *American Journal of Agricultural Economics*, **75**: 578–92.

Stelfox, J.G. (1983), 'Logging-wildlife Interactions', in Proceedings of the Symposium on Fish and Wildlife Resources and Economic Development, Edmonton, Alberta, edited by Alberta Society of Professional Biologists, Edmonton, Alberta, pp 20–51.

Stelfox, J.G. (1988), 'Forest succession and wildlife abundance following clear-cut logging in west-central Alberta', Technical Report to Alberta Fish and Wildlife Division, Edmonton, Alberta, 152 pp.

Watson, D.O., L. Peters, P.C. Boxall, J. Englin and K. Chakraborty (1994), 'The economic value of canoeing in Nopiming Park in relation to forest and park management', A Report of the 1993 field season: Volume I, Canadian Forest Service Report, Canada–Manitoba Partnership Agreement in Forestry, Winnipeg, Manitoba, 136 pp.

PART III

Rivers and the Sea

12. A random utility model of beach recreation

George R. Parsons and D. Matthew Massey

1. INTRODUCTION

The purpose of this chapter is to estimate a random utility maximization (RUM) model of beach recreation and use it to value losses associated with beach closures and beach erosion. Our application is to 62 beaches in the Mid-Atlantic region of the USA. We estimate the model using a random sample of 400 beach users from the state of Delaware. The prominent beaches and the state are shown on the map in Figure 12.1. We estimate a simple multinomial and a mixed logit version of the RUM model. The latter allows us to account for general patterns of substitution among the sites (Train, 1999a). We consider day trips only in this analysis. Both versions of the model originally appeared in Massey (2002).

The RUM model is a 'discrete choice' travel cost model which considers an individual's choice of one recreation site from among many possible sites. The model yields per-trip values, which may be used to value sites or characteristics of sites. In our case the sites are beaches. The foundations for the model are found in a series of articles by Daniel McFadden (see McFadden, 1974, 1978, 1981, and 2001).

The RUM model was first applied to recreation demand by Hanemann (1978) and later developed more fully by Bockstael et al. (1986). The model has been applied to many types of outdoor recreation including fishing, swimming, boating, rock climbing, hunting, viewing, hiking, and so on. There are a number of beach use applications. Hanemann (1978), Bockstael et al. (1986), and Bockstael et al. (1987) applied the model to beach use in Boston. Bockstael et al. (1988) and Haab and Hicks (1997) applied it to swimming at beaches on the Chesapeake Bay. And, more recently, Murray et al. (2001) estimated a model of beach use on Lake Erie in Ohio.

Our application is novel in a number of respects. It is the first application to beaches in the Mid-Atlantic region. It is the first to consider a mixed logit version of the RUM model in beach use. And, it is the first to apply the model to valuing beach erosion losses. Due to sea rise and fairly dense

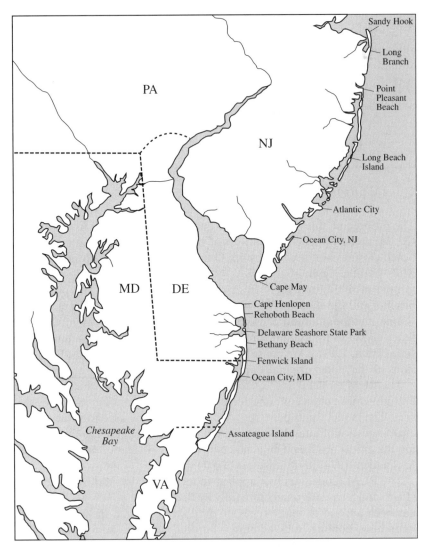

Figure 12.1   Mid-Atlantic region

development along beaches in the Mid-Atlantic region, beaches are prone to erosion or severe narrowing over time. State and federal government agencies routinely replenish these beaches with new sand at considerable cost. In our model we estimate the value of the recreation losses associated with some hypothetical erosion scenarios. In another application we consider the loss associated with hypothetical beach closures that may result for various reasons, major among these being an oil spill. Tanker traffic in this region is significant.

Our chapter is organized as follows. In Section 2, we present our RUM model. In Sections 3 and 4 we present the multinomial and mixed logit models for estimating the RUM model. In Section 5, we discuss the data set. In Sections 6 and 7 we present and analyse the parameter and welfare estimates. In Section 8 we conclude.

2. A RUM MODEL OF BEACH CHOICE

The RUM model considers an individual's choice of one recreation site from a set of many possible sites on a single choice occasion. In our application a site is a beach. There are 62 beaches in the choice set and the individual is deciding which beach to visit on a given choice occasion during the season. We assume that a trip to beach i gives an individual utility V_i where $i = 1,2,...,62$. We also assume that V_i is a linear function of the characteristics of the site. So,

$$V_i = \beta_p p_i + \beta_x x_i + \varepsilon_i, \tag{12.1}$$

where p_i is the trip cost of reaching site i, x_i is a vector of beach characteristics, and ε_i is random error term.

Trip cost includes the travel cost and time cost of reaching beach i from the individual's home. The further away the beach is from home, the higher the trip cost. The vector x_i measures the characteristics that matter to individuals when deciding which beach to visit. These might include things like presence of a boardwalk, natural areas, facilities, parking, beach width and so forth. In our application we use the characteristics listed in Table 12.1.

The error term captures unobserved beach and individual characteristics that matter in site choice. Individuals know the unobserved characteristics, but researchers do not. Put differently, V_i is deterministic to individuals but is the outcome of a random process determined by ε_i to researchers. From our perspective then, on any given choice occasion, an individual will have some *expected maximum utility of a trip* defined as

$$E^{base} = E\{MAX[(\beta_p p_1 + \beta_x x_1 + \varepsilon_1),(\beta_p p_2 + \beta_x x_2 + \varepsilon_2),...,$$
$$(\beta_p p_{62} + \beta_x x_{62} + \varepsilon_{62})]\}. \tag{12.2}$$

E^{base} is a random variable depending on the realization of $\varepsilon_1,\varepsilon_2,...,\varepsilon_{62}$. We superscript E^{base} with *base* because this is the baseline expected utility in our applications.

Table 12.1   Site characteristics*

Trip Cost	Trip cost (includes tolls, beach fees, transit costs, and parking fees) + time costs
Length	Length of beach in miles (logged)
Boardwalk	Boardwalk with shops and attractions present
Amusements	Amusement park, rides, or games available or nearby the beach
Park	State park, federal park, or wildlife refuge
Private	Private or limited access
Wide	Beach width from dune toe to berm greater than 200 feet
Narrow	Beach width from dune toe to berm less than 75 feet
Atlantic City	Atlantic City
Surfing	Recognized as a good location for surfing
High Rise	Highly developed
Park Within	Part of the beach is a park area
Facilities	Facilities such as bathrooms, showers, and food available on or just off the beach
Parking	Presence of adequate parking near beach
New Jersey	Beach located in New Jersey

Note: * Except for *Trip Cost* and *Length*, all are dummy variables.

Recall that we consider two scenarios: beach closure and beach erosion. To estimate the welfare loss in both cases we evaluate the expected maximum utility with and without the change in beaches. For example, the expected utility with the closure of beach 1 is

$$E^{close} = E\{MAX[(\beta_p p_2 + \beta_x x_2 + \varepsilon_2),(\beta_p p_3 + \beta_x x_3 + \varepsilon_3),...,$$
$$(\beta_p p_{62} + \beta_x x_{62} + \varepsilon_{62})]\}. \tag{12.3}$$

This is simply the expected maximum utility an individual can attain when choosing among all sites *except beach 1*. The per-trip welfare loss due to the closure then is

$$W^{close} = \{E^{close} - E^{base}\}/\lambda, \tag{12.4}$$

where λ is the individual's marginal utility of income that converts utility difference into monetary terms. Multiple site closures are considered by dropping many sites in the computation of E^{close}.

To estimate the loss due to beach erosion, or a change in any measured site characteristic, an expected maximum utility is computed with a change in the characteristic set. In our case we have

$$E^{erosion} = E\{MAX[(\beta_p p_1 + \beta_x x_1 + \varepsilon_1),(\beta_p p_2 + \beta_x x_2^* + \varepsilon_2),...,$$
$$(\beta_p p_{62} + \beta_x x_{62} + \varepsilon_{62})]\}. \tag{12.5}$$

where the vector x_2^* denotes that site 2 has less beach width than previously. Using the variables shown in Table 12.1 and assuming that beach 2 is initially more than 75 feet wide and less than 200 feet wide, we would set NARROW = 1 in computing $E^{erosion}$. The welfare loss due to erosion of site 2 then is

$$W^{erosion} = \{E^{erosion} - E^{base}\}/\lambda. \tag{12.6}$$

Again, it is easy to consider erosion at many sites by making the right changes in the expected utility computation.

In the empirical analysis, we estimate the parameters $\beta = (\beta_p, \beta_x)$ using observed data on beach trips. These estimates, in turn, are used to compute E^{base}, E^{close}, and $E^{erosion}$. As noted above, we use two methods of estimation: multinomial logit (MNL) and a mixed logit (MXL). The methods vary in how they treat the error term in equation (12.1). The MXL is less restrictive allowing for a more general pattern of substitution among beaches. We discuss the methods in turn beginning with the MNL.

3.   MULTINOMIAL LOGIT

In our beach visitation data we know the beaches visited by a random set of beach users. Recall from the discussion above that these choices, in the eyes of the researcher, are the outcomes of a random process. From our prospective then the beach actually visited on any given choice occasion is probabilistic. Assume an individual chooses beach k if $V_k > V_i$ for all $i = 1,...,62$. If so, the probability of observing an individual choose beach k is

$$pr(\beta_p p_k + \beta_x x_k + \varepsilon_k > \beta_p p_i + \beta_x x_i + \varepsilon_i) \text{ for all } i \neq k, \tag{12.7}$$

where the distribution assumed for ε_i determines the explicit form for the probability.

In the MNL model the error terms are assumed to be independently and identically distributed (iid) type-I extreme-value random variables. This yields a closed form for equation (12.7)

$$pr(k) = \frac{\exp(\beta_p p_k + \beta_x x_k)}{\sum\limits_{i=1}^{62} \exp(\beta_p p_i + \beta_x x_i)}, \tag{12.8}$$

The probability depends on the characteristics of beach k as well as the characteristics of all other 61 sites in the choice set as shown in the denominator in equation (12.8).

In our data, we observe 400 individuals each visiting at least one of 62 beaches. The log-likelihood of observing the actual pattern of visits using the MNL model then is

$$\ln(L(\beta)) = \sum_{n=1}^{400} \sum_{i=1}^{62} r_{ni} \ln \left\{ \frac{\exp(\beta_p p_k + \beta_x x_k)}{\sum\limits_{i=1}^{62} \exp(\beta_p p_i + \beta_x x_i)} \right\}, \tag{12.9}$$

where $r_{ni} = 1$ if individual n visited site i and $= 0$ if not. The data set on beach visits gives us values for r_{ni}. In estimation we search for the values of β that maximize $\ln(L(\beta))$ giving us parameter estimates for the RUM model in equation (12.1).

Since we observe individuals taking more than one trip during the season in our data set, we use a slightly modified version of equation (12.9). The likelihood function is the same as (12.9) but r_{ni} is now the number of trips to site i by individual n during the season. We assume that trips taken by any given individual are independent over the season when we form the likelihood function in this way. This is not a particularly realistic assumption. Ideally, we'd like to have information on the timing of trips over the season and then to explicitly account the relationship of trips taken over the season. However, we have no such information. See Haab (forthcoming) and Herriges and Phaneuf (2002) for examples of models that at least allow the error terms to be correlated over time for a given individual.

In the MNL model the expected maximum utility of a trip, equation (12.2), is $E = \ln[\sum_{i=1}^{62} \exp(\beta_p p_i + \beta_x x_i)]$. This follows from the distribution of the error term. So, our closure and erosion estimates for equations (12.4) and (12.6) are

$$W^{close} = \left\{ \ln \left[\sum_{i=2}^{62} \exp(\beta_p p_i + \beta_x x_i) \right] - \ln \left[\sum_{i=1}^{62} \exp(\beta_p p_i + \beta_x x_i) \right] \right\} 1 - \beta_p$$

$$\tag{12.10}$$

$$W^{erosion} = \left\{ \ln \left[\sum_{i=1}^{62} \exp(\beta_p p_i + \beta_x x_i^*) \right] - \ln \left[\sum_{i=1}^{62} \exp(\beta_p p_i + \beta_x x_i) \right] \right\} 1 - \beta_p$$

where we assume site 1 is closed in the first expression and x_i^* captures the alteration in site characteristics due to erosion in the second expression. The estimated parameter on trip cost $-\beta_p$ is the marginal utility of income and is used to convert the expected maximum utility differences into monetary terms. All else constant this parameter tells us how much a person's utility for a site drops with increases in cost.

The MNL model, while useful and easy to estimate, imposes rather restrictive assumptions on how individuals substitute one beach for another. Its property of independence of irrelevant alternatives (IIA), which manifests this restriction, is a direct result of the assumption that the error terms ε_i are independent. This result is well documented in the literature (see for example Train, 1986). IIA implies that the relative odds of selecting any single beach over another is independent of all other beaches. For example, if an erosion rate at beach 2 were to cause a 10 per cent decrease in the probability of visiting that beach, there would have to be a commensurate increase of 10 per cent in the probability of visiting *all* other sites. There must be a proportionate increase in all other probabilities. If some beaches are better substitutes for the beach experiencing the erosion than others, this is unrealistic. We would expect a larger increase in the probability of visiting the beaches that are good substitutes.

The restrictiveness of the MNL model has led researchers to consider models that relax the assumption of IIA and allow for more realistic patterns of substitution across sites. The two most common approaches are the nested and mixed logit. The latter is more general and is the next method we used to estimate our RUM model.

4.   MIXED LOGIT

Unlike the MNL model, the MXL allows for correlation among site utilities. In our MXL model an individual's utility for visiting site i is

$$V_i = \varphi_p p_i + \varphi_x x_i + \mu_p p_i + \mu_x x_i + \varepsilon_i, \tag{12.11}$$

where φ_p and φ_x are the usual parameters on trip cost and site characteristics, and μ_p and μ_x are new random terms with mean 0. The error term ε_i still has a type-1 iid extreme-value distribution, but the full random component is now $\mu_p p_i + \mu_x x_i + \varepsilon_i$.

To see how utilities are correlated in the MXL model, consider a simple example. Let x_i^{park} be the element in x_i corresponding to the dummy variable for whether or not a beach is a park. The *fixed* coefficient φ_x^{park} (an element in φ_x) gives the mean increase (or decrease) in site utility for all 'park' beaches relative to other beaches, while the *random* coefficient μ_x^{park} (an element in μ_x) gives a variable effect on utility for 'park' beaches. Since μ_x^{park} is shared by all 'park' beaches, the random components in these utilities move together and so are correlated. More generally, since there is a vector of random terms, μ_x, there is the potential for a diverse pattern of correlation across the beach utilities.

Rewriting our MXL model in equation (12.11) as

$$V_i = (\varphi_p + \mu_p)p_i + (\varphi_x + \mu_x)x_i + \varepsilon_i, \qquad (12.12)$$

and setting $\beta_p = \varphi_p + \mu_p$ and $\beta_x = \varphi_x + \mu_x$ gives a RUM model with a random parameter for each site characteristic. The probability of visiting site k, equation (12.7), in the MXL model then is written as

$$pr(k) = \int L_k(\beta)f(\beta|\varphi,\mu)d(\beta)$$

$$\text{where } L_k = \frac{\exp(\beta_p p_k + \beta_x x_k)}{\sum_{i=1}^{62} \exp(\beta_p p_i + \beta_x x_i)} \qquad (12.13)$$

where $f(\beta|\varphi,\mu)$ is a probability density function for β with mean φ and standard deviation μ. This density function is called a mixing distribution. Notice that the MXL probability of visiting site k is just a weighted average of MNL probabilities L_k. The weights are the probabilities of each β combination.

The MXL likelihood function using equation (12.13) then is

$$\ln[L(\varphi,\mu)] = \sum_{n=1}^{400} \sum_{i=1}^{62} r_{ni} \ln \left\{ \int \frac{\exp(\beta_p p_k + \beta_x x_k)}{\sum_{i=1}^{62} \exp(\beta_p p_i + \beta_x x_i)} f(\beta|\varphi,\mu)d\beta \right\} \qquad (12.14)$$

where, once again, $r_{ni} = 1$ if individual n visited site i and $= 0$ if not. And again, given that individuals take many trips to many sites, we let r_{ni} be the number of trips to site i by individual n during the season.

In the MXL model the parameters φ and μ are estimated. This is done by simulation methods, which circumvents the integration in equation (12.14). The 'simulated' version of the log-likelihood function is

$$\ln[L(\varphi,\mu)] = \sum_{n=1}^{400} \sum_{i=1}^{62} r_{ni} \ln \left\{ \frac{1}{D} \sum_{d=1}^{D} \frac{\exp(\beta_p^d p_k + \beta_x^d x_k)}{\sum_{i=1}^{62} \exp(\beta_p^d p_i + \beta_x^d x_i)} \right\}, \quad (12.15)$$

where the term inside the log operator is the simulated probability. To calculate that probability, we specify a form for the mixing distribution $f(\beta|\varphi,\mu)$ and assign hypothetical starting values for φ and μ. Then, D values of β are drawn from the mixing distribution. Each draw is used to calculate one of the d logit probabilities inside the summation in equation (12.15). The average of these over D draws is the simulated probability for individual n. This is repeated for each of the 400 individuals in our sample and a simulated log-likelihood is computed. The values of φ and μ that maximize $[L(\varphi,\mu)]$ are the simulated maximum likelihood estimates.

In our application we use GAUSS-based software developed by Ken Train at the University of California at Berkeley to estimate the MXL model. We assume that the mixing distribution for each variable is normal and we use 150 'Halton' draws in our simulation. Halton draws enable faster estimation with fewer draws (Train, 1999b).

The expected maximum utility of a trip in the MXL model is $E^{base} = 1/D \sum_{d=1}^{D} \ln \sum_{i=1}^{62} \exp(\beta_p^d p_i + \beta_x^d x_i)$, and the welfare loss for closure and erosion are

$W^{close} =$

$$\left\{ \frac{1}{D} \sum_{d=1}^{D} \ln \sum_{i=2}^{62} \exp(\beta_p^d p_i + \beta_x^d x_i) - \frac{1}{D} \sum_{d=1}^{D} \ln \sum_{i=2}^{62} \exp(\beta_p^d p_i + \beta_x^d x_i) \right\} / - \beta_p^d$$

$$(12.16)$$

$W^{erosion} =$

$$\left\{ \frac{1}{D} \sum_{d=1}^{D} \ln \sum_{i=1}^{62} \exp(\beta_p^d p_i + \beta_x^d x_i) - \frac{1}{D} \sum_{d=1}^{D} \ln \sum_{i=1}^{62} \exp(\beta_p^d p_i + \beta_x^d x_i^*) \right\} / - \beta_p^d$$

where again site 1 is closed and x_i^* measures erosion. W^{close} and $W^{erosion}$ are simulated means. D draws of β are made from our mixing distribution. Values for the log-sum inside equation (12.16) are computed for each draw.

The advantage of the MXL model is its ability to allow for flexible patterns of substitution (Train, 1999a). This follows directly from the correlation of the error terms. Independence of irrelevant alternatives is broken and the proportionate reduction (or increase) in visitation to sites no longer needs to hold as a single site or group of sites is altered. In particular, as the correlation across sites for any givenf characteristic increases, the 'similarity' of the sites sharing that characteristic is said to be greater and changes in visitation patterns in response to alterations will reflect these similarities. All else constant, individuals will tend to substitute a similar site following an alteration (closure or erosion in our application) at one or more sites. That similarity will be determined by the parameters on the random terms in the MXL model.

5. DATA

As mentioned at the outset, our application is to day-trips taken by 400 Delaware residents to 62 beaches in the Mid-Atlantic region in the USA. Delaware and the Mid-Atlantic beaches are shown in the map in Figure 12.1.

The trip data were gathered by a stratified random mail survey. An equal number of surveys were sent to each of Delaware's three counties. This stratification was necessary to avoid a sample concentrated on the heavily populated portion of the state in the north. Individuals were sent a survey in early October asking about recreation trips in 1997 to date. One week later they received a reminder postcard. Two weeks later they received a second copy of the survey. A cover letter asked for the adult member of the household with the next birthday to complete the survey. An adult was anyone sixteen years old or older. The survey took about 5 to 15 minutes to complete depending largely on the number of trips taken. In the end, we had 565 completed surveys to analyse with a response rate of approximately 55 per cent.

Respondents were asked to report the number of day, short-overnight, long-overnight, and side trips taken to each of the 62 beaches in the region. The beaches were listed in the survey. They were also asked to report trips taken outside the region by state. We asked several demographic questions as well covering age, income, work status, and so forth. Of the 565 respondents, 400 had taken at least one day-trip to one of the 62 beaches. The total number of day-trips over this sample was 9330. We focus on these 400 beach users in our application.

The raw participation rate in our sample of 565 is 71 per cent, where participation is defined as taking at least one day-trip in 1997. The participation rate adjusting for stratification is 65 per cent. The rate drops because we intentionally oversampled the two less populated counties closer to the beaches. Applying 65 per cent to the entire population of Delaware assumes that the residents choosing to respond to the survey are representative of the entire population. To be conservative and accept that non-respondents are less likely to be beach goers, we calculate a third participation rate. This rate assumes all non-respondents are non-participants. If so, the predicted participation rate drops from 65 per cent to 36 per cent. While not as tight as we might like it to be, it seems safe to say that the rate of participation for day-trips to the Mid-Atlantic beaches by Delaware residents is between 36–65 per cent. The raw mean number of day trips in our sample of 400 over the year is about 23, and the adjusted mean is about 16. While these numbers may still seem high, it is worth keeping in mind that our sample is limited to a population living fairly close to the beaches. Furthermore, our definition of a day trip to a beach is broadly defined to include any type of beach recreation such as a simple stroll on a boardwalk, surfing, fishing, and so forth.

The 62 Mid-Atlantic beaches shown in Figure 12.1 run from Sandy Hook, New Jersey in the north to Asseategue Island, Virginia in the south. The beach names are listed in Table 12.2 in geographic order. The most prominent among these appear on the map. For each beach, we gathered the characteristic data listed in Table 12.1. We used a variety of resources to compile the data set including travel guides, field trips, interviews with resource managers in Delaware and New Jersey, and geological maps. The resource managers were particularly helpful; not only in compiling the data but also in deciding what characteristics are likely to matter to individuals in choosing a beach. Table 12.3 reports summary statistics for all of the site characteristics used in the model.

Our measure of trip cost includes travel and time cost as well as the cost of highway tolls, a ferry toll, and beach fees. The components of trip cost are reported in Table 12.4. Distance and time were calculated for each of the 400 individual's hometowns to each of the 62 beaches using PC Miler, a software package that generates measures along roads using optimal routing and accounting for speed variation across different roads. We use 35 cents per mile in our travel cost calculation: $0.35 times the round trip distance to a site. We use one-third of annual income divided by 2080 as a proxy for an individual's hourly wage in our time cost calculation: wage times the round trip time to a site. We assume on-site time is constant, so it drops out of the RUM model in estimation.

The highway and ferry toll data came from the relevant system operators. For each route we simply incorporated the toll cost if relevant. The ferry toll was for the Cape May–Lewes Ferry that travels across the mouth of the Delaware Bay from New Jersey to Delaware. This route was used for trips from southern Delaware to New Jersey. The beach fees applied only to beaches in New Jersey. While most beaches had various package deals for a week, weekend, or even season, we used the daily beach fee. The relative sizes of these different costs are shown in Table 12.4. The average trip cost

Table 12.2　　Mid-Atlantic beaches from north to south

New Jersey: North Shores
1. Sandy Hook
2. Sea Bright
3. Monmouth Beach
4. Long Branch
5. Deal
6. Asbury Park
7. Ocean Grove
8. Bradley Beach
9. Avon-by-the-Sea
10. Belmar
11. Spring Lake
12. Sea Girt
13. Manasquan

New Jersey: Barnegat Peninsula
14. Point Pleasant Beach
15. Bay Head
16. Mantoloking
17. Normandy Beach
18. Chadwick Beach
19. Ocean Beach
20. Lavallette
21. Ortley Beach
22. Seaside Heights
23. Seaside Park
24. Island Beach State Park

New Jersey: Long Beach Island
25. Barnegat Light
26. Loveladies
27. Harvey Cedars
28. Surf City
29. Ship Bottom
30. Long Beach
31. Beach Haven
32. Holgate

New Jersey: Atlantic City Area
33. Brigantine
34. Atlantic City
35. Ventnor
36. Margate
37. Longport

New Jersey: South Shore
38. Ocean City
39. Strathmere
40. Sea Isle City
41. Avalon
42. Stone Harbor
43. North Wildwood
44. Wildwood
45. Wildwood Crest
46. Cape May

Delaware
47. Cape Henlopen State Park
48. North Shores
49. Henlopen Acres
50. Rehoboth Beach
51. Dewey Beach
52. Indian Beach
53. Delaware Seashore State Park
54. North Bethany Beaches
55. Bethany Beach
56. Sea Colony
57. Middlesex Beach
58. South Bethany Beach
59. Fenwick Island State Park
60. Fenwick Island

Maryland/Virginia
61. Ocean City, MD
62. Assateague Island

Table 12.3   Site characteristic variable summary statistics

	Delmarva 16 beaches	New Jersey 46 beaches	All Beaches
Continuous variable mean values*			
Trip Cost ($)	49.49	147.28	122.04
	(0.00 to 184.76)	(57.63 to 310.85)	(0.00 to 310.85)
Length (Miles)	1.20	1.93	1.86
	(0.40 to 22.00)	(0.50 to 10.60)	(0.40 to 22.00)
Percentage of beaches with each characteristic			
Boardwalk	6.25	47.83	37.10
Amusements	12.50	13.04	12.90
Park	25.00	4.35	9.68
Private	37.50	21.74	25.81
Wide	18.75	28.26	24.19
Narrow	6.25	17.39	14.52
Atlantic City	0.00	2.17	1.61
Surfing	43.75	32.61	35.48
High Rise	6.25	30.43	24.19
Park Within	0.00	19.57	14.52
Facilities	50.00	34.78	38.71
Parking	43.75	45.65	45.16
New Jersey	0.00	100.00	74.19

Note: * The top number in each cell is the variable's mean value among the area's beaches and the numbers in parentheses give the variable's range over those beaches.

Table 12.4   The components of trip cost

Component	Mean	Maximum	Minimum
Tolls	$12.07	$108.40	$0.00
Day Fees	$2.63	$7.00	$0.00
Distance (miles)	106.86	230.10	0
Hours	2.32	4.47	0
Parking Fees	$2.44	$6.00	$0.00
Income	$51 600.00	$125 000.00	$5 000.00
Kids Under 16	0.74	6	0
N*	24 800		

Note: * The values in the table are the mean values for the 400 participants over their 62 possible beach choices.

to a Delaware beach was about $50 and to a New Jersey beach was about $150.

6. PARAMETER ESTIMATES

The parameter estimates and implicit prices for the MNL and MXL models are shown in Tables 12.5 and 12.6. The implicit price for a characteristic is its coefficient divided by the negative of the coefficient on trip cost. It gives the value of a characteristic assuming a person is constrained to visit the site. It helps in making comparisons across models. We will begin with a discussion of the MNL results in Table 12.5.

Table 12.5   The MNL random utility model

Variables	Coefficient	t-Statistic	Implicit Price ($)
Trip Cost	−0.047	43.0	1.00
Length	−0.011	0.3	−0.25
Boardwalk	0.700	5.2	14.62
Amusements	1.256	24.9	26.24
Private	−0.387	7.1	−8.09
Park	0.371	2.7	7.75
Wide	−0.752	15.3	−15.70
Narrow	−0.266	3.5	−5.75
Atlantic City	1.474	12.0	30.78
Surfing	0.869	18.8	18.15
High Rise	−0.417	6.6	−8.72
Park Within	1.561	14.7	32.59
Facilities	−0.381	4.3	−7.96
Parking	0.612	4.1	12.80
New Jersey	−1.073	11.3	−22.40
Day Trips	9330		
# of Participants	400		
Mean Log Likelihood	−2.49776		

With a few exceptions the coefficient estimates have expected signs and are statistically significantly different from zero. The coefficient on trip cost which plays a pivotal role in the welfare analysis as the denominator in equations (12.10) works as we had expected, negative and with a low standard error. All else constant higher trip cost lowers site utility.

Length is included more as a control for size than as an actual attribute.

All else constant, if the size of a beach doubles, there is more space for beach use and hence greater potential visitation. Think of combining two beaches with nearly equivalent attributes into a single large beach. It seems to pick up little of this type of effect in the MNL model. The coefficient is insignificant and has a low implicit price.

The attraction to busy beaches with boardwalks and amusements is evident. The coefficients for *Boardwalk* and *Amusements* are positive and significant. Beaches with amusements, as we have defined them, are basically boardwalk beaches with more attractions such as amusement rides, shopping, and so forth.

There is also evidence of a preference for natural beaches – beaches with parks located within their boundaries or beaches designated as local, state, or federal parks. The coefficients on *Park* and *Parks Within* are positive and significant. It is worth noting that the coefficient on *Parks Within* is larger than the coefficient on *Amusements* and that these two characteristics had among the highest implicit prices in the MNL model at roughly $33 and $26. Consistent with a preference for more 'natural' beaches, is a negative coefficient on *High Rise* – a variable intended to capture the degree of development along a beach. Visitation is high on developed beaches, but this is due mostly to overnight, not day, trips. Since most surf fishing in this region is done on park beaches, this 'natural' effect is picking up some of this influence as well.

Two variables in our model measure access to a beach: *Private and Parking*. Primarily overnight visitors use private beaches. Day-trippers are usually excluded. The negative coefficient on *Private* then is as expected. Most day trips involve some time in a car and the need to park the car. If parking is limited – far from the beach or expensive – this 'lowers' access to the beach. Our *Parking* variable is a qualitative attempt to distinguish beaches with good parking. Resource managers in Delaware emphasized the importance of having such a measure. The empirical evidence supports their argument.

Facilities was intended to capture the presence of bathhouses, concession stands, and other near-beach conveniences on each beach. We expected facilities to be important on day-trips to beaches, but it gives a negative and significant coefficient. Measurement error is a possibility. It is also likely that boardwalk and amusements pick up much of this effect alone. The coefficient stays negative in the MXL model as well.

Beach erosion is a topic of much concern in the Mid-Atlantic region as it is elsewhere. Due to development and natural forces beach width diminishes over time. New Jersey, Delaware, and Maryland regularly nourish beaches to maintain width. To capture the importance of width in beach choice we have included two variables in our model: *Narrow* and *Wide*.

Narrow denotes a beach that is less than 75 feet wide. *Wide* denotes a beach that is more than 200 feet wide.

In our initial specification we had used a continuous variable measured in feet as an explanatory variable. Its coefficient was near zero and insignificant. We took this as evidence that width was not particularly important in beach choice. Later it was pointed out to us, again by resource managers in the area, that individuals have a distaste for narrow as well as extremely wide beaches. On wide beaches the effort of actually reaching the water apparently lowers the desirability of the beach. This may have explained our result on the continuous measure for width. So, by creating two coefficients, one for narrow and one for wide beaches, we hoped to pick up this dichotomous effect. Again, the resource managers' judgement appears to be validated by our model. Narrow and wide beaches lower utility relative to beaches of moderate width (between 75 and 200 feet). In the MNL model extremely wide beaches actually lower utility more than the narrow beaches. The implicit price of *Wide* is about − $16 while the implicit price of *Narrow* is about − $6.

Based on travel guides and interviews we identified beaches noted for their quality of surfing. We designated fifteen beaches in New Jersey and eight in Delaware as surfing beaches. No doubt, this variable is capturing more than the simple attraction to surfers. Beachcombers, swimmers, and others are drawn to beaches with more wave action as well. The coefficient estimate is positive, significant and higher than we had expected relative to other variables with an implicit price is about $18.

Finally, we included dummy variables for beaches located in *New Jersey* and for the beach in *Atlantic City*. The latter obviously captures the attraction of Atlantic City as a center of gambling and nightlife. It certainly stands apart from the other beaches in this regard. The *New Jersey* dummy attempts to sweep-up any shared unobserved effects that New Jersey may have which are missed in our variable list. *Atlantic City* has a positive coefficient, as we had expected, and *New Jersey* has a negative coefficient. We had no strong priors on the latter.

Now let's turn to MXL model in Table 12.6. The MXL model reports estimates for the means and standard deviations of the coefficients – φ and μ in $f(\beta|\varphi,\mu)$ in equation (12.13). The t-statistics associated with each are reported in the table. Notice that the coefficients on *Trip Cost* and *Length* are fixed – no standard deviation is estimated. We wanted to avoid negative and zero measures for the marginal utility of income on the *Trip Cost* variable. Since *Length* is included simply as a weighting factor in the model we saw little reason to measure variability in that coefficient. While qualitatively similar, the MXL and MNL models have some striking quantitative differences. First, the coefficient on *Trip Cost* in the MXL model is nearly double the MNL estimate, − 0.0883 versus − 0.0479. All else constant this

Table 12.6   The MXL random utility model

Variable	Coefficients				Mean implicit price ($)
	Mean		Standard Deviation		
	Estimate	t-statistic	Estimate	t-statistic	
Trip Cost	−0.088	41.6	–	–	1
Length	0.276	7.7	–	–	3.13
Boardwalk	0.950	6.4	0.483	1.9	10.76
Amusements	0.919	16.3	0.161	1.1	10.41
Private	−0.933	3.8	1.267	4.0	−10.56
Park	0.132	0.8	0.451	2.4	1.50
Wide	−1.674	7.0	2.318	6.7	−18.96
Narrow	−2.673	3.2	2.699	4.6	−30.27
Atlantic City	−0.686	1.3	3.279	6.9	−7.77
Surfing	0.771	15.5	0.421	3.1	8.73
High Rise	−0.476	6.6	0.477	3.5	−5.39
Park Within	0.676	5.1	0.707	2.5	7.65
Facilities	−0.232	2.4	0.187	0.8	−2.63
Parking	0.294	1.7	0.239	1.3	3.33
New Jersey	−2.550	8.8	4.920	20.3	−28.88
Day Trips	9330				
# of Participants	400				
Mean Log Likelihood	−2.46239				

implies lower characteristic values in absolute terms. Indeed, this is seen in many of the mean implicit prices in Table 12.6 for the MXL versus MNL model. The prices do not, however, drop proportionately and some actually rise. So, the change cannot be attributed to a decline in the coefficient on *Trip Cost* alone. The relative sizes of the characteristic coefficients are changing as well.

The sign on the coefficient for *Atlantic City* changes from positive in the MNL to negative in the MXL model. At the same time it carries one of the largest estimated standard deviations. The coefficient on *Narrow* becomes roughly ten times larger in the MXL model. Shortly, we will see how this raises losses for the hypothetical erosion scenarios in the MXL versus MNL model. Like the *Atlantic City* variable, the estimated standard deviation on *Narrow* is quite large. It appears as though large adjustments in the mean values of coefficients (and their implied prices) are accompanied by larger standard deviation estimates.

Overall the coefficients exhibiting the greatest variability in the MXL model are *Narrow*, *New Jersey*, *Atlantic City*, *Wide*, and *Private*.

7. WELFARE ESTIMATES

Again, we'll begin with the MNL Model, and then turn to the MXL. The welfare losses for the beach closure scenarios are reported in Tables 12.7 and 12.8. These are computed using the first equation in equations (12.10). All values are reported in per-person per-trip terms and are population weighted sample means so they are representative of the residents of the state who use the beaches. In Table 12.7 we report the losses for individual beach closures assuming all other beaches remain open. In Table 12.8 we report closure losses for groups of beaches. These are geographically contiguous beaches or beaches with similar amenities. The labels in Table 12.8 are self-explanatory. 'All Delmarva' is a closure of all Delaware, Maryland, and Virginia beaches, 'Northern Delaware' includes the six northernmost beaches in the state, and so on. Closures due to oil spills typically affect more than one beach. The geographical groups may mimic such losses. In particular, the Northern Delaware beaches are most vulnerable to spills due to their proximity to tanker shipping lanes.

Among the individual beach closures in Table 12.7, Rehoboth, the largest and most popular beach in Delaware, has the largest mean loss at $5.27 per-person per-trip. Cape Henlopen State Park has the second largest loss at $2.21. These two beaches are shown on the map in Figure 12.1. It is no surprise that Rehoboth is the highest valued beach. It is the most visited in the Mid-Atlantic by Delaware residents and has many desirable characteristics. Moreover, Rehoboth is a northern beach making it one of the most accessible to residents in the state. Cape Henlopen State Park, like Rehoboth, is located in the north and offers some of the same characteristics. Unlike Rehoboth, it is an undeveloped park beach.

The next highest valued beaches are Ocean City, MD and Atlantic City, NJ. Ocean City is a large and highly developed beached in Maryland just below the Delaware–Maryland state line. These beach closures are valued at $1.65 and $1.57 per-person per-trip. The fifth highest is Bethany. Bethany is the most popular among the beaches in the southern portion of the state. Its closure is close in mean value to Ocean City, MD and Atlantic City, NJ at $1.42. Again, all three beaches are shown on the map.

While these may seem like low values for such popular beaches, keep in mind the number of available substitutes in this scenario. In each case one beach is closed, 61 remain open. Also, keep in mind that these are per-trip, not seasonal measures. To arrive at a seasonal measure for day trips multiply by about 16, the mean number of trips. This gives seasonal losses for Rehoboth of about $84, for Cape Henlopen $35, and for Bethany $23.

The values for the remaining beaches in the MNL are all under $1 per-person per-trip, again reflecting the good substitutes in the region. As one

Table 12.7   Mean per-person per-trip loss due to the closure of individual beaches

MNL Model		MXL Model	
Beach	Estimate	Beach	Estimate
Rehoboth Beach, DE	$5.27	**Rehoboth Beach, DE**	$3.62
Cape Henlopen St. Park, DE	2.21	**Cape Henlopen St. Park, DE**	1.48
Atlantic City, NJ	1.65	Atlantic City, NJ	1.36
Ocean City, MD	1.57	Ocean City, MD	1.08
Bethany Beach, DE	1.42	**Delaware Seashore St. Park, DE**	0.86
Delaware Seashore St. Park, DE	0.88	**Bethany Beach, DE**	0.75
Fenwick Island, DE	0.79	**North Shores, DE**	0.61
Dewey Beach, DE	0.79	**Dewey Beach, DE**	0.53
North Shores, DE	0.64	**Fenwick Island, DE**	0.39
Fenwick Island St. Park, DE	0.56	**Fenwick Island St. Park, DE**	0.24
Ocean City, NJ	0.47	**Henlopen Acres, DE**	0.21
Sea Isle City, NJ	0.41	Sea Isle City, NJ	0.20
Cape May, NJ	0.36	**Indian Beach, DE**	0.19
Henlopen Acres, DE	0.35	**North Bethany Beaches, DE**	0.17
South Bethany Beach, DE	0.33	Ocean City, NJ	0.16
Indian Beach, DE	0.32	**South Bethany Beaches, DE**	0.16
Assateague Island, MD	0.29	Strathmere, NJ	0.15
Strathmere, NJ	0.28	Assateague Island, MD	0.14
Stone Harbor, NJ	0.26	Cape May, NJ	0.12
North Bethany Beaches, DE	0.23	Wildwood, NJ	0.10
Seaside Heights, NJ	0.23	Stone Harbor, NJ	0.10
Middlesex Beach, DE	0.22	**Middlesex Beach, DE**	0.10
Seaside Park, NJ	0.21	Seaside Heights, NJ	0.09
North Wildwood, NJ	0.20	Seaside Park, NJ	0.08
Brigatine, NJ	0.20	North Wildwood, NJ	0.08
Point Pleasant Beach, NJ	0.19	**Sea Colony, DE**	0.08
Holgate, NJ	0.19	Avalon, NJ	0.08
Sea Colony, DE	0.16	Brigatine, NJ	0.06
Wildwood, NJ	0.14	Point Pleasant Beach, NJ	0.06
Avalon, NJ	0.12	Ship Bottom, NJ	0.04
Manasquan, NJ	0.09	Surf City, NJ	0.04
Ship Bottom, NJ	0.09	Harvey Cedars, NJ	0.04
Beach Haven, NJ	0.08	Holgate, NJ	0.04
Harvey Cedars, NJ	0.07	Lavallette, NJ	0.03
Surf City, NJ	0.07	Long Beach, NJ	0.03
Ortley Beach, NJ	0.06	Manasquan, NJ	0.02
Avon-by-the-Sea, NJ	0.06	Ventnor, NJ	0.02
Lavallette, NJ	0.06	Ortley Beach, NJ	0.02
Long Beach, NJ	0.06	Beach Haven, NJ	0.02
Spring Lake, NJ	0.06	Island Beach State Park, NJ	0.02

Table 12.7   (continued)

MNL Model		MXL Model	
Beach	Estimate	Beach	Estimate
Barnegat Light, NJ	$0.06	Loveladies, NJ	$0.02
Long Branch, NJ	0.04	Long Branch, NJ	0.02
Belmar, NJ	0.05	Longport, NJ	0.02
Island Beach State Park, NJ	0.04	Wildwood Crest, NJ	0.01
Ventnor, NJ	0.04	Belmar, NJ	0.01
Loveladies, NJ	0.04	Avon-by-the-Sea, NJ	0.01
Longport, NJ	0.03	Spring Lake, NJ	0.01
Bradley Beach, NJ	0.03	Barnegat Light, NJ	0.01
Ocean Grove, NJ	0.03	Asbury Park, NJ	0.01
Bay Head, NJ	0.02	Bradley Beach, NJ	0.01
Asbury Park, NJ	0.02	Ocean Grove, NJ	0.01
Mantoloking, NJ	0.02	Chadwick Beach, NJ	0.01
Ocean Beach, NJ	0.02	Bay Head, NJ	0.00
Chadwick Beach, NJ	0.02	Ocean Beach, NJ	0.00
Wildwood Crest, NJ	0.01	Sea Girt, NJ	0.00
Normandy Beach, NJ	0.01	Margate, NJ	0.00
Sea Girt, NJ	0.01	Mantoloking, NJ	0.00
Margate, NJ	0.01	Normandy Beach, NJ	0.00
Sandy Hook, NJ	0.01	Sandy Hook, NJ	0.00
Deal, NJ	0.01	Deal, NJ	0.00
Monmouth Beach, NJ	0.00	Monmouth Beach, NJ	0.00
Sea Bright, NJ	0.00	Sea Bright, NJ	0.00

Note: Delaware beaches are in bold text.

might expect, the Delaware beaches (shown in bold type in Table 12.7) tend to rank higher. A few New Jersey beaches stand out as important – Ocean City, Sea Isle City, and Cape May. As one goes north along the New Jersey shore, the per-person per-trip values more or less fall to zero. Many of the beaches in the northern part of New Jersey take three or more hours for Delaware residents to reach, lowering their values considerably.

Table 12.8 shows the closures losses for different geographic and amenity groups. Losing groups of beaches yield much higher welfare losses. The per-person per-trip loss for closing the entire beach area on the Delmarva Peninsula, a major loss to say the least, is $47.73. The average per person seasonal loss is $764. It is interesting to note that closing all Delaware beaches, which differs from the Delmarva scenario only by leaving Ocean City, MD and Assateague Island, VA open, gives a significantly lower loss at $25.40. The value of the southern substitutes is quite evident. This result,

Table 12.8   Mean per-person per-trip loss due to the closure of groups of beaches

Beach Group	MNL Model	MXL Model
Geographic Groups:		
All Delmarva	$47.73	$70.11
Cape Henlopen St. Park DE to Assateague Island VA		
All Delaware	25.40	27.10
Northern Delaware Beaches	13.81	11.14
Cape Henlopen St. Park, North Shores, Henlopen Acres, Rehoboth Beach, Dewey Beach, and Indian Beach		
Southern Delaware Beaches	4.09	2.19
Delaware Seashore St. Park, North Bethany Beaches, Bethany Beach, Sea Colony, Middlesex Beach, South Bethany Beach, Fenwick Island St. Park, and Fenwick Island		
All New Jersey Beaches	8.42	8.78
Amenity Type:		
Beaches with Amusements	11.74	7.42
Point Pleasant Beach NJ, Seaside Heights NJ, Atlantic City NJ, Ocean City NJ, Wildwood NJ, Cape May NJ, Rehoboth Beach DE, and Ocean City MD		
Park Beaches	4.28	3.03
Sandy Hook NJ, Island Beach St. Park NJ, Cape Henlopen St. Park DE, Delaware Seashore St. Park DE, Fenwick Island St. Park DE, Assateague Island MD and VA		
Surfing Beaches	13.01	9.24
Long Branch NJ, Avon-by-the-Sea NJ, Belmar NJ, Manasquan NJ, Point Pleasant Beach NJ, Bay Head NJ, Mantoloking NJ, Seaside Heights NJ, Loveladies NJ, Harvey Cedars NJ, Surf City NJ, Ship Bottom NJ, Long Beach NJ, Beach Haven NJ, Holgate NJ, Cape Henlopen State Park DE, North Shores DE, Dewey Beach DE, Delaware Seashore St. Park, Bethany Beach DE, Fenwick Island DE, Ocean City MD, and Assateague Island MD and VA		

of course, ignores the effect of congestion on these two beaches that may result if such a closure were to occur. In general, these findings must be tempered somewhat keeping in mind that such scenarios are well beyond the range of the data. We never observe individuals facing 'no beaches on the peninsula' in our data. Furthermore, our model does not account for non-participation and some people may opt for no trip with such a large closure. For models incorporating participation into the decision using these data see von Haefen et al. (2002).

The loss of all northern and southern beaches is much as expected. Both are significantly less than losing the entire state, and the northern beach loss is greater than the southern loss by a factor of three, $13.81 versus $4.09. Again, the population of the state mostly resides in the north. The loss of New Jersey beaches is $8.42 per-person per-trip.

The second half of Table 12.8 shows the value of lost beaches sharing the same beach amenities. These are unlikely scenarios but give us a sense of the relative value of some the characteristics beyond simple implicit prices. All surfing beaches are valued at $13.01 per-person per-trip, amusement beaches at $11.74, and park beaches at $4.28.

Our final loss scenario involves beach erosion on the Delaware and Maryland beaches. Unlike the closure analyses this involves a change in beach characteristics. We simulate beach erosion over four different groups of beaches. All of these are beaches presently managed for erosion through beach nourishment projects. The four groups are Northern Delaware, the Bethany Area, Fenwick Island and Ocean City, and All Delmarva. The first three groups are consistent with the management units in the region. That is, beaches are usually nourished in these groups. In all cases the natural park beaches, Cape Henlopen, Delaware Seashore, Fenwick Island State Park, and Assateague Island are excluded from the analysis. These beaches are not managed for erosion and in the absence of coastal development are not likely to erode.

The scenarios assume that all beaches in a group narrow to 75 feet in width or less. We set *Narrow* = 1 and *Wide* = 0 for all beaches in the group to simulate this effect. The losses are calculated using the second equation in equations (12.10) and are reported in Table 12.9. The per-person per-trip loss for the northern beaches is $1.46 and for the Bethany group is $0.73. For Fenwick Island and Ocean City the losses are actually negative. This is because Ocean City MD has a wide beach (*Wide* = 1 for Ocean City in the data). In our simulation when we set *Wide* = 0 and *Narrow* = 1, Ocean City is actually a more desirable beach in our model because the parameter on *Wide* is larger in absolute value than the parameter on *Narrow*. This also explains why the loss on the northern Delaware beaches is larger than the loss on all the beaches on Delmarva. This result changes

Table 12.9   Mean per-person per-trip loss due to the erosion of Delmarva beaches

Beaches narrowed	MNL Model	MXL Model
Northern Delaware Beaches North Shores DE, Henlopen Acres DE, Rehoboth Beach DE, Dewey Beach DE, and Indian Beach DE	$1.46	$2.78
Bethany Area Beaches North Bethany Beaches DE, Bethany Beach DE, Sea Colony DE, Middlesex Beach DE, and South Bethany Beach DE	0.73	0.80
Delaware/Maryland Border Fenwick Island DE and Ocean City MD	−0.21	1.36
All Delmarva North Shores DE, Henlopen Acres DE, Rehoboth Beach DE, Dewey Beach DE, Indian Beach DE, North Bethany Beaches DE, Bethany Beach DE, Sea Colony DE, Middlesex Beach DE, South Bethany Beach DE, Fenwick Island DE, and Ocean City MD	1.23	6.42

in the MXL model where the mean value of the *Narrow* coefficient exceeds *Wide*.

The MXL welfare results are reported along side the MNL results in Tables 12.7–12.9. Going from the MNL to MXL model we see significant decreases in predicted losses for individual beaches in Table 12.7. The Delaware beaches are still toward the top of the list, Rehoboth and Cape Henlopen still rank first and second, but their values are lower by roughly 30 per cent. Overall the value of Delaware beaches decline anywhere from 2 per cent to 57 per cent. Similar changes are seen for New Jersey beaches.

There are two forces driving this result. First, the *Trip Cost* coefficient is nearly twice as large absolutely in the MXL as in the MNL model. Since the *Trip Cost* coefficient is used as a measure of marginal utility of income to monetize changes in expected utility, welfare measures are sensitive to its value. A larger marginal utility of income, all else constant, implies smaller welfare losses (see the denominator in equations (12.10) and (12.16)). This, no doubt, explains much of the drop in site values in the MXL model.

Second, the MXL model does a better job of accounting for site similarity and hence ease of substitution between sites (see Train, 1999, pp. 123–4 and 127). Given the size and significance of many of the coefficients for standard deviation, our model appears to be capturing a richer pattern of substitution than the MNL model. When only a single site is lost, one can count on other similar sites being in the choice set. The MXL model captures that similarity and hence gives lower values for individual site closures.

When groups of sites are lost, the same forces are at work but the importance of accounting for substitutes appears to play a larger role. For example, when all Delmarva beaches are closed the welfare loss in the MXL model is significantly *larger* than in the MNL model, $70.11 versus $47.73, even with the larger marginal utility of income in the MXL model (see Table 12.8). When a fraction of the Delmarva beaches are closed, just the northern or just the southern Delaware beaches, the loss is *smaller* in the MXL versus MNL model. For example, for the southern beaches MXL gives a loss of $2.19, while MNL gives $4.09. The Delmarva beaches are fairly similar. When all are lost, few good substitutes remain in the choice set – beachgoers are forced to go to New Jersey beaches that are quite different in character. When a subset of Delmarva beaches is lost, good substitutes remain. The MXL model, relative to the MNL, seems to pick up this effect. It is as though the Delmarva beaches are 'nested' together. If one or a few are lost within the nest, good substitutes remain. If the entire nest is lost, the alternatives do not look so good.

The MXL welfare losses over the set of beaches of similar amenity type, also shown in Table 12.8, are all lower than the MNL model. Given that the implicit prices of each of these characteristics dropped in the MXL versus MNL model and that the standard deviation on each is rather small, this is not surprising.

The losses in the erosion scenarios all increase in the MXL over the MNL model. The per-person per-trip losses rise from $1.46 to $2.78 for the northern beaches and rise from $0.73 to $0.80 on the Bethany area beaches. The sign on the Fenwick Island/Ocean City MD scenario has the correct sign in the MXL model and is even larger than the Bethany area values at $1.36. These results are easily accounted for by the significantly higher coefficients on the *Narrow* variable in the MXL model.

8. CONCLUSIONS

The day-trip data from a 1997 Mid-Atlantic beach mail survey appear to fit a RUM recreation demand model well. The parameter estimates were much as expected and statistically significant. The welfare estimates for individual beach closures gave much higher losses for popular beaches close to population centers but also generated higher losses for more distance beaches with special characteristics. The per-trip loss for the closure of any single beach, assuming all others remain open, was rather low. Most were well below $1 per-trip. This reflects the large number of good substitutes available. The values for the most popular five beaches ranged from about $1.00 to $5.00 depending on the beach and model used. The distance beaches in central to northern New Jersey generated little or no loss to Delaware residents.

When groups of beaches were closed, the welfare increased significantly. The per-trip loss for all Delaware beaches was about $25, while the northern and southern beaches alone were valued at $12 and $3. The loss of all Jersey beaches to Delaware residents was valued at about $8 per trip.

In all beach closure scenarios it is important to keep in mind the restrictions on substitution in the models. First, there is no participation decision built into the model. So, choosing 'no beach' is not an alternative. For the closure of a single beach for a short time in the season this restriction is probably fine. People are likely to go to alternate beaches, so our model will capture a realistic behavioral effect. For the closure of groups of beaches where individuals are more likely to stop making beach trips altogether, the assumption is more questionable and may lead to overstated losses. At the same time, the model assumes a costless substitution between sites, which may be unrealistic. Individuals are likely to be familiar with a small number of beaches for which they easily substitute one for the other. For many sites, however, individuals must incur some costs in learning about the sites and actually making the substitution from one site to another. This would suggest an understatement of values if such substitution were predicted in the simulation. Finally, the model fails to capture any trip-substitution across time periods. For example, many people may react to a one-week closure of Rehoboth Beach in June by simply delaying their trips to the beach till later in the season. Our model, like most RUM models, does not pick up this type of substitution. To the extent that this is a realistic response, the model overstates the loss.

We also consider some hypothetical erosion losses on Delaware beaches. We considered scenarios where once wide beaches were narrowed to 75 feet or less. The per-trip losses range from about $0.75 to $3 for small groups of Delaware beaches depending on the model and area to about $5 for erosion of all Delmarva beaches. Again, many large park beaches in this region were assumed to be unaffected in this scenario leaving a good number of wide beach substitutes in the simulation.

ACKNOWLEDGEMENT

This work was funded by the National Oceanic and Atmospheric Administration's Delaware Sea Grant Program.

BIBLIOGRAPHY

Bockstael, N.E., W.M. Hanemann and C. Kling (1987). 'Estimating the value of water quality improvements in a recreational demand framework', *Water Resource Research*, **23**(5): 951–60.

Bockstael, N.E., W.M. Hanemann and I.E. Strand (1986), 'Measuring the Benefits of Water Quality Improvements Using Recreation Demand Models', report prepared for the Environmental Protection Agency under Cooperative Agreement CR-811043-01-0, Washington D.C.

Bockstael, N.E., I.E. Strand and K. McConnell (1988), 'Benefits from Improvements in Chesapeake Bay Water Quality', Benefit Analysis Using Indirect or Imputed Market Methods. Vol. 2, U.S. EPA, Washington D.C. [EPA contract No. CR-811043-01-0].

Haab, Timothy C. and Robert L. Hicks (1997), 'Accounting for choice set endogeneity in random utility models of recreation demand', *Journal of Environmental Economics and Management*, **34**: 127–47.

Haab, Timothy C. (forthcoming), 'Temporal correlation in recreation demand models with limited data', *Journal of Environmental Economics and Management*.

Hanemann, W.M. (1978), 'A methodological and empirical study of the recreation benefits from water quality improvements', PhD dissertation, Department of Economics, Harvard University.

Herriges, Joe and Dan Phaneuf (2002), 'Controlling for Correlation Across Choice Occasions and Sites in a Repeated Logit Model of Recreation Demand', *American Journal of Agricultural Economics*, **84**(4): 1076–90.

Massey, D.M. (2002), 'Heterogeneous Preferences in Random Utility Models of Recreation Demand', PhD dissertation, Department of Economics, University of Delaware.

McFadden, Daniel (1974), 'Conditional Logit Analysis of Qualitative Choice Behavior', in Paul Zarembka, (ed.), *Frontiers in Econometrics*, New York: Academic Press, pp. 105–42.

McFadden, Daniel (1978), 'Modeling the Choice of Residential Location', in Anders Karlqvist, Lars Lundqvist, Folke Snickars, and Jorgen Weibull (eds), *Spatial Interaction Theory and Planning Models*, Amsterdam: North Holland, pp. 75–96.

McFadden, Daniel (1981), 'Econometric Models of Probabilistic Choice', in Charles Manski and Daniel McFadden (eds), *Structural Analysis of Discrete Data with Econometric Applications*, Cambridge, MA: MIT Press, pp. 198–272.

McFadden, Daniel (2001), 'Economic choices', *The American Economic Review*, **91**(3): 351–78.

Murray, C., B. Sohngen and L. Pendleton (2001), 'Valuing water quality advisories and beach amenities in the Great Lakes', *Water Resources Research*, **37**(10): 2583–90.

Parsons, G.R. and D.M. Massey (2000), 'Familiar and favorite sites in a random utility model of beach recreation', *Marine Resource Economics*, **14**: 299–314.

Train, K. (1986), *Qualitative Choice Analysis*, Cambridge, MA: MIT Press.

Train, K. (1999a), 'Mixed Logit Models for Recreation Demand', in Joseph A. Herriges and Catherine L. Kling (eds), *Valuing Recreation and the Environment*, Northampton, MA: Edward Elgar Publishing Limited, pp. 141–61.

Train, K. (1999b), 'Halton Sequences for Mixed Logit', University of California Berkeley Working Paper.

von Haefen, R.H., D.J. Phaneuf and G.R. Parsons (2002), 'Modelling Consumers' Demand for a Large Set of Quality Differentiated Goods: Estimation and Welfare Results from a Systems Approach', Manuscript.

13. A finite mixture approach to analyzing income effects in random utility models: reservoir recreation along the Columbia river

J. Scott Shonkwiler and W. Douglass Shaw

1. INTRODUCTION

In much applied work, for example on the benefit side of cost–benefit analysis, the goal is to estimate welfare measures for changes in prices or attributes of goods or activities (hereafter, 'alternatives'). Consumption is likely to be dependent on income. Due to the nature of the alternatives, or at least the nature of data available on the consumption levels, discrete choice forms of the random utility model (RUM) have been applied to estimate the probability of choosing each alternative. Utility-theoretic welfare measures are derived from the same model.

However, we are aware of only a few papers in which the authors use the RUM approach to estimate the probability of choices of goods or alternatives and assume the presence of income effects or assume that there is a non-constant marginal utility of income (for example Gertler and Glewwe, 1990; Herriges and Kling, 1999). In most models, the utility function is assumed linear in its arguments, which may include prices, income, characteristics of the alternatives and the individual. For those arguments that do not change across alternatives, the argument drops out. This is a result of the fact that RUMs examine utility differences, and in the case where income enters the indirect utility function linearly, the income term has a constant effect that disappears when examining these differences. A consequence of this assumption is that the Hicksian measures of consumer's surplus, the compensating and equivalent variation (CV and EV), are identical to ordinary (Marshallian) consumer's surplus. Yet this may not be an attractive feature of the model.

There are several possible approaches to relaxing the assumption of linearity (see Karlstrom, 1999). We offer another here: introducing a finite mixture distribution. As an illustrative example we compare a traditional linear-in-arguments RUM to a finite mixture conditional logit model. Our mixture approach allows groups of individuals to have different marginal utilities of income, leading to differences in consumer's surplus across different groups. The issues motivating the development of our model are presented in Section 2 along with the statistical characterization of the finite mixture conditional logit model. Next follow a short discussion of the data (Section 3) and estimation results (Section 4). Our summary is presented in Section 5.

2. THE MODEL

2.1 Issues

Assume that a relevant population chooses from $i = 1,2,...,G$ mutually exclusive alternatives on a given choice occasion. Let an indirect utility function represent the consumer's $(n = 1,2,...,N)$ level of satisfaction associated with the ith alternative, according to:

$$U_{ni} = f_i(I_n - p_{ni}) + \gamma' x_i + \varepsilon_{ni} = V_{ni} + \varepsilon_{ni} \tag{13.1}$$

where I_n is money income, p_{ni} is n's cost of obtaining the ith alternative, and **x** is a vector of attributes associated with each alternative.

Consider equating expected utilities under two different levels of the attributes (x and x^*). This can be done by adjusting or compensating income with the monetary amount C according to:

$$E \max_i U[f_i(I - p_i - C), x_i^*, \varepsilon_i] = E \max_i U[f_i(I - p_i), x_i, \varepsilon_i] \tag{13.2}$$

Next, define B_{ih} as the event that alternative i is chosen under **x** and alternative h is chosen under x^* with the compensation C.

If the individual chooses alternative i at attribute level **x** and alternative h at attribute level x^* then C equals the difference in the two levels of utility normalized by the marginal utility of income:

$$C_{ih} = f_h^{-1}(U_h - U_i) \tag{13.3}$$

McFadden (1999) denotes the expected income compensation for a quality improvement (or the mean willingness to pay) as:

$$E\ C(I,p,x,x^*,\varepsilon) = \sum_{i=1}^{G} \sum_{h=1}^{G} \text{Prob}(B_{ih}) E[C_{ih}|B_{ih}] \tag{13.4}$$

Here, when $f_i(\cdot)=\alpha(I-p_i)$, then the function is linear and the marginal utility is constant across alternatives and thus C_{ih} becomes equal to:

$$p_i-p_h+[\gamma'(x_h-x_i)+\varepsilon_h-\varepsilon_i]/\alpha \qquad (13.5)$$

If the f_i are nonlinear or vary by the alternative, McFadden (1999) points out that the evaluation of $\mathbf{E}[C(\cdot)]$ may be difficult, depending on the stochastic properties of ε. For example, he shows that by adopting the generalized extreme value distribution (GEV) for ε, this necessitates the use of a Markov Chain Monte Carlo simulator. This is quite computationally complex (although Karlstrom (1999) claims that alternative simpler numerical techniques may be used in certain circumstances). Furthermore, there is a serious additional consequence for determining proper welfare measures.

2.2 Welfare Measures

Many applications seek to extrapolate welfare measures for a sample and generalize these to a population. The manner in which the extrapolation is done varies, but the basic unit of observation for microtheoretic demand estimation is the individual. Chipman and Moore (1980) (among others) have considered the conditions under which compensating variation (the CV is an exact measure of consumer's surplus) can be used to quantify changes in social welfare.

Consider the form of the indirect utility function (U_i):

$$U_i=f_i(I-p_i)+\gamma'x_i+\varepsilon_i \qquad (13.6)$$

A property of U_i is homogeneity of degree zero in p and I. We can satisfy this by assuming that P and I have been normalized by the fixed price of some composite commodity. Chipman and Moore show that if preferences are parallel with respect to this composite commodity then the consumer's surplus provides a valid measure of welfare change. One implication of specifying this representation of preferences is that the resulting demand functions for all goods other than the composite good depend only on the prices, so that the marginal utility of income is indeed constant (Chipman and Moore, 1980, p. 941). Now if it is possible to sort consumers into groups ($j=1, 2, ..., K$) which have homogenous preferences, then the Chipman and Moore result is not particularly restrictive. Each group is assumed to have a constant marginal utility of income. Under these conditions, an unambiguous welfare measure, C_j, can be calculated for each group. Suppose there are n_j individuals in each group. Because C_j provides a uniquely defined cardinal indicator of welfare change, a natural social welfare function to consider is $S = \Sigma C_j$. (Such a social welfare function does not define highest and best welfare, but does map welfare changes into monetary units.)

As shown above, unless $f_i(\cdot) = \alpha(I - p_i)$, then the demand functions that result from a specification for U_i will involve I, and/or have varying marginal utilities of income. While a compensated income level C^* which will keep expected utility constant may exist, it will therefore not be optimal in the sense that aggregated individual preferences represent social preferences (McFadden, 1999). If the assumption is made that the marginal utility of income is constant for each group, then the assignment of individuals to the 'proper' group will condition the welfare estimates. This is plausible, but requires a method that segregates consumers and estimates welfare conditional on the segregation. This is what we propose below.

2.3 The Mixture Model

Assume that the indirect utility function can be defined to be additive in income and attributes as in equation (13.1). The probability that the ith alternative (again suppressing individual subscripts) yields maximum utility across the G alternatives is given by:

$$\text{Prob}[U(I,p_i,x_i,\varepsilon_i) > U(I,p_h,x_h,\varepsilon_h)] \text{for all } h \neq i \qquad (13.7)$$

Now obtaining an operational estimator requires finding a joint distribution for the errors such that evaluation of the probability above is not computationally burdensome. Assume errors are identically distributed according to the joint cumulative distribution function

$$\exp(-e^{\varepsilon 1}, -e^{\varepsilon 2},..., -e^{\varepsilon G}) = F(\varepsilon) \qquad (13.8)$$

which is of extreme value form. If we define:

$$H(e^{V1}, e^{V2},..., e^{VG}) = w_1 + w_2 + ...w_G \qquad (13.9)$$

where $w_i = e^{Vi}$, we obtain the well-known multinomial logit model (MNL). For the MNL, the probability of selecting the ith alternative is

$$P_i = e^{Vi} \bigg/ \sum_{h=1}^{G} e^{Vh} \qquad (13.10)$$

McFadden (1999) shows that when the elements of ε are characterized by a generalized extreme value distribution (GEV) and the indirect utility function is as in equation (13.6), then expected maximum willingness to pay (WTP) can be written:

$$EC(I,p,x,x^*,\varepsilon) = \alpha^{-1}[E \max_i U(I,p_i,x_i^*,\varepsilon_i) - E \max_i U(I,p_i,x_i,\varepsilon_i)] \qquad (13.11)$$

where x^* denotes the new levels of the attribute for the ith alternative. The closed form solution to this is given by

$$\alpha^{-1}\left[\ln \sum_{i=1}^{G} w_i^* - \ln \sum_{i=1}^{G} w_i \right] \qquad (13.12)$$

where

$$w_i^* = \exp[\alpha(I - p_i) + \gamma' x_i^*] \qquad (13.13)$$

Maximum likelihood estimation (MLE) of the parameters in equation (13.10) requires the joint probability mass function (PMF) implied by equation (13.8). For a single observation, this PMF has the general form:

$$f(y|z,Y,\theta) = \text{Prob}(Y_1 = y_1, Y_2 = y_2,..., Y_G = y_g|z,Y,\theta) \qquad (13.14)$$

where z denotes a vector of conditioning variables, θ denotes a vector of unknown parameters, and $Y = \Sigma y_i$. This is a conditional multivariate discrete distribution (conditional on Y) and the joint probability mass function specifically is

$$f(y|z,Y,\theta,) = \frac{Y! \prod_{i=1}^{G} P_i^{y_i}}{\prod_{i=1}^{G} y_i!}. \qquad (13.15)$$

Maximization of the likelihood derived from (13.15) yields the estimates of θ for the MNL when the probabilities P_i are defined as they are in equation (13.10) above. We next modify this basic MNL structure through the introduction of a set of mixing parameters.

2.4   A Finite Mixture Approach

Given the joint PMF for the single observation above, a finite mixture representation can be written

$$f(y|z,\psi) = \sum_{j=1}^{K} \pi_j f(y|z,\theta_j) \qquad \pi_j \geq 0; \ \sum_{j=1}^{K} \pi_j = 1 \qquad (13.16)$$

where ψ subsumes all parameters contained in π and θ (here and subsequently we drop the conditioning variable Y as an explicit argument). An extensive treatment of finite mixture models can be found in Titterington et al. (1985); and we draw heavily on this text in what follows. When both the π_i and θ_i are unknown, MLE can be used to maximize the log likelihood

$$\sum_{n=1}^{N} \ln f(y_n | z_n, \psi) \qquad (13.17)$$

over the observed sample. The global ML estimator for the parameters in (13.17) is strongly consistent if: (i) a proper subset of the parameter space which includes the true ψ is where the search takes place (Redner, 1985), and (ii) if certain regularity conditions are met (Titterington et al., 1985). However, another issue for the case of the MNL model is that of identification.

The MNL is a multivariate model whose marginals are independent binomial logit models. Both these statistical distributions are conditional on $Y = \Sigma y_i$. Identification of the individual univariate models is necessary for identification of the multivariate form. Substantial attention has been devoted to identifying the finite mixture binomial model (see Johnson et al., 1992). Conditions are dependent on the range of Y and the number of observations. However, these conditions provide rules of thumb only when Y varies from observation to observation – as would be expected in most applications. Thus, we advocate an empirical approach that implies parametric identification when the estimated Fisher information matrix is positive-definite upon convergence of the optimization algorithm (Titterington et al., 1985, p. 92).

In general, the π_j would themselves be parametric functions of the conditioning variables. These variables can vary with the individual so that for the nth observation we can specify

$$\pi_{nj} = \exp(\delta_j' q_{nj}) \Bigg/ \sum_{m=1}^{K} \exp(\delta_m' q_{nm}) \qquad (13.18)$$

where δ_j is a vector of parameters modifying the conditioning variables q_{nj}. The probability of the nth individual choosing the ith alternative is then

$$P_{ni} = \sum_{j=1}^{K} \pi_{nj} w_{nij} \Bigg/ \sum_{h=1}^{G} w_{nhj} \qquad (13.19)$$

where it is clear, that the choice probabilities may differ for different individuals in the sample.

There are two quite important features of the mixture MNL model. First, the independence from the usually assumed irrelevant alternatives property (IIA) need not hold. This assumption can usually only be relaxed in the linear in income RUM context by using the nested multinomial logit approach (McFadden, 1996), a random parameters MNL approach (see Train, 1996), or a different distribution for the ε. In equation (13.19), however, the ratio of the probabilities has arguments which include the systematic utilities from other alternatives, not just those for the pair being considered.

The second feature of the model regards interpretation of the probabilities. A posterior analysis of the probability of membership in a given regime, $f(y|z, \theta_j)$ for each observation is gained. Assume that there are only two regimes and consider (suppressing the observation index) the estimated joint PMF. MLE provides

$$P(y|z, \hat{\psi}) = \hat{\pi}f(y|z,\hat{\theta}_1) + (1 - \hat{\pi})f(y|z,\hat{\theta}_2) \qquad (13.20)$$

Membership in a given regime is denoted by one of two states of nature, Ω_1 or Ω_2. For $\Omega = \Omega_1$ an observation belongs to regime one, hence we can write

$$P(y|z, \hat{\psi},\Omega = \Omega_1) = f(y|z,\hat{\theta}_1) \qquad (13.21)$$

and if π denotes the probability of Ω_1 then

$$P(y \text{ and } \Omega = \Omega_1|z, \hat{\psi}) = \hat{\pi}f(y|z,\hat{\theta}_1) \qquad (13.22)$$

Straightforward application of Bayes Theorem consequently results in

$$\text{Prob}(\Omega = \Omega_1|y,z, \hat{\psi}) = \hat{\pi}f(y|z,\hat{\theta}_1)/\text{Prob}(y|z,\hat{\psi}) \qquad (13.23)$$

Define the above posterior probability as ζ_1. In the next section, we very briefly describe the data used to estimate the model. As an example of the approach, we estimate a two-component mixture conditional logit model.

3.   THE DATA

The data used to estimate the model were obtained from a subset of data collected using a mail survey of a sample of individuals who live in the Pacific Northwest.[1] The larger data set was developed for use in examination of water reallocation policy issues (see Callaway et al., 1995), the most important being related to flushing salmon smolts down the Columbia

River from spawning areas. The survey questionnaire focuses mainly on reservoirs on the Columbia, and we select four such reservoirs as destinations for the analysis: Lake Roosevelt (behind Grand Coulee Dam), Dworshak, Lower Granite, and Lake Pend Oreille. We use only the actual behavior data for the analysis below, rather than the actual *and* the contingent behavior data used by Cameron et al. (1996). Because we use the travel costs to the sites to proxy the price of a trip, one can interpret the model below as a recreation demand, or travel cost model (for example Hausman et al., 1995).

In addition to the travel cost variable, which mainly drives the empirical model, we also use the summer average deviation of each water level away from its full pool level (for example, a negative ten means ten feet below full pool). We recognize that our sample contains all different types of recreators (for example anglers, water skiers, those who just like to sit on the shore of the lake), and so we have no a priori expectation on the direction of influence this variable should have on trips. One might hypothesize that shore-oriented users like more shore to be available, suggesting a negative coefficient on a deviation below full pool, and the reverse might be true for boaters who like high water. To parameterize the switch to a different regime, we use a function of the education level and age of the individual. This captures some individual-specific measures that may be associated with a different marginal utility of income.

4. EMPIRICAL RESULTS

4.1 Estimated Coefficients

Results for a straight multinomial logit model are in column 2 of Table 13.1 and results for the finite mixture model are in column 3. The log likelihood is significantly improved using the finite mixture model. A likelihood ratio (LR) test of the null hypothesis that $\pi = 1$ or $\pi = 0$ (that is that the standard MNL model is appropriate) does not yield a test statistic with the proper asymptotic distribution due to a parameter space boundary problem (see Titterington et al., 1985, pp. 152–6). However, under an approximation to the LR test they suggest, we conclude that $0 < \pi < 1$ with greater than 99.99 per cent confidence.

Travel cost has the expected sign in the MNL model for both regimes. The water level deviation variable is negative for regime I (people in this group prefer lower water level), but positive for regime II (showing the preference for higher water levels). For the mixture model, the probability of membership in either regime depends on the switch variables: a constant

Rivers and the sea

Table 13.1   Estimated models

		Mixture MNL	
Variable	MNL	Regime I	Regime II
Price	−0.0761	−0.0394	−0.1571
	(0.0069)*	(0.0039)	(0.0277)
Deviation from full pool	−0.0138	−0.0310	0.0512
	(0.0133)	(0.0127)	(0.0242)
Constant(π)			−22.1528
			(9.3204)
Education(π)			1.4161
			(0.6394)
Age(π)			0.3319
			(0.1645)
Education·Age(π)			−0.02179
			(0.01135)
Log likelihood	−650.98		−480.78

Note: * White's robust standard errors appear in parentheses.

Table 13.2   Properties of the estimated probabilities of membership in Regime I

Probability	Estimated mean	Number of observations with values between 0.25 and 0.75
π	0.374	118
ζ_1	0.374	62

term, education, age, and an interaction variable. Education represents the number of years of schooling (mean = 14.4). The positive signs on education and age along with the negative sign on the education/age interaction variable indicate that slightly older, more highly educated individuals tend to fall into regime I. Taken together, the price and water level coefficients may suggest that this group prefers more shore (a higher deviation away from full pool).

Finally, the mixture model allows estimation of both the conventional and posterior probability of being in either regime (see equations (13.18) and (13.23)). Table 13.2 shows that the average estimated posterior probability of being in regime I is identical to the average estimated prior

Table 13.3   Some average welfare measures

Change	MNL Model	Mixture MNL Model		
		Weighted total	Regime I	Regime II
Increase price of site 1 by $5.00	−2.56	−2.61	−1.56	−3.08
Draw down site 1 by 10 additional feet	0.98	−0.59	2.66	−2.02

probability. However, the posterior probability is much sharper, as indicated by the fact that 118 individuals have prior probabilities of membership in Regime I between 0.25 and 0.75, while only 62 individuals have a posterior probability in the same range (Table 13.2). Thus the posterior analysis can provide an improved method of classifying recreators when information regarding their observed choices is taken into account.

4.2   Estimated Consumer's Surplus

We examine welfare estimates for two scenarios, a price increase, and a ten foot decrease in the deviation from full pool at site 1, Lake Roosevelt. All recreators are unambiguously assigned to one of the regimes according to whether the calculated ζ_1 is less than or equal to 0.5, that is the rule for regime indicator R is:

$$R = 1 \text{ if Prob } (\zeta_1 \geq 0.5) \quad (13.24)$$

where $R = 1$ denotes assignment to regime I. Those recreators not assigned to Regime I are by default assigned to Regime II. This assignment rule results in about 30.5 per cent of the individuals in the sample falling into Regime I. We assume a price increase of $5 at Lake Roosevelt caused by a site fee increase. (We merely wish to illustrate the differences in welfare measures between our two models.) The conventional CV for the simple MNL is identical to ordinary consumer's surplus, as no income effects are assumed. We obtain an estimate of $−2.56 from the MNL model and a pooled estimate of $−2.62 from the mixture model (see Table 13.3). In this case, the straight logit model closely corresponds to the average weighted response of both sets of recreators identified by the finite mixture model. Note, however, that recreators in Regime II incur losses in per trip consumer surplus of almost twice those as the Regime I recreators.

Next, we conduct similar analysis for a water level change at site 1 (see Table 13.3). While the straight logit model unambiguously assigns an average positive per trip consumer surplus measure for a reduction in water level, the finite mixture model clearly distinguishes the differential effects of such a change. Regime I recreators, who may more likely participate in shore activities, actually value a reduction in water levels. Contrast this to Regime II recreators who appear to regard this change as a disamenity. Additionally since these latter recreators comprise about 70 per cent of the sample, the weighted average welfare measure calculated from the mixture MNL model is of a different sign than for the MNL model. Apparently our ability to discriminate between types of recreators with the mixture model more precisely reflects the average welfare effects of a change in water levels.

5. SUMMARY

Several papers in the literature note that common outdoor recreation random utility models typically assume that there are no income effects. In general, however, microeconomic theorists might hypothesize that outdoor recreation activity rises with income, and that valuation of an amenity which is an attribute of a recreation site also differs with income. Our findings support the notion that the marginal utility of income can differ between groups of individuals. Rather than introduce a complicated simulation problem to obtain welfare measures based on indirect utility functions with nonlinear income terms, we have introduced an alternative finite mixture approach here. Our results indicate that differential income effects are important to allow for, and our model allows a nice interpretation of the posterior probabilities that stem from it. Furthermore, we identify a case where an alternative's attribute can be valued differently by different groups of recreators.

Finally, though our particular data set does not necessarily provide a compelling interpretation of the distinguishing characteristics of the two groups identified, it is possible to imagine applications where this would be the case. Consider, for example, using our approach to examine the differences in response to fish consumption advisories for those anglers who fish for food, and those who fish for sport.[2] Similarly, consider an application to recreation in an urban setting, where individuals drawn from the urban population might differ greatly in income or other personal characteristics.

ACKNOWLEDGEMENTS

Our thanks to V. Kerry Smith, Kenneth Train, and also to seminar participants in the Department of Agricultural and Resource Economics at

University of California-Davis for their comments. We also thank Mac Callaway and Matt Rea for access to the data, which were collected as part of research for the U.S. Army Corps of Engineers, Bureau of Reclamation, and Bonneville Power Administration. Research partially supported by the Nevada Agricultural Experiment Station.

NOTES

1. The sample of 203 respondents used for our example visited waters near their home and we have information on trips taken in 1993 from one of four regional survey versions. Other details can be found in Callaway et al. (1995), or in Cameron et al. (1996).
2. We thank Paul Jakus for providing this example at the 1997 AERE summer session.

REFERENCES

Callaway, J.M., S. Ragland, S. Keefe, T.A. Cameron and W.D. Shaw (1995), 'Columbia River Systems Operation Review Recreation Impacts: Demand Model and Simulation Results', Final report prepared for the U.S. Army Corps of Engineers, Portland, Oregon, by RCG/Hagler, Bailly, Inc., Boulder, CO 80306 (July).

Cameron, T.A., W.D. Shaw, S.E. Ragland, J.M. Callaway and S. Keefe (1996), 'Using actual and contingent behavior data with differing levels of time aggregation to model recreation demand', *Journal of Agricultural and Resource Economics*, **21**: 130–49.

Chipman, J.S. and J.C. Moore (1980), 'Compensating variation, consumer's surplus, and welfare', *American Economic Review*, **70**(5): 933–49.

Gertler, P. and P. Glewwe (1990), 'The willingness to pay for education in developing countries: evidence from rural Peru', *Journal of Public Economics*, **42**: 251–75.

Hausman, J., G. Leonard and D. McFadden (1995), 'A utility-consistent, combined discrete choice and count data model: assessing recreational use losses due to natural resource damage', *Journal of Public Economics*, **56**: 1–30.

Herriges, J. and C. Kling (1999), 'Nonlinear income effects in random utility models', *Review of Economics and Statistics*, **81**: 62–72.

Johnson, N.L., S. Kotz and A. Kemp (1992), *Univariate Discrete Distributions*, 2nd edn, New York: John Wiley and Sons.

Karlstrom, A. (1999), 'Hicksian welfare measures in a nonlinear random utility framework', unpublished mimeograph.

McFadden, D. (1999), 'Computing Willingness to Pay in Random Utility Models', in J.R. Melvin, J.C. Moore and R. Riezman (eds), *Trade, Theory and Econometrics*, New York: Routledge.

Redner, R.A. (1985), 'Note on the consistency of the maximum likelihood estimate for non-identifiable distributions', *Annals of Statistics*, **9**: 225–8.

Titterington, D.M., A.F.M. Smith and U.E. Makov (1985), *Statistical Analysis of Finite Mixture Distributions*, New York: John Wiley & Sons.

Train, K. (1996), 'A random parameters multinomial logit model', Unpublished paper, Dept. of Economics, University of California – Berkeley.

14. Whalewatching demand and value: estimates from a new 'double-semilog' empirical demand system

Douglas M. Larson and Sabina L. Shaikh

1. INTRODUCTION

Whalewatching is an increasingly-popular form of winter recreation in California and along much of the rest of the western coasts of the United States and Canada. The annual migration of grey whales along the coast, from summer feeding grounds in the Bering Sea off Alaska to the Gulf of Mexico for calving, is well-documented and publicized in the popular media. The southward migration runs closer to shore and may last for a period of 1–4 weeks, peaking in mid-December in central and Northern California. In the northward migration, whales travel farther offshore and its peak occurs in March. In many ports along the coast, offering whale-watching cruises is an important supplement to the winter incomes of fishing guides, party boat operators, and other boat owners. In addition to regularly-scheduled boat cruises and tours in ports up and down the coast, there are many opportunities for shore-based viewing of the migration from major headlands and promontories.

The value of whalewatching, as with other forms of recreation, is assessed in models of consumer demand that reflect the constraints on choice and the opportunities for consumption. When the behavior of interest is recreational use, often the substitution between sites is important to measuring the value of any given site. A common approach is the random utility model, which predicts the probability of a site being chosen on a given choice occasion. As an alternative, the demand systems popularized in the literature on demands for market goods have recently been applied to the recreation demand and nonmarket valuation setting (for example, Fugii et al., 1985; Shaikh and Larson, 2003).

One attractive feature of the demand systems approach is that it accounts for both the number of trips and the distribution of trips among sites within a utility-theoretic framework. Random utility models are best at predicting the distribution of trips, that is, the probability that a site will be chosen given a trip is taken. One can augment this model with a number of trips model, but it is difficult to reconcile both as having arisen from the same set of underlying preferences except under rather extreme restrictions. Another approach, repeating the site choice model some number of times to generate a number of trips taken, requires information on the number of choice occasions or (equivalently) the number of times a trip was not taken, which is typically not observable and makes a difference to the model estimates. So the self-contained nature of demand systems with respect to predicting where and how often people go is appealing, and merits further exploration in the literature, particularly in light of the advent of flexible functional forms for demand.

While the flexible functional forms are attractive for their ease of use and familiarity to economists working with market goods demands, some interesting nuances arise in their application to the nonmarket setting. One of these is in the measurement of the total worth, or 'access value', of the activity being consumed. It is not uncommon for recreation demands to be price-inelastic at the observed levels of consumption. Depending on the demand system being used, this can lead to problems with measuring access value.

For example, in the Almost Ideal Demand System (Deaton and Muellbauer, 1980), whose focus is explaining budget shares and elasticities, some ranges of parameter values imply that budget share increases with price, which leads to an infinite Hicksian choke price (not, by itself, necessarily a problem) and an infinite willingness to pay for access. In the Linear Expenditure System (Stone, 1954) applied to the nonmarket goods setting, the parameter interpreted as a 'subsistence quantity' of each good may be negative, and in fact must be negative for access value to be finite (Kling, 1988). Another, more commonly used functional form in empirical practice, the Cobb–Douglas demand system (LaFrance, 1986), implies that goods are necessities, with infinite access values, when they are own price-inelastic.

In each of these demand systems, the findings of infinite access value for some parameter ranges are artifacts of the convergence properties of the demand systems as own price for a good rises and quantity consumed goes to zero. This problem diminishes their appeal for empirical nonmarket valuation where determining the total value of resource-based activities is the goal.

In contrast, the 'semilog' demand system, which relates log of quantity consumed to the levels of the independent variables, has finite access values, even though the Hicksian choke price is infinite and quantity consumed goes to zero only in the limit. This makes the semilog model a more attractive option for empirical recreation demand analysis, and it is often used in single equation models (for example, Bateman et al., 2002). However, LaFrance (1990) has shown that demand systems based on this functional form are quite restrictive, with cross-price effects that are either zero or the same across all goods, and income effects that are also either zero or the same for all goods.

This chapter proposes a variation of the semilog demand system, the 'Double Semilog' (DS) system, which retains its attractive features with respect to measuring access values, while achieving somewhat greater flexibility with respect to cross-price and income elasticities. The key differences between the DS and semilog systems are (a) each good can have a different income elasticity in the DS system, whereas all goods have the same income elasticity in the semilog system; and (b) elasticities for price and quality in the DS system are essentially the elasticities in the semilog system with the addition of an income elasticity adjustment.

The first part of the chapter develops the basic demand system and its properties, then its implementation in situations where both time and money are important constraints on demand (as is usually the case with recreation demand) is discussed. Finally, the DS demand system is illustrated with a sample of whalewatchers who visited the three northern California sites. The empirical model jointly estimates the shadow value of leisure time and the 2-constraint whalewatching demand system for the three sites. The demand model estimates are in conformity with the integrability conditions, and are highly significant for two of the three sites, with expected signs on quality effects and on the price–income relationships for all three. The marginal value of time implied by the model estimates is about \$6/hr, with a range in the sample from about \$0.50 per hour to \$13/hour. The demand parameters imply finite access values in spite of demands being price-inelastic at baseline prices and quantities, which illustrates a potential advantage of the DS system relative to some of the other flexible forms.

2.   THE MODEL

The DS model begins with an *expenditure function* of the form

$$e(\mathbf{p}^n,u) = \theta(\mathbf{p},M)\cdot[-e^{\gamma_0+\Sigma\gamma_i p^n_i} + u e^{\Sigma\beta_j p^n_j}] \tag{14.1}$$

where $p^n_i = p_i/\theta(\mathbf{p},M)$ are normalized prices, with $\theta(\mathbf{p},M)$ being any function of prices and income that is homogeneous of degree 1 in $(\mathbf{p},M)$. The use of normalized prices and income imposes the desired homogeneity properties on demands, expenditure, and indirect utility (LaFrance and Hanemann, 1983).

One can also define the *normalized expenditure function* as

$$e^n(\mathbf{p}^n,u) = e(\mathbf{p}^n,u)/\theta(\mathbf{p},M) = [-e^{\gamma_0+\Sigma\gamma_i p_i^n} + ue^{\Sigma\beta_j p_j^n}]. \tag{14.2}$$

Equation (14.2) can be rewritten to solve for the *indirect utility function*

$$\begin{aligned}
V &= [M^n + e^{\gamma_{i0}+\Sigma\gamma_i p_i^n}]e^{-\Sigma\beta_j p_j^n} \\
&= M^n e^{-\Sigma\beta_j p_j^n} + e^{\gamma_0+\Sigma(\gamma_i-\beta_i)p_i^n}
\end{aligned} \tag{14.3}$$

where $M^n = M/\theta(\mathbf{p},M)$ is normalized income. From equation (14.3), it can be seen that in this model, the utility index is strictly positive.

Differentiating (14.2) with respect to p_i^n, the Hicksian demands are

$$x_i^h(\mathbf{p}^n,u) = -\gamma_i e^{\gamma_0+\Sigma\gamma_k p_k^n} + \beta_i ue^{\Sigma\beta_j p_j^n}, \tag{14.4}$$

and the corresponding Marshallian demands, obtained by substituting in the indirect utility function (14.3), are

$$x_i(\mathbf{p}^n,M^n) = (\beta_i - \gamma_i)e^{\gamma_0+\Sigma\gamma_j p_j^n} + \beta_i M^n. \tag{14.5}$$

These Marshallian demands have a functional form that is a hybrid of the semilog and linear demand functions: the price effects are similar to those of the semilog system while the income effects are linear. Notably, the income effects β_i in (14.5) are not restricted as they are in the semilog demand system, where they must all take on a single value.

In the DS system, the Marshallian income slope is $\partial x_i(\mathbf{p}^n,M^n)/\partial M^n = \beta_i$, so that each good has a separate income effect (β_i), unlike the semilog demand system, where all income effects must be the same. The *income elasticity* for good i is, then,

$$\varepsilon_{iM} \equiv \frac{\partial x_i(\mathbf{p}^n,M^n)}{\partial M^n} \cdot \frac{M^n}{x_i} = \frac{\beta_i M^n}{x_i} = \frac{\beta_i p_i^n}{\alpha_i} \tag{14.6}$$

where $\alpha_i \equiv p_i x_i/M$ is the Marshallian budget share of good i. Each good has an independent income effect, unlike the semilog system, where all income effects must be equal.

The Marshallian *own-* and *cross-price elasticities* ε_{ii} and ε_{ij} are, respectively,

$$\varepsilon_{ii} \equiv \frac{\partial x_i(\mathbf{p}^n M^n)}{\partial p_i^n} \cdot \frac{p_i^n}{x_i} = \gamma_i p_i^n \left[1 - \frac{\beta_i p_i^n}{\alpha_i}\right] \tag{14.7}$$

and

$$\varepsilon_{ij} \equiv \frac{\partial x_i(\mathbf{p}^n, M^n)}{\partial p_j^n} \cdot \frac{p_j^n}{x_i} = \gamma_j p_j^n \left[1 - \frac{\beta_i p_i^n}{\alpha_i} \right], \tag{14.8}$$

where $\alpha_i \equiv p_i^n x_i / M^n$ is the budget share of good i. Noting, from (14.6), that $\beta_i p_i^n / \alpha_i$ is the income elasticity for good i, (14.7) and (14.8) can also be written as

$$\varepsilon_{ii} = \gamma_i p_i^n [1 - \varepsilon_{iM}] \tag{14.9}$$

$$\varepsilon_{ij} = \gamma_j p_j^n [1 - \varepsilon_{iM}]. \tag{14.10}$$

In comparing these to the own- and cross-price elasticities of the standard semilog model (Table 14.1), both have an extra term involving own income elasticity $(1 - \varepsilon_{iM})$ which allows more flexibility in the values the elasticities can take.

Table 14.1 *A comparison of Marshallian elasticities in the semilog and double semilog models*

Elasticity	Semilog	Double semilog
Income (ε_{im})	βM^n	$\beta_i M^n / x_i$
Own Price (i)	$\gamma_i p_i^n$	$\gamma_i p_i^n (1 - \varepsilon_{im})$
Cross Price (j)	$\gamma_j p_j^n$	$\gamma_j p_j^n (1 - \varepsilon_{im})$
Own Quality (i)	$\gamma_{iz} z_i p_i^n$	$\gamma_{iz} z_i \cdot (1 - \varepsilon_{im})[p_i^n - 1/(\beta_i - \gamma_i)]$
Cross Quality (j)	$\gamma_{jz} z_j p_j^n$	$\gamma_{jz} z_j p_j^n \cdot (1 - \varepsilon_{im})$

As with the semilog system, in the DS system the own- and cross-price elasticities have the relative relationship *within* a given Marshalian demand,

$$\varepsilon_{ij}/\varepsilon_{ik} = \gamma_j p_j^n / \gamma_k p_k^n,$$

though it has greater flexibility in the elasticity of a given price in own demand relative to other demands,

$$\varepsilon_{ij}/\varepsilon_{kj} = [1 - \varepsilon_{iM}]/[1 - \varepsilon_{kM}]$$

which depends on the income elasticities of both goods. In the semilog system, by contrast, $\varepsilon_{ij}/\varepsilon_{kj} = 1$.

While (14.6)–(14.8) indicate that the DS system has a greater flexibility in representation of Marshallian elasticities, it still embodies some restrictions, due to its relatively simple functional forms for estimation and relatively small number of parameters to be estimated. From (14.9) and (14.10), it can be seen that the own- and cross-price elasticities of demand for good i are related to the income elasticity; this relationship is

$$\frac{\varepsilon_{ij}}{\gamma_j p_j^n} = [1 - \varepsilon_{iM}] = \frac{\varepsilon_{ii}}{\gamma_i p_i^n}. \quad (14.11)$$

As always in specifying empirical demand and valuation systems, the trade-off is between flexibility and relative ease of use and estimation. The DS system largely preserves the convenience and usefulness for measuring access values of the semilog system, while increasing its flexibility to represent price and income effects on demand.

3. ADDING QUALITY EFFECTS ON DEMAND

A convenient way to represent quality effects is to allow the price coefficients to vary with quality. In (14.5), one can define $\gamma_j = \gamma_{j0} + \gamma_{jz} \cdot z_j$, and substituting these into (14.5), each site demand function is a function of own- and substitute site quality levels. With this addition, the own-quality slopes are

$$\partial x_i / \partial z_i = \gamma_{iz} p_i^n (\beta_i - \gamma_i) e^{\gamma_0 + \Sigma \gamma_j p_j^n} - \gamma_{iz} e^{\gamma_0 + \Sigma \gamma_j p_j^n}$$

$$= \gamma_{iz} e^{\gamma_0 + \Sigma \gamma_j p_j^n} (p_i^n (\beta_i - \gamma_i) - 1).$$

The sign of the Marshallian own-quality slope of demand, which is expected to be positive, depends not only on the quality parameter γ_{iz} but also the magnitude of normalized price p_i^n relative to $(\beta_i - \gamma_i)$.

The *Marshallian own-quality elasticities*,

$$\varepsilon_{iz_i} \equiv \frac{\partial x_i}{\partial z_i} \cdot \frac{z_i}{x_i}$$

can be written as

$$\varepsilon_{iz_i} = \gamma_{iz} z_i \cdot (1 - \beta_i p_i^n / \alpha_i)[p_i^n - 1/(\beta_i - \gamma_i)],$$

$$= \gamma_{iz} z_i \cdot (1 - \varepsilon_{iM})[p_i^n - 1/(\beta_i - \gamma_i)], \quad (14.12)$$

where α_i is the budget share of good i. Again, in comparison with the semilog demand system where quality enters in a similar way (Table 14.1), the semilog own quality elasticity has additional terms involving ε_{iM} and $(\beta_i - \gamma_i)$, which gives increased flexibility.

The Marshallian cross-quality slopes are given by

$$\partial x_i / \partial z_j = \gamma_{jz} p_j^n (\beta_i - \gamma_i) e^{\gamma_0 + \Sigma \gamma_j p_j^n}$$

$$= \gamma_{jz} p_j^n (x_i - \beta_i M),$$

and the *Marshallian cross-quality elasticities* are

$$\varepsilon_{iz_j} \equiv \frac{\partial x_i}{\partial z_j} \cdot \frac{z_j}{x_i} = \gamma_{jz} z_j p_j^n \cdot (1 - \beta_i p_i^n / \alpha_i) = \gamma_{jz} z_j p_j^n \cdot (1 - \varepsilon_{iM}). \qquad (14.13)$$

Similarly to the price effects, the cross-quality effect in the DS system has an extra term, $(1 - \varepsilon_{im})$, relative to the semilog system (Table 14.1). Combining (14.12) and (14.13) with (14.11), the full set of relationships between quality, price, and income effects within a given demand function are

$$\frac{\varepsilon_{iz_j}}{\gamma_{jz} z_j p_j^n} = \frac{\varepsilon_{ij}}{\gamma_j p_j^n} = [1 - \varepsilon_{iM}] = \frac{\varepsilon_{ii}}{\gamma_i p_i^n} = \frac{\varepsilon_{iz_i}}{\gamma_{iz} z_i [p_i^n - 1/(\beta_i - \gamma_i)]}. \qquad (14.14)$$

4.   WELFARE MEASUREMENT

As noted in the Introduction, a principal purpose of introducing the DS model is to evaluate its use for the purposes of measuring access value, the take-it-or-leave-it measure of the worth of recreational opportunities. This welfare measure, when applied to the value of a particular site, is defined with reference to a change in price from initial level p_i^0 to infinity, which causes quantity consumed to change from the initial level x_i^0 to zero.

Welfare measures for smaller changes in price that leave the individual consuming the good before and after the price change are also often of interest. However, because they are straightforward to calculate in the DS model, as with other models, they are not pursued further in this chapter. Instead, price elasticities of whalewatching demand at the observed price and quality levels are presented. A similar approach is taken for quality effects, since they too are straightforward to evaluate in the DS and other models.

In general the integrability conditions for the model are satisfied for the following ranges of the income (β_i) and own-price (γ_i) parameters:

(a) $\beta_i < 0, \gamma_i < 0$

(b) $\beta_i = 0, \gamma_i < 0$

(c) $\beta_i > 0, \gamma_i < 0$

(d) $\beta_i > 0, \gamma_i > \beta_i$

For the purpose of measuring access values, in the different parameter ranges the DS model has characteristics similar to those of the other common demand systems. For parameter ranges (a) and (d), where $\text{sgn}(\gamma_i) = \text{sgn}(\beta_i)$, the model has finite 'choke'[1] prices and access values, similar to the linear demand system or the LES system with negative subsistence quantities. For parameter range (b), it resembles the semilog demand system and the AIDS or Constant Elasticity systems with own price-elastic demands, in that the 'choke' price is infinite but access value is always finite. For range (c), the model resembles the LES system with positive subsistence quantities in that demand converges to a positive quantity as own price goes infinite.[2]

4.1 Choke Prices

When finite [that is, when $\text{sgn}(\beta_i) = \text{sgn}(\gamma_i)$], the normalized Hicksian choke price $\hat{p}_i^n$ is defined implicitly as

$$x_i^h(\hat{p}_i^n, \mathbf{p}_{-i}^n, \mathbf{z}, u) = -\gamma_i e^{\gamma_i(\hat{p}_i^n - p_i^{n0})} e^{\gamma_0 + \sum_k \gamma_k p_k^{n0}} + \beta_i u e^{\beta_i(\hat{p}_i^n - p_i^{n0})} e^{\sum_j \beta_j p_j^n} \equiv 0,$$
(14.15)

where $\text{sgn}(\beta_i) = \text{sgn}(\gamma_i)$. The Hicksian demand now depends explicitly on the vector of qualities $\mathbf{z} = (z_1, ..., z_n)$ at different sites since the price coefficients $\gamma_j = \gamma_{j0} + \gamma_{jz} \cdot z_j$ depend on quality. Using the indirect utility function (14.3) evaluated at initial prices $\mathbf{p}^{n0}$ and M^n to identify the utility index u, the choke price $\hat{p}_i$ can be written explicitly in terms of observables as

$$\hat{p}_i^n = p_i^{n0} + \frac{1}{\gamma_i - \beta_i} \ln \left\{ \frac{M^n - x_i^0/\gamma_i}{M^n - x_i^0/\beta_i} \right\}.$$
(14.16)

where $x_i^0 = (\beta_i - \gamma_i) e^{\gamma_0 + \sum \gamma_j p_j^{n0}} + \beta_i M^n$ is the Marshallian demand at initial prices.

In contrast, where it exists and is finite (that is, for $(\beta_i - \gamma_i)\beta_i < 0$), the normalized Marshallian choke price $p_i'^n$ sets Marshallian demand to zero, so is defined implicitly as

$$x_i(p_i'^n, \mathbf{p}_{-i}^n, \mathbf{z}, u) = (\beta_i - \gamma_i) e^{\gamma p_i'^n} e^{\gamma_0 + \sum_{k \neq i} \gamma_k p_k^n} + \beta_i M^n \equiv 0,$$

and simplifies to a form similar to (14.16),

$$p_i'^n = p_i'^{n0} + \frac{1}{\gamma_i} \ln \left\{ \frac{M^n}{M^n - x_i^0/\beta_i} \right\}.$$
(14.17)

4.2   Access Value and Consumer's Surplus

Access value for good i is defined as the change in expenditure resulting from the price change $\hat{p}_i^n \to p_i^{n0}$; that is,

$$
\begin{aligned}
AV &\equiv e_i(\hat{p}_i^n,\mathbf{p}_{-i}^n,\mathbf{z},u) - e(p_i^{n0},\mathbf{p}_{-i}^n,\mathbf{z},u) \\
&\equiv e(\hat{p}_i^n,\mathbf{p}_{-i}^n,\mathbf{z},u) - M.
\end{aligned}
\tag{14.18}
$$

Using the indirect utility function (14.3) evaluated at initial prices $\mathbf{p}^{n0}$ and M^n to identify the utility index u, the expenditure function evaluated at the choke price for good i is

$$
\begin{aligned}
e(\hat{p}_i^n,\mathbf{p}_{-i}^n,\mathbf{z},u) &= \theta(\mathbf{p},M)\cdot[-e^{\gamma_i(\hat{p}_i^n-p_i^{n0})}e^{\gamma_0+\Sigma\gamma_j p_j^{n0}} \\
&\quad +(M^n+e^{\gamma_0+\Sigma\gamma_j p_k^{n0}})e^{\beta_i(\hat{p}_i^n-p_i^{n0})}].
\end{aligned}
\tag{14.19}
$$

Using (14.19) in (14.18) and simplifying, access value can be written as

$$
AV = \frac{\beta_i+\gamma_i}{\gamma_i}M^n - \left[\frac{\beta_i+\gamma_i}{\gamma_i}M^n - x_i^0/\gamma_i\right]\left\{\frac{M^n-x_i^0/\gamma_i}{M^n-x_i^0/\beta_i}\right\}^{\frac{\beta_i}{\gamma_i-\beta_i}}
\tag{14.20}
$$

The Marshallian consumer's surplus approximation to access value is the integral of the Marshallian demand over the interval $(\hat{p}_i^n,p_i^{n0})$,

$$
AV^M = \int_{p_i^{n0}}^{\hat{p}_i^n}[(\beta_i-\gamma_i)e^{\gamma_0+\Sigma\gamma_j p_j^n}+\beta_i M^n]dp_i
$$

which, when integrated and simplified, can be expressed as

$$
AV^M = x_i^0/\gamma_i - \frac{\beta_i}{\gamma_i}M^n\cdot\ln\left\{\frac{M^n}{M^n-x_i^0/\beta_i}\right\}.
\tag{14.21}
$$

5.   THE DS MODEL WITH TWO CONSTRAINTS ON CHOICE

The foregoing discussion developed the new DS system in terms of a money expenditure function only, which is appropriate for standard money-constrained choice problems that are used in most areas of demand analysis. When choice is constrained by time in addition to money, as is likely with most recreational activities, a two-constraint version of the model is needed. The properties of two-constraint choice models have been discussed elsewhere (Bockstael et al., 1987; Larson and Shaikh, 2001). In particular, Larson and Shaikh (2001) have identified the parameter restrictions on demand systems that follow from the assumption that time is costly. It is straightforward to show that the Marshallian demand system in (14.5) satisfies these conditions.

Two-constraint demand systems have two expenditure functions dual to indirect utility: one is the money expenditure function given the time budget and utility level, and the other is the time expenditure function given money budget and utility. In the DS system with two constraints on choice, the money expenditure function is

$$e(\mathbf{p}^n, \mathbf{z}, u) = \theta(\mathbf{p}, \mathbf{M}) \cdot [-e^{\gamma_0 + \Sigma \gamma_i p_i^f} + u e^{\Sigma \beta_j p_j^f} - \rho^n \cdot T^n] \qquad (14.22)$$

which is similar to (14.5), with two major differences:

(a)   the normalized prices p_i^n in (14.5) are replaced by 'full' prices $p^{fi} = p_i^n + \rho^n \cdot t_i^n$, ρ^n is the normalized value of time,[3] and $t_i^n \equiv t_i / \psi(\mathbf{t}, T)$ and $T^n \equiv T / \psi(\mathbf{t}, T)$ are time price and time budget normalized by the deflator $\psi(\mathbf{t}, T)$, which is homogeneous of degree 1 in $(\mathbf{t}, T)$;
(b)   it has an additional term involving the normalized value of time and time budget, $-\rho^n \cdot T^n$.

The Hicksian and Marshallian demands are obtained from the two-constraint money expenditure function (14.22) in the usual way, namely, by differentiating with respect to money price and initializing the utility term in terms of full budget and full prices. The functional form of the Marshallian demand system in (14.5) is unaffected, though the money prices p_j^n and money budget M^n are replaced by full prices p_j^f and full budget M^f. Similarly, if the normalized shadow value of time is independent of budget arguments (which satisfies the homogeneity requirements for it), the Hicksian and Marshallian access values have the same functional form as (14.20) and (14.21), with M^f replacing M^n.[4]

Empirically, the marginal value of time spent on a recreation trip can be treated in at least three ways. If the individual is jointly choosing labor supply and recreation demands, the marginal value of time is equated to an observable parameter (the marginal wage) which can be used in its place (Becker, 1965; Bockstael et al., 1987). The second is to identify it through auxiliary choices, such as the labor supply decision if that is predetermined with respect to the recreation choices (Heckman, 1974; Feather and Shaw, 1999). The third is to treat it as endogenous to the recreation choices and to estimate it jointly with recreation demands (McConnell and Strand, 1981; Larson and Shaikh, 2002). In this case, the marginal value of time function must satisfy the requirements of choice subject to two constraints (Larson and Shaikh, 2001).

The strategy here is to use a simple version of the latter approach, where the normalized marginal value of time is constant, which satisfies the homogeneity requirements with respect to money and time budget arguments. This also implies that the 'absolute' marginal value of time, scaled to the levels of actual budgets and prices, varies across people if they have different prices or budget levels. The reason is that the relationship between the relative and absolute marginal values of time is

$$\rho(\mathbf{p},\mathbf{t},M,T) = \rho^n \cdot \theta(\mathbf{p},M)/\psi(\mathbf{t},T); \qquad (14.23)$$

that is, the absolute marginal value of time is the relative marginal value of time scaled by the ratio of the deflators used to normalize the money and time budgets (Larson and Shaikh, 2001). The end result is an estimate of the marginal value of time for each person that is a constant dollar per hour, similar to the approach taken in Hausman et al. (1995), with the per-hour value varying across the sample according to each person's time and money budgets.

6. DATA

The data used to illustrate the model are from on-site intercepts of whale-watchers at three sites in Northern California during the winter of 1991–92. Two sites, Point Reyes and Half Moon Bay, are in the San Francisco area, with Point Reyes to the north of the Golden Gate Bridge and Half Moon Bay on the Pacific coast south of San Francisco. The third site, Monterey, is further to the south, some 110 miles from San Francisco. As these data are discussed in some detail elsewhere (Loomis and Larson, 1994), a relatively brief description is provided here.

Grey whale migration occurs on the Pacific coast in the winter months. The southward migration from the Bering Sea to Mexico generally occurs from November to January followed by several months of the return trip north. The whales travel very close to the shore and swim at about 3–5 miles per hour, making them very visible from the 16 shore or a boat. Whales are viewed from the shore at Point Reyes, and predominantly from boats in Half Moon Bay and Monterey. The boat trips normally consist of a 2–4 hour excursion to view whales. Since the survey took place during the whale migration, which is in the winter months, most people were on the coast for the primary purpose of whale watching and not summer beach activities.

Each site visit has both a money price (p_j) and a time price (t_j). The

Table 14.2 Quantities, prices and qualities by site

Variable	Mean	Std Dev	Minimum	Maximum
Point Reyes (N=258)				
Actual Trips	2.2519	2.8230	1.0000	40.0000
Normalized Money Price	0.0010	0.0036	0.0000	0.0488
Normalized Time Price	0.0005	0.0005	0.0000	0.0049
Expected Sightings	4.1938	6.8532	0.0000	50.0000
Predicted Trips	2.1616	0.5450	−0.7509	5.0324
Half Moon Bay (N=72)				
Actual Trips	1.4306	1.0322	1.0000	8.0000
Normalized Money Price	0.0015	0.0019	0.0003	0.0136
Normalized Time Price	0.0008	0.0002	0.0004	0.0015
Expected Sightings	9.6944	9.7730	0.0000	50.0000
Predicted Trips	1.1572	0.0484	1.0942	1.4350
Monterey (N=102)				
Actual Trips	1.7843	2.4439	1.0000	24.0000
Normalized Money Price	0.0022	0.0042	0.0001	0.0402
Normalized Time Price	0.0009	0.0006	0.0001	0.0028
Expected Sightings	13.0588	10.6006	0.0000	50.0000
Predicted Trips	1.6444	0.6305	−1.1666	3.4718

money travel costs include round trip vehicle cost per mile, plus other travel expenses. On-site time is considered largely exogenous because most of the whalewatching at two of the three sites, Monterey and Half Moon Bay, occurs on boat trips of fixed length. Variations in onsite time are relatively small at the third site, Point Reyes, and in all cases whalewatching was a day trip activity. Household income before taxes was the money budget variable, and the respondent's time spent not working is the leisure time budget; this is obtained from the average hours worked per week and the number of days of paid vacation per year. The money and time budget levels for each individual were used as the deflators, so normalized money price of site j is $p_j^n = p_j/M$, normalized time price of site j is $t_j^n = t_j/T$, normalized money and time prices are $M^n = 1 = T^n$, full prices are $p_j^f = p_j^n + \rho^n \cdot t_j^n$, and full budget is $M^f = 1 + \rho^n$, with ρ^n estimated as a constant. The quality variable, z_j, is the number of whales vistors to each site expect to see. Table 14.2 provides a summary description of these variables for each of the three sites.

The system of Marshallian demands in (14.5), with full prices and full budget variables, was estimated for the three Northern California whalewatching sites (Point Reyes, Half Moon Bay, and Monterey) via maximum likelihood, using Gauss MAXLIK Version 4.0.22. Because the data represented visitors intercepted at the sites (that is, those with positive quantities), the demand errors are likely to be truncated and this must be taken account of in estimation. If one writes the latent demand for site i as

$$x_i^*(\mathbf{p}^f, M^f) = (\beta_i - \gamma_i)e^{\gamma_0 + \Sigma \gamma_j p_j^f} + \beta_i M^f + \varepsilon_i, \qquad (14.23)$$

then a positive quantity $x_i(\mathbf{p}^f, M^f)$ is observed when $x_i^*(\mathbf{p}^f, M^f) > 0$, or when

$$\varepsilon_i > -[(\beta_i - \gamma_i)e^{\gamma_0 + \Sigma \gamma_j p_j^f} + \beta_i M^f].$$

Due to the truncation, the expectation of ε_i is not zero and must be accounted for in estimation (Heckman, 1974; Greene, 1993). The inverse mills ratio

$$E\{\varepsilon_i | \varepsilon_i > 0\} = \phi(w_i)/\Phi(-w_i)$$

with $w_i \equiv -[(\beta_i - \gamma_i)e^{\gamma_0 + \Sigma \gamma_j p_j^f} + \beta_i M^f]$, was included in an additional regressor in estimating the demand systems (14.5) to ensure that the estimation error has expectation zero.[5]

7.   RESULTS

The estimation results are presented in Table 14.3. The estimates for all three sites satisfy the integrability conditions for the parameters to represent a valid demand model, and the price, quality, and budget parameters are highly significant for the Point Reyes and Monterey trips, though not so for Half Moon. The model predicts the actual mean trips at each site relatively well: the predicted (actual) trips for Point Reyes was 2.16 (2.25), for Half Moon it was 1.15 (1.43), and for Monterey it was 1.64 (1.78). The Half Moon results are not too surprising in light of the relatively small number of people intercepted there (72) relative to the other sites, and the fact that there is less variation in the number of trips taken there.[6] The Point Reyes and Monterey results, though, illustrate some of the interesting features of the DS model.

First, the budget parameters β_j are the only ones whose sign directly indicates the direction of impact of the corresponding demand slope. The significant coefficients (β_1 and β_3) indicate that demand at Point Reyes has a positive income effect, while at Monterey it has a negative income effect. The finding of negative income effects is relatively common in recreation demand, and probably reflects the cross-sectional pattern of usage by

Table 14.3   Estimation results

Variable	Parameter	Estimate	Asymptotic Std. Error
Pt. Reyes Price	γ_{10}	16.3725	5.464
Pt. Reyes Sightings	γ_{1z}	−0.0637	−9.664
Pt. Reyes Budget Slope	β_1	6.8902	2.214
Half Moon Price	γ_{20}	3.8157	1.227
Half Moon Sightings	γ_{2z}	−0.0026	−0.297
Half Moon Budget Slope	β_2	1.7373	1.208
Monterey Price	γ_{30}	−17.4486	−5.936
Monterey Sightings	γ_{3z}	−0.0350	−4.968
Monterey Budget Slope	β_3	−6.3731	−2.125
Value of Time Constant	$-\sqrt{\rho^n}$	−0.7778	−1.518
Pseudo R^2		0.421	
Mean log-likelihood		−6.05	
Number of cases		432	

different income groups at a point in time more than the changes in an individual's consumption as his or her income increases.

For the quality and price parameters, the signs do not indicate the direction of impact, since the own- and cross-elasticities with respect to quality depend not only on the γ_{jz} but also on the income elasticities (equations (14.12) and (14.13)). The own- and cross-elasticities with respect to price depend on both the income and quality effects in addition to the γ_{j0} (equations (14.9) and (14.10)), since $\gamma_j = \gamma_{j0} + \gamma_{jz} \cdot z$.

The sample means of elasticities at observed price, quality, and budget levels are presented in Table 14.4.[7] Because these are Marshallian elasticities, the price elasticities are not perfectly symmetric, though their signs are.[8] All three demands are own-price inelastic, with elasticities ranging from −0.1 at Point Reyes to −0.55 at Monterey. As noted in the Introduction, it is this own-price inelasticity that invalidates the use of several common and/or flexible functional forms for measuring access values. The pattern of cross-price elasticities suggests that Point Reyes and Monterey are substitutes; the insignificant Half Moon price coefficient means its substitution relationship with the other sites cannot be determined.

The income elasticity estimates, interestingly, suggest that demand is highly income elastic at all sites. As noted above, this is likely reflecting the relative patterns of visitation by income groups in the different areas: in Point Reyes, those with higher budgets for leisure activities (higher income,

Table 14.4   Price, income and quality elasticity estimates

Elasticity of trips to	With respect to price at			With respect to income
	Point Reyes	Half Moon	Monterey	
Point Reyes	−0.1009 (0.0230)[a]	−0.0336 (0.0071)	0.1960 (0.0284)	6.1263 (0.104)
Half Moon	−0.0884 (0.0275)	−0.1193 (0.0294)	0.0767 (0.0155)	3.7578 (0.032)
Monterey	0.2095 (0.0448)	0.1499 (0.0265)	−0.5571 (0.1503)	−14.1127 (1.262)

Elasticity of trips to	With respect to expected sightings at		
	Point Reyes	Half Moon	Monterey
Point Reyes	0.0612 (0.0053)	0.0000 (9.62E-06)	0.0015 (0.0002)
Half Moon	0.0004 (7.22E-05)	0.0052 (0.0008)	0.0007 (0.0001)
Monterey	−0.0021 (0.0005)	−0.0001 (3.37E-05)	0.0961 (0.0216)

Note: [a] Standard errors of the means in parentheses.

more leisure time, or both) go more frequently, while in Monterey, those with lower leisure budgets go less often.

The own-quality elasticities for each site (Table 14.4) are all positive, as one would expect, and are larger in magnitude than the cross-site quality elasticities. Magnitudes of the own-quality elasticity for Point Reyes and Monterey, the two sites with significant quality effects, are large relative to the cross-effects. The elasticities of 0.06 and 0.10, respectively, mean that a doubling of expected sightings would yield 6 per cent and 10 per cent increases in trips taken to Point Reyes and Monterey, respectively.

A final point about the estimation results concerns the marginal value of time, which is significant at the 10 per cent level (1-tailed test) in Table 14.3. This parameter was estimated with a squared transformation to impose the requirement that the marginal value of time is nonnegative, and the estimate of −0.7778 implies that the relative marginal value of time is 0.605 for everyone (Table 14.5). Rescaling by the ratio of deflators M/T, the absolute marginal value of time is, on average, $5.87 per hour, and varies from a low of $0.45/hr to a high of $13.60/hr in the sample.

Access value estimates are presented in Table 14.6. The consumer's

Table 14.5 Normalized and absolute shadow values of time (n = 432)

Shadow value of time	Mean	Std Dev	Minimum	Maximum
Normalized	0.6050	0.0000	0.6050	0.6050
Absolute ($/hr)	5.8698	3.2893	0.4507	13.6010

Table 14.6 Hicksian and Marshallian estimates of access value

	Welfare measure of access value	
Site[a]	Consumer's surplus	Compensating variation
Point Reyes	779.09	833.98
	(36.74)[b]	(42.56)
Monterey	128.71	125.58
	(6.96)	(6.72)

Notes:
[a] Estimates not provided for Half Moon as demand coeffients are insignificant.
[b] Standard errors of the mean in parentheses.

surplus estimates of willingness to pay for access at prevailing price conditions are $779 for Point Reyes and $129 for Monterey, while the compensating variation estimates are $834 and $126, respectively. The magnitudes of the Hicksian and Marshallian measures are close, reflecting a small overall income effect at each site. Also, the compensating variation measure is larger at Point Reyes, since it is a normal good, while consumer's surplus is larger at Monterey, because of its negative income effect. Measured relative to the mean number of trips, the access value on a per trip basis is approximately $779/2.16 \approx $360/trip at Point Reyes, and about $129/1.64 \approx $79/trip at Monterey. While the range in per-trip values may seem a bit large, in fact it is consistent with the difference in prices of whalewatching and in income elasticities at the two sites. Because most trips in Monterey are taken on boats, the price of a whalewatching trip is higher than at Point Reyes; because of this, access value will be lower at Monterey, all else equal. Similarly, the pattern of visitation being heavier among those with lower leisure budgets at Monterey suggests willingness to pay is lower.

8. CONCLUSIONS

This chapter has introduced and illustrated a new empirical demand system that may be of some use in measuring access values for recreation activities that are commonly price-inelastic. Like the standard 'semilog' demand system which relates demand covariates to log-quantities, the 'double semilog' or DS system generates finite access values, or total consumer's surplus, estimates for own-price inelastic demands. This does not occur with several other common and/or flexible demand forms, including the Almost Ideal Demand System, the Linear Expenditure System, and the Cobb–Douglas demand models. In addition, the DS model has somewhat greater flexibility than does the semilog system to represent price, quality and income elasticities. Each demand has a separate income coefficient in the DS model, while all income coefficients are the same in the semilog model. Similarly, the price and quality elasticities in the DS model involve more parameters, including the income elasticity in every case and, for own-quality effects, additional parameters beyond that.

The model was developed initially for the standard single-constraint setting, then extended to the case of two binding constraints on choice, as is often expected with consumption of time-intensive goods such as recreation. The marginal value of time is a parameter or function that can be estimated jointly within the model, provided it meets certain homogeneity requirements implied by the two-constraint choice theory, or it can be assumed to be predetermined as is common in many other recreation demand studies.

An illustration of the model is provided, using data on whalewatching in Northern California at a system of three sites in relatively close proximity that one might expect act as three substitutes in consumption. The demand model satisfies the integrability conditions and estimates for two of the three sites, Point Reyes and Monterey, are highly significant with the expected signs. The estimated marginal value of time is approximately $5.90 per hour, with a range from $0.45/hr to $14/hr. Despite the fact that demands are highly price-inelastic, the model readily produces access value estimates of approximately $360 per trip for Point Reyes and $79 per trip for Monterey. Several characteristics of demand that differ between the two sites suggest that this difference in per-trip values is plausible.

While the model works well for the case study at hand, with a small number of sites (3) and quality attributes (1), it has not yet been applied to resources with large numbers of sites or attributes. Thus it is hard, at present, to gauge the practical limitations of the approach in these dimensions. It seems likely that the main challenges posed are data-related: having enough data, and enough variation in the data, to implement the model for many sites or attributes. This is clearly an important area for further work.

Several other lines of analysis are suggested by these results. It may be possible to estimate a more flexible, individual-specific normalized value of time within the model, consistent with the two-constraint choice requirements. Using a count rather than continuous demand error may improve the estimates further, though the available count data estimators for systems of more than two goods are somewhat inflexible with respect to the cross-equation covariances. Finally, it may also be possible to further improve the flexibility of the demand model itself through the introduction of additional parameters, though this may come at the cost of greater difficulty in using the model to evaluate access values analytically or in finding global maxima of the likelihood function.

NOTES

1. 'Choke' prices are the minimum prices that choke off demand to zero; thus they are the price on the demand curve (whether Hicksian or Marshallian) for which quantity equals zero. In measuring access values, Hicksian choke prices are used; they are infinite for models where quantity consumed approaches zero asymptotically with price.
2. This latter case is the problemmatic one, for all demand systems, as it implies the good is a necessity, which is implausible for specific recreation activities; thus one would not expect to see this case in practice.
3. The normalized marginal value of time, $\rho''(\mathbf{p}, \mathbf{t}, M, T)$, is the ratio of the marginal utility of time and the marginal utility of money in the normalized choice model and, as such, is potentially a function of all variables in the choice problem. Larson and Shaikh (2001) show that $\rho''(\mathbf{p}, \mathbf{t}, M, T, \mathbf{s})$ is homogeneous of degree zero in $(\mathbf{p}, M)$, $(\mathbf{t}, T)$, and $(\mathbf{p}, \mathbf{t}, M, T)$.
4. With ρ'' independent of the budget arguments, one can measure the money compensating variation of welfare change either as a difference in the money expenditure function or as a difference in full expenditure, since the term $\rho'' \cdot T'$ does not change with money prices.
5. Because the truncation was at the same threshold, 0, it is not possible to estimate a scale coefficient so it is normalized to 1.
6. This was typically the case for other demand models explored using these data as well.
7. To give a sense for variation in these elasticities due to differences in demand covariates, the standard errors of the sample means are also provided in Table 14.4.
8. The corresponding Hicksian elasticities (not shown) are symmetric as expected and required by theory.

REFERENCES

Bateman, I.J., A.A. Lovett, J.S. Brainard and A.P. Jones (2003), 'Using Geographical Information Systems (GIS) to estimate and transfer recreational demand functions', in Nick Hanley, W. Douglass Shaw and R.E. Wright (eds), *The New Economics of Outdoor Recreation*, Cheltenham: Edward Elgar.

Becker, G. (1965), 'A theory of the allocation of time', *Economic Journal*, **75**: 493–517.

Bockstael, N.E., I.E. Strand and W.M. Hanemann (1987), 'Time and the recreation demand model', *American Journal of Agricultural Economics*, **69**: 293–302.

Deaton, A. and J.J. Muellbauer (1980), 'An almost ideal demand system', *American Economic Review*, **70**: 312–26.

Feather, P. and W.D. Shaw (1999), 'The demand for leisure time in the presence of under-employment and over-employment', *Economic Inquiry*, **38**: 651–66.

Fugii, E.T., M. Khaled and J. Mak (1985), 'An almost ideal demand system for visitor expenditures', *Journal of Transport Economics and Policy*, **15**: 161–71.

Greene, W.H (1993), *Econometric Analysis*, 2nd edn, New York: Macmillan.

Hausman, J.A., G.K. Leonard and D. McFadden (1995), 'A utility-consistent, combined discrete choice and count data model: assessing recreational use losses due to natural resource damage', *Journal of Public Economics*, **56** (January): 1–30.

Heckman, J. (1974), 'Shadow prices, market wages, and labor supply', *Econometrica*, **42**: 679–94.

Kling, C.L. (1988), 'Comparing welfare estimates of environmental quality changes from recreation demand models', *Journal of Environmental Economics and Management*, **15** (September): 331–40.

LaFrance, J.T. (1986), 'The structure of constant-elasticity demand models', *American Journal of Agricultural Economics*, **68**: 543–52.

LaFrance, J.T. (1990), 'Incomplete demand systems and semilogrithmic demand models', *Australian Journal of Agricultural Economics*, **34** (August): 118–31.

LaFrance, J.T. and W.M. Hanemann (1983), 'On the integration of some common demand systems', Staff Paper No. 83–10, Department of Agricultural Economics and Economics, Montana State University.

Larson, D.M. and S.L. Shaikh (2001), 'Empirical specification requirements for two-constraint models of recreation choice', *American Journal of Agricultural Economics*, **83**: 428–40.

Larson, D.M. and S.L. Shaikh (2003), 'Recreation demand choices and revealed values of leisure time', *Economic Inquiry,* forthcoming.

Loomis, J.B. and D.M. Larson (1994), 'Total economic values of increasing grey whale populations: results from a contingent valuation survey of visitors and households', *Marine Resource Economics*, **9** (Fall): 275–86.

McConnell, K.E. and I.E. Strand (1981), 'Measuring the cost of time in recreation demand analysis: an application to sportfishing', *American Journal of Agricultural Economics*, **63**: 153–6.

Shaikh, S.L. and D.M. Larson (2003), 'A two-constraint almost ideal demand model of recreation and donations', *Review of Economics and Statistics*, forthcoming.

Stone, J.R.N. (1954), 'Linear expenditure systems and demand analysis: an application to the pattern of British post-war demand', *Economic Journal*, **64**: 511–27.

15. Estimating recreational trout fishing damages in Montana's Clark Fork River Basin: summary of a natural resource damage assessment

Edward R. Morey, William S. Breffle, Robert D. Rowe and Donald M. Waldman

1. INTRODUCTION

Southwestern Montana contains some of the most popular cold-water trout fishing rivers and streams in the United States, such as Rock Creek, the Big Hole River, and the Madison River. However, among these trout fishing jewels, a century of heavy metal releases from mining waste has completely eliminated trout from the 20-mile long Silver Bow Creek between Butte, Montana and the start of the upper Clark Fork River, and has significantly reduced trout stocks in a 125-mile stretch of the upper Clark Fork River from its headwaters to Missoula (Lipton et al., 1995). The State of Montana filed suit in 1983, under federal Superfund law and its state counterpart, against the Atlantic Richfield Co. (ARCO), the current owners of the mining operations, for compensable damages and restoration costs for these recreational fishing and other damages. The intent of the research presented here was to conduct a natural resource damage assessment (NRDA) to estimate the compensable damages to the anglers who fish the cold-water trout rivers and streams of southwestern Montana. This chapter summarizes the work of the economists working for the State of Montana, although space will not accommodate all of the details. For all of the specifics, see Morey et al. (1995). The economics assessment for ARCO was conducted by Desvousges and Waters (1995b).

We develop and estimate an individual-based utility-theoretic model of where and how often an angler will fish as a function of travel costs, expected catch rates, other characteristics of the fishing sites in the choice set, and characteristics of the individual. From this demand model of participation and site choice, we derive an estimate of each angler's annual expected compensating variation, E(CV), associated with increasing the expected catch rates to their no-injury levels. This E(CV) can be interpreted as the annual willingness to pay (*WTP*) for the expected catch rates that would exist in the absence of injury.

The model includes both resident anglers and nonresident anglers who currently fish in Montana, and allows them to have different preferences.[1] This issue is important because the cold-water rivers and streams of southwestern Montana are nationally known as premier trout fishing destinations that draw large numbers of nonresidents each year.

A goal in recreation studies is to cost-effectively collect relevant data on sites and anglers, while minimizing potential sampling biases. In this study, we used an *intercept/subsample/follow* (*ISF*) procedure: anglers were *intercepted* at 26 study sites, a *subsample* of anglers was selected to reflect the actual population trip-taking proportions to the study sites based on supplemental information, and these anglers received *follow-up* surveys through the fishing season. Because we have a choice-based sample, the sampled anglers have a higher level of avidity than the study angler population. We use avidity weights to correct for this bias. Thus, the *ISF* procedure, with independent information on avidity and site trip-taking proportions, cost-effectively collects the required catch rate and angler data and eliminates potential sampling biases.

Parameters in the travel-cost portion of the model were jointly estimated along with the sites' expected catch rates, which determine site choice. This method was used, rather than using just the simple observed average catch rates; the amount of catch data in the sample varies significantly across the sites in our choice set, being particularly low for many of the injured sites and thus resulting in unreliable averages at some sites. This joint estimation technique was developed by Morey and Waldman (1993 and 1998). The joint estimation was controversial and criticized by the economists working for ARCO (Desvousges and Waters, 1995a; McFadden, 1995). The advantages and disadvantages of joint estimation are discussed in Morey and Waldman (2000) and Train et al. (2000). In summary, joint estimation is appropriate and improves efficiency if all important explanatory variables of site choice are included in the model, but may lead to biased parameter estimates if important explanatory variables are omitted. The damage estimates are significantly dependent on whether simple averages are used for the expected catch rates or catch rates are jointly estimated with the parameters in the travel-cost model, as discussed at the end of the chapter.

2. TROUT FISHING IN SOUTHWESTERN MONTANA: THE CHOICE SET, DATA AND TRIP COSTS

To group fishing sites in the choice set, we divide southwestern Montana into four study regions around four population centers: Missoula (M), Butte/Dillon (BU), Helena (H), and Bozeman (BZ). We chose 26 river and stream sites within the four regions for intensive study, although trip data were collected for all trout rivers and streams in southwestern Montana that were visited by sampled anglers. The 26 intensively studied sites and the four regions in southwestern Montana are listed and defined in Table 15.1. The 26 sites include all of the injured sites: Upper Clark Fork 1–5 and Silver Bow Creek. The criteria for choosing the set of sites for intensive study included geographic dispersion over southwestern Montana, variability in expected catch rates, and variability in site size. For the study sample, approximately 73 per cent of all resident trips and 82 per cent of all nonresident trips to southwestern Montana were to the 26 sites. While we focus on angler choice in southwestern Montana, trips to Montana rivers and streams outside of southwestern Montana are also included in the trip data by assigning them to a broad region encompassing the rest of Montana.

Individual per-trip catch data were obtained for the 26 sites by intercepting and interviewing at the sites following a stratified random sampling procedure across sites, days, and times of the day from May through August 1992. From these interviews, catch data from 1344 individual fishing trips were collected. Anglers were also asked survey questions about their perceptions of expected catch rates at several of the sites. Based on fishing time observed during the intercept survey, anglers spent considerably less time fishing at the sites they perceive to have low catch rates than at the sites they perceive to have high catch rates, which indicates there is a strong relationship between demand for a site and angler perceptions about expected catch rates. For example, Madison 2 was given the highest average perceived catch-rate rating, and there are 847 hours of fishing reported at that site. Upper Clark Fork 2 and 3 received the lowest perceived catch-rate rating, and only 69 hours were reported for those two sites combined. This difference in fishing hours is dramatic given that interviewers spent approximately half as much time collecting data at Madison 2 than at Upper Clark Fork 2 and 3.

Data on trips and angler characteristics were collected by on-site, telephone, and mail surveys using an *ISF* sampling procedure.[2] Approximately one-half of anglers initially intercepted on-site were targeted to be followed through the rest of the season. An in-field postcard survey was conducted

Table 15.1   List of 26 intensively studied sites by region[a]

Missoula Nest (M)
   Upper Clark Fork 1 (*UCF*1) – Bonner to Rock Creek
   Upper Clark Fork 2 (*UCF*2) – Rock Creek to Flint Creek
   Upper Clark Fork 3 (*UCF*3) – Flint Creek to L. Blackfoot
   Middle Clark Fork (*MCF*) – Spurgin Rd. to Huson
   Rock Creek (*RC*) – 1 mile up from Clark Fork to Siria
   Flint Creek (*FC*) – Maxville to Black Pine Rd.
   Bitterroot 1 (*BT*1) – Maclay Br. to Chief Looking Glass
   Bitterroot 2 (*BT*2) – Angler's Roost to Hannon Mem.
   Lolo Creek (*LC*) – Mormon Cr. to Lolo Hot Springs
   Blackfoot (*BF*) – Bonner to Whitaker Br.
   Little Blackfoot (*LBF*) – Cutoff Rd. to Elliston

Butte/Dillon Nest (BU)
   Upper Clark Fork 4 (*UCF*4) – L. Blackfoot to Perkins L.
   Upper Clark Fork 5 (*UCF*5) – Perkins L. to Pond 2 Outfall
   Silver Bow Creek (*SBC*) – Ponds to Butte
   Warm Springs Creek (*WSC*) – Fish Hatchery to Meyer's Dam
   Big Hole 1 (*BH*1) – Pennington Br. to Brown's Br.
   Big Hole 2 (*BH*2) – Melrose to Divide
   Jefferson 1 (*J*1) – Willow Cr. to Cardwell
   Jefferson 2 (*J*2) – Waterloo to Twin Bridges
   Beaverhead (*BV*) – Barretts to Clark Canyon

Helena Nest (H)
   Missouri (*MS*) – Dearborn R. to Holter Dam

Bozeman Nest (BZ)
   Lower Yellowstone (*LY*) – Springdale to Livingston
   Gallatin (*G*) – Shedd Br. to Spanish Cr.
   East Gallatin (*EG*) – Spain L. Br. to Griffen Dr.
   Madison 1 (*MD*1) – Cobblestone to Beartrap
   Madison 2 (*MD*2) – Varney to Lyons

Note: [a] Region and site abbreviations used with models are identified after each region or site name.

at the 26 intensively studied sites concurrently with the intercept survey and was used as a method to count angler visitation at each site and to determine the follow-up sampling proportions for anglers intercepted at each of the 26 sites.

This subsampling was undertaken because the proportions of intercepted anglers at the sites may misrepresent actual proportions of anglers, as a result of limitations on survey agents' time. Because postcards were placed on every automobile at all sites, the postcard proportions of anglers across sites provide reliable estimates of the proportions of anglers at each of the 26 sites. The postcard survey includes questions relating to party size, the number of individuals participating in fishing and nonfishing recreational activities, time on-site, and other fishing data. It was used as a method to count angler and nonangler recreation visitation at each of the 26 intensively studied sites. All license plate numbers of automobiles on which postcards were placed were recorded to monitor postcard return rates. Response rates average 47 per cent across all sites but differ across sites, which was taken into account in the estimation of site proportions. We demonstrate later that the implicit site weighting in the sampling plan appears to be sufficient.

Trip patterns for the 1992 fishing season were obtained for a sample of 443 anglers, comprising 291 residents and 152 nonresidents. Multipurpose trips were not included.[3] Single-site trips to each of the 26 sites were coded to the specific site. Multisite trips where all of the sites were to one region were coded as a trip to that region but were not assigned to a specific site. Trips to sites in southwestern Montana other than the 26 intensively studied sites were designated as *other sites* by region, and trips to Montana rivers and streams outside of southwestern Montana were aggregated as the separate, fifth *other region*. All other trips were coded as a trip being taken, but no site or region was coded.

Of the 26 intensively studied sites, the six most popular sites in terms of seasonal visitation (Rock Creek, Bitterroot 2, both Big Hole sites, Missouri, and Madison 2) account for 52 per cent of all the trips to the 26 sites. The five injured upper Clark Fork sites and Silver Bow Creek account for only 6 per cent of all of the fishing trips to the 26 sites, even though they run between two major population centers.

Larger rivers and streams attract and support more anglers than smaller rivers and streams. To account for this, a size index was created by multiplying the length of each study river/stream segment by the average flow in the segment, measured in cubic feet per second. The largest seven sites account for 43 per cent of trips to the 26 intensively studied sites over the season. The smallest seven account for only 13 per cent. Data on other site characteristics that influence trip taking were also collected. We found that the presence of campgrounds increases visitation. With two exceptions, whether a site is suitable for effective float fishing is determined solely by size. The two exceptions are the Gallatin, where floating is prohibited, and the Beaverhead, which is suitable for floating even though it is small.

The cost of a trip to site j has four components: transportation costs, lodging costs, variable per-trip equipment costs (such as tackle and guide fees), and the opportunity cost of the individual's time in travel and while at the site. Specifically, trip cost is determined by the driving distance to the site, the angler's wage rate, average equipment and lodging costs by one-way distance category (0–25 miles, 26–50 miles, 51–150 miles, and more than 150 miles), and average on-site time by distance category.[4] Distance and per-mile vehicle operating costs ($0.14 per vehicle occupant)[5] were used to determine transportation costs for residents and all nonresidents for whom driving was less expensive than flying, and airfares and car rental rates were used to calculate transportation costs for distant nonresidents. Trip costs vary significantly in percentage terms across sites for each resident angler but vary less significantly across sites for nonresidents. Time costs are converted to money costs by multiplying travel and on-site time by the opportunity cost of the individual's free time. The per-hour opportunity cost of the individual's free time is assumed to be some fraction of the individual's wage rate, β_w, which was estimated within the recreation demand model.[6]

3.   THE JOINT MODEL OF PARTICIPATION, SITE CHOICE AND EXPECTED CATCH RATES

The recreation demand model has two components: a travel-cost component and a catch-rate component. The travel-cost component is a repeated three-level nested logit model of participation and site choice. Because nested logit models of recreational demand are becoming increasingly common, only the specific details of the travel-cost component are presented here.

As noted above, the two components of the model were jointly estimated because the observed trip patterns contain information about expected catch rates (*ceteris paribus*, anglers take more trips to sites with high expected catch rates and fewer trips to sites with low expected catch rates). Our estimate of an expected catch rate is a weighted average of the site's observed average catch rate and the maximum likelihood catch rate parameter that would best explain trip patterns in the absence of any observed catch data (see Morey and Waldman, 1998). The weight on the site's observed average catch rate is a decreasing function of its sampling variation relative to the sampling variation in the observed trip patterns.

We assume the trout fishing season consists of 60 periods such that in each period an angler can take no more than one fishing trip. There is no stipulation that each period is of equal length; we chose 60 periods because only 10 of the 443 anglers in our follow-up sample took more than 60 trips.[7]

In each period, the individual simultaneously decides whether to fish at a river or stream in Montana and, if so, which one. The angler has 31 river and stream trout fishing sites from which to choose: 26 specific sites and five *other* sites. In each period, each angler must choose one of 32 alternatives where one of the alternatives is nonparticipation. The sites are grouped by regions that correspond to the major cities in southwestern Montana because resident anglers are more likely to visit sites near their homes. The angler's choice set for each period (other than nonparticipation), and the regional nesting structure for fishing, is presented in Table 15.1.

This recreation demand model determines the per-period probability that individual *i* will choose alternative *j*. The predicted number of trips angler *i* will take to site *j* is therefore the per-period probability that individual *i* will choose site *j* multiplied by 60, and the predicted number of trips angler *i* will take to all sites in Montana during the summer season is the sum of his or her predicted trips to the 30 sites.

The utility the individual receives during period *p* if he chooses alternative *j* is:

$$U_{jp} = V_j + \varepsilon_{jp}; \quad j = 0, \; UCF1, \; UCF2, \; UCF3, \; MCF, \; RC, \; FC, \; BT1, \; BT2, \; LC,$$
$$BF, \; LBF, \; RMo, \; UCF4, \; UCF5, \; SBC, \; WSC, \; BH1, \; BH2,$$
$$J1, \; J2, \; BV, \; RBUo, \; MS, \; RHo, \; LY, \; G, \; EG, \; MD1, \; MD2,$$
$$RBZo, \; R5, \tag{15.1}$$

where $j = 0$ is the nonfishing alternative. The full names of the 26 intensively studied sites are listed in Table 15.1. *RMo*, *RBUo*, *RHo*, and *RBZo* are collectives of all the other sites in the Missoula, Butte, Helena, and Bozeman regions. *R5* is a collective of all the river and stream sites in Montana that are not in one of the four regions in southwestern Montana, denoted region 5.

The term V_j depends on the cost and characteristics of alternative *j*. Assume that the unobserved random components, ε_{jp}, are drawn from the generalized extreme value distribution with cumulative distribution function

$$F(\varepsilon) = \exp[-e^{-\varepsilon_0} - [(E_M)^{t/s} + (E_{BU})^{t/s} + (E_H)^{t/s} + (E_{BZ})^{t/s} + (E_5)^{t/s}]^{1/t}], \tag{15.2}$$

where *s* is a statistical parameter that influences the degree of unobserved correlation between the utility from trips to any two sites in the same region, *t* is a statistical parameter that influences the degree of unobserved correlation between the utility from trips to any two fishing sites,[8] and

$$E_M = e^{s\varepsilon}UCF1 + e^{s\varepsilon}UCF2 + e^{s\varepsilon}UCP3 + e^{s\varepsilon}MCF + e^{s\varepsilon}RC + e^{s\varepsilon}FC +$$
$$e^{s\varepsilon}BT1 + e^{s\varepsilon}BT2 + e^{s\varepsilon}LC + e^{s\varepsilon}BF + e^{s\varepsilon}LBF + e^{s\varepsilon}RMo, \tag{15.3}$$

$$E_{BU} = e^{s\varepsilon}UCF4 + e^{s\varepsilon}UCF5 + e^{s\varepsilon}SBC + e^{s\varepsilon}WSC + e^{s\varepsilon}BH1 + e^{s\varepsilon}BH2 +$$
$$e^{s\varepsilon}J1 + e^{s\varepsilon}J2 + e^{s\varepsilon}BV + e^{s\varepsilon}RBUo, \tag{15.4}$$

$$E_H = e^{s\varepsilon}MS + e^{s\varepsilon}RHo, \tag{15.5}$$

$$E_{BZ} = e^{s\varepsilon}LY + e^{s\varepsilon}G + e^{s\varepsilon}EG + e^{s\varepsilon}MD1 + e^{s\varepsilon}MD2 + ee^{s\varepsilon}RBZo, \text{ and} \tag{15.6}$$

$$E_{R5} = e^{s\varepsilon}R5, \tag{15.7}$$

This generalized extreme value function generates a three-level nested logit model of participation and site choice. Given this cumulative distribution function (CDF), the per-period probability that an individual will choose not to fish is

$$\text{Prob}_0 = \frac{e^{V_0}}{e^{V_0} + [(I_M)^{t/s} + (I_{BU})^{t/s} + (I_H)^{t/s} + (I_{BZ})^{t/s} + (I_{R5})^{t/s}]^{1/t}}, \tag{15.8}$$

where

$$I_M = e^{sV}UCF1 + e^{sV}UCF2 + e^{sV}UCF3 + e^{sV}MCF + e^{sV}RC + e^{sV}FC + e^{sV}BT1 +$$
$$e^{sV}BT2 + e^{sV}LC + e^{sV}BF + e^{sV}LBF + e^{sV}RMo, \tag{15.9}$$

$$I_{BU} = e^{sV}UCF4 + e^{sV}UCF5 + e^{sV}SBC + e^{sV}WSC + e^{sV}BH1 + e^{sV}BH2 + e^{sV}J1 +$$
$$e^{sV}J2 + e^{sV}BV + e^{sV}RBUo, \tag{15.10}$$

$$I_H = e^{sV}MS + e^{sV}RHo, \tag{15.11}$$

$$I_{BZ} = e^{sV}LY + e^{sV}G + e^{sV}EG + e^{sV}MB1 + e^{sV}MB2 + e^{sV}RBZo, \text{ and} \tag{15.12}$$

$$I_{R5} = e^{sV}R5. \tag{15.13}$$

The per-period probability the individual will choose site j in the Missoula region ($j = UCF1$, $UCF2$, $UCF3$, MCF, RC, FC, $BT1$, $BT2$, LC, BF, LBF, RMo) is

$$\text{Prob}_j = \frac{e^{sV}[(I_M)^{t/s} + (I_{BU})^{t/s} + (I_H)^{t/s} + (I_{BZ})^{t/s} + (I_{R5})^{t/s}]^{(1/t)-1} + (I_M)^{(t/s)-1}}{e^{V_0} + [(I_M)^{t/s} + (I_{BU})^{t/s} + (I_H)^{t/s} + (I_{BZ})^{t/s} + (I_{R5})^{t/s}]^{1/t}}.$$
$$\tag{15.14}$$

The per-period probabilities for the intensively studied sites in the three other regions (Butte, Helena, and Bozeman) are defined similarly. The per-

period probability the individual will choose a site in Montana that is not in one of the four regions in southwestern Montana is

$$\text{Prob}_R = \frac{e^{sV_{RS}}[(I_M)^{t/s} + (I_{BU})^{t/s} + (I_H)^{t/s} + (I_{BZ})^{t/s} + (I_{R5})^{t/s}]^{(1/t)-1}(I_{R5})^{(t/s)-1}}{e^{V_0} + [(I_M)^{t/s} + (I_{BU})^{t/s} + (I_H)^{t/s} + (I_{BZ})^{t/s} + (I_{R5})^{t/s}]^{1/t}}.$$

(15.15)

Specifically, assume the V_j for a fishing trip to site j, where j is one of the 26 intensively studied sites, is a function of the following variables: the angler's per-period income, PPY; the angler's cost of a trip to site j, $COST_j$; the expected catch rate at site j, ECR_j; the size of site j, SZ_j;[9] a variable that takes the value one if there is a campground adjacent to the site and zero otherwise, D_{CG}; a variable that takes the value one if the river has low flow but is suitable for float fishing (only the Beaverhead) and zero otherwise, D_{LFF}; and a variable that takes the value one if the site is high flow but is unsuitable for float fishing (only the Gallatin) and zero otherwise, D_{HFNF}.[10] $COST_j$ is a function of β_w, which is estimated endogenously in the recreation demand model.

$$V_j = [\beta_o(1 - NRES) + \beta_{ONR}(NRES)](PPY - COST_j)$$
$$+ [\beta_C + \beta_{CSK}(1 - NRES)SK + \beta_{CNR}(NRES)](ECR_j)$$
$$+ \beta_{SZ}(SZ_j) + \beta_{CG}(D_{CG}) + \beta_{LFF}(D_{LFF})$$
$$+ \beta_{HFNF}(D_{HFNF}),$$

(15.16)

where $NRES = 1$ if the angler is not a resident of Montana and zero if the angler is a resident. Note $(PPY - COST_j)$ is the amount of income the individual has left to spend on other commodities in period p if the individual takes a trip to site j. Resident and nonresident anglers are allowed to have different catch and price parameters. We feel that the estimated model included all the significant determinants of site choice, while the economists for ARCO disagreed.

If the trip is to a site in one of the four regions (Missoula, Butte, Helena, or Bozeman), but not to one of the intensively studied sites, assume

$$V_j = [\beta_0(1 - NRES) + \beta_{ONR}(NRES)](PPY - AveCOST_{Rk}) + \alpha_o,$$ (15.17)

where the individual's cost of a trip to the *collective* site in region k is assumed to be the average of the individual's trip costs for the intensively studied sites in region k. Since the collective sites are catch-alls for trips to sites other than the intensively studied sites, there is unobserved variation across trips to each collective site in terms of site size, expected catch rate, and other characteristics. Therefore, characteristics cannot be included as explicit determinants of the utility an angler receives from a trip to a collective site. Their influence is replaced with a constant term, α_O.

If the trip is to a site that is not in one of the four explicit regions in southwestern Montana, assume

$$V_{R5} = [\beta_0(1 - NRES) + \beta_{ONR}(NRES)](PPY) + \alpha_{R5}. \qquad (15.18)$$

Note in this case there is no information about trip costs, so even though trip cost is positive it cannot be included as an explicit determinant of the utility the angler receives from a trip to this *fifth* region. Its influence must be accounted for by the fifth-region constant, α_{R5}.

If an individual does not take a fishing trip in period p, that individual will have PPY to spend on other goods, and V_0 is

$$V_0 = [\beta_0(1 - NRES) + \beta_{ONR}(NRES)](PPY) + \beta_G(G) + \beta_{SK}(SK)$$
$$+ \beta_{MTF}(MTF) + \beta_{FT}(FT) + \beta_A(A) + b_V(V) +_{\beta PNR}(NRES) + \alpha_p, \qquad (15.19)$$

where G is the angler's gender (1 = female), SK is self-assessed fishing skill, MTF is years fished in Montana, FT is reported hours of free time in a typical weekday, A is age, V is weeks of paid vacation, and α_p is a constant term. While each angler's utility is an increasing function of his or her income, the choice probabilities are not a function of income because an increase in income affects the utility from all of the alternatives equally. *Ceteris paribus*, residents and nonresidents are allowed to have different preferences for trout fishing in Montana relative to other activities. This feature, in addition to the separate catch and price parameters for residents and nonresidents, and along with the variation between residents and nonresidents in travel costs, skill, and other included variables, allows the model to reflect significant differences in preferences between resident and nonresident anglers.

The catch rate component of the model assumes the probability that a representative angler will catch a certain number of fish at a site depends on the expected catch rate for that site and the number of hours fished, and is increasing in both. Specifically, it assumes that catch is Poisson distributed as a function of the expected catch rate and the number of hours fished.[11] The Poisson distribution correctly restricts the observed catch to be a nonnegative integer and is consistent with the large number of observations with zero catch (almost half). Expected catch rates are the link between the catch rate and travel-cost components of the model in that they are parameters in both components.

We define x_{kj} as the reported catch for intercept trip k to site j and h_{kj} as the number of hours of fishing associated with that catch. Set $\lambda_{kj} = h_{kj} ECR_j$. Assume that catch has a Poisson distribution such that the probability of catching x_{kj} fish in h_{kj} hours of fishing is

$$\text{Prob}(x_{kj}) = \frac{e^{\lambda_{kj}} \lambda_{kj}^{x_{kj}}}{x_{kj}!} \tag{15.20}$$

$j = 1, 2, ..., 25$ and $x_{kj} = 0, 1, 2, ...$

Sites with high perceived catch rates have many observations on catch while sites with low perceived catch rates have only a few observations, even though approximately the same amount of time was spent interviewing at each of the 26 intensively studied sites (except Silver Bow Creek which received about 48 per cent of the interviewing time received by other sites, enough to confirm that virtually no fishing was occurring). The number of observations on catch varies from 0 at Silver Bow Creek to 176 at Madison 2, and the reported fishing time for which we have catch data varies from 7 hours at Warm Springs Creek to 847 hours at Madison 2.[12]

The simple average for a site with few hours of reported catch will be an imprecise estimate of the site's expected catch rate relative to sites with many hours of reported catch. For example, the simple average for Upper Clark Fork 4, 1.5 fish per hour (based on 21 hours of reported catch from 9 trips) is, relatively speaking, an imprecise estimate of the site's expected catch rate, whereas the simple average for Madison 2, 0.72 (based on 847 hours of reported catch from 172 trips) is a relatively precise estimate of the expected catch rate at Madison 2. Therefore, when one has limited catch data for some sites, we argue that assuming the expected catch rates are the simple observed averages is not the best way to proceed. Since data are available on both individual observed catch and individual trip patterns, the best statistical estimate of a site's expected catch rate is a weighted average of these two separate estimates, where the weight on a site's simple average observed catch rate is an increasing function of the number of hours of fishing at the site for which catch is reported.

For each of the 443 anglers in the recreation demand model data set, there is a record of how many fishing trips he or she took during the 1992 summer season, but not a complete record of where each angler went for each trip. An angler's fishing trips were allocated to one of the following 36 site categories on the basis of the information available for each trip:

$T_{UCF1}, T_{UCF2}, ..., T_{MD2} =$ Number of trips to each of the 26 intensively studied sites in Table 15.1 (26 variables).

$T_{Xo}=$ Number of trips to a single site in one of four study regions, but not to an intensively studied site, where $X = RM$ for Missoula, RBU for Butte, RH for Helena, and RBZ for Bozeman.

$T_X=$ Number of trips where each trip involved multiple sites in one of four study regions, but no sites in other regions, where X is as defined as for T_{Xo}.

$T_{R5}=$ Number of trips to rivers or streams in Montana that are outside of the 4 study regions.

$T_O=$ Number of trips that involved multiple regions or where there is no information about the site(s) visited except that the trip involved trout fishing in Montana.

The number of periods the individual chose not to fish, N, is 60 minus the individual's total number of fishing trips.

The per-period probability of a trip to multiple sites in region k ($k = M$, BU, H, BZ) is modeled as the per-period probability that region k will be chosen. Denote this per-period probability Prob_{Rk}. For example, Prob_{RM} is the per-period probability the Missoula region will be chosen, where $\text{Prob}_{RM} = \text{Prob}_{UCF1} + \text{Prob}_{UCF2} + ... + \text{Prob}_{LBF} + \text{Prob}_{RMo}$.

Because of the intercept nature of the sampling, the 443 individuals in the data set take, on average, more trips than anglers randomly chosen from the population who fish for trout at rivers and streams in Montana. To adjust for overavidity, choice-based avidity weights were used (Manski and Lerman, 1977). All observed choices (fishing or nonfishing) were weighted, separately for residents and nonresidents, by the ratio of the population probability of the choice to the sample probability. Let $w_f = (1 - NRES) \times w_f^r + NRES \times w_f^{nr}$ be the weight for a fishing trip, where w_f^r equals the ratio for residents, which is the mean number of trips per season for the population (based on state data) relative to the sample: $6.356/17.880 = 0.355$, and w_f^r is the same ratio for nonresidents: $w_f^{nr} = 1.342/3.816 = 0.352$. Let $w_{nf} = (1 - NRES) \times w_{nf}^r + NRES \times w_{nf}^{nr}$ be the weight for nonparticipation, where w_{nf}^r equals the ratio of the mean number of periods of nonparticipation in the population to the mean number in the sample for residents: $w_f^r = (60 - 6.356)/(60 - 17.880) = 1.274$, and w_{nf}^{nr} is the same ratio for non-residents: $w_{nf}^{nr} = (60 - 1.342)/(60 - 3.816) = 1.044$. The impact of avidity weights on estimated consumer surplus is discussed in the section below on damage estimates.

The log likelihood function for the travel-cost component of the model is

$$L_{tc} = \sum_{i=1}^{443} \{W_{nf}[N\ln(\text{Prob}_0)] + w_f[T_o\ln(\text{Prob}_o) + T_{R5}\ln(\text{Prob}_{R5})$$

$$+ T_{RMo}\ln(\text{Prob}_{RMo}) + T_{RBUo}\ln(\text{Prob}_{RBUo}) + T_{RHo}\ln(\text{Prob}_{RHo})$$

$$+ T_{RBZo}\ln(\text{Prob}_{RBZo}) + T_{RM}\ln(\text{Prob}_{RM}) + T_{RBU}\ln(\text{Prob}_{RBU})$$

$$+ T_{RH}\ln(\text{Prob}_{RH}) + T_{RBZ}\ln(\text{Prob}_{RBZ}) \tag{15.21}$$

$$+ \sum_{j=1}^{26} T_j\ln(\text{Prob}_j)]\},$$

where the T variables and all the probabilities (Prob) are indexed by i; the i subscript is suppressed for notational simplicity. This component of the log likelihood function is a function of all parameters in the model, the data on site characteristics, and the data for each of the 443 anglers on trips, trip costs, gender, age, residency, skill, years fished in Montana, free time, and weeks of paid vacation.

The catch component of the model adds the following term to the log likelihood function:

$$L_c = \sum_{j=1}^{26} \sum_{k=1}^{K_j} [-h_{kj}ECR_j + x_{kj}\ln(h_{kj}ECR_j) - \ln(x_{kj}!)], \tag{15.22}$$

where K_j is the number of intercept trips to site j with catch information. This component of the log of the likelihood function is a function of the expected catch rate parameters and the observed catch data. The likelihood function for the joint model of participation, site choice, and expected catch rates is $L = L_{tc} + L_c$.

4. THE ESTIMATED MODEL

Gauss was used to find those values of the parameters that maximized the likelihood function using FIML (see Morey, 1999). On the basis of asymptotic t statistics, all included variables are statistically significant.[13] The parameter estimates are reported in Table 15.2.

The 1991 National Survey of Fishing, Hunting and Wildlife-Associated Recreation (U.S. DOI, 1993) estimates an average of 8.8 trips annually by residents to rivers and streams in Montana. Our model predicts 9.4. Both our model and the National Survey estimate 1.4 trips annually by non-residents who currently fish in Montana. The correlations between the actual and predicted site proportions for the 26 intensively studied sites are 0.71 for the full sample, 0.70 for residents, and 0.67 for nonresidents.

Table 15.2   Parameter estimates

Parameter		Estimate	t statistic
Expected catch rates	$ECUCF1$	0.434	6.967
	$ECUCF2$	0.222	2.941
	$ECUCF3$	0.423	4.783
	$ECMCF$	0.447	8.883
	$ECRC$	0.926	20.598
	$ECFC$	0.877	9.268
	$ECBT1$	0.240	5.546
	$ECBT2$	0.739	14.833
	$ECLC$	0.683	8.698
	$ECBF$	0.267	6.203
	$ECLBF$	0.731	5.244
	$ECUCF4$	0.846	7.660
	$ECUCF5$	0.784	8.851
	$ECWSC$	0.771	5.429
	$ECBH1$	0.899	17.930
	$ECBH2$	0.812	14.428
	$ECJ1$	0.280	6.994
	$ECJ2$	0.326	7.696
	$ECBV$	0.637	17.164
	$ECMS$	0.760	17.577
	$ECLY$	0.382	11.238
	ECG	0.884	11.481
	$ECEG$	1.051	11.184
	$ECMD1$	0.413	11.602
	$ECMD2$	0.7260	–
Parameter explaining the influence of the expected catch rates	β_C	0.126	1.581
	β_{CNR}	0.246	2.218
	β_{CSK}	2.604E-2	1.633
Parameters explaining the influence of trip costs	β_0	7.224E-3	3.739
	β_{0NR}	6.150E-4	3.819
	β_W	0.110	3.479
Parameters explaining the influence of gender, age, skill, years finished in Montana, free time, vacation, and residency	α_P	4.414	23.203
	β_G	0.239	2.349
	β_A	5.20E-3	2.565
	β_{SK}	−0.480	−20.029
	β_{MTF}	2.380E-2	10.412
	β_{FT}	−0.040	−5.997
	β_V	0.093	5.927
	β_{PNR}	1.840	19.758

Table 15.2 (continued)

Parameter		Estimate	t statistic
Parameters explaining the influence of	β_{SZ}	0.213	3.207
size, campgrounds, and suitability for	β_{CG}	0.131	3.368
floating	β_{LFF}	0.100	2.151
	β_{HFNF}	-0.168	-2.782
Other parameters	α_O	0.431	3.270
	α_{R5}	-0.052	-0.878
	s	8.746	7.179
	t	7.327	3.723

As mentioned above, the opportunity cost of time is 11 per cent of the angler's wage rate; this value was estimated as a parameter in the model, not preselected. This percentage is lower than the percentage used in many travel cost studies.[14] Estimating this percentage is preferred to forcing the percentage to take the value from another study or model. Estimates from one study should not, in general, be used in another travel-cost model: the estimated percentage can be sensitive to model specification and the assigned values to travel costs, and one would expect the disutility associated with travel to sites to vary across sets of sites.

In terms of estimated expected catch rates, the top five sites include some of the most famous trout streams in the United States. In contrast, four of the ten sites with the lowest estimated expected catch rates are impacted sites in the upper Clark Fork River Basin (Upper Clark Fork 1–3 and Silver Bow Creek). Most of the expected catch rates estimated by the recreation demand model are similar to the simple Poisson catch rates, except at those sites with few observed hours of trout fishing. For example, the Beaverhead, with 464 hours of fishing over 172 trips, has a simple Poisson average catch rate of 0.6331, and a jointly estimated catch rate of 0.6366. In contrast, the simple average for Upper Clark Fork 4 is 1.5 trout caught per hour, based on only 21 hours of reported catch from nine trips, but the model estimated catch rate is 0.85.

5. THE RELATIONSHIP BETWEEN TROUT STOCKS AND EXPECTED CATCH RATES

Biological injuries are related to economic damages through their impact on stock sizes which in turn affect angler catch rates. Stock estimates (trout per hectare) were available for 1992 for eight of the study sites

(Don Chapman Consultants, 1995) and were combined with the estimated expected catch rates to estimate the stock-catch function: $ECR_j =$
0.1539 ln $(STOCK_j + 1)$ with $R^2 = 0.93$ and $t = 9.91$.

This functional form of the regression allows for a nonlinear stock-catch
relationship and the regression predicts zero expected catch when stocks are
zero.[15] The estimated function indicates decreasing rates of increase in
expected catch rates from increasing fish stocks. The stock-catch model and
estimates of baseline (no-injury) stocks were then used to predict expected
catch rates at the injured sites under baseline conditions in the absence of
past releases of heavy metals. Specifically, the baseline expected catch rate
for each Clark Fork site was calculated by adjusting the current expected
catch rate by the percentage change in expected catch rates (from current
to baseline conditions) predicted by the stock-catch model. For Silver Bow
Creek, which currently has zero stock, the best estimate of the expected
catch rate under baseline conditions is that predicted directly by the stock-
catch model. Injuries have caused proportionately large reductions at all of
the impacted sites except Upper Clark Fork 5. Aggregating across sites and
adjusting for site lengths, expected catch rates would be almost twice as
high under baseline conditions.

6.   USE UNDER BASELINE

The recreation demand model predicts that if baseline conditions were
restored at the impacted Upper Clark Fork River and Silver Bow Creek
sites, an average resident angler active in river and stream trout fishing in
southwestern Montana would take 0.36 more trips per year to the impacted
sites and 0.32 fewer trips to other sites in Montana. The predicted trips
to the impacted sites under baseline conditions represent a 66 per cent
increase relative to the predicted trips under current conditions. The
average nonresident angler would take 0.07 more trips to the impacted sites
and 0.06 fewer trips to other sites. The net change is more than a doubling
of the total number of trips to the impacted sites for nonresidents. In
summary, when the impacted sites are returned to baseline conditions few
new trips are predicted to be taken by existing anglers, but approximately
5 per cent of trips to other sites are predicted to be substituted to the
impacted sites.

The increase in visitation to the impacted sites under baseline conditions
varies across sites, reflecting the variability in increased expected catch
rates. For example, under baseline conditions the expected catch rate at
Upper Clark Fork 2 would increase by 123 per cent, and the site would have
a higher expected catch rate than other well-known sites such as Bitterroot

1, Blackfoot, and the Jefferson River sites. Compared to current conditions, the predicted visitation increases by 83 per cent under baseline conditions at Upper Clark Fork 2. Visitation at Upper Clark Fork 2 is predicted to exceed visitation at Jefferson 2, Yellowstone, Madison 1, and other popular sites. This reflects the relatively high expected catch rate at the impacted site under baseline conditions, the size of the site, and that this site is closer than other substitute sites for residents of nearby cities such as Missoula, Helena, and Butte. Remediating injuries would also have a substantial impact on Silver Bow Creek, making it an excellent small stream for trout fishing. That anglers will substitute fishing visits from other sites to the upper Clark Fork River and Silver Bow Creek sites indicates that anglers are currently taking trips to sites that, under baseline conditions, would be less desirable because of lower catch rates or increased travel distances.

7. E(*WTP*) FOR THE ABSENCE OF INJURIES

For anglers who are residents of Montana, the estimated expected annual willingness to pay, E(*WTP*), for the absence of injuries ranges from $0.01 to $42.96 with a mean of $6.31 and a median of $4.54 (in 1992 dollars). The standard deviation of mean E(*WTP*) for residents is $3.13.[16] For nonresident anglers who fish in Montana, estimated E(*WTP*) ranges from $1.19 to $40.35 with a mean of $14.17 and a median of $12.62. The standard deviation of mean E(*WTP*) for nonresidents is $6.59. E(*WTP*) varies across individual anglers because trip costs and the other determinants of E(*WTP*) vary across anglers. Consider the angler with the highest estimated E(*WTP*) ($42.96), and compare this angler to an angler with an E(*WTP*) that is effectively zero. The angler with an E(*WTP*) of $42.96 resides near Silver Bow Creek, is a 52-year-old male, reports a skill level of 6 on a scale of 1 to 7, and reports 11 hours of free time on a typical weekday. This is an angler with low trip costs for the injured sites and a higher than average skill level and amount of free time. In contrast, the angler with an E(*WTP*) of effectively zero is a 42-year-old male who reports a skill level of 4, reports five hours of free time on a typical weekday, and lives approximately 270 miles from the injured sites. This angler has high trip costs and lower skill and free time. The distributions of the resident and nonresident E(*WTP*) are similar to a log-normal distribution in that they have a long tail extending into higher E(*WTP*) values.

For residents, $6.31 is approximately 8 per cent of the average trip cost, and $14.17 is only 2 per cent of the average trip cost for nonresidents: nonresidents spend an average of $221 for lodging and $193 for equipment and guides, so $14.17 does not appear to be much to pay per year for the opportunity to have significantly better fishing along 145 miles at the injured sites. Viewed in terms of what it would cost to travel to substitute sites rather than the injured sites, the mean E(WTP)s would cover 36 additional round-trip miles of annual fishing travel by a resident, and 66 additional round-trip miles by a nonresident.

It is relevant, but not surprising, that nonresidents who currently fish the cold-water rivers and streams of southwestern Montana have higher estimated fishing damages per year in southwestern Montana than active resident anglers. These nonresident anglers, while taking fewer trips to southwestern Montana than resident anglers, spend more per trip on Montana fishing than most residents (for example, the mean trip cost for nonresidents is $840, whereas the mean trip cost for residents is only $77) and have a lower estimated marginal utility of money; further, their selection of Montana fishing sites is more responsive to expected catch rates than is the case for residents.

8.   AGGREGATE DAMAGE ESTIMATES

On the basis of State of Montana angler license data and data collected by the 1991 National Survey (U.S. DOI, 1993; see also Morey et al., 1995), we estimate that approximately 71 000 resident anglers and 65 000 nonresident anglers were active in river and stream trout fishing in southwestern Montana in 1992. The residents anglers took an estimated 629 000 fishing trips to rivers and streams in Montana, and the nonresidents took an estimated 92 000 trips. Applying the mean annual damages of $6.31 per resident angler results in aggregate annual damages to residents of $448 000 (in 1992 dollars). Applying the mean nonresident annual damages of $14.17 results in aggregate annual damages to nonresidents of $921 000.

9.   SENSITIVITY OF DAMAGE ESTIMATES

When the model is estimated without the avidity weights, E(WTP) estimates are upwardly biased by more than an order of magnitude. If the simple average Poisson catch rates are used rather than estimating the expected catch rates as model parameters using both catch and trip data, the mean damage estimates are 58 per cent lower for residents and 30 per cent lower for nonresidents.

To test for potential differences between the sample and population proportions of trips to the 26 sites, site weights were constructed as the ratio of the population shares to the sample shares of trips to the intensively studied sites. Three different sets of weights were derived from three different estimates of the population shares, based on the number of anglers receiving postcards per interviewer visit, anglers receiving postcards per hour of interviewer time, and anglers who returned postcards. The model was re-estimated using each of these three sets of weights. Site weighting results in mean E(*WTP*)s ranging from $5.93 to $6.88 for residents, and from $13.27 to $15.32 for nonresidents. These alternative methods do not provide much variation in results, with the means of E(*WTP*) from the model that does not include the additional site weights falling in the middle of these ranges (which span ±10 per cent). This suggests that the implicit weights in the *ISF* procedure were reliable without the complications of further weights.

The model of participation and site choice was also estimated with only the 291 resident anglers. The estimated mean E(*WTP*) is $5.97, 5 per cent lower than the estimate from the model that includes both residents and nonresidents. The damage estimates for nonresident anglers are more sensitive to model specification, which is most likely due to sample sizes (291 residents versus 152 nonresidents) and more variation in trip costs among resident anglers than nonresident anglers. The nonresident travel-cost data do not have enough variation to estimate a completely separate model of participation and site choice for the 152 nonresidents.

To further examine the sensitivity of the estimates, we estimate a site-choice-only model (without participation) separately for non-residents and for residents, which will result in a lower-bound estimate of E(*WTP*) for the absence of injuries (Morey, 1994 and 1999). With this model, the estimate is $9.41 for non-residents and $4.71 for residents.

10.   CONCLUSIONS AND EPILOGUE

Mining wastes have injured Montana's Silver Bow Creek and Upper Clark Fork River. This chapter describes the NRDA sampling and modeling procedures used to estimate damages to anglers, and presents results relevant to policy and Superfund litigation. In the model, residents and nonresidents are allowed to have different preferences. Nonresident anglers, who are often excluded in similar analyses, are found to have larger damages than resident anglers. A stock-catch function is estimated, linking expected catch rates, which are key in determining demand and economic values, to trout stock data and biological injuries. The potential need for weights in the likelihood function as a result of the *ISF* sample is investigated, and the *ISF* survey technique is found to be both cost-effective and appropriate if one has independent estimates of avidity and site proportions. Maximum likelihood expected catch rates are estimated endogenously in the model.

In June 1998, the State of Montana and ARCO entered into a partial settlement for the amount of $215 million for environmental damages. This settlement covers the State's claims for compensable damages, including those to anglers.

ACKNOWLEDGEMENTS

We thank Rob Brooks, Trudy Cameron, Rob Collins, John Duffield, Bob McFarland, Chris Neher, Douglass Shaw, and two anonymous reviewers for help and advice. This chapter is based on work prepared by the authors and Hagler Bailly, Inc. for the State of Montana, Natural Resource Damage Program.

NOTES

1. If one constrains resident and nonresident anglers to have identical preferences, nonresident anglers will have lower damage estimates than residents because nonresidents face higher trip costs.
2. The response rates to these three surveys were 98 per cent, 83 per cent, and 63 per cent, respectively.
3. The exclusion of trips that were not primarily for the purpose of fishing may have an effect on the valuation, but modeling multipurpose trips was beyond the scope of this research. The proportion of trips that were for multiple purposes was much greater for nonresidents than for residents.
4. Mean equipment expenses were about $10 for all of the distance categories under 150 miles, and were $23 for anglers traveling more than 150 miles. On-site time averaged 3.5 hours for trips less than 25 one-way miles, 6.3 hours for trips of 26–150 one-way miles, and 8.7 hours for trips in excess of 150 one-way miles. Categorical averages are used rather than individual-level measures so that the cost associated with on-site time would be an exogenous cost. A model such as the one in this chapter could be extended to make on-site time endogenous.
5. The State of Montana paid $0.275 per mile for job-related activities, and similarly the federal government allowed a tax deduction of $0.28 per mile. We allocated the vehicle operating costs across two anglers (the median number traveling together).
6. By way of comparison, the ARCO economic analysis (Desvousges and Waters, 1995b) assumed $0.05 per mile and assumed one-third of the wage rate for travel time, but no opportunity cost for time spent on site. These and other factors result in much lower damages than reported here.
7. Note that truncating the maximum number of trips to 60 will cause the estimates of both total trips and damages to be biased downward.
8. A sufficient, but not necessary, condition for this density function to be well-behaved is $s \geq t \geq 1$. This condition is fulfilled.
9. A site's size is defined as the site's average flow from May through August (in cubic feet per second) multiplied by the site's length. Sizes of the sites are important determinants of both the total number of fishing trips to southwestern Montana and which sites are

chosen because, everything else constant, larger sites have more access points and more places to fish.

10. A parameter for sites that are exceptionally aesthetically unattractive (only Silver Bow Creek) and a parameter for sites with both bad bank access and that are unsuitable for float fishing (only Upper Clark Fork 3) were both found to be insignificant determinants of participation and site choice.

11. McConnell et al. (1995) first used the Poisson distribution to characterize catch. The expected catch rate for Silver Bow Creek is zero, as there are no fish due to high pollution levels. The expected catch rate for Madison 2 was normalized to its simple Poisson average catch rate (0.726). Madison 2 is the site with the most recorded fishing time. This anchors the expected catch rates for the other 24 sites on the zero expected catch rate for Silver Bow Creek and the simple Poisson average for Madison 2.

12. When the number of observations is small, the simple average is often unduly influenced by a few extreme observations. For example, one of the individuals intercepted at Upper Clark Fork 4 reported catching 18 fish in three hours. Eliminating this one observation drops the simple average from 1.5 to 0.77 fish per hour.

13. Programs, specific parameter estimates, and their t statistics can be obtained from the second author.

14. See, for example, McConnell and Strand (1981), Smith et al. (1983), and Bockstael et al. (1987).

15. A linear model gave a much poorer fit. When an intercept term was included it was not statistically significant.

16. Details on the calculation of E(WTP) for nested logit models without income effects can be found in Hanemann (1999) and Morey (1999). Standard deviations for the estimated mean of the per angler damages were estimated through repeated simulations of the recreation demand model using the Krinsky–Robb procedure.

REFERENCES

Bockstael, N.E., I.E. Strand and W.M. Hanemann (1987), 'Time and the recreation demand model', *American Journal of Agricultural Economics*, **69**(2): 293–302.

Desvousges, W.H. and S.M. Waters (1995a), *Volume II: Critique of the State of Montana's Recreation Study*, Submitted to United States District Court, District of Montana, Helena Division, State of Montana v. Atlantic Richfield Company No. CV-83-317-HLN-PGH July.

Desvousges, W.H. and S.M. Waters (1995b), *Volume III: Report on Potential Economic Losses Associated with Recreation Services in the Upper Clark Fork River Basin*, Submitted to United States District Court, District of Montana, Helena Division, State of Montana v. Atlantic Richfield Company No. CV-83-317-HLN-PGH, July.

Don Chapman Consultants, Inc. (1995), 'Assessment of Injury to Fish Populations: Clark Fork River NPL Sites, Montana' (Appendix G to Lipton et al., 1995), prepared for the State of Montana, Natural Resource Damage Litigation Program.

Hanemann, W.M. (1999), 'Welfare Analysis with Discrete Choice Models', Chapter 2 in C. Kling and J. Herriges (eds), *Valuing the Environment Using Recreation Demand Models*, Northampton, MA: Edward Elgar Publishing, pp. 33–64.

Lipton, J., H. Bergman, D. Chapman, T. Hillman, M. Kerr, J. Moore and D. Woodward (1995), 'Aquatic Resources Injury Assessment Report', Upper Clark Fork River Basin, prepared by RCG/Hagler Bailly, Inc. for the State of Montana, Natural Resource Damage Litigation Program.

Manski, C.F. and S.R. Lerman (1977), 'The estimation of choice probabilities from choice-based samples', *Econometrica*, **45**(8): 1977–88.

McConnell, K.E. and I. Strand (1981), 'Measuring the cost of time in recreation demand analysis: An application to sport fishing', *American Journal of Agricultural Economics*, **63**: 153–6.

McConnell, K.E., I. Strand and L. Blake-Hedges (1995), 'Random utility models of recreational fishing: Catching fish with a Poisson process', *Marine Resource Economics*, **10**: 247–61.

McFadden, D. (1995), 'Report on Montana's and ARCO's Travel Cost Reports', submitted to United States District Court, District of Montana, Helena Division, State of Montana v. Atlantic Richfield Company No. CV-83-317-HLN-PGH July.

Morey, E.R. (1999), 'TWO RUMs UnCLOAKED: Nested-logit models of site choice and nested-logit models of participation and site choice', in C. Kling and J. Herriges (eds), *Valuing the Environment Using Recreation Demand Models*, Northhampton, MA: Edward Elgar Publishing, pp. 65–120.

Morey, E.R. and D.M. Waldman (1993), 'Measurement Error in Recreation Demand Models: The Joint Estimation of Participation, Site Choice and Site Characteristics', Discussion paper, Department of Economics, University of Colorado, Boulder, CO 80309-0256.

Morey, E.R. and D.M. Waldman (1998), 'Measurement error in recreation demand models: The joint estimation of participation, site choice and site characteristics', *Journal of Environmental Economics and Management*, **35**: 262–76.

Morey, E.R. and D.M. Waldman (2000), 'Joint estimation of catch and other travel-cost parameters: Some further thoughts', *Journal of Environmental Economics and Management*, **40**: 82–6.

Morey, E.R., D.M. Waldman and R.D. Rowe (1995), 'Assessment of Damages to Anglers and Other Recreators from Injuries to the Upper Clark Fork River Basin', Prepared by Hagler Bailly Consulting, Inc. for the State of Montana Natural Resource Damage Litigation Program.

Smith, V.K., W. Desvousges and M. McGivney (1983), 'The opportunity cost of time in recreation demand models', *Land Economics*, **59**: 259–77.

Train, K., D. McFadden and R. Johnson (2000), 'Discussion of Morey and Waldman's measurement error in recreation demand models', *Journal of Environmental Economics and Management*, **40**: 76–81.

U.S. DOI. (1993), *1991 National Survey of Fishing, Hunting and Wildlife-Associated Recreation: Montana*, Washington, DC: U.S. Fish and Wildlife Service.

This chapter is reprinted from the *Journal of Environmental Management* (2002), **66**(2), Edward R. Morey, William S. Breffle, Robert D. Howe and Donald M. Waldman, 159–70, with permission from Elsevier Science.

Index